Improving Policy Coherence in South Asia

Improving Policy Coherence in South Asia

Edited by
Manas Bhattacharya

International Labour Office
Geneva

Academic Foundation
New Delhi

First published in 2010 by

Academic Foundation
4772/23 Bharat Ram Road, (23 Ansari Road), Darya Ganj,
New Delhi - 110002, India.
email: books@academicfoundation.com
www.academicfoundation.com

Manas Bhattacharya (ed.)
Improving Policy Coherence in South Asia

ISBN 978-81-7188-820-7

Designed and typeset by Italics India, New Delhi
Cover design copyright: Academic Foundation
Printed and bound in India

Contents

List of tables, figures, boxes and appendices

TABLES

FIGURES

BOXES

APPENDICES

Preface

The term "policy coherence" first entered the development literature lexicon in the early 1990s, a coinage of the OECD's Development Assistance Committee. At that time, the focus on policy coherence referred mainly to the need to review the extent that the development policies and programmes of OECD countries, and indeed their own domestic policies, were consistent in promoting their intended aim of development. The need for a good rethinking of the policies and channels through which development assistance occurs was paramount, and extended well beyond limits of poorer countries' capacities to absorb and make productive use of the assistance they received. Consider, for example, a poor country in sub-Saharan Africa in the late 1990s receiving no fewer than 1,000 visits from a variety of overseas agencies in the multinational system in a given year. A surfeit of uncoordinated technical advice is tantamount to receiving no advice of any useful nature whatsoever. With the new millennium, both the roll out of Poverty Reduction Strategy Papers (PRSPs) and, more globally, the Millennium Development Goals (MDGs) have made major strides in improving donor coordination.

Since then, policy coherence has usefully acquired a richer and broader meaning. Three reasons are primarily responsible for this. Over a period of five years in the first decade of the new millennium, developing countries were living through a sustained episode of quite respectable levels of output growth. While, at this writing, the global economy is challenged by the continued weakness of credit markets brought about by the unwinding of the "sub-prime" crisis originating in the US housing market, as well as by soaring prices in energy- and non-energy commodity markets, this does not obscure the fact that there has been growth, and good growth – and still is in much of the developing world. The problem, however, is that this output growth has been accompanied by a decline in many countries in its employment content. The latter, moreover, is not necessarily captured by movements in the unemployment rate. Rather, it is the fact that even respectable rates of growth have failed to translate into productive jobs for millions of working men and women. In other words, there is no shortage of work; there is a shortage of productive jobs.

This phenomenon conveys the stark message that growth alone is not enough: it is the pattern of growth that matters. And this, in turn, has its own implications. For example, many developing countries are understandably proud to have regained stability in their macroeconomic policy frameworks. But, in an open world economy, the price of that stability has been to circumscribe sufficient policy space for the use of monetary, fiscal, and exchange rate policies as flexible tools to shore up domestic economic and employment growth. "Counter-cyclical" spending in a downturn, for example, is largely unavailing in developing countries seeking to preserve hard-won fiscal stability.

With globalization, therefore, efforts to influence the pattern of growth toward generating productive employment lead inevitably to other policy spheres – the coherence amongst which was less important in more closed economies. Thus, trade policy, for example, becomes employment policy, as does industrial policy, product market regulation, or commercial taxes. The present volume is both thorough and eloquent in isolating the different policy spheres that need to be harnessed in a coherent way if the objective is to increase productive employment. For example, trade liberalization may have pay-offs, but if domestic industrial policy has not single-mindedly focused on upgrading domestic industries, then the penalty is deindustrialization and job loss. One of the critical lessons of this volume is that the *mix, the sequencing, and the coherence* of policies are vital to maximizing employment gains.

The second way in which the notion of policy coherence has evolved is that it no longer necessarily – indeed, perhaps primarily – pertains to improving the coordination of the multilateral system. The latter is an essential objective, to be sure, and is beginning to bear fruit in the context of UN Reform. The laudable aim of the latter is to have one UN, speaking with one voice, in one country. Policy coherence now, however, has a meaningful application to the domestic policy environment. The conference upon which the chapters in this volume are based represented a structural innovation of sorts: the conference succeeded in bringing together the key economic agencies from South Asian countries, the Planning Commissions and the Finance Ministries, around the same table with ILO constituents, the Labour Ministries and the worker and employer organizations, to seek commonality of views and the coherence needed to forge this on ways to improve the linkage between growth and productive jobs. Representing not only different mandates, but also different constituencies in the economy, this was no mean feat. Widespread agreement over the conclusions reached by the conference is thus an earnest of the progress achieved.

Third, and finally, policy coherence has become the essential mechanism through which the ILO can deliver on its own mandate of Decent Work. Not any job can be described as a decent job, even in purely economic terms. The volume offers ample empirical support for the proposition that merely increasing the employment intensity of growth is not an unalloyed positive outcome – particularly when increasing that intensity results from crowding more and more people into less productive work: increasing the employment content of growth does not and should not mean increasing the quotient of working poor people, and all the more in a subregion where that quotient, after sub-Saharan Africa, is already the highest in the world, and where most working men and women eke out their livelihoods in the informal economy. In economic terms, a Decent Work strategy for making productive employment central to macroeconomic policies requires a simultaneous focus on the productivity, labour-absorption capacity, and demand for specific sectors.

But Decent Work is not just about economics and incomes. It is also about rights, such as those against discrimination in labour markets on the basis of gender or caste or ethnicity. Decent Work is a concept that acknowledges that labour, unlike product markets, requires the capacity to adapt ("flexibility"), and the wherewithal to do so ("social protection"). It is finally a concept in which the right to participate in the terms under which a worker is engaged in his or her livelihood, and the right to have a say in shaping those terms is a fundamental human, social, political, and economic right. The promotion of Decent Work resides in the simultaneous and coherent interaction of economic and social policies.

A prominent recommendation of the World Commission on the Social Dimension of Globalization was the call for the multilateral system to engage in a Policy Coherence Initiative on Growth, Investment, and Jobs (PCI). Nine meetings of that Initiative have been held since 2004. Held in April 2007, in New Delhi, the Policy Coherence Initiative for South Asia, upon which this volume is based, was the first effort to transpose this initiative "closer to home" in two regards. First, while diversity clearly prevails across the countries in South Asia, so often do shared cultures, traditions, the obvious feature of contiguity, and a set of shared challenges. Second, in this transposition to the subregional level, the dialogue brought together not merely the agencies of the multilateral system active in the subregion, but the national economics ministries with the constituents of the International Labour Organization. The outcome, reflected in this volume, is a prismatic view of the salience of how policies interact in the promotion of development and Decent Work.

Duncan Campbell
Director
Department of Economic and Labour Market Analysis
International Labour Organization

Acknowledgements

This book is the fruit of the ILO initiative to organize the 'High-Level Tripartite Meeting on the Nexus of Growth, Investment, and Decent Work for the South Asian Region' held in New Delhi, 4 April 2007. The initiative was spearheaded by Duncan Campbell, the then Director of the Policy Integration Department of the ILO headquarters in Geneva, in collaboration with Leyla Tegmo-Reddy, ILO Representative and Director of the ILO Subregional office for South Asia, Delhi. I am indebted to them for their unending support and inspiration while editing this work.

This High-Level Meeting would not have taken place without the active involvement and effort of K.M. Sahani, the then Secretary to the Government of India, Ministry of Labour and Employment; I.P. Anand, formerly Governing Body Member and Employers' representative of India to the ILO, and N.M Adyanthaya, ILO Governing Body Member and Workers' representative. I am grateful to them since this book would not have been what it is today without this meeting.

This Meeting was graced by several dignitaries from the Government of India, including Oscar Fernandes, Minister of Labour and Employment; C. Rangarajan, Chairman of the Economic Advisory Council to the Prime Minister of India; Arjun Sengupta, Chairman of the National Commission for Enterprises in the Unorganized Sector (also Independent Expert on Human Rights and Extreme Poverty, Human Rights Commission, Geneva); Ashok Lahiri, Chief Economic Adviser to the Government of India and Sudha Pillai, Secretary to the Ministry of Labour and Employment. I am thankful to all of them.

A.F.M. Jamiluddin, Ingrid Christensen, Moazam Mahmood, Nita Neupane, Shengjie Li and Tine Staermose from the ILO and Ali Farzin from the UNDP were instrumental in identifying and selecting the authors. I am also thankful to Sukti Dasgupta, Senior Employment Specialist at

ILO-Delhi, who, apart from helping in author selection, offered insightful suggestions while reviewing the papers.

Clare Nora Schenker and Barbara Collins from the ILO headquarters and Anjana Chellani and Jolly Dawar from the ILO subregional office in Delhi extended invaluable assistance in all organizational, financial and administrative matters.

I owe my gratitude to Rolph van der Hoeven, Director of the Policy Coherence Group, ILO, Geneva, who meticulously read through the volume, extended guidance for improvements and was very supportive of the effort in publishing the work.

I wish to express special thanks to Professor Arup Mitra of the Institute of Economic Growth, Delhi, in helping me plan this publication. Comments from two anonymous referees helped me in improving the thematic coherence between the chapters. Our publisher, Academic Foundation, has shaped the book into its final form with admirably high-quality professionalism and expertise.

Finally, I am indebted to the contributors to this volume who have been so patient with me and responded to the editorial requirements promptly. These eminent authors were the prime movers of the deliberations in the meeting and this book derives its worth from their knowledge and expertise.

Contributors

Ahmad Ahsan, Lead Economist, World Bank, Washington DC, USA

Manas Bhattacharya, Senior Technical Specialist, International Labour Organization, Geneva, Switzerland

Dipak Dasgupta, Lead Economist, World Bank, New Delhi, India

Nadeem Ul Haque, Director, Pakistan Institute of Development Economics, Islamabad, Pakistan

K.P. Kannan, Member, National Commission on Enterprises in the Unorganized and Informal Sector, Government of India, New Delhi, India

Paula Kantor, Senior Research Manager, Afghanistan Research and Evaluation Unit, Kabul, Afghanistan

Dilli Raj Khanal, Member, UN Expert Committee on Global Economy and Chairman, Institute of Policy Research and Development, Kathmandu, Nepal

Ashish Narain, Economist, World Bank, New Delhi, India

Shyamali Ranaraja, Consultant, International Labour Organization, Colombo, Sri Lanka

Mohammed Ali Rashid, Professor, North South University, Dhaka, Bangladesh

Hassan Taee, Professor, Allameh Tabatabai University, Tehran and former Deputy Head, Parliament Research Center, Tehran, Islamic Republic of Iran

Abbreviations

ACBAR	Agency Coordinating Body for Afghan Relief
AISA	Afghanistan Investment Support Agency
ANDS	Afghanistan National Development Strategy
AREU	Afghanistan Research and Evaluation Unit
CSO	Central Statistical Office
CWS	Current Weekly Status
DGET	Directorate General of Employment and Training
EPF	Employees' Provident Fund
ESAF	Enhanced Structural Adjustment Facility
ETF	Employees' Trust Fund
FDI	Foreign Direct Investment
GDP	Gross Domestic Product
GSDP	Gross State Domestic Product
HRDP	Human Resource Development Planning and Policy Making
I-ANDS	Interim Afghanistan National Development Strategy
IDA	Industrial Disputes Act (1948)
IFI	International Financial Institution
ILO	International Labour Organization
IMF	International Monetary Fund
IRPHE	Institute for Research and Planning in Higher Education
LFS	Labour Force Survey
MDGs	Millennium Development Goals

MoCI	Ministry of Commerce and Industry
MoLSAMD	Ministry of Labour, Social Affairs, Martyrs and Disabled
MPO	Management and Planning Organization
MTEF	Medium-Term Expenditure Framework
NCEUS	National Commission for Enterprises in the Unorganized Sector
NCVT	National Council for Vocational Training
NGO	Non-Governmental Organization
NHDR	National Human Development Report
NLSS	Nepal Living Standard Survey
NPDWSL	National Policy for Decent Work in Sri Lanka
NRB	Nepal Rastra Bank
NREG	National Rural Employment Guarantee
NRVA	National Risk and Vulnerability Assessment
NSDP	National Skills Development Programme
NSS	National Sample Survey
NSSO	National Sample Survey Organization
OECD	Organisation for Economic Co-operation and Development
PCD	Policy Coherence for Development
PCI	Policy Coherence Initiative
PE	Public Enterprise
PRSP	Poverty Reduction Strategy Paper
QR	Quantitative Restriction
RNF	Rural Non-Farm
SAARC	South Asian Association for Regional Cooperation
SAP	Structural Adjustment Program
SC	Scheduled Caste

SMP	Staff Monitored Program
ST	Scheduled Tribe
TEVC	Technical Education and Vocational Training Commission
TEVT	Technical Education and Vocational Training
TEWA	Termination of Employment of Workmen Act
TFP	Total Factor Productivity
TYDF	Ten Year Development Framework
UNCTAD	United Nations Conference on Trade and Development
UNDP	United Nations Development Programme
UPS	Usual Principal Status
UPSS	Usual Principal and Subsidiary Status
WTO	World Trade Organization

1 Policy coherence, growth, investment and decent work in South Asia

Some reflections

Manas Bhattacharya

Growth, employment and decent work connect with many policy areas ... Policy coherence is necessary. It is the result of an overall national development approach that is capable of overcoming the often segmented nature of decision-making.

Juan Somavia, Director-General of the International Labour Office[1]

1.1 Introduction

Policy Coherence for Development (PCD) is about ensuring that, in simultaneous pursuit of a range of development goals, policies do not undermine each other. This is, however, a restrictive way of defining it; to say what it should prevent from happening. Being more positive, PCD implies exploitation of maximum potential synergies between multiple policy domains, so that policy made in one area enhances the effectiveness of policy in a related area. According to the OECD, PCD involves "the systematic promotion of mutually reinforcing policy actions across government departments and agencies creating synergies towards achieving the agreed objectives" (*OECD Observer* (2004) cited in Picciotto, 2004). In an ideal situation, policies would cohere over space and time to achieve an optimal set of predefined objectives. In reality, there are various obstacles, which create difficulties in achieving the

---

1. Excerpts from the address by Juan Somavia, Director-General of the International Labour Office to the Asian Employment Forum at Beijing, China, 13 August 2007 available at *www.ilo.org*

best solutions.[2] Recognizing these impediments, identifying trade-offs and synergies across various policies and making the choices more explicit through continued policy dialogue and minimizing policy conflicts mark the beginning of Policy Coherence Initiatives (PCIs).

Policy coherence had been a recurrent theme in international policy discourse. In the early 1990s, policy coherence became an issue within the international community in the context of aid-effectiveness. This was borne out of the realization that, to be effective, aid policies require coherence with other public policies in the industrialized countries, and that this has a strong impact on the developing countries.

PCI in the multilateral system

The term "policy coherence for development" was coined by the Development Assistance Committee of the OECD around 1991 for promoting coherent policy among its members. Subsequently, the principle of coherence became an objective of the European Union and was included in the Maastricht Treaty of 1992 (ECDPM and ICEI, 2005). The concept of coherence was inherent in the notion of a "balanced strategy at country level among multiple development partners" which underpinned the Comprehensive Development Framework of the World Bank in early 1999. In the following year, the United Nations Millennium Declaration resolved "to ensure greater policy coherence and better cooperation" within the multilateral system, including the international financial institutions (IFIs).[3] "Coherence" was also pivotal in the framework of the Monterrey Consensus[4] on financing for development, adopted in 2002.

---

2. A discussion on why policy coherence is important yet difficult to achieve is available in *OECD Observer*, July 2003. Also see Picciotto (2004).
3. *http://www.un.org/millennium/declaration/ares552e.htm*
4. The United Nations International Conference on Financing Development held in 2002, known as Monterrey Conference, led to certain agreements among the participating governments on issues relating to financing development. These agreements are generally referred to as 'Monterrey Consensus' in international dialogues on development and cooperation. 'Monterrey Consensus' includes, apart from agreements relating to 'financing for development', systemic issues like coherence and consistency of policies.

A number of multilateral organizations have promoted policy coherence in their respective policy domains. The World Trade Organization (WTO), following the Ministerial Meeting in Singapore, has undertaken an initiative to mainstream trade in national development plans, including in the Poverty Reduction Strategy Plans. These plans, in turn, are expected to provide platforms for the coordination of domestic policies and donor support in different projects and programmes. In this initiative, the WTO is a partner with the World Bank, the International Monetary Fund (IMF), the United Nations Conference on Trade and Development (UNCTAD), the United Nations Development Programme (UNDP) and the International Trade Centre in an integrated framework (WTO, 2004: 194). In pursuit of the recommendation of the World Commission on the Social Dimension of Globalization, the ILO has undertaken, as a part of its PCI, a joint study with the WTO to review the relationship between trade and employment to identify the key policy issues that need to be addressed to strengthen the impact of trade on job creation (Jansen and Lee, 2007). The United Nations High Level Task Force on the Right to Development, established in 2004 as an independent body of experts to advise the inter-governmental Working Group on the Right to Development, brings together human rights experts, among others, and representatives of the IMF, World Bank, WTO, UNCTAD, UNDP with a view to ensuring that human rights in international economics are implemented through existing structures such as trade, aid and debt relief (Saloman, 2006: 27). Likewise, the UN General Assembly recognized the need for "a coherent and coordinated international strategy on employment" and supported "the comprehensive International Labour Organization programme on Decent Work".[5] In July 2006, the Ministers on the UN's Economic and Social Council invited all international organizations, including the IMF and the World Bank, to give explicit consideration to how their activities can contribute to the goals of full employment and decent work for all.

---

5. Commitment 3 of the 24th Special Session of the General Assembly (United Nations, 2000).

The expanding domain of the concept

Wider acceptability of the concept of coherence has been commensurate with the expanding connotations, forms and complexities that underpin PCI. The theme of coherence has not remained circumscribed within the domain of donors' policy coordination. Policy coherence within national government, between different types of public policies, multiple departments and various layers of governance, has become important. The scope extends beyond national frontiers to accommodate the challenge of coherence between national, regional and global policies.

In a restricted sense, policy coherence is about potential policy conflicts and trade-offs. This aspect needs to be distinguished from "policy imbalance": policy incoherence is certain to manifest in policy imbalance, but the reverse is not necessarily true. Mere policy imbalances may exist even before a country had reached the limits of policy choice, where the policies exhibit trade-offs. It might simply be a situation where the one or the other policy is simply not in place,[6] not necessarily a case where one policy objective has to be sacrificed in order to achieve another. More often, society faces the challenge of policy coherence in the simultaneous pursuit of multiple objectives, especially economic and social, like growth and income distribution, or growth and poverty eradication. Viewed from this perspective, policy coherence means policies aimed at growth objective must be coherent with—or not incoherent with—the policies that are directed towards income redistribution or poverty eradication.

Policy coherence is important for any nation striving to reach economic and social goals. Coherence is needed between different agencies within the multilateral system, since different agencies have specialized mandates (e.g., the ILO has jurisdiction on labour standards as its mandate, the WTO deals with the international trading system) and it is necessary to ensure that the pursuit of respective mandates by these agencies is suitably orchestrated. The same is true for donor agencies, where coordination is needed between the donor agencies, the

---

6. This does not take into account implementation failure, which can lead to an unbalanced outcome even if balanced policies are in place.

multilateral organizations and national governments. It is necessary to ensure that the policy advice given by these agencies to national governments is not incoherent.

National governments have a key role in promoting policy coherence, since they are present in the governance structure of the multilateral systems and it is for the governments to accept or reject any policy advice, depending upon whether it is suited to national objectives. While global initiatives can strengthen coherence in policies and approaches within the multilateral system, a simultaneous effort is needed on the part of national governments to synchronize domestic compulsions with international commitments. One could ask, if globalization is the rule of the game, how much policy space is available for national governments to exercise coherence in policy-making at the national level? A more pertinent issue is how we contextualize policy coherence in a global policy environment—an issue touched upon briefly in the following subsection.

Finally, the policy domains that are candidates for coherence are many and encompass broad subject areas, such as trade, investment, agriculture, education, health, environment, employment, poverty and human rights. There are multiple stakeholders and the forms of coherence will vary according to the partners involved. The task of achieving overall coherence is, therefore, complex and difficult.

Policy coherence and globalization

Policy coherence is perceived to be beneficial for a fair globalization. The OECD policy brief observed that "greater development coherence in OECD governments' policy stances will allow the benefits of globalization to be more equally distributed and shared" (*OECD Observer,* 2004). The World Commission on Social Dimension of Globalization had observed that the benefits of globalization have been unequally distributed, creating growing polarization between the winners and the losers. By putting primacy of market expansion over other considerations, the international rules and policies seem to have undermined those economic and social policies that are needed to achieve inclusive globalization based on a better balance between economic and social objectives. In order to mobilize action for change, the Commission recommended that international organizations should launch PCIs to design a more coherent set of policies for achieving a fair and inclusive globalization. It also supported ILO action in cooperation with other interested international organizations to promote dialogue and support research to develop improved methods of monitoring and measurement for better policy developments (ILO, 2004a: 134–138). To start with, as recommended by the Commission, the PCI should address the question of growth, investment and employment in the global economy (ILO, 2004a: xiv).

The present volume is a collection of papers that attempt to evaluate coherence among policies that are designed to promote growth, investment and decent work[7] at the national level. It aims to improve the understanding of global imbalance in growth and job opportunities through a bottom-up approach based on an analysis of imbalances at country level.

The framework that has been used for assessing the policy conflicts/coherence with special reference to employment and decent work objectives starts with an evaluation of the comparative performance of growth and employment in order to explore the notion of 'jobless growth' or 'growth-job-disconnect' and how to arrive at a meaningful measure of this phenomenon. It has been sought to demonstrate that the conventional employment elasticity measures convey very limited information for understanding whether a particular employment-growth nexus could potentially enhance decent work prospects. Elasticity figures can simply go up due to an increase in the number of working poor that have been counted as employed. Likewise, a decline in growth can be associated with a rise in employment elasticity because of the downward stickiness of employment in terms of 'head-count'; however, the income of workers may fall and the number

---

7. Securing decent work for people everywhere is a primary ILO goal and is a converging focus for all four of its strategic objectives: the promotion of rights at work, employment, social protection and social dialogue. It implies promoting opportunities for women and men to obtain decent and productive work, in conditions of freedom, equity, security and human dignity. The ILO's *Decent Work* report (ILO, 1999) contains elaborate discussions on the theme of decent work, including a regional perspective. The report is available at *http://www.ilo.org/public/english/standards/relm/ilc/ilc87/rep-i.htm*

of working poor increase under such circumstances. The exogenously determined supply of labour can increase the value of elasticity. In a typical developing country with an overcrowded agricultural sector and a large informal economy, a substantial portion of the addition to the labour force is confined to agriculture and informal employment (or self-employment), thereby contributing towards a rise in the overall head-count in employment. All this does not enhance the potential for decent work. Later in this chapter, it will be shown how supply-side pressure in the labour market impacts on the values of employment elasticity in the respective countries discussed. Underpinning this discussion is the notion that supply-side issues need to be carefully disentangled from the overall employment data for a better understanding of the nexus between growth and decent work. In the absence of refined employment data that segregates working poor, the analytical framework that is used in this chapter presumes that an increase in employment elasticity with a decline in the per capita output of workers is not conducive towards decent work. Conversely, a decline in employment elasticity, if accompanied by an increase in the output per worker and faster employment growth, enhances decent work potential.

The major thrust of the framework is to examine the macro-economic policies aimed at stimulating investment and growth, and to understand their decent work implications.

To sum up, the framework looks at the observed imbalance between growth and decent work, and explores whether the policies that seek to promote investment and growth are coherent with the goal of achieving decent work.

The persistent imbalance in the global economy

The global economy is experiencing a persistent imbalance characterized by joblessness amidst robust global growth. This shows that decent work is not a guaranteed outcome in a market economy, even if the economic policy levers perform well in achieving the growth objectives. The global number of unemployed people increased by 22 per cent over the past 10 years, with global unemployment rate sluggish at 6.3 per cent, despite an estimated increase in the annual global gross domestic product (GDP) growth rate from 4.3 per cent in 2005 to 5.2

per cent in 2006. In terms of absolute numbers, the total number of unemployed people in 2006 was 195.2 million. Although the share of working poor to total unemployed declined from 54.8 per cent in 1996 to 47.4 per cent in 2006, the absolute number of working poor continued to grow. In 2006, 1.37 billion workers lived on US$2 or less per day (ILO, 2007a). The share of national income that goes to labour is declining, and it has been noticed that in most countries this tends to coincide with the advent of globalization (Lübker, 2007). There are severe risks of such tendencies potentially undermining the prospects of achieving the Millennium Development Goals. From the policy perspective, two important issues arise in this context. First, is the outward manifestation of a mismatch between growth and decent work a reflection of incoherent policies? Second, if so, has globalization got anything to do with it? The inquiry has direct relevance to the Global Employment Agenda of the ILO, which includes "pro-employment macroeconomic framework" as one of its pillars (ILO, 2003). A major concern in this respect is to explore the extent to which policies get circumscribed[8] under the forces of globalization.[9] An understanding of this is essential for the analysis of the macroeconomic context in which the ILO's Decent Work Country Programmes[10] function.

Emerging from this perspective, the ILO organized a "High-level tripartite meeting on the nexus of Growth, Investment and Decent Work" for the South Asian subregion.[11] This was a part of the ILO's PCI bringing together policy-makers (governments), representatives from the employers' and the workers' organizations, multilateral institutions

8. For a discussion, see the issue of "policy space" in Jenkins *et al.* (2007: 28-29); see also Akyüz (forthcoming).

9. For an interesting discussion on how greater policy coherence between international and national financial, economic and employment policies can give greater attention to employment and incomes, see van der Hoeven and Lübker (2006).

10. "Decent Work Country Programmes put ILO's knowledge, instruments and advocacy at the service of" the ILO's constituents to "promote decent work as a key component of development policies" at the national level. For details, see ILO (2004b).

11. The South Asian subregion includes seven countries: Afghanistan, Bangladesh, India, Iran, Nepal, Pakistan and Sri Lanka.

(including the IFIs), donor communities and researchers for a technical discussion to identify the major constraints to achieving employment-rich growth and the main policy issues facing the countries of this subregion in this context. The meeting was exploratory in nature, a part of the "search underway for a sustainable development approach to growth that balances in a fair way economic, social and environmental objectives".[12]

The collection of papers included in the present volume were commissioned from authors from the seven subregional countries. The authors were asked to write about the experiences of their respective country to highlight the aspects of policy coherence and policy sequencing that they would consider relevant for understanding the relationships between growth, investment and decent work, and the trade-offs and the synergies. The papers[13] were presented and discussed in the high-level meeting. Each paper is treated as a separate chapter in this volume, and the paper presented by the World Bank is focused on India.

Growth and employment in South Asia

We now look into some of the general features of the growth and employment situation in the South Asia region. South Asia[14] registered an annual average GDP growth rate of 6.1 per cent over the decade 1996–2006,[15] higher than any other region in the world except East Asia. With an annual average labour force growth rate of 2.1 per cent during this period, the unemployment rate increased from 4.4 per cent in 1996 to an estimated 5.2 per cent in 2006. The proportion of working poor earning US$1 a day to total employment declined from 53.8 per cent in 1996 to 34.4 per cent in 2006, the largest reduction of any region in the world. However, in 2006, South Asia had the second largest share of

12. Excerpts from the address by Juan Somavia, Director-General of the International Labour Office, to the Asian Employment Forum at Beijing, China, 13 August 2007.

13. The papers reflect the personal views of the authors.

14. Here, "South Asia" includes Bhutan and Maldives but not Iran; the "South Asian subregion", also referred to in this volume, contains seven ILO member countries, including Iran but excluding Maldives and Bhutan.

15. 2006 data in this discussion are preliminary estimates.

total employment in the "poor" category, next to sub-Saharan Africa, the same relative position as in 1996. In terms of absolute number of working poor, South Asia tops the list in both 1996 and 2006.[16] Consistently over this period, South Asia ranked number two in the world in terms of percentage share of total employment in agriculture, next to sub-Saharan Africa (the share itself declined, but it still accounted for over half of total employment) (ILO, 2007a). Thus, despite being a good growth performer, the region exhibits certain persistent characteristics of lack of development.

The region is also conspicuous in terms of gender disparities. The gender gap in South Asia in terms of the number of economically active females, at 41.8 per 100 males, was the second lowest in the world in 2006, the lowest being Middle East and North Africa. In the same year, female labour force participation rate in South Asia, at 36 per cent, was the second lowest in the world, just above Middle East and North Africa. Conversely, the male participation rate for that year in South Asia, at 82.2 per cent, was one of the highest in the world, next to sub-Saharan Africa and South-East Asia. Despite the low female participation rate, the unemployment rate for females is higher than that for males, having increased over the decade 1996–2006. While the female unemployment rate grew from 4.9 per cent in 1996 to 6.2 per cent in 2006, the unemployment rate for males increased from 4.2 per cent to 4.9 per cent over the same period. South Asia has the distinction of having the highest share of female workers employed in agriculture compared with other regions, a feature typical of underdevelopment. This relative position remained unchanged over the decade 1996–2006. Over 60 per cent of working women in South Asia are classified as contributing family workers (highest proportion in the world), 20 per cent as own-account workers and 15 per cent as wage and salaried workers (lowest proportion in the world)—features that have strong correlations with the incidence of working poverty at the US$2 a day level (ILO, 2007b). The relative positions of South Asia did not alter over the decade 1996–2006 despite reasonably robust growth.

16. The total number of working poor declined from 250.8 million in 1996 to 196.9 million in 2006.

Youth unemployment poses another serious challenge to this region. Despite a low labour force participation rate of 47.1 per cent, youth in this region are 2.8 times more likely to be unemployed than adults, according to 2006 data. Low literacy rates, absence of social protection for the overwhelming majority of workers, crowding out of female workers in the labour market (described as "discouraged workers") and low wages—sufficiently indicative of poor working conditions (ILO, 2007a)—are serious obstacles to achieving decent work objectives.

What happened in each of the seven countries of the subregion? Are they experiencing jobless growth? Are they experiencing labour market developments that are conducive to the achievement of decent work objectives? Are they facing discrete erosion in their policy spaces? Are policy mismatches occurring? Are there issues of inappropriate sequencing of policies? The following section is devoted to these themes. It draws largely from the background papers prepared for the high-level meeting by the present author and from the papers presented by the authors from the participating countries and the World Bank. The discussion and debate that took place in the meeting are outside the scope of this work.

The subsequent discussion in this chapter is divided into five sections. Section 1.2 presents a statistical analysis of the link between growth and employment. Section 1.3 discusses linkages between policies and employment outcome, and also highlights the challenges that these countries face in achieving a better balance between macro growth and employment objectives. Section 1.4 brings out how the growth–employment nexus affects the prospects for decent work. Section 1.5 presents a brief discussion on each of the following chapters, and section 1.6 concludes the chapter.

1.2 Growth and employment

Statistical exploration of the growth–employment disconnect

Country-level analysis reveals that the nexus between growth and employment did not follow a unique pattern in all countries of the subregion. Pakistan, for example, has been experiencing a robust growth at an average annual rate of 7 per cent between 2004 and 2007 and over 7.5 per cent between 2005 and 2007, with a steady decline in employment growth. However, the disconnection between growth and jobs in this case reflects improvements in productivity. The unemployment rate has come down from 8.3 per cent in 2001/02 to 6.2 per cent in the second quarter of 2005/06 (Government of Pakistan, 2006).

In Bangladesh, on the contrary, the rate of growth decelerated from 5.9 per cent in 1990 to 5.3 per cent in 2003 (with the growth rates going down as low as 4.9 per cent and 4.4 per cent in some of the years in between). Employment fell steeply, by 12 per cent, during this period,[17] indicating jobless growth. Unemployment rate increased from 1.9 per cent in 1990/91 to 4.3 per cent in 2002/03. The disconnection between growth and employment could possibly be explained by the fact that total factor productivity (TFP) has been the main growth driver in Bangladesh for a long period.[18] Similarly, a recent study of Sri Lanka using a growth accounting framework found that labour was a dominant factor in growth in the 1980s. However, the role of labour declined over time and was overtaken by TFP and, to a lesser extent, by physical capital accumulation (Duma, 2007).

Aggregate relationships often mask important differences between different sectors in respect of differential growth–employment nexus. Several countries of this subregion had labour market slacks in one or two sectors, and yet experienced labour market tightening that supported transition of surplus labour from the low-productivity to the high-productivity sector. In Sri Lanka, for example, the average annual growth rate of output declined from 5.2 per cent in the 1990s to 4 per cent during 2000–2004. The decline has been shared both by agriculture and industry while the service sector has succeeded in improving its performance marginally. For the economy as a whole, employment

17. Estimated from the data available in the *Labour Force Report* 1999-2000 and 2002-03 cited in Chapter 2 in this volume. Data on GDP growth rate are from ILO (2006a).

18. According to one estimate, between 1975 and 2000, TFP growth explained about 80 per cent of GDP growth above its long term average growth rate (World Bank, 2005a).

growth has fallen from 2.4 per cent in the 1990s to 1.8 per cent during 2000–2004. The fall in employment growth has been brought about by a steep decline in employment growth in the service sector due to substantial improvements in productivity. In both agriculture and industry, productivity[19] fell in the wake of a rise in the growth in employment and a substantial decline in the growth of output (Table 1.1). The economy failed to move surplus labour from agriculture to industry and from industry to the service sector. Growth in the service sector was not high enough to pull excess workers out from agriculture and industry. The unemployment rate in Sri Lanka increased from 7.6 per cent in 2000 to 8.5 per cent in 2004. The increase has occurred in both rural and urban areas and in male and female categories. In 2004, the unemployment rate among females was more than double that among males. Stagnation in agriculture and industry and productivity-led marginal growth in the service sector all contributed to a rise in unemployment.

Table 1.1

Sri Lanka: Average annual growth rates of output and employment, 1990s and 2000/2004

(percentage)

Sector	*1990s*		*2000-2004*	
	Output	*Employment*	*Output*	*Employment*
GDP	5.2	2.4	4.0	1.8
Agriculture	2.6	-0.5	0.4	0.5
Industry	6.8	3.2	3.4	3.8
Services	5.4	5.9	5.6	1.9

Source: Tilakaratna *et al.*, 2006.

In India, the three successive quinquennial surveys on employment and unemployment conducted in 1993/94, 1999/2000 and 2004/05[20] reveal that between the first two survey periods (i.e., between 1993/94 and 1999/2000) and the second two survey periods (i.e., between 1999/2000 and 2004/05), the growth of employment more than doubled

19. In this chapter, "productivity" means output per worker.

20. Each survey covers the period July to June.

whereas average annual growth of output came down from 6.53 per cent to 6 per cent, implying a fall in productivity. The decline in productivity was observed in the primary and tertiary sectors, where the annual average growth rates in output had declined but employment growth had increased. In contrast, a large increase in the growth rate of output in the secondary sector led to increased productivity despite higher employment growth (Tables 1.2 and 1.3). There was supply-side pressure in the labour market, with annual growth of the labour force nearly doubled over this period from 7.6 to 14.7 per cent. Unemployment rates also went up for rural, urban, male and female categories, substantially for females (Table 1.4).

Table 1.2

India: Average annual growth in output and employment, 1993/94–1999/2000

(percentage)

	1993/94 to 1999/2000		
Sector	*Employment growth*	*Value added growth*	*Elasticity*
Primary	0.03	2.88	0.01
Secondary	2.91	6.91	0.42
Tertiary	2.27	8.66	0.26
Whole economy	1.07	6.53	0.16

Source: Government of India, various rounds of NSS; and Government of India, 2007.

Table 1.3

India: Average annual growth in output and employment, 1999/2000–2004/05

(percentage)

	1999/2000 to 2004/05		
Sector	*Employment growth*	*Value added growth*	*Elasticity*
Primary	0.85	1.76	0.49
Secondary	4.64	9.72	0.48
Tertiary	4.67	7.64	0.61
Whole economy	2.60	6.00	0.43

Source: Same as Table 1.2.

Table 1.4

India: Unemployment rates (rural/urban and male/female), 1999/2000 and 2004/05, on current daily status basis

(percentage)

Category	*1999/2000*	*2004/05*
Rural males	7.2	8.0
Rural females	7.0	8.7
Urban males	7.3	7.5
Urban females	9.4	11.6

Source: Highlights on unemployment rates from National Sample Survey (NSS) 61st Round.

In Nepal, employment elasticity for the period 1981–1990 was 0.081, which increased to 0.363 during 1990–2005. Output per worker (at constant prices) in 2005 was more than double that of 1990.[21]

In Iran, apparently, there is no jobless growth. Employment growth increased from 0.5 per cent in 1998 to 3 per cent in 2001. GDP growth during this period increased from 3.9 per cent to 4.8 per cent (Table 1.5). Iran had the highest employment elasticity measured over the period 1991–2003 when compared with the other subregional countries (Table 1.6). However, as Table 1.5 indicates, Iran is an example of higher employment growth as a result of higher productivity. Despite a low rate

Table 1.5

Iran: Growth of annual output and employment, 1998–2001

(percentage)

Year	*1998*	*1999*	*2000*	*2001*	*Average 1997–2001*
GDP growth	3.9	1.5	5.7	4.8	3.6
Employment growth	0.5	2.0	2.7	3.0	1.8
Labour productivity growth	3.4	-0.5	2.9	1.7	1.8
Capital stock growth	7.5	7.7	7.8	8.0	7.8
Capital productivity	-3.2	-5.8	-1.9	-3.0	-3.9
Capital per worker	7.0	5.5	5.0	4.9	5.9
TFP growth	0.4	"2.9	0.9	-0.3	-0.5

Source: *Economic and performance evaluation report: Second year of the third development plan, 2002*, Management and Planning Organization (MPO), Islamic Republic of Iran cited in ILO, 2005a.

21. See Tables 5.6 and 5.7 in this volume.

of labour force participation (62 per cent for males and 12 per cent for females), Iran faces high unemployment rates. In 2001/02, the unemployment rate was 13.3 for males and 18.3 for females. There was no sign of jobless growth; employment growth was achieved in the face of a decline in the TFP growth.

There is a methodological issue here: how do we meaningfully measure growth–job disconnect (or connect) or jobless growth if employment data tend to conceal underemployment? (Fall in labour productivity can be one proxy to capture growing underemployment.) The use of the conventional measure of elasticity has serious disadvantages in this regard since high employment elasticity may simply reflect supply-side pressure due to growth in the labour force without divulging information on the demand side of the labour market. This is typically the situation in the countries of the South Asia subregion. As Figure 1.1 (a graphical depiction of data from Table 1.6) indicates, the variation of employment elasticity across the countries within this group mimics the variation in labour supply. The observed growth in employment in such cases may simply be the result of growth of underemployment (or disguised unemployment). Higher employment elasticity, therefore, does not necessarily imply strengthening of the growth–employment[22] nexus, in the same way that lower elasticity does not mean weakening of it. A meaningful assessment in this context needs to take into consideration the changes in productivity.

Table 1.6

Employment elasticity driven by labour supply, 1991–2003

	1991–2003	
Country	*Elasticity*	*Annual average growth in labour supply*
Iran	1.17	3.17
Bangladesh	0.44	2.18
India	0.33	2.10
Pakistan	0.91	2.74
Nepal	0.64	2.23
Sri Lanka	0.49	2.07

Note: Data for Afghanistan not available.

Source: World Bank, 2004a.

22. When employment means productive employment.

Figure 1.1

Labour supply driving employment elasticity

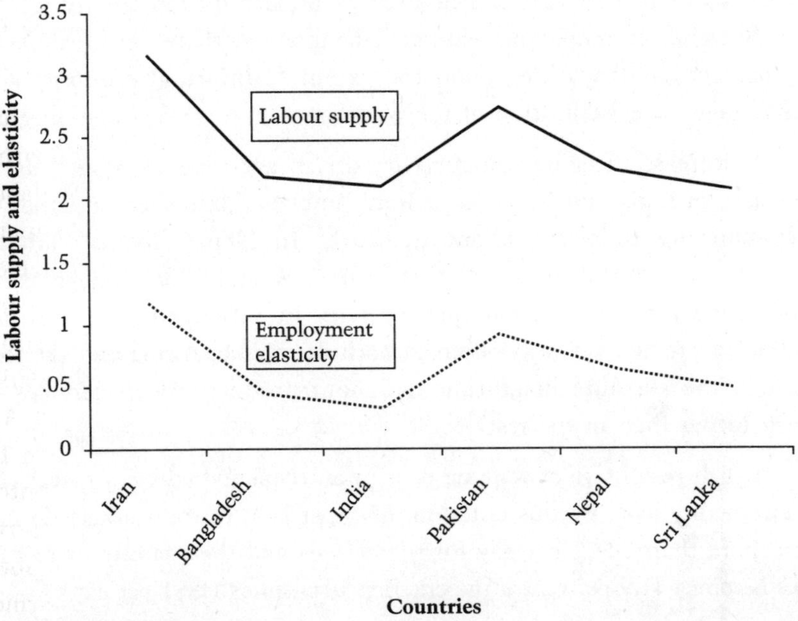

Source: Data in Table 1.6.

To sum up, going by the broad labour market indicators such as employment or unemployment rates and employment elasticity, there is no generalized evidence of a growing disconnect between growth and jobs in different countries of this subregion. According to the available recent data, in India the unemployment rate increased, employment grew and employment elasticity increased. In Pakistan, unemployment rate, growth of employment and employment elasticity all came down. These broad measures of employment or unemployment, however, are not reliable indicators of the inherent potential of economic growth to create productive jobs because these data hide underemployment. A study of the relationship between growth and productive employment, therefore, has to reconcile changes in employment with the changes in productivity. Furthermore, because the aggregate measure of the growth–employment nexus does not reveal intersectoral differences, there is need to observe this relationship at a disaggregated level by looking at the growth dynamics and labour absorption in each sector.

Job quality

In this subsection, we report on some of the broad characteristics of the labour market that can be used as proxies for job quality. These include trends in output per worker (labour productivity) and real wage, the percentage of working poor, the extent of informal economy and trends towards casualization of the workforce.

A decrease in labour productivity (in an aggregate measure), as in the cases of India and Nepal (also Iran), implies diminished potential in the economy to advance decent work. In Nepal, overall labour productivity declined marginally between 2000 and 2005, though there was strong growth in labour productivity in agriculture. Substantial decline in productivity was observed both in manufacturing and services (though the absolute magnitude of labour productivity in services is much higher than in the rest).

A high percentage of working poor in an economy reflects a prevalence of low-quality jobs. By this criterion, 87.5 per cent of the workers do not earn more than US$2 per day for themselves and their family in Nepal. This becomes 41.9 per cent if the criterion is taken as US$1 per day.

A decline in real wages implies deterioration in job quality. In Sri Lanka, except government employees,[23] workers faced a decline in real wage for most of the years between 2000 and 2004 (Table 1.7), and casualization[24] is growing in relation to both male and female workers.

Table 1.7

Sri Lanka: Annual average percentage change in real wages by sector, 2000–2004

Sector	*2000*	*2001*	*2002*	*2003*	*2004*
Agriculture	-3.6	-9.8	-1.5	2.5	-5.9
Industry and commerce	-2.7	-6.1	-2.0	-3.8	-3.8
Services	-5.7	2.8	-5.9	-5.9	2.9
Government employees	1.9	5.9	6.4	-6.0	14.1

Source: IMF, 2005a.

23. In 2004, out of 7.3 million employed persons, 1 million were employed by government.
24. Casual work, as opposed to regular work, is associated with inferior job quality attributes.

Furthermore, there are also reports of unsatisfactory working conditions in some of the new areas of employment growth. Working conditions (and also living conditions) in the free trade zones have been at the focus of attention in this regard.[25] Complaints are also received about the hostile and insecure work atmosphere that unskilled and semi-skilled migrant workers find in the host countries. Women account for the bulk of the workforce in both these categories.

Pakistan, like most of the countries in the subregion, has to deal with high proportion of jobs being in the informal economy. Informal jobs are characterized by low productivity, low incomes and poor and hazardous working conditions and the workers are outside the scope of labour laws and social protection. A very small proportion of the labour force is unionized and has access to collective bargaining. This does not augur well for the aims of promoting social dialogue and a rights-based labour market.

Bangladesh has about 95 per cent of the workforce in the informal economy, with a time-related underemployment of nearly 31 per cent. Fewer than 3 per cent of all workers fall under the purview of protection of labour laws. Furthermore, temporary, casual and subcontract work seems to have increased over time. Temporary workers as percentage of employees increased from 15 per cent during 1985–1990 to 24 per cent during 1995–2000 (Muqtada, 2003). The index of rural wages (1989/90 = 100) at constant prices for agricultural workers declined from 106.5 in 1993/94 to 94.5 in 1999/2000.[26] For the economy as a whole, formal economy employment seems to have declined further due to "shedding of labour in civil service, privatization processes and restructuring and closure of enterprises" (Muqtada, 2003: 18).

In India, the entire net increase in employment during 2000–2004 seems to have occurred in the informal economy. The 61st round of the National Sample Survey, pertaining to the year 2004/05, is the most reliable and comprehensive source of recent labour market information

25. For a discussion on unsatisfactory working conditions in the free trade zone in Sri Lanka, see Kelegama and Epaarachchi (2003). Conditions are reportedly no better in Bangladesh; see Chapter 2 in this volume.

26. Agriculture accounted for 51 per cent of total employment in 1999-2000.

in India. Certain findings of this survey point towards deteriorating job quality, as evident from a decline in wage employment and an increase in self-employment. Self-employment currently accounts for nearly half of the Indian workforce. For rural women, nearly two-thirds of all jobs are in self-employment. The survey also revealed that nearly half of the self-employed workforce did not find their work remunerative.[27] Interestingly, the decline in wage employment was associated with a decline in real wages for most of the workers. The gender gap in wages is quite large and has tended to increase. The other interesting facet of the decline in the real wage is that over the period 1999/2000–2004/05, women faced a substantial decline in average daily real wages for all categories of educational level (Chandrasekhar and Ghosh, 2006).

On the basis of the data published by the Annual Survey of Industries, which cover the organized manufacturing industries in India, it is seen that industries are gradually increasing their use of contract workers. It is also observed that the proportion of labour costs to the total production costs is falling: the two series are plotted in Figure 1.2. Between 1999/2000 and 2003/04, the proportion of contract workers to all workers increased from 20 to 25 per cent.[28] The proportion of labour costs[29] to total costs of production came down from 7.84 to 6.82 per cent during the same period.

Over the period 2000 to 2004, employment in the organized sector declined: the entire net increase in employment in India took place in the informal economy. Table 1.8 shows the trend in organized sector employment in India. The figures in the table indicate virtual stagnation in employment in the organized sector. Thus, the expansion of output of the organized sector during this period has been achieved with no growth in employment. Whatever growth in employment has been seen, it has been in the informal economy.

---

27. For more than 40 per cent of rural workers and about 30 per cent of urban workers, the perception of the level of satisfactory remuneration reportedly varied between US$1 and 2 per day. If by this criterion self-employment is found to be non-remunerative, it means that for many, earnings in self-employment are not even US$2 per day.

28. It was 12 per cent in 1990.

29. Labour cost also includes contract labour costs.

Figure 1.2

India: Increasing incidence of contract work—contract workers as a percentage of all workers and labour costs as a percentage of total production costs, 1999–2004 (indexes, 1999/2000 = 100)

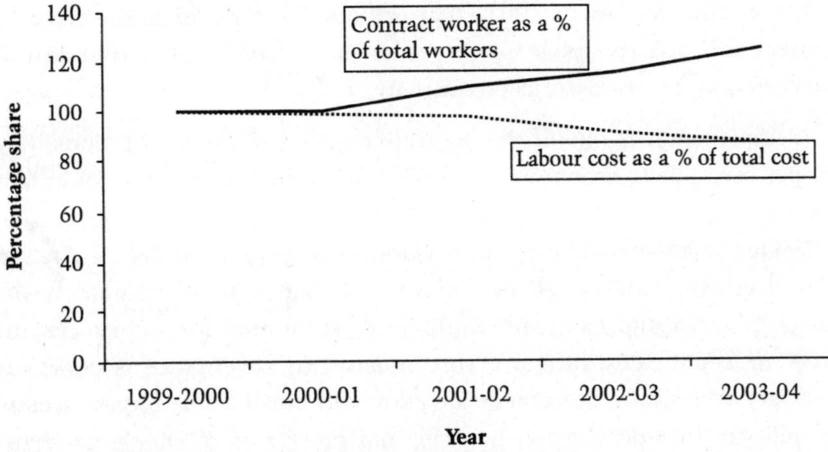

Note: The figure relates to the organized manufacturing sector in India.

Source: Computed on the basis of data released by the Ministry of Labour and Employment (*http://labourbureau.nic.in* visited on 9 March 2007).

Table 1.8

India: Employment in the organized sector, 1994–2004

(million persons)

Sectors	*1994*	*2000*	*2004*
Public sector, of which:	19.44	19.31	18.20
Primary	0.55	0.51	0.49
Secondary	4.90	4.49	4.03
Tertiary	13.99	14.31	13.68
Private sector, of which:	7.93	8.65	8.24
Primary	0.88	0.90	0.92
Secondary	4.82	5.26	4.65
Tertiary	2.22	2.48	2.68
Total (public and private), of which:	27.37	27.96	26.44
Primary	1.43	1.42	1.41
Secondary	9.73	9.76	8.67
Tertiary	16.22	16.79	16.36

Source: Computed from data reported in Government of India, 2007.

In Iran, towards the late 1990s, employment tended to rise faster than output, leading to a decline in labour productivity in agriculture, construction and trade. For the other sectors, output increased faster than employment, implying an increase in productivity (ILO, 2005a: 12). However, real manufacturing wage indices increased from 100 in 1995 (1995 = 100) to 128 in 2001 (ILO, 2006a). This might have served to protect job quality, at least in terms of earnings, even if it is not supported by an increase in productivity.

Afghanistan is one of the poorest countries of the world. Some 80–90 per cent of the economy is informal, with illicit production of opium accounting for one-third of the GDP in 2003, the bulk of which is of subsistence nature. The median value of sales per worker of Afghan manufacturing firms is about one-third of that of small manufacturing firms in India and Pakistan. Agriculture accounted for 47 per cent of GDP in 2003. State infrastructure is nascent, governance is poor and judiciary and legal enforcement are extremely weak. "The biggest sectors in industry include plastics, bottlers, and processors of simple packaged foods – all aimed at the local market ... Afghan enterprises are nascent and unable to effectively compete against imports to enter the export market" (World Bank, 2005b). "Eighty five per cent of the rural labour force is either self-employed or paid casual daily wages. ... Most businesses are owned by a family and employ only one or two workers (or owners)" (World Bank, 2005c). There are very strong locally entrenched business interests; regional and local warlords have very strong holds over the functioning of the economy. Capacity to implement the labour code (from the 1970s) does not exist. In the near absence of a legal framework, informal arrangements dictate working relations and rights. Due to the non-availability of comparable data over time, it is difficult to track changes in job quality, more so in view of the informal nature of the functioning in the economy.[1]

1.3 Growth inducing policies and their implications for employment growth

The economies of this subregion are at different levels of economic and social development and at differential stages of advancement of economic reform and structural adjustment. The lowest on the ladder of progress in reform are Afghanistan and Iran. It is possible to draw up some commonalities of policy compulsions for the rest. This section presents discussions on the commonalities and compulsions emerging from the growth strategies adopted by Bangladesh, India, Nepal, Pakistan and Sri Lanka, followed by discussions on Iran and Afghanistan.

Policy compulsions and commonalities

Wedded to a policy combination of stabilization as a part of a structural adjustment programme and liberalization aided by reduction in tariffs and taxes that adversely affected government revenue, Bangladesh, India, Nepal, Pakistan and Sri Lanka face the challenges of fiscal restraints and, consequently, their governments have serious incapacity to undertake the developmental spending necessary to create productive employment. These countries fall short of meeting the requirements of much needed public investment in the rural sector and on infrastructure, which would draw in the private investment necessary for the expansion of diversified agriculture and the non-farm sector, critical for the generation of productive employment.

In Sri Lanka, for instance, revenue forgone due to trade policy reforms, tax incentives and exemptions used to promote investment has not been compensated by an increase in tax buoyancy from overall growth in the economy (IMF, 2005b).[30] Total government revenue as a share of GDP declined from 19 per cent in 1996 to 15.3 per cent in 2004. The decline was contributed to by a falling share of all forms of taxes and non-tax revenue. The expansionary fiscal policy, in the face of falling revenue share, was aided by deficit financing. On an average, fiscal deficits have been close to 9.5 per cent of the GDP over the past 25 years, from mid-1970s until 2004, and public debt has exceeded 100 per cent of GDP. The high fiscal burden impaired the ability of the Government to undertake investment in infrastructure, much needed to boost private sector investment. This also constrained fresh public

30. It has been observed that the effectiveness of these incentives and exemptions in attracting FDI or in promoting domestic investment is yet to be proven. These may well work as means of granting rents to investors rather than as effective investment incentives.

investment in agriculture and the maintenance of existing rural assets. The infrastructure bottleneck hampered distribution of agricultural produce. Weak transport has been identified as the single most important bottleneck to rural firms (World Bank and ADB, 2005). Due to lack of maintenance, only 10 per cent of the paved road network is in good condition (World Bank, 2005d).

In Nepal, agriculture was considered to be a sector having big potential for ensuring a sustained high growth rate, generating more employment opportunities and thereby reducing poverty. Such was the vision of the Agriculture Sector Perspective Plan, prepared under the guidance of Professor John Mellor. However, the policies were in contrast with the government commitments to implement the long-term Agriculture Sector Perspective Plan. Subsidy in agriculture was abruptly abolished in 1998. The farmers were badly hit. The situation became worse after 2001, when domestic terms of trade started moving against agriculture in the wake of competition with subsidized agricultural products from India. Nepali farmers suffered high input costs and low output prices. Furthermore, the share of government development expenditure has reduced drastically in recent years.[31]

Accelerated growth in agriculture has helped to reduce poverty in Nepal. However, sustaining this growth would require increasing farm productivity, improving market efficiency and strengthening the capacity of the farmers to respond to domestic and international market opportunities. This in turn would require not only reforms of land and credit policies and agricultural trade regulations, but also removing the barriers to increased private sector participation and investment in rural infrastructure and agriculture. These requirements need to be viewed against the backdrop of the fact that: "With a tax to GDP ratio of around 9% of GDP, Nepal's tax effort is, (alongside Bangladesh), the lowest in the region" (World Bank, 2005e).

Fiscal compulsions hamper public spending in the social sector, and this can potentially be a critical obstacle in achieving the objectives for decent work. A study by the World Bank benchmarked Pakistan

31. See Chapter 5 in this volume.

against the top 25 per cent of the developing-country distribution in respect of several growth determinants. The comparison revealed that Pakistan was fairly close to the top 25 per cent in respect of trade openness but lagged behind substantially in three areas: education, public infrastructure and financial depth (World Bank, 2006a: 24).[32] Clearly, decent work deficits cannot be addressed without building a competent and skilled workforce through investing in human capital[33] and making substantial public investment in infrastructure that paves the way for an inclusive and broad-based growth. The fiscal trends do not align well with this objective. With fiscal liberalization in Pakistan, tax revenue as a percentage of GDP at market prices came down from 13.2 per cent in 1997/98 to 10.0 per cent in 2004/05 (revised estimate). On top of this, the economy faces the challenge of an almost unsustainable burden of public debt. The ability of the government to make investment, therefore, is severely limited by fiscal constraints. Public spending on education in Pakistan as a percentage of GDP is the lowest in South Asia. The proportion, however, increased from 1.8 per cent in 2000/01 to 2.1 per cent in 2005/06.[34] The government launched a package entitled the Education Sector Reform. The targets set for literacy and enrolment for the primary and middle school levels for 2005 were not achieved (Government of Pakistan, 2006: Chapter 11).

Important questions that need to be explored are to what extent a strategy of export-led growth can be an option in these countries and whether such an option can be compatible with employment objective. Bangladesh, India, Nepal and Sri Lanka have increased their export–GDP ratios significantly over the past one and a half decades. Policies favouring increased openness and better management of the exchange rate, among other factors, have helped to continue export-led growth

32. Pakistan underperformed relative to other countries with similar per capita income with respect to expenditure and outcomes across education, health and nutrition. The discrepancies were particularly large for women, manifesting in a "gender gap" that reinforced the "social gap"; see World Bank (2002).

33. Pre-school and early childhood programmes create a solid foundation for subsequent learning. Primary and secondary education provides workers with basic skills that help them to learn the new skills that are required to cope with the changes induced by new technology; see OECD (1996).

34. Even then, however, it is lower than Bangladesh, India and Sri Lanka.

and employment for some time. However, exports from these countries are dominated by a few items,[35] and diversification—which figures prominently on their export agendas—will take time. There are several reasons why this strategy cannot lead to a win–win situation for both growth and employment promotion in the future.

Much of the growth in export has been due to the Multi-Fibre Agreement (MFA) and preferential access to somc of the destination countries. Competitive survival in the export market in the medium term would take the form of upgrading technology to enter overseas markets for higher value added items at the upper end of the value chain. The first move in the competitive game would be in the form of a "race to the bottom", which would create local unemployment. At the next stage, labour shedding is likely to result from of the introduction of more sophisticated and advanced technology in the "race to the top".

Sri Lanka's garment sector, for example, contributes around 50 per cent of total exports and 44 per cent of industrial outputs, and it employs about 5–6 per cent of Sri Lanka's labour force directly and roughly 1 million workers indirectly. The question is whether continued reliance on the same strategy will achieve growth with decent employment. In the post-MFA scenario, the leaders of Sri Lanka's garment industry had taken measures to move up the value chain to higher value added products. However, there are risks of disruption among small exporters, who account for about 70 per cent of the exporters and 35 per cent of the employment in this sector (World Bank, 2005d: 23). If the future of Sri Lanka's export success continues to hinge on the race to move up the value chain and a quick shift to out-of-quota goods, its precise impact on labour absorption is uncertain. Productivity is going to play a key role in this competitive gain. The winning strategy in the near term could be to compress labours' shares in value added, or to fly to low labour cost countries. Reports of production being moved away from Sri Lanka to China and India to take advantage of the low

35. Sri Lanka's garment sector contributes half of the country's total exports; garments and carpets led exports from Nepal; ready-made garments accounted for three-quarters of the export earnings of Bangladesh; textiles and apparel account for around 65 per cent of merchandise exports from Pakistan.

labour costs in these countries have already been received (IMF, 2005b: 10). Another option is to raise productivity by operating with much higher levels of capital;[36] in other words, capital deepening of the production process. In any of these scenarios, the export-led growth strategy may not help in maximizing productive employment.

Countries that would tend to adopt supportive measures to promote an export-led growth strategy—for example through access to concessional credit and tax exemptions—might, by making capital available relatively cheaply, indirectly encourage substitution of labour with capital. Countries with low real rates of interest (resulting from expansionary monetary policy leading to inflation) may also create the same inducements. Sri Lanka, for instance, used fiscal policy to support an export-led investment strategy through tax exemptions, tax holidays and export incentive to companies operating under a Board of Investment.[37] Views have been expressed that these measures not only adversely affected the budget, but also did not bring commensurate benefits of foreign direct investment (World Bank, 2005d: 23).

Due to slow progress in institutional reforms in these countries (in state-owned enterprises, public utilities, the power sector and banking), infrastructure could soon become a binding constraint, eroding the initial comparative advantages of cheap labour. The competitive strategy in such an instance might take the form of introducing better and more sophisticated technology to win the race, and this might affect labour absorption. Similar consequences could result if the skills gap became a binding constraint due to lack of adequately skilled personnel in the economy.

Some of these economies are supplementing domestic savings with substantial foreign savings (high remittances contributed significantly to foreign savings) to support relatively high levels of investment and

36. It is reported that in this industry, value added per worker in Sri Lanka is 28 per cent lower than in China, and that the latter operates with a much higher level of capital (World Bank, 2004b).

37. According to an estimate by the Government, exemptions of corporate tax, mainly to the Board of Investment companies, accounted for about 1 per cent of the GDP (IMF, 2005b).

export-led growth. However, insufficient progress in institutional reforms and infrastructure bottlenecks may soon create supply-side constraints in the domestic economy. Progressively, higher demand in such cases would have to be met through imports. Import dependence of export may, in consequence, tend to further weaken the linkages between the external sector and the domestic economy, affecting employment prospects adversely. Employment elasticity would fall and a progressively higher import–GDP ratio (not necessarily competing imports) would create a wedge between growth and employment. The situation could get worse if labour shedding occurs because of deindustrialization due to increased competition with imports.

As an example, about 800,000 Nepalese work abroad and remit approximately US$800 million, amounting to 12 per cent of GDP. This caused GNP to grow at a faster rate than GDP, with consequent impacts on demand (World Bank, 2005e). It may be seen from Table 1.9 that a progressively larger gap between domestic savings and total investment (both expressed as ratios of GDP) is concomitant with an increasing difference between exports and imports (both expressed as ratios of GDP).

Table 1.9

Savings–investment and export–import gaps in Nepal, 1971–2003

Year	*GAP I_1*	*GAP II_2*
1971–1980	-7.3	-4.7
1981–1990	-9.4	-9.4
1991–2000	-10.5	-11.2
2001	-9.1	-11.5
2002	-13.6	-11.3
2003	-15.5	-14.6

Notes: [1] GAP I = gross domestic savings in proportion to GDP–investment in proportion to GDP.
[2] GAP II = exports to GDP ratio–imports to GDP ratio.

Source: Computed on the basis of data given in Table 1.1 in World Bank, 2005e.

Nepal has been affected in both ways. For example, exports in Nepal are heavily dependent on imported raw materials, with virtually no backward linkages (linkages with domestic agriculture and the non-farm sector). Furthermore, Nepal has experienced deindustrialization and consequent labour shedding due to competition with imports. The worst casualties were cottage and small-scale industries (Chapter 5 in this volume).

To be broad-based, economic growth should generate enough domestic productive activities to lead to growth in domestic income and domestic savings. In Pakistan, domestic savings in proportion to GDP have shown a consistent decline, from 18.1 per cent in 2001/02 to 14.4 per cent[38] in 2005/06. The fact that growth in investment is supported by a growth in foreign savings gives rise to a doubt about whether the growth process is capable of generating the broad-based domestic activities that might lead to higher incomes and higher savings in the domestic economy, a prerequisite for increased domestic income generation and employment.

Investment rates in Pakistan improved, however. After a decline and stagnation over three years, both public and private investment improved during 2003/04–2005/06. Consequently, total investment as a percentage of GDP increased from 16.6 to 20.0 per cent, reflecting, partly, increased public sector investment in infrastructure and involvement in various development programmes. Growth in private sector investment took place mainly in agriculture, manufacturing, mining and quarrying, construction, transport and communication, wholesale and retail trade. This, by itself, is no doubt a healthy development given the background of declining private investment in the 1990s and low and falling public investment in agriculture (World Bank, 2002a). However, demand-led growth did spill over the external sector, leading to an increased import–GDP ratio—from 14.4 per cent in 2001/2002 to 18.5 per cent in 2004/05—without a concomitant growth in the export share in GDP. The potential for sustaining a demand-led growth strategy without destabilizing the external sector is open to question; there is also no conspicuous link with possible improvement of decent work outcomes. This limitation underscores the need to address supply-side factors that could potentially drive growth and at the same time, cohere with the need to achieve the decent work goals.

An important question that needs to be explored is whether a "fallacy of composition" is involved if an export-led strategy is adopted by

38. Provisional estimate.

labour-surplus economies in order to exploit their comparative advantage of cheap labour. An interesting study of Bangladesh shows that along with the growth in unskilled labour-intensive exports, there has been a concomitant growth in unskilled labour-intensive imports. The growth in unskilled labour-intensive imports largely explained by a sharp increase in the import of textiles required for the production of garments for export (wearing apparel accounted for 72 per cent of total manufacturing exports in 1996/1998). The net employment effects of unskilled labour due to increased integration of Bangladesh with the global market is, therefore, not obvious. One estimate places aggregate employment effects of exports to be marginally higher than that of imports (Sen, undated).

How does globalization affect a country such as India, which has a large domestic market? To the extent that the logic of competitive survival *vis-à-vis* import into the domestic market would dictate investment in the manufacturing of high value added products based on technology upgrading, there is a potential for labour displacement. Since 2003/04, the Indian economy has entered into a high-growth trajectory and has been running at an average growth rate of 8.5 per cent up to 2006/07. A good number of supportive macro policies seem to be yielding results, a noteworthy achievement being a steady rise in the tax–GDP ratio of the centre from 8.8 per cent in 2002/03 to 10.3 per cent in 2005/06, with fiscal deficit declining to 4.1 per cent of GDP in 2005/06. The savings of the public sector, which were negative until 2002/03, have turned positive.

A notable feature of the high growth was the resurgence of the manufacturing sector. However, it has been observed that, within manufacturing, the industries that registered high growth were skills-intensive and produce relatively high value added products. These industries include chemicals, basic metals, machinery and transport equipment. Conversely, industries that are employment-intensive and local-resources based, such as food products and leather, did not perform well. The economy in general and the manufacturing sector in particular is investing in improved technological sophistication of the production process. This is reflected in greater increases in the prices of capital goods compared with general price levels (Government of India, 2007).

The trend, therefore, clearly indicates a tendency towards increase in capital intensity consistent with reductions in labour costs as a proportion of the total cost of production.

The above discussion drives home the point that under a "business as usual" scenario, it is likely that the policies being pursued in the South Asia subregion would tend to weaken the growth–employment nexus. Under the pressure of globalization, growing technological sophistication will be the key to competitive survival in the domestic market (as in the example of India) or in the export market (as discussed with reference to the Sri Lankan experience). The supply pressure of labour in such circumstances would tend to show up in higher employment elasticity and lower labour productivity in those sectors that are outside the scope of rapid technological progress. Growth will emerge in certain segments of the economy where investments are made. The increased premium on skilled workers would tend to widen the income gap between skilled and unskilled workers.

An added concern is that if diversification of agriculture is delayed, import dependence of consumption is likely to increase. This would further deter private investment in agriculture and prevent growth of employment. Statistical evidence suggests that with the growth of income, the consumption basket is getting more and more diversified and the proportion of income being spent on staple foods such as rice and wheat is coming down.[39] Middle and upper income consumers are improving their diets and, consequently, demand for fruits, vegetables, fats and livestock products is showing accelerated growth (Landes and Gulati, 2004). If domestic production is not able to meet the demand from domestic consumers, the demand will be met through imports, with adverse implications for the domestic demand for labour.

It is clear that growing openness is a double-edged sword; it cuts both ways, through channels of exports and imports. It could also potentially undermine the development of labour market if coherence between the mainstream growth strategy and the labour market is not

39. A detailed discussion on diversification is available in Joshi *et al.* (2004), and an interesting discussion on policy compulsions of farm sector reforms in India is available in Landes and Gulati (2004).

forged through necessary intervention. A coherent macro strategy would dictate that investment is promoted in agriculture and infrastructure to create a dynamic synergy with the manufacturing and service sectors. Skill development is an essential adjunct to this process.

Afghanistan and Iran

Starting from a low base, the annual GDP increase in Afghanistan was 29 per cent in 2002 and 16 per cent in 2003. Out of a total GDP of US$6.9 billion in 2003, foreign aid and opium exports contributed US$4 billion in 2003/04. Afghanistan also received remittances of hundreds of millions of dollars per year. However, government revenue accounted for just over 4 per cent of the official GDP in 2003 (official GDP[40] was US$4.6 billion in that year). The reconstruction programme, agriculture, the opium economy and donor funding are the key drivers of growth. State building and governance are still in their infancy, with near absence of state capacity, judiciary and a legal framework. More than 90 per cent of the economy is informal, with warlords and the mafia network running parallel informal governments. The major challenge that the economy faces, therefore, is one of transition from an informal economy, with a large part of its income generated by criminal activities, to a formal economy with progressive decriminalization. This would help to attract private investment.

The government is running the National Emergency Employment Program and other Safety Net Programs (World Bank, 2005c). The ILO project in Afghanistan is geared towards strengthening the capacity of the Ministry of Labour and Social Affairs and improving access to labour market services (ILO, 2006b). Coherence at three levels—among donors' approaches and policies, within different ministries and agencies of the Government, and between donors and the Government[41]—is essential to ensure availability of funding support to maintain the growth momentum and to sequence economic reforms in such a way as to avoid disruptive impacts on the labour market.

---

40. Unofficial GDP is sourced from the opium economy.

41. An interesting discussion on donor and aid harmonization efforts in Nepal is available in World Bank (2005e, Box 2.1).

Iran faces the major challenge of raising the growth rate to a sufficiently high level to clear the existing backlog of unemployment and absorb the annual growth of the labour force. According to the estimates of the World Bank, annual labour supply growth in Iran is now 5 per cent, which, if added to the existing stock of unemployed, would require more than 8 per cent growth in GDP per year (there are, however, differences in figures: the World Bank estimates that unemployment is 16 per cent). This would require an additional investment of 10 per cent of GDP, which is less than the "large and inefficient" energy consumption subsidy that Iran spends every year (World Bank, 2003). Institutionally, this means moving progressively away from a public sector dominated economy (characterized by inefficiency and overemployment) to an enabling environment for private sector investment and growth. The transition needs to be coordinated and sequenced in a planned manner so as to avoid disruptive consequences for the labour market.

1.4 Growth–Employment nexus: Decent work implications and coherence

It is evident from the foregoing discussions that, under the programmes of economic reform and fiscal stabilization, there is a reduction of policy space for the government, and that this is likely to influence the employment outcome of growth in the short and medium terms. The growth-inducing policies do not cohere with the objective of employment promotion. Nevertheless, it is noteworthy that elements of decent work are reflected in policies and programmes being implemented by different ministries in countries of this subregion (ILO, 2006b).[42] Reviews of the functioning of these programmes and policies suggest weak implementation and poor coordination between the different agencies involved. This leads to waste rather than efficiency, overlap, thinning of resources and fragmented efforts that fail to reach the critical threshold level required for an impact. To cite just one instance,[43] there are many social protection schemes in Nepal. Lack of

42. Some of the countries, such as Pakistan and Sri Lanka, have adopted decent work as an explicitly stated major policy objective.

43. There are many examples available in the literature cited in this chapter.

coordination reduces their effectiveness, and in some cases their impact is not clear. Some are based on short-term funding and their continuity is not certain. For example, the assistance programme, which encourages good practices such as food for education, depends upon the availability of food surpluses from the donor countries in the World Food Programme. This is clearly outside the control of the Government of Nepal. Even the pensions and the provident fund in the formal economy is likely to pose an unsustainable fiscal burden unless monitored and managed effectively. Furthermore, the impacts of these schemes on labour market flexibility, labour mobility and the relation with the productivity gains is not known (World Bank, 2005e).

Incoherence leads to pervasive mismatches: between supply and demand for skills; between education, skills development and jobs; between the need for and the provision of social protection; between social protection and its linkage with labour market flexibility, to name but a few. Furthermore, there are issues of coherence in approach and coordination of efforts between different layers of governance—central, state and local—for implementing policies of decentralized development. Efforts to strengthen coherence need to encompass the community of donors and the multilateral system; they are important stakeholders in the process.

In order to design effective mechanisms for policy and institutional coordination, there needs to be an improved understanding of the reasons for the unintended incoherence. The explanation may devolve on organizational and inter-organizational aspects, encompassing a wide range of issues, including incentives and transaction costs, turf protection, information asymmetries and social, cultural and political barriers.

It is apparent that a lack of coherence between growth and employment is a source of critical weakness in achieving decent work goals. If unemployment increases, or, as is increasingly the case, employment is created in the informal economy, it becomes the weak link in the chain and affects all other components of decent work. Unemployment and underemployment, and employment without rights in the informal economy, potentially undermine the prospects for social dialogue and decrease social protection. In India, for example, the decay of trade union power started in the 1980s, when there was large-scale closure of mills after a protracted period of lockouts which led to extensive job losses without compensation (Mazumdar and Sarkar, 2004). This development reportedly reduced the incentive for workers to join trade unions, and with the closure of many mills, trade union membership, including in the service sector, declined from 8.18 million in 1986/87 to 5.61 million in 1996/97 (Uchikawa, 2002, cited in Mazumdar and Sarkar, 2004). Many factors contributed towards the growing ineffectiveness of protective labour regulation. These include downsizing of the public sector and lack of growth in employment in the organized sector, introduction of flexible labour practices, recruitment by employers of non-unionized workers to perform work meant to be carried out by the unionized categories of workers, increasing use of contract labour by the organized sector, and informalization and casualization of the labour force.

1.5 Highlights of the following chapters

We now briefly discuss some of the issues highlighted in the following chapters. The chapters bring together the recent development experiences of seven countries, not all of which share the same political and economic history and therefore, similar compulsions. A significant part of this subregion has been devastated by war and continues to reel under conflicts and insurgency, which have taken, and continue to take, a heavy toll on the ability of the governments involved to concentrate on progress. The development contexts, therefore, vary greatly between the countries discussed. There is the oil-rich outlier Iran with a resource endowment different from the rest of the subregion. Information, data, statistics are either non-existent or difficult to collect in strife-torn countries or regions. The diverting of resources towards security and defence preparedness inflicts a heavy burden on public exchequers, leaving very little money for spending on infrastructure, education and health. Against this wide variety of backgrounds and differences in setting, this volume presents the varying perspectives of the authors and their differences in the prioritization of issues, while approaching the same broad theme of growth, investment and decent work. The shift of emphasis in terms of content and coverage in the different chapters is therefore to be expected.

Bangladesh

The chapter on Bangladesh (Rashid, Chapter 2 in this volume) draws attention towards factors that constrain potential growth in private investment in the country—such as poor infrastructure, power shortage, corruption, government regulation and non-availability of adequate finance. According to the author, despite attempted reforms in the financial sector in Bangladesh, financial intermediation continues to be inefficient. The rate of borrowing and therefore, the costs of private investment remain high.

The trend in public investment is not encouraging either. Public investment as a percentage of GDP has fallen since 2000/01, with the result that total investment as a percentage of GDP in 2005/06 remained at a low level of 24.33 per cent against the national savings rate of 29.15 per cent in the same year.[44] With one of the lowest tax–GDP ratios in the world, the government faces a serious challenge in increasing public investment if fiscal deficit is to remain under control. Furthermore, the proportion of annual government development expenditure allocated to agriculture and water resources has shown a declining trend for about a decade. This has threatened the prospects for agricultural diversification, which could have been a source of potential demand for productive employment. Similarly, a decline in investment in the power sector had also affected agricultural production and investment.

Import liberalization has adversely affected inefficient, import-competing domestic industry but has also improved efficiency in some others: both of these effects have a negative impact on employment. Tariff liberalization has halted the growth of the nascent domestic engineering and the capital goods industries. This growth could have potentially facilitated technological adaptation and upgrading of the traditional domestic industry in the informal economy and the forging of subcontracting relationships with the large firms.

44. Provisional estimates.

The investment policy in Bangladesh has not spelt out any strategy to stimulate the growth of labour-intensive industries in rural areas. Thus, it cannot be said that employment is central to macroeconomic policy in the country. During the period of economic reforms, which also included financial sector reforms, the share of bank advances to agriculture and to small and cottage industries declined whereas the share for large scale manufacturing has increased. Thus, credit support to the more employment-intensive sector has been proportionately less and less.

Chapter 2 clearly shows that policy developments during the period of reforms and their impacts were not conducive for maximizing productive employment. There is a need for further work to assess how better matching and sequencing among these policies could advance the goals of decent work. Concerns have been expressed in this chapter about the challenges of governance involved in implementing the decent work agenda in growing informal economies, a common feature in most of the countries. The author brings attention to the fact that even in the formal economy, the norms of decent work are bypassed (the example of the export-oriented ready-made garments sector in Bangladesh has been cited in this connection). Another governance issue referred to in this chapter relates to poor implementation of the Annual Development Programme in Bangladesh, which slows down the progress in infrastructure development and adversely affects the growth and employment prospects—an issue of inefficiency in public spending, which is not uncommon in other countries of this subregion.

India

In the first of two chapters on India (Chapter 3 in this volume), Kannan underscores the need for an indicator of "decent work" rather than "jobs" per se and suggests "regular work" as a second approximation of decent work. According to the author, this is much better than the "broad employment measure" commonly used. In the Indian context, the author provides a more refined estimate of decent work by capturing the regular employment where workers have access to rights, enjoy reasonable conditions of work, earn above minimum wages, have access to social dialogue and enjoy "legally backed social security benefits". The author categorizes such employment as "formal employment" rather than "formal economy employment". The number of those "self-employed" who have equivalent or better standards of consumption than regular workers (using an estimation based on consumer expenditure data) was added to the number of those in regular employment to arrive at a broad measure of the number of persons having access to decent work. Based on such measurements, the author finds that "the disconnect between growth and decent work is quite robust over a long period of time". Furthermore, the share of regular work is invariant to the sectoral shift in the pattern of employment that occurs as the economy transforms itself.

According to the author, despite being a continued concern, employment was never central to macroeconomic policy or planning in India. It remained an adjunct policy that supported creation of self-employment or wage employment through public works programmes. Some of the earlier support policies, which sought to promote employment indirectly in agriculture and the small scale sector, were subsequently relaxed in Indian economic policy as per the logic of economic reforms. As a strategy, the author recommends the promotion of public investment in rural areas, especially in infrastructure, combined with innovative programmes to generate direct employment for unskilled workers and to include women and those in self-employment in these programmes. This might lead to an increase in demand for wage goods. Any pressure on prices of wage goods that might result from such a strategy could be tackled by, as some economists in the country suggest, import of wage goods using the country's comfortable foreign exchange reserves. However, such a prescription comes in conflict with the goal of fiscal stability being pursued under the programme of economic reforms.

The author refers to a recent report by the Research and Information System for Developing Countries, which provides estimates of direct and indirect employment in Indian exports. According to these estimates, exports accounted for 3.5 per cent of total employment in India in 2004/05. The employment impact, therefore, is quite low, even when the likely adverse impact of import-competing activities on employment is not added. The author also points out that the employment strategy in India seeks to support the promotion of employment in export-oriented sectors, such as textiles and apparels, gems and jewellery, and that, as experience has shown, employment in such sectors will not necessarily be decent employment. Informal employment abounds in formal enterprises in some of the well known export-oriented industrial clusters and export processing zones in India.

If, as the author presumes, regular/formal/organized sector employment is the first approximation of decent employment, the question that arises is—and this is a part of one of the contemporary debates—whether current labour legislation is incompatible with the goal of expansion of employment in the organized sector. The author argues that there is not enough empirical evidence so far to support such an apprehension. However, according to the author, in a competitive environment, changes in technology should dictate the need for enterprise restructuring and labour legislation should not be a hindrance in it. The issue at stake that needs to be addressed is what combination of job security and income security the economy should strive to provide, "a social model that will have to be mediated by the state".

The author observes that there are multiple adjunct policies and programmes to promote employment; the question is whether "they add up to a meaningful whole". The employment impact of certain other policies, such as dereservation of certain items in the small scale sector and the setting up of Special Economic Zones (SEZs), should be added to the employment generated through the adjunct policies to assess the aggregate employment impact of different policies. The author argues in favour of the creation of special zones, similar to SEZs, for the micro and small enterprises in the existing clusters, particularly those which have rural linkages. It would have been interesting to know more about this concept of SEZs for micro and small enterprises and in what ways such a scheme could benefit the existing clusters.

Commenting on the potential conflict between the compulsion of fiscal stabilization and the need for increasing public investment to promote decent employment, the author expresses the view that in India, fiscal stabilization has been attempted through compression of capital expenditure by the government rather than by reducing the revenue deficit through improved revenue collection efficiency and/or taxing the rich and the corporate sector. The latter option is avoided on the ground that it might discourage private investment. According to the author, this "current orthodoxy" misses out on the point that public and private investments in a developing country are often seen as complementary, as demonstrated by the Chinese experience.

The author recommends balancing macroeconomic policies with macro social policies and identifies three important needs: to monitor whether aggregate economic growth leads to divergent growth patterns in the formal and informal economy; to balance inflation with employment; and to balance the notion of income poverty with supplementary information on infant mortality, availability of social protection, etc.

Finally, to arrive at a broad estimate of the number of people having access to decent work, the author included those self-employed who have standards of consumption equivalent to or better than regular workers. It would be useful to explore how the notion of consumption expenditure could be combined with some measures of rights and social security to evolve a more complete approximation of decent work dimensions. The decent work deficits on these counts may be acute among those in the lower-middle or lower deciles of the expenditure classes.

India (study by the World Bank)

The other study on India (Ahsan, Dasgupta and Narain, Chapter 4 in this volume)[45] argues that rapid economic growth in India in the 1990s led to a better labour market outcome and to "greater non-farm opportunities" of employment "drawing labour away from agriculture". The unorganized manufacturing sector gained in terms of growth in labour productivity and earnings. Thus, there was some evidence of labour market tightening. Along with the increase in productivity, real wages grew, benefiting all wage groups including the poor and the vulnerable. Wage differentials across regions and gender improved,

45. Contribution by the World Bank Country Office, Delhi.

although substantial differences still remain. An interesting observation mentioned in the chapter is that in most occupations, particularly in manual ones, women's wages were about half that of men's—a differential that could not be explained through industry or occupational characteristics.

More discussions of certain ideas put forward in the chapter could have enhanced the usefulness of the paper. For example, the authors cite improvement in real earnings as one indicator of the improvement in job quality. While an increase in real earnings is certainly desirable, such an increase is compatible with deterioration in job quality if the deficit in other elements of decent work (such as job insecurity, employment rights and freedom) increases. Furthermore, while real earnings can increase, the gap between the increase in productivity and real earnings can widen if the former progressively exceeds the latter.

Based on observed relationship between productivity growth and lagged employment growth, the authors find that in contrast to the regions (within India) with lower productivity growth, regions with higher productivity growth had higher employment growth with a lag. The relationship between growth in productivity and growth in employment, therefore, is more complex than an observed trade-off between the two in the short run would imply. Spreading the gains from productivity to the lagging regions of India and to the wider society, therefore, remains a challenge. Policies recommended to achieve this objective are:

- stimulate demand for labour through diversification into horticulture and high-value products; expand sustainable irrigation; remove any policy bias in the existing incentives structure that discourages labour-intensive crops and cropping practices; and develop an efficient agricultural supply chain;
- review the industrial incentives structure to remove any bias against the emergence of dynamic middle-sized manufacturing enterprises;
- improve the investment climate;
- reform labour market regulations;

- facilitate development of the informal economy through support facilities;
- expand and improve access to secondary education and market-relevant skills development facilities; and
- maintain good macro policies that keep inflation low and stable.

Analysis of the trade-offs and synergies involved in the simultaneous pursuit of these multiple policy objectives—the essence of any discussion on policy coherence—would be an interesting area of further work.

Like in the study on Bangladesh (Chapter 2 in this volume), the authors cite a number of regulatory and governance-related factors and weak infrastructure as deterrents to improvement in the investment climate.

In the other study on India (Chapter 3), Kannan recommends "taxing the rich and the corporate sector" as a part of the fiscal consolidation effort. Likewise, the authors in this chapter are critical of India's generous depreciation rate for investment in machinery and equipment for tax purposes, which according to them may encourage firms to be capital-intensive. An interesting agenda for future work could be a detailed examination of the rationale behind such recommendations, the considerations involved in such fiscal dispensations and an assessment of the likely impact of these policies on investment.

The authors of Chapter 4 discuss the dysfunctional aspects of labour laws in India, in particular the Industrial Disputes Act (IDA), and argue that "restrictive labour regulations emanating from the IDA constrain production and job growth in formal manufacturing, promotc the informal economy and deepen dualism". While one cannot deny the necessity of a review of labour laws (like any other regulations) to improve their effectiveness and efficiency, there is no conclusive empirical evidence in the literature that they are obstructive to the expansion of formal manufacturing enterprises and employment therein. A survey of literature for and against this argument is beyond the scope of our discussion here.

It would, however, be interesting to mention here that both studies on India included in this volume briefly touch upon the issue of whether existing labour laws hamper decent employment, a subject that merits detailed examination. The subject merits detailed examination and as such cannot be treated briefly, as in these two chapters. To bring out the contentious nature of the issue, one can cite just one example from these two chapters. The World Bank study indicates that "an important consequence of these costs imposed by IDA is that, firms are encouraged to remain small to remain outside the purview of the law". Conversely, Kannan finds empirical evidence to suggest that there has been no observable transition in average employment size from those categories of enterprises for which labour laws are applicable to those for which these laws are not applicable over a long period, stretching from 1981/82 to 2003/04.

The two papers on India, despite holding contrasting positions on several issues, together provide a comprehensive account of the growth dynamics, labour market and decent work issues and their policy contexts in that country. The first of these two papers (Chapter 3) attempts a measure of decent work and highlights the disconnect between the policies of growth, investment and decent work. The second paper (Chapter 4) touches upon a number of issues dealt with in Chapter 3, and analyses the changes in the composition of growth, investment and employment. This chapter uses the measurement yardsticks of the growth in regular wage employment and the increase in real earnings as indications of an improvement in job quality. A merit of this chapter is its approach to the labour market, both from the supply and the demand side. The chapter argues that growth in India was not jobless, though employment elasticity was low. It is also interesting to observe the contrasting stand taken by the two papers on the potential impact of labour regulation on labour demand. The issue is contentious. While Chapter 3 maintains that there is no evidence to support the argument that labour legislation hindered employment growth and investment, Chapter 4 takes the opposite view.

Chapter 4 uses data until 1999/2000. Extension of this work to include the data of 2004/05 to test the validity of the results would be a useful exercise as a future effort for the authors. In this context, it would be interesting to quote some of the findings of Sundaram (2007) who attempted a comparison of the 2004/05 results from the NSS with those of the earlier two rounds to capture the trend between 1983 and 1993/94, between 1993/94 and 1999/2000 and between 1999/2000 and 2004/05. According to Sundaram, regular wage-salary (RWS) workers, which, according to him, is a good indicator for tracking the growth of 'jobs' in the country, increased during these periods. The average annual increase in the number of RWS workers between 1993/94 and 1999/2000 was 1.46 million (more than double that of the average annual increment between 1983 and 1993/94), which increased to over 2.14 million per annum between 1999/2000 and 2004/05. However, for the economy as a whole, the growth of labour productivity fell significantly between 1999/2000 and 2004/05 in comparison with the growth of labour productivity between 1993/94 and 1999/2000. This was accompanied by a significant decline in the growth of real wage rates of rural casual labourers and an actual decline in real wage rates for urban adult casual labourers. Measuring changes in the number of workers in Above Poverty Line (APL) households as an indicator of the quality of employment (particularly of the self-employed), it was found that the annual increments to RWS workers in the APL households increased during this period. These increments far outpaced the increase in the number of working poor between 2000 and 2005.

Nepal

Major policy reforms in Nepal were implemented quite rapidly. These were based on donors' policy prescriptions; stakeholders were hardly consulted in the process. Much less priority was given to structural and institutional reforms than to the speedy opening up of the economy, withdrawal of subsidies and abolition of administered pricing. Consequently, as has been the experience in most countries, institutional and governance reform (in the public utility and infrastructure sector) lagged behind price reform, creating a mismatch between price and non-price factors. This inhibited market response to price reforms in agriculture and had an adverse impact on poverty reduction objectives (Khanal, Chapter 5 in this volume). The asymmetric progress on reforms coupled with fiscal and monetary tightening led to a decline in the competitiveness of trade and industry, reduced access to credit, fiscal compression and a squeeze in public spending on development, and finally a decline in economic growth that adversely affected employment.

During the period of economic reform, the agriculture sector was neglected. In recent years, there has been a drastic reduction in the proportion of government expenditure allocated to agriculture. This trend is at variance with an earlier commitment by the government to implement a long-term Agriculture Sector Perspective Plan, which consisted of an integrated plan of investment in roads, electricity, irrigation, inputs and technology. This strategy, according to the author, had potential to ensure a sustained high rate of growth with employment generation and reduction of poverty. A distraction from this plan had eroded the potential for employment growth in the economy. Some progress was achieved in poverty reduction due to massive inflow of remittances supporting consumption. However, remittances contributed very little to expansion of investment and employment.

There has been no explicit recognition in Poverty Reduction Strategy Papers (PRSPs) or the Millennium Development Goals (MDGs) of the role of employment in enhancing growth and reducing poverty. While import liberalization has led to increased import dependence in the economy, with adverse impacts on domestic industries and employment, no *ex-ante* assessment of likely impact of such policies in the context of PRSPs and MDGs was made. Exports, being dependent on imported raw materials, had very poor domestic linkages. The reforms in the financial sector also did not lead to the lowering of the cost of capital for industries. Financial services remained concentrated in urban and metropolitan areas. The link between financial deepening and employment remained weak. The other interesting observation was that PRSPs did not make any difference to sectoral allocation patterns in government expenditure in Nepal.

The author indicates two areas where cross-border coherence in policies needs to be established with India. One of them relates to subsidization of agriculture. Nepal abolished subsidy in agriculture since 1998. The high level of subsidy for agriculture in India—in a situation of free-trading arrangements for primary commodities through an open border and free convertibility of Indian currency in the Nepalese market—therefore, puts Nepalese primary producers at a disadvantage. Since 2001, the domestic terms of trade in Nepal moved against agriculture due to the dampening impact on prices under the pressure of subsidized imports from India. At the same time, the input prices were rising as a result of deregulation. The analysis by the author throws open an interesting area of research in policy coherence—the role of price and non-price factors in supply response to liberalization measures based on deregulation of prices; whether such liberalization measures deliver the intended results when non-price factors play significant roles.

The other area needing attention is the management of the exchange rate. In Nepal, the exchange rate is pegged with the Indian currency. Occasional adjustments are made to correct the mismatch with hard currencies based on cross-examination of the movement in exchange rates between the Indian currency and hard currencies. However, as the author shows, this could not prevent a continuous appreciation of real exchange rate of Nepal against the Indian currency. This means that the Nepalese currency is overvalued, and if it is not depreciated, this will encourage imports from India and discourage exports. The worse hit in this situation, according to the author, has been the agriculture sector. Appreciation of the Nepalese currency has also encouraged inflow of workers from the adjoining countries. An analysis of the role of productivity differentials between Nepal and India in explaining the exchange rate differentials between these two countries could have been an interesting supplement to this work.

Like in other countries, skills development programmes and vocational training in Nepal are of limited coverage and are deficient, ineffective and not market-driven. The same is true of the programmes for the development of small and medium-sized enterprises.

Manufacturing has become capital-intensive, even in labour-intensive sectors such as carpets, garments and other textiles. According to the author, rigidity in labour laws has encouraged informalization and encouraged capital-intensive production—an issue that could be probed analytically and empirically in the context of Nepal. However, the author does not provide any analytical or empirical support in favour of his argument.

The author stresses the need for a better policy mix and sequencing of reforms, with institutional and governance-related reforms being an integral part of the mix. The reform should be comprehensive and should include agriculture and infrastructure. Adequate care should be taken to ensure that small businesses and entrepreneurs can take advantage of the "liberal policy environment". This should include certain policy incentives and institutional arrangements for credit support and other facilities.

The other highlights on the economy are the high degree of informalization, the absence of stakeholders' voices in charting the course of economic reforms, and the absence of a comprehensive social protection system. All these factors lead to the prevalence of widespread decent work deficits in the country.

The need for labour policy reforms as a part of an overall reforms programme in favour of a flexible labour market supplemented by policies that contribute to raising skills and enhancing productivity has been underscored in this chapter. The author also recommends affirmative state action to abolish discrimination against women and other disadvantaged groups and suggests strengthening of "tripartism plus" institutions "to facilitate consensus-building processes through social dialogue in various contentious labour-related issues" based on continuous flow of information from the grass roots level.

Pakistan

Although Pakistan is in a transitional phase from a controlled regime and is on a path of gradual "opening up" and privatization (Haque, Chapter 6 in this volume), this intermediate stage is characterized by the persistence of a strong hold by the government in the economic sphere. The government seeks to promote exports through active engagement of government agencies such as the Export Development Board and the Ministry of Commerce. The engineering goods sector is subject to import substitution bias, with the Engineering Development Board (which comprises the owners of the industry) having a strong say in the protective policy for the sector. According to the author, domestic commerce and trade remained underdeveloped as a result of the lack of development of a competitive domestic market integrated with the global markets. This has eroded job prospects for most people, especially for most of the poor, who could have been employed in trade and commerce.

The author finds that the rate of growth of employment in Pakistan remained more or less insensitive to the growth of the economy. The incremental labour force is not being absorbed, while employment in the informal economy continues to rise. The author comments that since a sizeable labour force is locked up in the informal economy and the informal economy is labour-intensive, the policies should be directed towards encouraging this sector rather than forcing a transition from informal to formal. However, a counter-argument to this suggestion could be that there is a simultaneity between formality and development, i.e., development process entails transition from informality to formality. Furthermore, formality is a concept of "rights", without which rightful development cannot take place. The chapter also draws attention towards the underperformance of Pakistan on the educational front.

Pakistan's planning era continues to influence the prevailing paradigm against enlargement of competitive markets. The author argues that this policy mindset puts a premium on industrial development and neglects domestic commerce—the potential source of most pro-poor growth possibilities—and its promotion through appropriate policies and infrastructure.

The author puts emphasis on "establishing the rule of law and a good system of justice" as a prerequisite for good market development and emphasizes the need for civil-service reform and elimination of "rent seeking" to promote primacy of a merit-based incentive system. A number of recommendations has been advanced by the author in the chapter for reforming the civil service to achieve this objective.

While one would tend to agree with the author that the development of trade and commerce would create some job opportunities, the experiences in other countries show that these would not necessarily be decent work. Many such jobs are of the informal type. The tertiary sector is a huge absorber of underemployed in the developing world. The author's argument to develop competitive markets follows the conventional paradigm. However, a free market need not necessarily be free from pressures from non-market forces. As argued by Hussain (2007), functioning of markets "as they exist in Pakistan", if left free, would lead to unequal distribution of gains with the consequence that the poor and the working class will lose in the bargain due to the capture of the market by the dominant power group. The challenges of market failures are much more "central" and pivotal rather than "marginal" and peripheral and cannot be tackled by government regulation alone. It involves a huge task of "restructuring the system of power which has configured markets such that perverse functioning is inherent to their structure".

Although not explicit, the author's emphasis on the need to promote market orientation and institutional reforms in order to align with globalization, the establishing of the rule of law and a good system of justice, the encouraging of creativity and innovation could be construed as the author's prioritization of certain prerequisites to potentially strengthen the nexus between growth–employment–decent work. Interpreted this way, one can infer that a coherent set of policies that integrates institutional reforms with market orientation and the promotion of trade and commerce would achieve harmony between growth, investment and decent work.

Sri Lanka

With human development achievements comparable to many developed nations, Sri Lanka is well set to reach the MDGs in several areas, such as universal primary school enrolment, gender equality and maternal and infant mortality, ahead of schedule. However, the country faces the challenge of unemployment, poverty and inequality just as much as countries that have not made similar social progress. This underscores the need to restore a balance between social and economic progress through a review of the development strategy and objectives from the perspective of decent work.

In Sri Lanka, successive elections have led to one of the two major political parties coming into power alternately. The parties have diametrically opposite economic philosophies: one has a market-focused ideology and the other has a more nationalistic-socialistic attitude. This has resulted in disrupted continuity in policies and implementation (Ranaraja, Chapter 7 in this volume).

According to the author, there has been a marked disconnect between growth in employment and economic growth, especially since the 1990s. Despite having decent work in its national agenda, the same is not incorporated in the macro policy. The type of industrialization being pursued, with a focus on the apparel sector and based on cheap labour, is in direct contradiction with decent work objectives. Conditions of employment being created in this sector come nowhere close to fulfilling those objectives. There is a concern that granting the fair wage necessary for decent work would erode the competitive advantage of the Sri Lankan industry and that the employers may be forced to close down operation. Over the years, increases in productivity have not translated into an increase in wages. Policy coherence also suffers because in the sectoral approach to development, "linkages in related sectors are not developed in a systematic way".

A disturbing feature of the labour market from the perspective of the freedom of association and trade unionism is the declining proportion of unionized wage earners among the total number of private sector employees in the organized sector. The proportion declined from 53 per cent in 1995 to 20 per cent in 2002. This is happening at a time when employment in the public sector is declining steadily and private sector employment is increasing. There are many trade unions in Sri Lanka (in 2003, there were 400 trade unions), but the absence of an umbrella body for trade unions prevents a coherent approach by the workers on labour issues.

There are two other features that Sri Lanka shares with most other countries in the South Asia subregion. These are the absence of a well functioning universal social protection system, and a situation where multiple ministries have components of skill development and vocational training curriculum, which are uncoordinated and not driven by market demand.

The Termination of Employment of Workmen Act (TEWA) in Sri Lanka has been criticized as having the most restrictive severance pay systems in the world. There are also delays in the judicial review of disputes. Various ad hoc amendments carried out by the government from time to times increase in the number of labour tribunals, etc., and have not succeeded in expeditious resolution of industrial disputes. The country has an "over-burdened system of justice" due to the prevalence of an "unnecessarily legalistic" attitude towards the problems. The author advocates a participatory approach to reforms from the perspective of employment creation and investment promotion—a strategy that underscores the need to promote the culture of social dialogue. Besides, there also remains the challenge of extending workers' rights and benefits in the informal economy.

The author highlights the need to increase productivity, a crucial prerequisite for remaining competitive, while at the same time allowing real wage increases in a commensurate manner. As mentioned above, this has not been the case in Sri Lanka, especially in the manufacturing sector during the 1990s; the average growth in real wages lagged behind productivity growth. A mechanism therefore needs to be evolved, and in this case the proximate recourse would be the mechanism of social dialogue, to ensure that the growth in real wage tracks increase in productivity.

There are stark regional disparities in development in Sri Lanka. As rightly emphasized by the author, this requires a "dual policy approach" that would generate income and employment for the poor in the lagging regions rather than focusing "solely on income transfer programmes". The author recommends a broad-based development that would support formalization and hassle-free development of small and micro enterprises through the availability of credit and skills development. The nature of the dualistic development strategy needed to achieve a balanced development and how such a strategy could be coherent with sectoral development programmes would be an interesting agenda of research that flows from this paper. We have maintained earlier (Section 1.3, Policy compulsions and commonalities) that public investment in rural infrastructure and agricultural diversification will be the key to a broad-based development strategy in Sri Lanka. However, the fiscal hardship poses a challenge in following this approach. How to address this challenge remains a key question.

Afghanistan

In a state like Afghanistan, amidst weak state institutions and entrenched criminal vested interests, neoliberal advice and influence are gaining ground in national policies under the auspices of the IFIs to the complete neglect of concerns for employment (Kantor, Chapter 8 of this volume). Employment is not mainstreamed into the national investment and growth strategy. There is a sharp contradiction between pro-poor rhetoric in policy (Afghanistan has an interim PRSP document) and a neoliberal approach at the macro level; the latter puts emphasis on the investment climate rather than on workers' protection or employment. One reason for this could be the fear that any imposition of labour market conditionality (such as binding requirements to hire and train local workers) may discourage investments and potentially erode growth prospects. However, this approach fails to recognize that strengthening the market in its current form will increase the strong hold of the existing entrenched lobbies (traders, local commanders, warlords, etc.) that now control the market, and that it will exacerbate existing inequality and poverty, a concern expressed by Hussain (2007) in the context of Pakistan. Competitive pressure, on the other hand, may create negative externalities through recourse to cutting costs and working conditions and creating low-quality, low-paid jobs. The laws drafted recently focus on investors' protection and neglect workers' interests and therefore, offer no safeguards to workers against such a race to the bottom. It also needs to be recognized that low labour productivity is a problem in the Afghan economy. Productivity enhancement could, therefore, be possible through adding more capital to labour, implying that additional investment would not address the problem of raising overall employment levels if it has to raise productivity in the near term.

Furthermore, in Afghanistan, the present situation of reliance on foreign workers in a rush to complete projects undermines the medium- and long-term prospects of domestic labour market development to achieve the goals of decent work. An absence of domestically available skilled labour tends to increase the reliance on foreign workers, which in turn hinders development of a domestic labour market, creating a vicious circle. Attracting high-quality employment and building a skilled labour force to support it would be a recommended strategy. Lack of labour market information and data in Afghanistan stands in the way of implementing this strategy, and therefore addressing this problem should be a high priority in the policy agenda.

It is apparent that the short-run costs that the free-market strategy can inflict on the society are immense and the negative consequences could potentially be degenerating. There is no indication in theory or in practice of when this process would become self-limiting, if at all. This downslide could be arrested through a strategy of introducing a "social floor in every country according to its means" that "can mean, for example, a basic income, health care and education package—together with organization, rights at work and empowerment to voice and defend their interests. Taken together, these measures can no doubt enhance growth and productivity. But they are also justified by the enormous growth in wealth creation that has been taking place."[46] According to the author, the aid community can assist the national government in setting a realistic benchmark (social floor) through an open process and periodically adjusting the same with economic progress. The ongoing Afghanistan National Development Strategy process has thrown open an opportunity for the aid community to bring employment and pro-poor growth into policy dialogue.

Islamic Republic of Iran

The author draws attention to a fundamental issue that the particular stage of development of the bio space, knowledge space, political space, legal space and economic space impacts the labour market. Perhaps one could find implicit in this idea the notion that progress towards decent work is contingent upon the state of development in these "spaces". One can draw a parallel with Haque

46. Excerpts from the address by Juan Somavia, Director-General of the International Labour Office, to the Asian Employment Forum at Beijing, China, 13 August 2007.

(Chapter 6 in this volume) who narrates how the development paradigm shifted in Pakistan, how economic space evolved over the years, the nature and the role of eminent domain (the nature of political space) and recommended the need for alignment with globalization, encouraging creativity and innovation (knowledge space). In a way, both authors bring out explicitly the role of initial conditions, so important in any discourse on growth and decent work. It is interesting to supplement these ideas with the conviction that emerges in the writing of Kantor (Chapter 8 in this volume) that the development agents could intervene and shape the process of evolution in these "spaces". In Afghanistan, Multilateral Development Banks are actively involved with the national government in shaping the economic space in the country and there is no reason why the agenda of decent work cannot be a part of this construction.

In the Islamic Republic of Iran, Human Resource Development Planning and Policy Making (HRDP), a comprehensive research project within the framework of the Third and the Fourth Socio-Economic and Cultural Development Plans (2000–2004 and 2005–2009 respectively), presents detailed employment plans and sub-plans for the economy. Preparation of a national decent work development plan finds a mention in Article 101 of the Fourth Development Plan.

Iran relied on supporting private sector development and reducing reliance on the public sector for the expansion of employment (Taee, Chapter 9 in this volume). Between 1989 and 2003, the proportion of private sector employment in total employment increased from 67 per cent to 76 per cent, with a corresponding decrease in the share for public sector employment. Employment elasticity increased over this period. Income policy has been used to support decent earnings for the employed. Income distribution also improved. Although social security insurance exists, it is under pressure to meet the expanding needs of the population due to a decrease in funding and low levels of per capita savings by the insured population.

In the 1990s, the advent of new technology and knowledge-intensive production started to affect employment prospects adversely. The economy faced high inflation (15 per cent) and a high rate of unemployment (12 per cent).

The chapter provides detailed templates of employment plan. Connecting them to the underlying weaknesses in the macro fundamentals would considerably enrich the analytical content of the paper. A look at the broad macroeconomic indicators of Iran reveals that despite reasonably high savings and investment rates, the country has a relatively low growth of GDP. Declining total factor productivity and inefficiency in governance both contribute to this outcome. Pervasive mismatches in the skills market, lack of proper coordination between different government agencies, poor coverage of social security, a low-end small-scale sector stifled with myriad of regulation, welfare, and a piecemeal approach to job creation have all been documented in an earlier ILO study (ILO, 2005a) (which is not mentioned in the chapter). There are many areas that call for corrective and coordinated measures if the goals of decent work are to be achieved.

A major attraction of this volume is its presentation of a kaleidoscopic view of the development phases that these seven countries are passing through and how economic realities have influenced the perceptions of individual authors from the point of view of growth, investment and decent work. A coherent policy for decent work is yet to emerge in any of the countries under study. Kannan (Chapter 3 in this volume) argues cogently that it is "decent work" rather than "employment" that should be the target. While none of the countries has a coherent policy framework for decent work, in several countries policy asymmetries are creating conditions that make the attainment of decent work more difficult.

Policy asymmetries can occur in many ways. Lack of synchronization between institutional and governance reforms and reforms in prices can lead to lopsided development in an economy that could affect decent work prospects and pro-poor growth. In Nepal, deregulation of prices and the interest rate went far ahead of progress in reforms in governance and public utilities. As a result, the delivery of infrastructural services, where public utilities and public investment dominate, continues to remain inefficient and poor, making the cost of production in domestic enterprises high and uncompetitive. In this situation, liberalization of the import tariff would tend to flood the domestic market with cheap imports and domestic enterprises would fail to compete—a case of the deindustrialization that one finds evidence of in the papers on Nepal and Bangladesh. Haque in his chapter on Pakistan argues strongly that institutional and governance reforms be aligned with globalization; a prescription that has hardly been followed in any of these countries. The paper on Bangladesh indicates how weak governance led to poor implementation of the Annual Development Programme in the country, adversely affecting the pace of progress in infrastructure development and, consequently, the growth of employment. In Afghanistan, institutional strengthening is a top priority, since state institutions are weak (see Kantor in Chapter 8 on Afghanistan).

It is, therefore, important that any coherent policy framework should appropriately calibrate and sequence the different areas and components of reforms so as to avoid disruptive consequences in the economy. In Bangladesh, while import liberalization started affecting a number of uncompetitive domestic enterprises, no countervailing strategy was in place to promote labour-intensive industries in order to absorb labour displaced from affected domestic industries. Kannan (Chapter 3) observes that, in India, earlier support policies directed towards agriculture and the small-scale sector, which indirectly helped to promote employment in these sectors, were relaxed under the logic of economic reforms.

In Chapter 7 on Sri Lanka, Ranaraja draws attention to another instance of policy asymmetry that needs to be addressed. The National Policy for Decent Work in Sri Lanka (NPDWSL) has been incorporated into the government's Ten Year Development Framework (TYDF). However, in the chapter on industrial development in the TYDF, the thrust of the development strategy is to promote "knowledge-based" and "technology-intensive" industries rather than "resource-based" and "labour-intensive" industries. In Iran, in spite of a detailed employment plan and sub-plan, unemployment is as high as 12 per cent. The advent of technology and knowledge-intensive production in the 1990s adversely affected employment. A disconnect between employment policy or decent work policy and other policies seems obvious.

The link between financial sector reforms, the investment regime and employment generation too seems to be tenuous. While reforms in the financial sector are being carried forward in Bangladesh, the interest rates charged on agricultural loans and on loans made to small-scale industries were as high as the interest levied on medium- and large-scale industries. The share of annual bank advances to agriculture and small-scale and cottage industries significantly declined. Nepal too experienced a decline in lending in agriculture during the period of ongoing reform of the financial sector. Khanal (Chapter 5 on Nepal) points towards the anomaly that the lending rates applied to loans for durable consumer goods was about half that of the rate applied to the industrial sector. Rural areas—and especially marginal farmers—faced very high interest rates. Furthermore, in the course of reform, overall employment in the commercial banks was reduced by a third, primarily due to the downsizing of the state-owned commercial banks. Ranaraja (Chapter 7 on Sri Lanka) argues that high and uncompetitive interest rates was one reason why the domestic manufacturing sector could not compete with imports into Sri Lanka.

The fiscal stabilization attempted in many countries of this subregion has been a topic for debate on policy coherence as the goals of stabilization were sought through the compression of development expenditure by the governments concerned. In areas like agriculture and rural infrastructure, where investment is supportive of employment growth, private investment complements public investment and, as such, a decline in public investment is likely to discourage private investment and therefore, overall investment and employment. Kannan (Chapter 3 in this volume) holds that enhanced public investment in rural areas is critical for the generation of decent employment in India. Rashid (Chapter 2 in this volume) maintains that the slowing down of development expenditure by the government of Bangladesh acted as a disincentive for the growth of private investment. A critically important sector like power had been the victim of insufficient public spending. In the same vein, Khanal (Chapter 5 in this volume) maintains that the compression of development spending by the government in Nepal in the name of achieving fiscal stabilization had a harmful effect on those sectors which were critical for promoting pro-poor growth or non-farm employment. In the same chapter, Khanal also presents an interesting perspective on policy incoherence between exchange rate management, the deregulation of prices, the liberalization of tariffs and sectoral policy in agriculture—a framework worth emulating for research on policy coherence in other countries.

This volume draws out a common theme that agriculture and rural development had to bear the brunt of a squeeze in public spending in the course of economic reforms, primarily due to the overriding priority assigned to fiscal stabilization. Apart from eroding employment prospects, such a deprivation might have serious long-term implications in terms of an impending food crisis that could be a worst-case eventuality for people in poverty.

This volume evinces a scepticism regarding the ability of export—an important conduit of globalization—to emerge as a sector that can be trusted for the promotion of decent work. Kannan (Chapter 3) argues, based on another empirical study, that the employment impact of export in India is quite low. Ranaraja (Chapter 7) highlights the concern that decent work implies an increase in the cost of production on account of labour, which would make Sri Lankan exports uncompetitive *vis-à-vis* those of other countries. The implication of such a fear is obvious. The problem, characterized as a "race to the bottom", can only be addressed through a multilateral initiative to declare a social floor that disallows competitive cost-cutting below a certain level where decent work is at stake.

All the countries discussed in this volume have very large informal economies. Addressing the decent work deficit in the informal economy is in itself a formidable challenge. To make the matter worse, there is an emerging challenge to cope with, that of the flouting of decent work norms even in the formal economy (see Chapters 2, 3 and 7).

Ahsan, Dasgupta and Narain (Chapter 4 on India), Khanal (Chapter 5 on Nepal) and Ranaraja (Chapter 7 on Sri Lanka) argue that labour laws in these countries were rigid and constrained the growth of formal employment. Kannan (Chapter 3) holds that, empirically, it cannot be established whether organized sector employment in India is hindered by labour laws. The subject to-date remains debatable. However, labour laws are not the only issue. As this volume will suggest, there are many policy areas where establishing coherence is a priority. Achieving a consensus on the future path of reforms should be based on a discussion of these priorities among stakeholders. This volume provides a starting point for this dialogue.

1.6 Conclusions

Although most of the countries discussed in the volume have employment policy or decent work programmes and/or plans as parts of their national policies, a link between overall macroeconomic policy and employment policy is missing in all of them. There was no evidence of centrality of employment in macroeconomic policy. Given this background, as the countries proceed with their respective programmes of economic reforms, macroeconomic policies being pursued under the neoliberal influence are creating impacts that are incompatible with the interests of decent work. A calibrated and gradual approach to economic reforms with careful evaluation of the likely impact on the world of work is, therefore, necessary.

Market fundamentalism, which underpins the contemporary reforms agenda, misses out on the point that a certain level of institutional development is a prerequisite for the emergence of efficient and well-functioning product and factor markets. A sudden withdrawal of the state from the economic sphere will not automatically lead to this outcome. On the contrary, there are apprehensions that premature dismantling of state control could lead to the replacement of the state by perverse markets, and a stranglehold by powerful vested interests that would seriously undermine the prospects of decent work. A programme of institutional strengthening should, therefore, be an integral part of any reforms programme and should include, among other things, building a strong foundation of tripartism with a focus on decent work. The present situation is far from this. Growing informalization and weakening of the influence of tripartism in the workplace is increasingly making the connections between growth and decent work remote. Two imperatives follow from this: first, an abrupt transition from state to market without institutional intermediation of a strong and healthy tripartism would not serve the interests of decent work; second, decent work will have to be an integral part of the reforms process: employment as an "adjunct" policy (Kannan, Chapter 3 in this volume) or as a "social protection" measure (Kantor, Chapter 8 in this volume) will not achieve the goal.

As of now, the costs and benefits of the various policy decisions in terms of their impacts on decent work are broadly understood. The analytical challenge lies in carrying it forward to a much more atomistic level to make it amenable to handling by the policy-makers in terms of concrete decisions. An evaluation of existing policies being implemented by different ministries or agencies of government—their costs and benefits and their impacts on the labour market—could be a starting point in this investigation. How could the results of such investigations be used productively? First, they could be used to help the ILO constituents to engage in more informed dialogue, in terms of data and numbers. Second, these findings could be taken into consideration when designing Decent Work Country Programmes wherever relevant. Third, echoing what the Director-General of the ILO said, we could "help international agencies—including the Bretton Woods institutions—self-assess their policies in terms of employment and decent work outcomes with the same methodology. It will result in better ways to incorporate these goals in their policies, programmes and activities."[47]

Part of the maladies in the functioning of labour markets can be due to administrative, organizational and institutional reasons; the remedies for these have to be found accordingly. This might call for an investigation on the ground and the suggesting corrective actions through an appropriately designed programme of action and innovative reorientation of micro structures and processes. The knowledge of best practices would be of help. However, solutions on the ground also exist within a macroeconomic and macro social context, and that should not be lost sight of.

Finally, several issues require cross-border initiatives. Migration is certainly one of them. Most countries of this subregion benefit substantially from remittances. Cross-border coalitions and negotiations are important parts of the effective management of this process. There can be other bilateral or multilateral issues. For example, Chapter 5 in

---

47. Ibid.

this volume brings out the importance of harmonization of policies on subsidies and exchange rate arrangements between India and Nepal and their impacts on the labour market in Nepal. With the progress of integration into the global value chain, more and more issues might need to be mediated at subregional, regional and global levels.

2 Growth, investment and decent work in Bangladesh

The need for a better policy mix

Mohammed Ali Rashid

2.1 Introduction

A major challenge for policy-makers and development practitioners alike is the stubborn persistence of poverty at both the global and national levels. An important factor for reducing poverty significantly is achieving sustained high growth. This is forcefully brought out by the experience of countries that have achieved this result. Equally important is the empirical finding that achievement of high growth is not enough; the pattern and sources of growth, as well as the distribution of the benefits of growth, are equally important for poverty alleviation. And from this perspective, the importance of employment as the key link between growth and poverty alleviation is often emphasized.

The average productivity of the employed workforce assumes importance because it influences the real wage rate and earnings in self-employment. Labour productivity is important not only from the perspective of poverty alleviation, but also because it influences the level of employment, particularly in the formal manufacturing sector. Thus, if labour productivity is lagging behind the increase in real wages, it would have an adverse effect on employment levels. Conversely, an increase in labour productivity would lead to an increase in output growth and thereby, growth in employment and wages. In the short run, however, a rise in labour productivity may be accompanied by a slowing down in employment growth if output demand is not growing at a commensurate rate.

Clearly, macroeconomic policy has an important role to play in the achievement of employment-intensive or pro-poor growth. Thus, macroeconomic stability is necessary for achieving rapid economic growth, and fiscal, monetary, trade and exchange-rate policies have important roles to play in this regard. Fiscal and financial policy, by affecting the volume and sectoral pattern of investment, also directly affect employment creation in the economy. Sectoral policies also influence the level of employment by, on the one hand, promoting growth of labour-intensive sectors and, on the other hand, enhancing skill levels (through investment in the health and education sectors), which increase the employability of labour. In sum, an appropriate mix of polices is necessary for ensuring employment-intensive growth.

While the creation of jobs is crucially important, it is equally important to ensure that men and women can obtain "decent and productive work, in conditions of freedom, equity, security and human dignity". This is what the International Labour Organization (ILO) has called "decent work". Decent work involves the attainment of four strategic objectives: promotion of rights at works, employment, social protection and social dialogue. It is clearly seen from a consideration of the above that employment levels can be increased even though the objective of decent work is overlooked. It is the responsibility of the government to ensure not only that employment levels increase, but also that the the goals of decent work are achieved simultaneously, through prudent management and intervention in the labour market.

With nearly 40 per cent of its population living below the poverty line, Bangladesh is one of the poorest countries in the world. Rapid creation of gainful employment opportunities and conditions of decent work are therefore, of crucial importance in its fight against poverty. This would require an acceleration in the economic growth rate, to begin with, through the use of appropriate macroeconomic and sectoral polices. At the same time, policies have to be put in place to enhance labour productivity, particularly in view of the rapid increase in low-productivity employment in the informal economy in recent times.

The objective of this chapter is to assess the linkage between growth, investment and decent work in Bangladesh. The analysis will be carried out within the conceptual framework outlined above.

The chapter is organized as follows. In Section 2.2, the trend and status of economic growth, investment and employment in Bangladesh are examined for the period 1980 to 2005. In Section 2.3, an analysis is made of the macroeconomic policy regime operating in Bangladesh over the past two decades, with the specific objective of assessing the centrality of employment creation in macroeconomic policy. Special emphasis is placed on examining how the concern for decent employment has been addressed in fiscal and investment policy, financial policy and trade policy. The issue of labour productivity and employment is analysed in Section 2.4. While overall economic growth may generate employment growth, such employment may not embody the various dimensions of decent work even in the formal economy. This issue is flagged up in Section 2.5, where the quality of employment created in the ready-made garments industry, the fastest growing industry in the country, is examined. This highlights the point that the objective of decent employment cannot be achieved simply through accelerating economic growth; rather, growth needs to be supplemented by the operation of sound labour market institutions to ensure the growth of decent employment. Finally, concluding observations are presented in Section 2.6. Particular attention is paid to the following policy issues:

- the role of better policy mix to strengthen the linkages between economic growth, investment and decent employment;
- ways in which policies may be coordinated for enhancing decent employment;
- how to achieve policy consistency to promote the linkages between growth, investment and decent employment;
- how the above linkages are weakened by poor implementation of policies; and
- to what extent aid programmes could strengthen the above linkages.

2.2 Economic growth, investment and decent employment: The status

Since large-scale redistribution of income and wealth is not feasible, the only way that poverty can be reduced is through accelerated economic growth. However, "growth maximization" may have only limited favourable impact on poverty; rather, what is required is "pro-poor" growth, or growth that would maximize quality employment opportunities for the large mass of the poor. While some people may be unemployed because they do not possess marketable skills, the majority of them are unemployed because there is a deficient demand for labour. Reducing poverty would therefore, require increasing the demand for labour, and in a market economy this can be achieved by increasing the rate of economic expansion.

In a labour-surplus economy such as Bangladesh, the binding constraint on growth is the capital stock. Hence, the principal factor determining the rate of growth in Bangladesh is the rate at which the nation's capital stock is augmented; that is, the rate of investment. Apart from its volume, the efficiency or productivity of investment has an important influence on growth. This is determined by the sectoral pattern of investment.[1] Technological progress also plays a key role in increasing productivity of the economy.

It is within this conceptual framework that economic growth, investment and decent employment in Bangladesh are analysed in this section.

The economy of Bangladesh achieved modest acceleration in growth in the 1990s compared with the previous decade. This is shown in Table 2.1. The gross domestic product (GDP) growth rate was 3.7 per cent per annum during the 1980s. The GDP growth rate accelerated during the 1990s; the growth rate rose from 4.4 per cent in the first half of the decade to 5.2 per cent in the second half. With a further decline in the population growth rate, per capita GDP growth increased to 3.6 per cent per annum during the second half of the 1990s. During 2000/01–2004/2005, GDP and per capita GDP growth rose further to 5.4 and 4.0 per cent respectively. The level of per capita GDP gradually increased to reach US$441 by 2004/05.

1. Thus, investment in education, the infrastructure and health care has greater influence on the productivity of the national economy than, say, investment in building monuments. Similarly, investment in labour-intensive industries generates greater employment and income than does investment in capital-intensive industries.

Table 2.1

Growth of the Bangladesh economy, 1980/81–2004/05

(annual average percentage growth rate)

Sector	Five-yearly average				
	1980/81–1984/85	1985/86–1989/90	1990/91–1994/95	1995/96–1999/2000	2000/01–2004/05
GDP	3.72	3.74	4.39	5.21	5.43
Population	2.14	2.20	1.74	1.51	1.35
Per capita GDP	1.54	1.60	2.60	3.64	4.03

Source: BBS, 1987, 1999, 2006.

The economy experienced some structural change during this growth process. The contribution of agriculture to GDP gradually declined from 33 per cent in 1979/80 to about 22 per cent in 2004/05, while the contribution of industry rose from 17 to 28 per cent during this time. The service sector's contribution has remained unchanged at around 49 per cent between 1980 and 2005. The contribution of the manufacturing sector increased from about 9 per cent in 1980/81 to nearly 17 per cent in 2004/05. The contribution of the manufacturing sector is thus, relatively small in Bangladesh.

The sectoral contribution to GDP growth is shown in Table 2.2.

Table 2.2

Sectoral GDP contributions, 1980/81–2004/05

(annual average; at constant 1995/96 producer prices)

Sector	Five-yearly average				
	1980/81–1984/85	1985/86–1989/90	1990/91–1994/95	1995/96–1999/2000	2000/01–2004/05
GDP	3.72	3.74	4.39	5.21	5.43
Agriculture	2.68	2.40	1.55	4.88	2.50
Crop production	2.69	2.69	-0.43	4.09	2.22
Fisheries	3.06	1.64	7.86	8.56	1.35
Others	2.41	2.20	2.54	3.30	4.78
Industry	5.70	5.86	7.47	6.44	7.42
Manufacturing	4.70	5.27	8.20	5.59	6.84
Large and medium	4.44	5.43	8.41	5.49	6.59
Small scale	5.41	4.89	7.69	5.87	7.46
Construction	6.44	5.59	6.27	8.81	8.38
Others	11.49	10.66	6.46	4.89	7.85
Services	3.83	3.58	4.15	4.81	5.67
Total GDP	**3.72**	**3.74**	**4.39**	**5.21**	**5.43**

Source: Same as Table 2.1.

Table 2.2 shows that all three broad economic sectors—agriculture, industry and services—contributed to the growth acceleration of the 1990s. Manufacturing, construction, services, non-crop agriculture (mainly fisheries) and rural non-farm (RNF) activities contributed greatly to economic growth during the 1990s and beyond. All three broad economic sectors contributed to faster economic growth during the 1990s. At a disaggregated level, rapid growth of several subsectors was observed during the 1990s. Fishery emerged as the fastest growing subsector in agriculture. Manufacturing and construction were the two most dynamic subsectors of the industrial sector. In the case of the service sector, wholesale and retail trade, hotels and restaurants, and financial intermediaries emerged as the most rapidly expanding subsectors.

The growth of agricultural GDP accelerated from 2.5 per cent in the 1980s to 3.2 per cent in the 1990s. During this time, industrial GDP accelerated from 5.8 to 7.0 per cent, and the service sector GDP from 3.7 to 4.5 per cent. However, sectoral growth performance differed in the two halves of the 1990s. Agriculture had lagged behind in the first half of the decade, but it picked up strongly in the second half. Conversely, industrial growth accelerated in the first half of the decade but declined a little in the second half. Services, however, experienced a continuous acceleration in growth throughout the decade. During the period 2000/01–2004/05, while growth of agriculture declined quite sharply (mainly due to negative growth in 2001/02 and 2004/05 caused by floods) and fell to 2.5 per cent per annum, the industry and service sectors maintained their growth acceleration with their average annual growth rates rising to 7.4 and 5.7 per cent respectively.

Within agriculture, the average annual growth of the crops subsector declined from 2.7 per cent in the 1980s to 1.7 per cent during the 1990s. This decline occurred despite the sharp acceleration in growth in the second half of the 1990s. The growth in crop production over the years has been mainly attributable to growth in production of food grains, mainly rice. The rice-based agricultural growth had masked the unexploited potential that exists for higher agricultural growth through crop diversification (Mahmud *et al.*, 2000). Fisheries also grew rapidly during the 1990s, but average growth of this subsector fell sharply in 2000/01–2004/05.

The manufacturing and construction subsectors experienced an increase in growth in the 1990s compared with the 1980s; while the growth rate of the manufacturing sector rose from 5 to 6.9 per cent during these two periods, the growth rate of the construction sector increased from 6 to 7.5 per cent. This upward growth trend of manufacturing continued to hold during 2000/01–2004/05. It may be noted that growth of the manufacturing sector declined in the second half of the 1990s compared with the first half; this was the pattern both for medium- and large-scale as well as small-scale manufacturing.

Only five industries, with a combined industry weight of 19.53, accounted for 81 per cent of the manufacturing growth achieved during the 1980s (Bakht, 2000). Three of the five industries, namely ready-made garments, fish and seafood and leather tanning, are export-oriented industries: garments contributed about 43 per cent of manufacturing output growth. Thus, during the 1980s, most of the import-substituting industries stagnated, and whatever growth was achieved was attributable to export industries.

The picture changed somewhat during the first half of the 1990s. While garments continued to spearhead industrial growth in Bangladesh, the pattern of industrial growth became more broad based. The top five growth-contributing industries, with a combined industrial weight of 23.78, now accounted for 67 per cent of the sectoral growth. The other notable feature was that, except garments, the other four top industries were import-substituting industries, namely pharmaceuticals, *bidi* (indigenous cigarettes), books and periodicals, and steel re-rolling mills (for producing steel products from ship scrap).

Growth of large and medium-sized industries slowed down during the second half of the 1990s, mainly due to unfavourable exogenous factors such as the prolonged flood of 1998 and the adverse impact of the East Asian financial crisis. Export of ready-made garments, like other manufactured exports, experienced slower growth during this period. The dominant import-substituting industries also experienced a slowing down of growth. This was particularly true of the following industries: pharmaceuticals, fertilizers, steel re-rolling, soaps and detergents, and silks and synthetics. Fertilizers, re-rolling and silks and synthetics experienced negative growth, while pharmaceuticals and soaps and detergents stagnated at a growth rate of around 2 per cent rate.

A major factor contributing to the decline of domestic import-substituting industries was an unfavourable movement in Bangladesh's exchange rate relative to the Indian rupee. Between 1989/90 and 1995/1996, the Bangladeshi *taka* appreciated by nearly 35 per cent against the Indian rupee. This contributed to a significant increase in illegal imports from India, particularly in pharmaceuticals, soaps and detergents, etc., which displaced domestic products. At the same time, a lowering of import tariffs in Bangladesh led to an increase in legal imports of competing products, which adversely affected some of the domestic industries. Small industries have shown dynamism in growth, particularly during the 1990s; the average annual growth rate of this subsector rose from 5.1 per cent during the 1980s to 6.8 per cent during the 1990s. Trade liberalization measures of the early 1990s, which provided these industries with easier access to imported raw materials such as plastics and metals may have been the main stimulus behind their rapid growth. Since the small industry subsector is more labour-intensive and caters mainly to domestic low- and medium-income consumers, there has been relatively less displacement of this subsector's products by competing imports after trade liberalization.

It would thus, appear that strong export growth has succeeded in stimulating some parts of the economy, mainly manufacturing (through exports of ready-made garments) and fisheries (through shrimp exports). Since the late 1980s, Bangladesh has achieved a sustained and robust growth of exports, averaging about 15 per cent annually in nominal US dollar terms. Though the structure of the economy is changing, only slightly more than 10 per cent of GDP currently comes from large-scale manufacturing, and about 6 per cent comes from fisheries.

Among the other sources of growth, a large proportion of GDP originates from the so-called "informal economy" outside crop-based agriculture: small-scale processing and manufacturing and various informal services. According to the 1999/2000 Labour Force Survey, these informal activities employ about three-quarters of the country's non-agricultural labour force. The growth rates of these informal activities accelerated in the 1990s, contributing substantially to the acceleration of overall GDP growth. Many of these activities—being extremely labour-intensive and requiring very little capital investment—are largely demand-driven. They respond to three major sources of increased income: crop production, ready-made garments exports and workers' remittances, in that order of importance (see Osmani *et al.*, 2003).

Economic growth depends largely on investment, which in turn depends on savings and foreign borrowing. The saving and investment rates in Bangladesh for the period 1995/96–2006/07 are shown in Table 2.3. Gross domestic saving, comprising both public and private saving, is fairly low in Bangladesh. Remittances from overseas partially compensate for the inadequacy of domestic saving, and so the gross national saving is somewhat higher. The domestic saving rate rose from about 15 to 20 per cent during the above period, while the national saving rate increased from 20 to nearly 29 per cent during this time, thanks to a healthy growth in remittances. Despite this modest rate of saving, Bangladesh is unable to find investment outlets for all of it, reflecting the difficulties that investors encounter. This is clearly seen from Table 2.3.

The investment rate has risen from 20 per cent in 1995/96 to 24.3 per cent in 2006/07, reflecting a fairly slow growth. The growth in investment has been mainly caused by growth in private investment, as can be seen from Table 2.3; public investment has declined from 1999/2000 onwards.

The slowdown in private investment growth has led to the emergence of "idle savings" in Bangladesh. A recent World Bank study (World Bank and BEI, 2003) has shown, based on firm-level surveys, that five factors have acted as major deterrents to private investment expansion in Bangladesh; these are: poor and inadequate infrastructure, electricity shortage, corruption, government regulation and finance. A major challenge for economic growth and poverty reduction in

Table 2.3

Saving and investment as percentage of GDP, 1996/96–2006/07

(percentage of GDP)

Year	*Domestic saving*	*National saving*	*Public investment*	*Private investment*	*Total investment*
1995/96	14.90	20.17	6.42	13.58	19.99
1996/97	15.90	21.58	7.03	13.70	20.72
1997/98	17.41	21.77	6.37	14.26	21.63
1998/99	17.71	22.31	6.72	15.47	22.19
1999/2000	17.88	23.10	7.41	15.61	23.02
2000/01	18.00	22.41	7.25	15.84	23.09
2001/02	18.16	23.44	6.37	16.78	23.15
2002/03	18.63	24.87	6.20	17.21	23.41
2003/04	19.53	25.44	6.19	17.83	24.02
2004/05	20.01	25.84	6.21	18.32	24.53
2005/06	20.25	27.67	6.00	18.65	24.65
2006/07(p)	20.46	29.15	5.60	18.73	24.33

Source: BBS, 2000, 2006, 2007.

Bangladesh is to raise the investment rate from its current level of 24.3 per cent to over 30 per cent, and also to improve its efficiency (Government of Bangladesh, 2005a). This could increase the growth rate by 2 percentage points, which in turn would lead to an increase in employment creation and poverty reduction necessary to meet the Millennium Development Goals. Thus, appropriate government policy to overcome the obstacles to private investment (as noted above) is crucially important for meeting the objectives of employment generation and poverty alleviation.

The sectoral distribution of private investment is shown in Table 2.4. It is important to note the declining trend in private investment in the industrial sector after 1991/92. This explains the dip in the manufacturing growth rate in the second half of the 1990s and its failure to recover to the 1990/91–1994/95 level even in 2000/01–2004/05. Increasing private investment in the construction sector explains the continuous growth of this subsector. During the first half of the 1990s, about one-third of private investment went into the service sector, resulting in healthy growth in this sector over this period. From the perspective of employment creation, the decline in private investment in industry and its stagnation in agriculture are worrisome. This trend needs to be reversed through appropriate government policy to achieve the objectives of employment generation and poverty alleviation.

Table 2.4

Sectoral distribution of realized private investment (at 1989/90 prices) during the Fourth Five Year Plan (1990–1995) and plan outlay (at 1996/97 prices) during the Fifth Five Year Plan (1997–2002)

(percentage of total annual private investment)

Sector	*1990/91*	*1991/92*	*1992/93*	*1993/94*	*1994/95*	*1997–2002*
Agriculture	08.64	13.33	11.16	12.41	11.28	13.37
Industry	31.07	32.24	31.02	27.96	28.11	24.89
Housing and construction	13.94	13.35	14.42	17.17	16.94	18.03
Transport and communication	11.35	9.09	8.85	8.07	11.14	13.63
Trade and other services	35.00	31.99	34.54	34.38	32.53	26.86
Total	**100.00**	**100.00**	**100.00**	**100.00**	**100.00**	**100.00***

Note: * Includes a share of 3.22 per cent for power and gas sector.

Source: Government of Bangladesh, 2000.

Estimates of sectoral distribution of private investment are difficult to come by. Fortunately, some estimates of private and government investment going into different sectors are available for the second half of the 1990s (Bangladesh Bureau of Statistics, 2002). Data on estimates of private investment (at constant 1995/96 prices) by sectors are presented in Table 2.5. By comparing the data in Tables 2.4 and 2.5, a difference in the pattern of private investment can be observed between the first and second halves of the 1990s. The industry sector's share of total private investment went down sharply during the second half of the decade to reach 13.2 per cent in 1999/2000, while the housing and construction's share increased quite dramatically to reach nearly 50 per cent in 1998/99. Agriculture's share stagnated at around 10 per cent during the second half of the 1990s. Investment in trade declined dramatically from 35 per cent in 1990/91 to 1.8 per cent in 1999/2000. As noted earlier, the decline in private investment in agriculture and industry is worrisome from the perspective of employment.

Table 2.5

Private investment by industrial sector, 1996/97–1999/2000

(percentage of total annual private investment)

Industrial origin sector	*1996/97*	*1997/98*	*1998/99*	*1999/2000*
Agriculture	10.16	10.48	10.46	10.45
Mining and quarrying	–	–	–	–
Industry	16.54	15.27	13.82	13.23
Housing and construction	45.81	47.20	49.93	47.69
Power, gas, water and sanitary services	9.85	10.48	9.82	10.40
Transport, storage and communication	12.17	10.69	9.86	12.08
Trade service	1.56	1.67	1.71	1.75
Banking and insurance	2.15	2.26	2.34	2.40
Professional and miscellaneous services	1.75	1.95	2.06	2.01
Total	**100.00**	**100.00**	**100.00**	**100.00**

Note: Highly provisional estimates; – = negligible.
Source: BBS, 2002.

Data on total government investment (under the Annual Development Programme and the Revenue Budget) channelled to different economic sectors are presented in Table 2.6. Investment in the two directly productive sectors—agriculture and manufacturing—

Table 2.6

Government investment by economic sectors, 1995/96–2000/01

(percentage of total government investment)

Sector	*1995/ 96*	*1996/ 97*	*1997/ 98*	*1998/ 99*	*1999/ 2000*	*2000/ 01*
Agriculture	4.07	3.99	4.09	4.04	4.03	3.99
Mining and quarrying	2.24	4.03	3.82	3.78	3.30	3.27
Manufacturing	1.96	1.61	0.54	0.77	1.36	1.35
Construction	10.93	14.08	18.18	18.29	18.00	18.08
Power, gas, water and sanitary services	19.60	20.39	11.95	13.35	13.92	13.82
Transport, storage and communication	27.24	21.72	20.95	23.32	23.34	23.21
Housing services	9.00	9.82	16.49	15.88	15.05	14.98
Public administration and defence	7.85	7.41	11.91	9.50	9.59	9.88
Professional and miscellaneous	17.11	16.95	12.06	11.08	11.41	11.42
Total	**100.00**	**100.00**	**100.00**	**100.00**	**100.00**	**100.00**

Source: Same as Table 2.5.

stagnated in the second half of the 1990s. Investment declined in the power sector, and this adversely affected both agricultural and industrial production. However, investment in the transport and communication sector was substantial (a little less than a quarter of total government investment), and this undoubtedly helped production activity, particularly in the rural areas.

The sectoral allocation of public investment, as embodied in the Government's Annual Development Programme, is shown in Table 2.7. In order to maximize employment, investment has to be increased in labour-intensive industries and industries that support them. Since most of the unemployed and underemployed live in the rural areas, the strategy should be to promote the growth of rural industries through providing more public services in the rural areas. The current practice, however, is the concentration of industrial activities in urban areas, which encourage migration of the rural unemployed and underemployed to the urban centres. Also, new employment can be generated in the agricultural sector, although to a limited extent, through pursuing a strategy of promoting greater diffusion of the labour-intensive new agricultural technology, particularly in the area of growing new, higher value added crops. As indicated earlier, there is significant untapped potential in this area which could be realized through agricultural crop diversification. Let us examine the Government's development expenditure pattern from these perspectives.

Government development expenditure in agriculture and water resources shows a clearly declining trend, although expenditure in agriculture increased in 2005/06 and 2006/07. This has adversely affected agricultural production through, *inter alia*, affecting the provision of agricultural subsidy on which poor farmers are dependent for increasing production in the face of rising input costs. There has been an increase in government expenditure for rural development, which has positively affected the growth of rural industry. On an average, about 22–23 per cent of development expenditure has been allocated for transport and communication, which has helped to ease to some extent the infrastructural problems faced by private investors. Conversely, the allocation for the power sector has virtually stagnated (except in 2003/04 and 2004/05), and this has negatively affected growth of manufacturing

Table 2.7

Sectoral allocation of government annual development expenditure, 1994/95–2006/07

(percentage sectoral share)

Sector	*1994/ 95*	*1995/ 96*	*1996/ 97*	*1997/ 98*	*1998/ 99*	*1999/ 2000*	*2000/ 01*	*2001/ 02*	*2002/ 03*	*2003/ 04*	*2004/ 05*	*2005/ 06*	*2006/ 07*
Agriculture	5.3	4.5	5.0	4.5	4.9	4.7	4.5	4.4	3.7	4.0	3.1	5.1	7.2
Rural development	6.6	6.8	8.4	8.2	10.1	12.2	12.2	11.1	10.1	13.8	13.3	14.6	12.0
Water resources	6.3	5.6	8.2	8.1	7.0	6.9	6.1	5.4	4.3	4.0	4.9	3.1	3.3
Industries	1.3	1.5	1.4	0.8	0.8	1.7	3.3	1.9	1.1	2.7	2.7	1.6	1.8
Power	14.8	13.7	13.5	10.9	12.0	12.9	12.2	12.1	13.7	17.3	17.0	15.7	13.1
Gas, oil and natural resources	2.3	4.1	4.4	4.9	4.7	4.3	2.5	3.1	4.0	5.2	4.5	1.6	2.6
Transport	18.9	20.1	22.4	19.7	17.9	17.4	20.4	19.9	16.1	18.0	16.1	13.1	12.7
Communications	4.4	2.9	1.9	1.6	2.8	3.1	2.8	6.1	3.6	2.2	5.6	3.5	3.3
Physical planning and housing	4.7	4.6	5.4	5.1	5.4	7.0	7.5	6.6	5.6	5.9	7.2	6.9	5.1
Education and religion	14.2	13.0	13.2	12.9	13.5	12.8	13.3	14.2	13.9	12.3	10.5	14.1	15.5
Health and population	8.2	6.9	7.9	9.1	8.2	8.1	7.3	7.9	6.7	8.3	7.4	9.8	9.6
Other	13.0	16.4	8.1	14.1	12.8	9.1	7.8	7.4	17.0	6.2	7.5	10.9	13.8
Total annual development expenditure	**100.0**	**100.0**	**100.0**	**100.0**	**100.0**	**100.0**	**100.0**	**100.0**	**100.0**	**100.0**	**100.0**	**100.0**	**100.0**

Source: Government of Bangladesh, 2000, 2005b, 2007.

industry. The allocation for the social sectors (health and education) shows a declining trend until 2004/05, falling from 22.4 per cent in 1994/95 to 17.9 per cent in 2004/05; this has adversely affected human capital formation and labour productivity, which is so important for increasing output and employment. This trend has been reversed subsequently.

The sectoral distribution of total investment (public plus private) during the second half of the 1990s is shown in Table 2.8. From the viewpoint of employment generation, a declining trend in industrial investment and stagnation in agricultural investment can be considered to be undesirable developments. Substantial investment in housing and construction, a sector which flourished during this time, definitely helped to provide new employment opportunities; however, by its very nature, this sector provided temporary jobs to casual workers, both males and females, which cannot be termed as decent work.

Table 2.8

Total (public and private) investment by industrial sector, 1996/97–1999/2000

(percentage of total investment)

Sector	*1996/97*	*1997/98*	*1998/99*	*1999/2000*
Agriculture	8.26	8.31	8.37	8.42
Mining and quarrying	1.99	2.15	2.19	2.22
Industry	10.88	9.89	8.96	8.65
Housing and construction	45.75	46.10	46.76	46.87
Power, gas, water and sanitary services	10.37	10.82	10.95	11.10
Transport, storage and communication	12.57	13.37	14.09	14.29
Trade service	0.98	1.05	1.07	1.09
Public administration and defence	5.89	4.88	4.10	3.77
Banking and insurance	1.34	1.42	1.46	1.49
Professional and miscellaneous services	1.97	2.01	2.05	2.10
Total	**100.00**	**100.00**	**100.00**	**100.00**

Note: Highly provisional estimates.

Source: Same as Table 2.5.

In summary, although savings are currently not a constraint, they could become so if investment were to increase substantially—something that must happen if the growth rate is to be increased. A strategy to raise the investment ratio would, therefore, have to be complemented by a policy to mobilize domestic resources to finance investment. Efforts to increase private saving may be restricted by the lack of savings instruments that yield a reasonable return. The capital market is generally expected to mobilize a substantial portion of private savings, but it has had a chequered history in Bangladesh. The stock market crash of 1996 shook the confidence of savers to save in the capital market. The Government has undertaken reforms of the capital market to make it attractive once more to savers and investors. The public sector must also contribute to the saving effort of the nation. Besides eliminating losses of state-owned enterprises, this would call for reforming the tax system and increasing the efficiency of the National Board of Revenue, the tax revenue collecting organ of government.

It is important to note that open unemployment is seriously underestimated in Bangladesh, given the definition of unemployment used in the Labour Force Survey. Thus, rather than open unemployment, it is underemployment which is a more serious problem in Bangladesh. So, the policy challenge is not simply to provide job opportunities for unemployed persons, but more importantly, it is to bring about a change in the existing patterns of employment so that the economic condition of the working poor, particularly the presently underemployed, is improved.

The size of the labour force has increased through population growth; every year there are almost one million new entrants into the labour force. As Table 2.9 shows, the labour force increased from 50.7 million in 1989 to 56 million in 1995/96. Subsequently, after changes in the definition and coverage of the labour force,[2] it was estimated to be 40.7 million in the Labour Force Survey (LFS) of 1999/2000, and it increased to 46.3 million in 2002/03 according to the latest Labour Force Report available. Nearly 80 per cent of the labour force are males, but the labour force participation rate is slowly rising for females. The open

2. Up to 1995/96, a person of age 10 years and over was included in the civilian labour force. Subsequently, the minimum working age was raised from 10 years to 15 years. Hence, the labour force data up to 1995/96 are not quite comparable with the data after 1995/96.

unemployment rate is low, given the definition of unemployment,[3] but it is rising. It increased from 1.2 per cent in 1989 to 4.4 per cent in 1999/2000, but then it declined slightly to 4.3 per cent in 2002/03. In recent years, the unemployment rate for females has been higher than for males, reversing the trend of the earlier years.

Table 2.9

Composition of the labour force, 1989–2002/03

(million persons)

Characteristics	*LFS 1989*	*LFS 1990/ 91*	*LFS 1995/ 96*	*LFS 1999/ 2000*	*LFS 2002/ 03*
Civilian labour force	50.7	51.2	56.0	40.7	46.3
Male	29.7	31.1	34.7	32.2	36.0
Female	21.0	20.1	21.3	8.5	10.3
Employed population	50.1	50.2	54.6	39.0	44.3
Male	29.4	30.5	33.8	31.1	34.5
Female	20.7	19.7	20.8	7.9	9.8
Unemployed population	0.6	1.0	1.4	1.8	2.0
Male	0.4	0.6	0.9	1.1	1.5
Female	0.2	0.4	0.5	0.7	0.5
Unemployed rate (%)	1.2	1.9	2.5	4.4	4.3
Male	1.3	1.9	2.6	3.4	4.2
Female	0.9	2.0	2.3	8.2	4.8

Source: BBS, 2000, 2005.

It may be noted that the female labour force participation rate increased quite rapidly during the 1980s and 1990s. Thus, between 1983/84 and 1999/2000, the female labour force participation rate increased from 7 to 22 per cent in rural areas and from 12 to 26 per cent in urban areas. However, the unemployment rate for females has also increased. The probable reason behind this is that during this time period, there was a shift of labour from agriculture to the expanding RNF sector, as the LFS data of 1999/2000 show. But the female participation rate increased the most in agriculture, where employment opportunities

3. According to the Labour Force Survey, any person in the civilian labour force not doing any work at all or working less than 15 hours during the reference week is treated as unemployed.

were growing slowly. In fact, there was a decline in the share of the non-farm sector in the employment of rural females. So, females were not able to take advantage of increasing employment opportunities in the RNF sector. As a result, their unemployment rate increased.

Youth employment is another important issue to consider. Table 2.10 shows that when both sexes are taken together, the unemployment rate is highest for youths—aged between 15 and 24 years—in 1999/2000 and in 2002/03. The youth unemployment rate was much higher for females (45.5 per cent) compared with males (0.3 per cent) in 1999/2000. The picture changed in 2002/03, when the unemployment rate for male youths (13.9 per cent) was slightly higher than for female youths (12.2 per cent). A detailed analysis of the labour market would be needed to explain the observed pattern of youth unemployment.

Table 2.10

Rate of unemployment by age and sex, 1999/2000 and 2002/03

(percentage)

Age group (in years)	*Both sexes*		*Male*		*Female*	
	1999/2000	*2002/03*	*1999/2000*	*2002/03*	*1999/2000*	*2002/03*
15–19	1.9	5.1	0.2	5.5	31.6	4.3
20–24	11.2	8.3	0.1	8.4	13.9	7.9
25–29	4.2	5.8	3.9	5.7	3.8	6.0
30–34	1.0	5.8	1.1	5.7	0.8	6.0
35+	0.4	2.6	0.3	2.5	1.2	3.4
Total	**4.3**	**4.3**	**3.4**	**4.2**	**7.8**	**4.9**

Source: BBS, 2000, 2005.

The sectoral pattern of employment is shown in Table 2.11. The bulk of employment is generated in agriculture, though its share in total employment has gradually declined, from nearly 65 per cent in 1989 to 51.7 per cent in 2002/03. What is striking is the declining share of industry in total employment; the share of this sector fell from 15.4 to 13.5 per cent between 1989 and 2002/03. Within industry, there has been a marked decline in the employment share of the manufacturing subsector, its share in total employment fell from 13.9 per cent in 1989 to 7.5 per cent in 1995/96 but then recovered to 9.7 per cent in 2002/03. This employment pattern appears to be quite consistent with the pattern of growth of the manufacturing sector. Conversely, the employment share of the construction subsector gradually increased to reach 3.4 per cent in 2002/03. The share of the service sector in total employment increased from 18 per cent in 1989 to 36 per cent in 1999/2000, but then declined to about 28 per cent in 2002/03. Much of the increase in service sector employment has occurred in the informal economy.

Table 2.11

Employment in major sectors, 1989–2002/03

(percentage of total)

Sector	*LFS 1989*	*LFS 1990/91*	*LFS 1995/96*	*LFS 1999/2000*	*LFS 2002/03*
Agriculture	64.9	66.4	63.2	50.8	51.7
Industry	15.4	12.9	9.6	13.0	13.5
Mining and quarrying	0.2	0.03	0.04	0.5	0.2
Manufacturing	13.9	11.8	7.5	9.5	9.7
Electricity, gas, water	0.03	0.08	0.2	0.2	0.2
Construction	1.3	1.0	1.9	2.8	3.4
Services	18.0	20.6	27.1	36.1	27.8
Trade and restaurant	8.2	8.5	11.1	15.6	15.1
Transport, storage, communications	2.5	3.2	4.2	6.4	6.8
Finance, business services	0.5	0.6	0.4	1.0	0.7
Community and personal services	3.6	3.8	9.3	13.1	5.2
Household sector	3.2	4.5	2.1	–	–

Note: The data in each column may not add up to 100 per cent due to rounding effect; – = negligible.

Source: Same as Table 2.10.

At this point, we consider the labour absorption taking place in different sectors in the wake of output growth. For this purpose, we have computed the employment elasticity of output growth for the three major sectors and for the entire economy. Employment elasticity is measured as the proportionate change in employment divided by the proportionate change in output during a given period. Estimates of employment elasticity are presented in Table 2.12. It is seen that for the period 1991–1995, the employment elasticity for the whole economy was 0.40, indicating a low employment intensity of growth. A negative elasticity for industry reflects declining employment despite output growth; this is partly attributable to the negative effect of import liberalization on inefficient import-substituting industries and partly due to rising productivity, which was the result of increased import liberalization. An elasticity of 2.1 in the service sector reflects the highly labour-intensive nature of economic activities in this sector. In the 2000/2003 period, we notice an increase in employment elasticity in all sectors except services. This increase reflects a decline in productivity. The decline in elasticity in the service sector probably reflects a rise in labour productivity that resulted from an increase in the size of enterprises in the RNF sector (Mahmud, 2006).

Table 2.12

Employment elasticity of output growth, 1991–2003

	1991–1995			*2000–2003*		
	Employment growth (%)	*Output growth (%)*	*Employment elasticity*	*Employment growth (%)*	*Output growth (%)*	*Employment elasticity*
Agriculture	0.74	1.55	0.48	5.22	2.73	1.91
Industry	-4.89	7.47	-0.65	5.88	6.30	0.93
Service	8.68	4.15	2.09	1.65	4.63	0.36
Total GDP	**1.77**	**4.39**	**0.40**	**4.53**	**4.98**	**0.91**

Source: Calculated by the author.

The employment elasticities for 2000/03 reported in Table 2.12 should be treated with some caution since these appear to be quite high when compared with most international experience. The rather high elasticity estimates probably reflect problems of comparability of employment data over time in Bangladesh, arising from changes in definition of employment in various Labour Force Surveys, as indicated above. Also, the high employment elasticities may have captured a rise simply in labour absorption rather than any significant increase in productive employment. To the extent that the latter is true, this would have serious consequences for poverty reduction and decent work in an economy characterized by already low levels of income and earnings.

It would be instructive at this stage to examine the employment status of employed persons to gain a better insight into the employment dynamics in Bangladesh. Data in this regard are presented in Table 2.13. The table shows that wage employment in the formal economy (categorized in the table as "employees") has been low, although its contribution to total employment increased from 9.5 per cent in 1989 to 16.7 per cent in 1999/2000, thereafter declining to 13.8 per cent in 2002/2003. Self-employment has been the dominant category, its share of total employment rising to 45 per cent by 2002/03. The other important category of workers has been the "day labourers", whose share of total employment reached 20 per cent in 2002/03. The share of "unpaid family workers", mainly women who work on farms, has declined, which indicates that they have obtained work in the non-farm sector, either rural or urban. This pattern of employment status reflects the large-scale prevalence of underemployment.[4] In 1995/96, the underemployment rate in Bangladesh was estimated to be 38.5 per cent; the rate was 22.1 per cent in urban areas and 42.1 per cent in rural areas. It rose to 41 per cent in 2002/03. Thus, in Bangladesh, the high rate of underemployment is a more serious concern than open unemployment.

The substantial rise in self-employed category from about 30 per cent in 1989 to about 45 per cent in 2002/03 reflects the growing informalization of employment in Bangladesh during the 1990s. Rising landlessness in the rural areas, largely a result of a growing population, caused the large-scale migration of farm family members to the rural non-farm sector and urban industrial centres in search of jobs. Since large numbers of these migrants were unable to find employment, many of them set up small (often tiny) business enterprises in the informal economy. This explains the observed increase in self-employment between 1989 and 2002/03. It also partly explains the observed decline in the "unpaid family workers" category during this period. The exodus of farm family members from agriculture where they were previously working as unpaid family helpers brought down the numbers in the latter category; many of them, particularly female workers, found wage employment in the rural non-farm sector (Mahmud, 2006).

4. Any person working less than 35 hours during the reference week is considered as underemployed in the Labour Force Survey.

Table 2.13

Employment status breakdown, 1989–2003

(percentage of total)

Type of employment	*LFS 1989*	*LFS 1990/ 91*	*LFS 1995/ 96*	*LFS 1999/ 2000*	*LFS 2002/ 03*
Self-employed	29.6	26.8	29.6	47.0	45.2
Employees	9.5	11.7	12.4	16.7	13.8
Day labourers	15.1	13.9	17.9	24.3	20.0
Unpaid family workers	45.8	47.2	40.1	12.0	18.2

Note: The data in each column may not add up to 100 per cent due to rounding effect.
Source: Same as Table 2.10.

As indicated earlier, according to the LFS 1999/2000, approximately three-quarters of the non-agricultural labour force belonged to the informal economy, while the rest were employed in the organized sector. By far, the larger part of informal economy employment is in the rural areas. This is because the RNF sector accounts for the larger share of the country's total non-farm labour force and is predominantly informal in nature.[5] Over the years, there has been a shift of labour from agriculture to the RNF sector.

The rural population has increasingly found employment in the RNF sector, as shown by Table 2.14. While about 34 per cent of the rural inhabitants were employed in the non-farm sector in 1983/84, this proportion rose to nearly 39 per cent by 1999/2000, and while participation of males in non-farm activities increased, that of females decreased.[6] Table 2.14 also indicates that the shift of male labour from agriculture to the RNF sector slowed during the 1990s.

5. According to the Population Census of 1991, nearly 60 per cent of the total non-agricultural labour force was rural. The proportion goes up to 70 per cent if semi-urban areas are treated as rural.

6. This was a period of rapid increase in female labour market participation: the participation rate increased from 7 to 22 per cent in rural areas, and from 12 to 26 per cent in urban areas. The declining non-farm proportion of female labour therefore, did not represent a genuine labour shift. Rather, female participation rates increased in all the broad sectors, but the increase was greatest in agriculture. See Mahmud (2006).

Table 2.14

Trends in the non-farm sector share of the total employed rural population, 1983–2000

(percentage)

Sex	*1983/84*	*1984/85*	*1990/91*	*1995/96*	*1999/2000*
Both sexes	34.3	34.3	38.6	37.8	38.7
Male	28.5	29.4	35.1	35.0	38.6
Female	89.5	88.8	61.3	51.0	39.0

Note: Calculated from Labour Force Survey.
Source: Mahmud, 2006.

Data on rural incomes available from the Household Expenditure Surveys indicate that the proportion of self-employed workers in the RNF sector declined in the 1990s after having remained more or less static in the 1980s. This implies a rise in the proportion of wage-based enterprises, which are likely to be somewhat larger in scale and more productive than the enterprises involving mainly self-employed workers that predominated in the 1980s. While the shift of agricultural labour to even low productivity self-employment generally results in an income gain (Mahmud, 1996), it would be more desirable to increase wage employment in relatively more productive jobs through the gradual scaling up of enterprises. An appropriate combination of these two paths could thus, create a virtuous cycle of higher income and demand for income-elastic products and services of the RNF sector and higher growth of both self-employment and wage employment.

The barriers faced by the poor in getting access to salaried or permanent wage employment as compared with employment as casual or daily wage labour are characteristic of the labour market and assume some importance in the context of any strategy for employment creation. This condition is seen from Table 2.15.

The table shows that the percentage of the poor (both extreme and moderate poor) in self-employment is lower than that of non-poor in both the farm and non-farm sectors. The difference is striking in the case of salaried jobs in the non-farm sector; here, the percentage of the poor in salaried jobs is about half that of the moderate non-poor. Differences in various types of endowments are responsible for these

Table 2.15

Distribution of poverty status of household workforce in rural areas by mode and sector of employment, 1999/2000

(percentage)

Poverty status	*Farm*		*Non-farm*		
	Self-employment	*Casual wage labour*	*Casual wage labour*	*Self-employment*	*Salaried wage labour*
Extreme poor	26.5	41.1	14.1	12.0	6.3
Moderate poor	35.4	29.7	12.8	15.4	6.7
Moderate non-poor	39.7	19.6	11.0	18.1	11.6
Rich non-poor	42.1	9.7	7.7	23.6	18.5
All poor	32.0	34.0	13.4	13.9	6.7
All non-poor	41.1	15.2	9.1	20.5	14.4
All households	36.2	25.0	11.2	17.3	10.2

Note: Estimated from the primary data of Household Expenditure Survey (HES), 2000.
Source: Osmani *et al.*, 2003.

differences in access; the most important are the differences in ownership of human capital and physical assets. These impede access to self-employment and permanent wage employment opportunities for the poor and must be removed so that the poor can escape the poverty trap.

2.3 Macroeconomic policy and decent employment

Any strategy to increase employment opportunities should have both a supply and a demand dimension. On the supply side, effort must be made to improve employability of the workforce by enhancing their marketable skills. A more severe constraint on the expansion of employment opportunities is, however, imposed by demand conditions. There are simply not enough jobs created in the market, particularly in the high-wage formal economy. The result is a large number of unemployed and underemployed young persons. In other words, the problem is mainly one of deficient demand for labour. This problem can be overcome through achieving growth in the economy, particularly in sectors where the employment elasticity of growth is highest. In the context of Bangladesh, these sectors would include agriculture and the RNF sector, as the analysis in the previous section indicated. Promoting agricultural growth would improve the capacity of small farmers to stay in agriculture. They would therefore, not join the ranks of landless agricultural labour or add to the overcrowding of low-productivity RNF self-employment. Agricultural growth is also extremely important for boosting the RNF sector, through various linkage effects and by absorbing the surplus landless labour. The growth of the RNF sector also needs to be stimulated directly so as to enable these enterprises (through scaling up) to make a shift from largely self-employment based to wage-employment based activities. Finally, labour absorption in the formal manufacturing sector has to be enhanced rapidly through achieving acceleration in growth of the sector.

Macroeconomic policy has a crucial role to play in the success of the employment strategy delineated above. On the one hand, it can provide the resources for investment required to achieve the desired growth rate. On the other hand, it can ensure that investment is channelled to the right areas and in the desired amounts. It is from this perspective that the macroeconomic policy regime of Bangladesh is examined in this section.

Bangladesh has been pursuing market-oriented liberalizing policy reforms since the mid-1980s, with the declared objective of accelerating growth and alleviating poverty. Here, we shall selectively discuss only those areas of policy reforms that have direct relevance for the promotion of employment. It may be noted that employment creation as an objective of planned development has been emphasized in the various Five Year Plan documents of Bangladesh.

Macroeconomic stability

Macroeconomic stability provides a conducive environment for accelerated economic growth. The Government of Bangladesh has been committed to the goal of achieving and maintaining macroeconomic stability since the early 1980s. The key aspects of macroeconomic stability include low and stable inflation, a low budget deficit and a sustainable external balance. The Government has used prudent fiscal and monetary policy and a supportive external sector policy to achieve these objectives.

The budget deficit has been reduced, from 9 per cent of GDP in 1980/81 to 4.5 per cent in 2004/05. Inflation came down from 16.3 per cent in 1981/82 to 1.6 per cent in 2000/01, but thereafter it has gradually increased to reach 7.3 per cent in 2004/05. The current account deficit in the balance of payments as a proportion of GDP was reduced from 12 per cent in 1981/82 and converted to a small surplus of 0.5 per cent by 2001/02 (and 0.6 per cent in 2002/03), but there was then a small deficit in 2004/05.

The above objectives were achieved through implementing a contractionary demand management policy, which involved reducing government expenditures and curtailing the growth of bank credit to the private sector. The government expenditure–GDP ratio was reduced from 18.4 per cent in 1980/81 to 14.6 per cent in 2004/05. However, in its effort to reduce its total expenditures, the Government reduced development expenditures but increased its current or non-development expenditures. Thus, while development expenditure as a proportion of GDP declined from 6.6 per cent in 1994/95 to 5.1 per cent 2004/05, the non-development expenditure–GDP ratio rose from 6.6 to 9 per cent during the same period. The annual growth rate of bank credit to the private sector was brought down from an average of 33.4 per cent during 1980/81–1984/85 to 14.1 per cent in 2003/04 and 17 per cent in 2004/05.

High inflation increases risk and uncertainty associated with investment and economic activities, both in urban and rural areas. Thus, reducing inflation doubtlessly had a salutary effect on private investment. Conversely, the lesser availability of credit for the private sector slowed down the growth of private investment, particularly in the manufacturing sector, and prevented this sector from achieving a faster growth rate. As pointed out above, private investors have identified shortage of finance as a major impediment to increasing investment.

Table 2.16 shows the slowing down of investment growth during the period 2001–2005. Since private investment forms a major part of total investment, and since public investment has virtually stagnated, a deceleration in growth of total investment largely reflects a slowing down of private investment growth. The other thing to be noted from Table 2.16 is the smaller growth of investment compared with domestic savings, probably the result of a declining enthusiasm for investment options. Three factors may have been operating simultaneously to dampen incentives for investment (Rahman, 2003):

- the social environment for investment was not conducive;
- the rate of interest on bank loans was high; and
- government investment financed by borrowing from the banking system had a "crowding out" effect on private investment.

Table 2.16

Growth rates of savings and investments, 1996–2005

Period	*Growth rate of gross domestic savings*	*Growth rate of investment*	*Growth rate of GDP*	*Growth rate of industry*
1986–1990	12.28	6.85	3.74	5.86
1991–1995	26.21	6.77	4.39	7.47
1996–2000	22.45	10.18	5.21	6.44
2001–2005	8.59	8.82	5.43	7.42

Source: Government of Bangladesh, 2000, 2005b, 2006.

The "crowding in" effect of public investment on private investment in developing countries is well known. By slowing down the growth of its development expenditure, the Government has dampened the incentive of private investors to increase their investment at a faster rate. The infrastructure and power sectors have been hit the hardest by insufficient development expenditure by government. By contrast, the Government's fiscal operations have had a "crowding out" effect on private investment since the late 1990s. Even though the budget deficit has been reduced, the Government has resorted to increased borrowing from domestic sources, particularly the banking system, to finance its budget deficit. As a result, public investment has crowded out private investment.[7]

The Government has been forced to keep its development expenditure from growing at a desirable rate because of the resource constraint that it has faced. Bangladesh's tax revenue–GDP ratio is one of the lowest in the world. Even in 1994/95 it was 7.9 per cent, and it increased sluggishly to 8.7 per cent by 2004/05. As noted above, insufficient development expenditure by government has constrained

7. For detailed analysis, see Rahman (2003).

private investment and thereby, prevented the economic growth rate from rising at a faster rate. Furthermore, a rapid increase in tax revenue would have enabled the Government to reduce its budget deficit without having to cut down its development expenditure. The clear policy implication is that taxation efforts need to be strengthened so that the tax–GDP ratio can be increased quickly.[8]

Financial sector reforms

The specific objectives of Bangladesh's financial sector reforms were to:

- remove interest rate (negative real rate) and credit distortions;
- remove impediments to competition;
- strengthen the financial sector infrastructure;
- strengthen financial institutions; and
- strengthen the macroeconomic environment.

Achieving a free and market-based interest rate structure was the major objective of banking sector reforms. This was expected to bring improvement in resource allocation as well as market competition. Until 1990, Bangladesh had an administered interest rate regime, which reduced the margins of the banks and reduced the incentive to mobilize savings. In 1991, a liberalized interest rate policy was introduced, in which there was a band of deposit interest rates and a market-determined lending interest rate, except in the agriculture, small-scale industry and export sectors. After 1993, deposit interest rates also became market-determined. However, this market-oriented change in interest rate policy did not yield any remarkable results. The deposit interest rate remained low but the lending rate remained very high, resulting in a large spread between the deposit and the lending interest rates. This indicates that market distortions have remained and the desired level of competitiveness is yet to be achieved. While some analysts have held loan default responsible for this market distortion,

8. Tax policy reforms have been underway in Bangladesh since the late 1990s but evidently have not yet been very effective.

this alone cannot explain the high level of spread. Government-induced distortions (e.g. high interest rates for government debentures) are also responsible for the unusually high spread (Centre for Policy Dialogue, 2001). Liberalization of the interest rate regime also resulted in an increase in the real rates of interest.

Other reforms were also carried out, which include the following. Two nationalized commercial banks were been denationalized and new private commercial banks have been allowed to operate. Directed credit programmes for priority sectors were stopped. A number of accounting, supervisory and management-oriented reform measures were undertaken; of these, loan classification and capital adequacy were the most significant. There were several legal reforms to strengthen the weak legal infrastructure, which was largely responsible for non-recovery of default loans and thus, for deterioration in the quality of overall credit management in Bangladesh.

How have the reforms affected the allocation of loans by the commercial banking system? Table 2.17 is used to answer this question.

Table 2.17

Loan advances by commercial banks as a proportion of sectoral GDP

(three-year average percentages)

Sector	*1986/87–1988/89*	*1991/92–1993/94*	*1995/96–1997/98*
Agriculture (crops and animal farming)	0.96	0.90	0.77
Large and medium-scale industry	2.85	3.17	3.27
Small-scale and cottage industry	1.05	0.60	0.51

Source: Same as Table 2.14.

The estimates in Table 2.17 show the trends in the amounts of loans advanced by the commercial banks to certain sectors as a proportion of the share of these sectors in the country's GDP in the respective years. It is seen from the table that the proportionate shares of annual bank advances going to agriculture and small and cottage industries have significantly declined, while the share of large-scale manufacturing has increased. Clearly, the former had adverse effects on employment creation.

The highly labour-intensive nature of agriculture and small and cottage industries (in the RNF sector) means that these two sectors offer scope for achieving large increases in employment through output growth. But output growth is constrained by a shortage of credit. The farmers and small entrepreneurs are largely deprived of access to formal sources of credit. Consequently, they resort to borrowing from informal sources, at much higher interest rates.

In recent years, low deposit rates have allowed banks to lower interest rates on loans. However, the lending rates are still relatively high, as can be seen from Table 2.18.

Table 2.18

Lending rates of nationalized commercial banks by sector

(percentage)

Sector	*Sonali Bank*		*Janata Bank*		*Agrani Bank*		*Rupali Bank*	
	2001	*2005*	*2001*	*2005*	*2001*	*2005*	*2001*	*2005*
Agriculture	12.5–13.0	8.0–9.0	11.0–14.5	8.0–10.0	13.5	8.0–10.0	13.0	9.0
Large and medium industry	10.0	11.0	13.0	9.0–11.0	13.0	10.0–12.25	13.5	11.25
Working capital	14.0	11.0	14.5	10.0–11.0	15.5	11.0	14.5	11.5
Export	10.0	7.0	9.0	7.0	10.0	7.0	10.0	7.0
Other commercial loans	16.0	12.0	15.0	12.5	16.0	12.0	15.0–18.0	12.0–12.5
Small industry	13.0	10.0–10.5	11.5	10.0	11.5	10.5	11.0	10.0–10.5
Others	12.0–18.0	10.0–15.0	12.0–15.0	12.5	11.0–16.0	13.0	15.0–18.0	10.0–12.0

Source: Bangladesh Bank, *Annual Report*, 2002, 2006.

Table 2.18 shows that the lending rates of all four nationalized commercial banks were reduced between 2001 and 2005. This was part of the Government's interest rate rationalization policy intended to encourage growth of the private sector. However, lending rates were still quite high in 2005. Moreover, the interest rates charged on agricultural loans in that year were nearly as high as the interest rates on loans made to the large and medium industries. What is worse is that interest rates charged on loans made to small industries have been nearly as high as interest rates on loans to large and medium industries. The saving grace has been the relatively low interest rate charged on loans made to export industries in 2005.

Agriculture and small and cottage industries have to be provided with adequate credit at moderate interest rates if the objective of employment generation is to be achieved. One way to overcome the problem of inadequate credit for small farmers and small entrepreneurs in the RNF sector is to fill in the "missing middle" between microcredit and formal banking (Mahmud, 2006). In order to help progressive microcredit group members to expand their micro enterprises, the major non-governmental organizations (NGOs) have started to provide them with larger loans. While deepening of microcredit in these areas is likely to be beneficial for employment generation, it can hardly be used to meet the entire credit needs of small farmers and entrepreneurs simply because of a funds constraint. It is the commercial banks that command enough funds to play the major role in addressing the problem of the "missing middle". There could be collaboration between NGOs and commercial banks, or some of the NGOs may be turned into rural banks under an appropriate legal framework. The Government must come to grips with these issues in order to generate more employment in the economy.[9]

Trade liberalization

Bangladesh initiated a process of trade policy reform in the early 1980s, through the reduction in the number of quantitative restrictions (QRs) and average tariff rates, to pursue an outward-oriented growth strategy. The objective of trade policy reform throughout the 1990s was to promote rapid export growth by reducing and eliminating the anti-export bias prevalent in the economy. Bangladesh pursued an extensive liberalization process by reducing its tariffs, harmonizing tariff rates on similar products and eliminating many QRs on imports. Moreover, several export promotion measures were put into operation to stimulate export growth.

---

9. For a detailed analysis of these issues, see Mahmud (2006).

The unweighted average customs duty rate was reduced from 47.4 per cent in 1992/93 to 13.5 per cent in 2004/05, while the import-weighted average duty rate came down from 23.6 to 9.6 per cent during this time. The number of tariff bands was reduced from 18 in 1990/91 to four in 2004/05. During this time, the maximum tariff rate was brought down from 350 to 25 per cent. The revised tariff structure is, however, cascading in nature, with higher tariffs imposed on final consumer goods and lower tariffs on capital goods and on raw materials and intermediate inputs. The effects of such a cascading tariff structure have been to provide higher effective protection to domestic production activities compared with the nominal protection they received before. The rate of tariff reduction has been fastest for capital goods (the unweighted average tariff rate fell from 16.1 per cent in 1999/2000 to 7.3 per cent in 2004/05). The unweighted average tariff rate has also been brought down significantly for consumer goods (from 31 per cent in 1999/2000 to 18.2 per cent in 2004/05).[10]

The coverage of all QRs was brought down from 15.6 per cent of four-digit tariff headings in 1991 to 5.1 per cent in 2003. The coverage of trade-related QRs declined from 6.4 per cent of four-digit tariff headings in 1991 to 1.9 per cent in 2003. The Import Policy 2003–2006 proposed to slash the number of items covered by QRs by almost half, but it also added many procedural restrictions, thus leaving in place many trade-related QRs.

Various export-promotion measures are used in Bangladesh to accelerate export growth. These operate mainly to provide exporters with access to imported inputs on a duty-free basis (e.g. the bonded warehouse facility).

The World Bank (1999), among studies by other authors, has assessed the effects of trade liberalization in Bangladesh. It is argued that the rapid growth in garments export, which was the major factor behind the robust export growth of 15 per cent annually, was fostered by the availability of innovative export promotion schemes, such as the bonded warehouse, together with the Multi-Fibre Arrangement quota

10. See Rashid (2008) for a detailed discussion.

system. The World Bank reported that most manufacturing industries registered significant expansion according to the official quantum index of manufacturing (ibid.). Out of the 57 identified manufacturing activities, only 18 import-competing activities showed output contraction over the 1990s: these included vegetable oil, cotton textile, jute textile, paper, insecticides, rubber footwear, iron and steel basic structures, fabricated metal, and some machinery and equipment. These 18 contracting activities accounted for about 17 per cent of large and medium manufacturing industries. An enterprise-level survey on manufacturing firms showed that in 1997/98, 28 out of 90 enterprises reported employment decline. About half of these firms undertook investment for expansion, diversification, quality improvement and modernization.

The above evidence suggests that the manufacturing sector seems to have performed well, although some import-competing firms may have been adversely affected by trade liberalization. Also, available evidence show that small-scale manufacturing activities (excluding the handloom and cottage industries) have fared better than large-scale manufacturing in the post-liberalization period; the former is estimated to have grown at 9.2 per cent annually between 1991/92 and 1999/2000 while the latter grew at 7 per cent. Small-scale informal-economy activities benefited from the liberalized import of inputs and capital machinery. Moreover, since the products of small-scale enterprises were mostly remote substitutes for imported items, the import-displacement effect of increased imports resulting from import liberalization policy was much weaker for these firms compared with their large-scale counterparts.

An important effect of the tariff reforms has been to stifle the growth of the domestic engineering and capital goods industry. This has been largely overlooked because of the small size of the industry, but this ignores the potential role of a domestic capital goods industry in technological adaptation, which is especially important for upgrading the traditional technology in the informal economy and for facilitating subcontracting arrangements with large-scale firms.

In addition, exports from the informal economy cannot take advantage of the duty-free access to imported inputs, as provided through the system of duty-drawback and the bonded warehouse scheme. Only handloom cloth, along with cloth in general, was given a cash incentive for export, including indirect exports in the form of sales to the export-oriented garments industry. However, this is being phased out to reduce the budgetary burden. There has, therefore, been discrimination against direct and indirect exports of the informal economy. However, in recent years the facility of cash incentives for export (at 5–10 per cent of the value of export) have been extended to include some goods produced by the small-scale and informal economy, such as processed food, cut flowers and light-engineering goods.

Investment policy

After the birth of Bangladesh in December 1971, about 90 per cent of fixed assets in the modern industrial sector were put under public ownership. The scope of the private sector and foreign investment in manufacturing was largely delimited. However, within two years the restrictions on private investment were partially relaxed. With political changes in 1975, the restrictions on private investment were relaxed further, and they were subsequently brought to a minimum. These measures culminated in the announcement of the New Industrial Policy of 1982, which provided the setting for a determined push towards privatization and assigned the private sector the major role in industrial development. Various liberalization measures were introduced in the New Industrial Policy, including the waiving of regulatory provisions pertaining to investment sanctioning, shifting from an import substitution to an export-led growth strategy, liberalizing import procedures and providing greater incentives for foreign private investment. The Revised Industrial Policy of 1986 and subsequent policy reforms were designed to strengthen these measures further.

During the 1990s, there was greater coordination of industrial policy with trade and fiscal policy. With regard to the sectoral focus of investment plans, the industrial policies placed greater emphasis on agro-based and agro-supportive industries as well as greater emphasis on investment in efficient intermediate and basic manufacturing. Industries with potential for high value addition and foreign exchange earning capacity were particularly encouraged in the 1990s.

Various measures were used during the 1990s to encourage private investment. These included the following:

- gradual reduction of "reserved lists" and the opening up of almost all sectors (except four reserved sectors) for private investment;
- guarantee of security of private investments from government control and ownership;
- increased incentives for investment in export-oriented industries in the form of liberalization of imports of raw materials and capital machinery, cash incentives, bonded warehouse facilities with back-to-back letters of credit, interest subsidy and working capital loan support (to the extent of 90 per cent of requirements);
- reactivating the capital market; and
- government provision of improved infrastructural and institutional support for private investment.

Under the current industrial policy, all but four reserved sectors have been kept open for private investment. Under the policy, foreign investors do not require government permission to invest in any sector except for the four reserved ones. A host of other incentives are also offered to encourage private investment, including relaxation of the Foreign Exchange Control Act, increased tariff rebates, tariff rebates for imported capital machinery for 100 per cent export-oriented industries and tax holidays. The telecommunications sector has been opened up for private investment, both domestic and foreign. Private investment is also encouraged in infrastructure development and in the service sector.

By and large, the investment policy focused on promoting industrial activities in the modern sector located in urban areas. Unemployed and underemployed people, who are mainly located in the rural areas, would thus have to migrate to the urban centres to avail of the employment opportunities created in the modern industrial sector. Not only has such rural-to-urban migration exacerbated the already serious congestion problem in the major urban centres, more importantly, labour absorption in the formal industrial sector has been limited in view of the relatively higher capital intensity of production in this sector. What is required from the perspective of employment-intensive growth is the stimulation of growth in labour-intensive industries in rural areas. Since such a strategy appears to have been largely ignored, one can legitimately question the centrality of employment creation in investment planning in Bangladesh.

The foregoing analysis of various government policies focused on enhancing decent employment in Bangladesh indicates some degree of lack of policy coherence. Thus, the Government has reduced its development expenditures (particularly in agriculture and water resources) to reduce the budget deficit, but this adversely affected output and employment growth in agriculture, which is a major source of employment in the country. Investment in the power sector has virtually stagnated with adverse effects on private investment and employment in the formal manufacturing sector. Again, the slowing down of the growth of bank credit has constrained investment and employment growth in the formal manufacturing sector as well as in the rural non-farm sector, both of which are important from the perspective of employment growth.

Financial liberalization failed largely to have the desired benefit because market distortions remained. The resultant increase in the real rates of interest discouraged investment with an adverse effect on employment growth. Also, poor recovery rates of default loans impacted negatively on overall credit management and hence, investment output and employment growth.

Many import-competing firms have experienced a contraction in output and employment as a result of import liberalization. Had the liberalization process been slower and accompanied by appropriate reforms in other sectors, the story may have been different.

Investment policy has focused primarily on promoting investment in the urban areas. However, most of the unemployed and underemployed are living in rural areas. Employment-intensive growth would require stimulating the growth of labour-intensive industries in rural areas, which sadly has not been the case in Bangladesh.

2.4 Labour productivity and employment

To analyse the relationships between output growth, employment and labour productivity and their implications for household income levels (which is important from the perspective of poverty alleviation), the conceptual framework provided by Islam (2006) is adopted here. Low levels of real wages and low levels of earnings in self-employment result from a low level of average productivity of the employed workforce. In turn, low labour productivity is caused by a relatively low capital intensity in production and the use of backward technology. Since rising capital intensity in production accompanies economic growth, the latter would lead to the generation of employment opportunities with rising productivity. In the process of economic growth, therefore, the unemployed and the underemployed would be absorbed in gainful employment in expanding sectors. They would benefit in terms of higher income (wages), either in their existing occupations or through shifting to new occupations involving higher level skills and/or better technology.

Employment-intensive growth requires a higher employment elasticity of growth. However, employment elasticity reflects the inverse of labour productivity. Therefore, the policy-maker has to be cautious not to focus solely on raising the employment elasticity as that would mean a further decline in productivity in economies where there already exists widespread low-productivity employment. In other words, the policy-maker must be aware of the potential trade-off between higher employment and lower labour productivity.

The contribution of agriculture and manufacturing to total employment (Table 2.11) increased respectively from 59 per cent and 9 per cent in 1983/84 (not shown in the table) to 65 per cent and 14 per cent in 1989, and 66 per cent and 12 per cent respectively in 1990/91. During this time, the contribution to GDP of agriculture declined from 31.5 per cent in 1984/85 to 29.5 per cent in 1989/90, while the contribution of manufacturing increased from 10 per cent in 1983/84 to 12.5 per cent in 1989/90. Thus, labour productivity in agriculture and manufacturing clearly declined between 1983/84 and 1989/90. The contribution of agriculture to GDP continued to fall, and reached 21.9

per cent in 2004/05. As Table 2.11 shows, the employment share of agriculture in 1990/91 and 1995/96 was higher than in 1983/84. This indicates that labour productivity in agriculture continued to decline throughout the first half of the 1990s. The employment share of agriculture dropped sharply in the LFS 1999/2000 data; this was partly due to a change in the definition of "employment" in the LFS and partly due to a shift of some agricultural labour to the RNF. The share of agriculture in employment rose again in the LFS 2002/03, but the fall in the contribution of agriculture to GDP during this time reflects declining labour productivity during the second half of the 1990s.

The manufacturing sector's contribution to GDP remained more or less unchanged, at about 15 per cent, between 1994/95 and 1999/2000; during this time, as Table 2.11 shows, the employment share of this sector increased from 7.5 per cent in 1995/96 to 9.5 per cent in 1999/2000. This indicates a declining trend in labour productivity in the manufacturing sector during the second half of the 1990s. This is confirmed by the World Bank's finding that annual value added per worker in manufacturing in Bangladesh declined from US$1,820 in 1980–1984 to US$1,711 in 1995–1999 (World Bank, 2000).

Table 2.19 shows that labour productivity declined in some major industries—jute and paper—between 1995/96 and 2002/03. As argued by Ahmed and Mondal (1993), the productivity situation in the manufacturing sector was in some ways worse between 1985/86 and 1990/91; out of six industries studied, there was a systematic decline in productivity in four—jute textile, cotton textile, TSP fertilizer, and pulp and paper—with productivity rising only in the cement and sugar industries.

Labour productivity is crucial in the determination of the real wage, with a positive relationship between the two. If productivity is low, the real wage would tend to be low, unless there is government intervention in the labour market in the form of minimum wage legislation. We will now examine the trends in real wages to better understand the link with labour productivity and their probable impact on employment (Table 2.20).

Table 2.19

Productivity indices for production workers in selected industries at constant prices

(1988/89 = 100)

Period	Jute	Cotton	Paper	Steel	Cement	Fertilizer	Petroleum products	Paints and varnish
1995/96	103.56	116.70	120.37	211.92	109.44	130.15	90.62	211.94
1996/97	106.25	127.12	102.25	441.98	158.34	103.88	106.73	264.29
1997/98	104.13	122.49	71.05	523.84	141.51	116.77	115.64	267.72
1998/99	96.00	128.23	96.22	462.42	188.84	103.66	85.88	311.50
1999/2000	89.24	136.09	90.56	468.74	295.80	110.37	127.56	349.49
2000/01	93.88	142.79	86.72	494.36	341.32	123.49	137.41	413.55
2001/02	94.66	142.48	69.85	–	335.10	106.96	144.25	380.65
2002/03	89.79	152.48	93.54	–	353.00	143.00	136.00	411.00
2003/04	80.99	201.92	114.49	–	362.82	144.11	132.72	473.17
2004/05	82.55	251.28	113.10	–	413.94	142.62	106.99	617.39
2005/06	76.02	287.38	107.68	–	435.50	134.38	115.78	577.40

Note: – = not available.
Source: BBS, 2000, 2006.

When growth takes place, if the growth is employment-intensive the labour market will tighten, leading to an increase in wage rates, particularly for low-wage day labourers. These workers are generally employed in agriculture or in non-farm activities, including construction. We have seen earlier that there has been acceleration in GDP and sectoral growth in Bangladesh. In spite of such growth, the real wage rates in agriculture have shown a declining trend since 1993/1994, and in construction there was a declining trend during the 1990s. The agricultural real wage rose from the late 1980s to the early 1990s, but then declined subsequently. A similar trend was observed for wages in the construction sector (which can be taken to be representative of the non-farm informal economy). It therefore, appears that acceleration of GDP growth failed to create enough employment to tighten the labour market and push up wage rates in the predominant agricultural and informal economy. The declining trend in real wage rates in agriculture seems to be consistent with the declining trend in labour productivity in that sector. In other words, agriculture and the informal

Table 2.20

Trends in rural wages, 1986/87–1999/2000

(1989/90 = 100)

Sector	*1986/87*	*1987/88*	*1988/89*	*1989/90*	*1990/91*	*1991/92*	*1992/93*	*1993/94*	*1994/95*	*1995/96*	*1996/97*	*1997/98*	*1998/99*	*1999/2000*
Construction	91.1	101.2	102.2	100.0	93.1	90.5	92.0	90.2	83.6	85.2	87.6	88.2	88.0	89.5
Agriculture	90.5	94.9	93.0	100.0	98.0	101.1	105.1	106.5	101.5	100.1	101.3	98.1	94.0	94.5
Manufacturing	95.0	94.0	96.0	100.0	99.0	98.0	103.0	105.0	105.0	107.0	113.0	119.0	114.0	119.0

Source: Mahmud, 2006.

economy seem to have been trapped in a low productivity–low real wage vicious circle.

We get a slightly different picture from the manufacturing sector. Here, we find an increasing trend in the real wage.[11] How did this happen despite declining labour productivity in this sector? The answer lies in the segmented nature of the labour market and the bargaining power of organized labour, which capitalizes on the minimum wages set by the Government. This disconnect between real wages and labour productivity could be an important factor in constraining employment growth in the formal large and medium manufacturing sector despite its healthy growth in output. The increase in real wages in the construction industry reflects a rising demand for construction workers in the wake of the construction boom during the second half of the 1990s.

2.5 The quality of employment in the formal manufacturing sector

The quality of employment in an activity is indicated in the concept of "decent work" enunciated by the ILO. Decent work includes the following characteristics:

- equal employment opportunities for both males and females;
- acceptable work;
- absence of forced, bonded or child labour;
- fair and equal treatment for males and females in employment;
- adequate wages for all work done corresponding to a fair living wage and work of equal value should receive equal pay;
- decent hours of work;
- safe working environment;
- stability and security at work;

11. The World Bank has also estimated that labour cost per worker per year in manufacturing in Bangladesh has risen from US$556 in 1980–1984 to US$671 in 1995–1999 (World Bank, 2000).

- social protection; and
- social dialogue.

Most of these conditions are absent in informal-economy employment in Bangladesh. This is understandable given the informal nature of the sector itself. However, many of these conditions are not fulfilled even in formal manufacturing-sector employment, particularly in the export-oriented ready-made garments industry, as has been shown by many studies. The implication is that economic growth alone cannot ensure decent employment in a labour-surplus economy such as Bangladesh. The Government has an important role to play in this regard by monitoring the conditions and quality of work and enforcing the national labour laws as well as the ILO conventions to which it is a signatory.

The export-oriented garments industry in Bangladesh has achieved phenomenal growth during the 1980s and 1990s. Employment has also increased to about 2 million workers (mostly female) as a result of the expansion in output. However, a number of studies have shown that working conditions in the garments industry are poor and many of the conditions of decent work are absent.[12] National labour law requires that all workers should receive an appointment letter, as this protects labour rights and provides security to the workers; however, studies found that only 5 per cent of garments workers, most of them men, received this document. Violation of this law has not only resulted in widespread job insecurity in the garments industry, it has also enabled factory owners to pay lower wages because a worker without a formal appointment letter is treated as a "casual" worker and hence, paid lower wages. This has also made it possible for employers to dismiss workers without prior notice. Studies also found that a large number of female garments workers, estimated to be more than 32 per cent, did not receive the minimum wage. Female workers are also deprived of any severance payment even through they are frequently dismissed. Studies also showed that the use of child labour was widespread in the garments industry until the mid-1990s.

12. For a list of these studies and a more detailed discussion on these issues, see Paul-Majumder (2002).

Garments factory workers, particularly the female workers, have also been deprived of non-wage benefits. Due to the absence of a formal appointment letter, they are largely deprived of non-wage benefits such as accommodation, transport, meal and medical allowances, bonuses, maternity benefit, pension, provident fund and insurance benefits.

Decent work conditions are also absent from some of the other formal economy manufacturing industries (Jabbar, 2006). For example, workers in the export-oriented shrimp and frozen food industry are paid on a daily or weekly basis. Their earnings are very low and no welfare benefits are provided. The state-run industries do not have good working conditions, such as health and safety provisions.

2.6 Conclusions

The foregoing analysis has shown that although Bangladesh has achieved healthy GDP growth, more than one-third of the labour force have remained unemployed or underemployed. The main reason behind this has been the relatively slow growth of agriculture and the non-farm sector, particularly the RNF sector. Agriculture and the RNF sector have, however, been the major sources of employment in Bangladesh. So, to ensure rapid employment growth, growth of these sectors needs to be accelerated. This calls for a better policy mix to strengthen the linkage between economic growth and decent employment. Investment in these sectors needs to be increased. This would require provision of adequate credit facilities to agriculture and the RNF sector. The interest rate on loans to the formal manufacturing sector needs to be lowered. Trade policy has to be designed with the needs of both the formal and informal manufacturing sectors in mind. At the same time, government policies are required to increase domestic savings (such as capital market development). The investment climate also needs to be improved through good governance.

Policies also need to be better coordinated. For example, the policy of import liberalization has to be designed in such a manner that it is consistent with financial sector reforms to ensure growth of a healthy manufacturing sector. Similarly, monetary and fiscal policy should be coordinated properly to ensure growth of agriculture and the RNF sector.

Poor implementation of policies has weakened the linkage between growth and employment in Bangladesh. Of particular importance in this regard has been the rather slow pace of implementation of the Government's Annual Development Programme. This has slowed down progress in the areas of infrastructure development, power and gas supply to manufacturing industries in the formal and informal economy, and agriculture. The result has been slow growth of production and employment in these sectors.

Aid programmes can help to strengthen these linkages, particularly through developing infrastructure in the economy. Aid can also contribute to growth and employment creation by providing resources.

3 India: A case for strengthening policy coherence

K.P. Kannan

3.1 Introduction

In most countries, the unfolding of the paradigm of globalization over the past 25 years has almost eclipsed the Keynesian paradigm of macroeconomic policies and the attendant welfare state. The process started in the late 1970s and intensified after the collapse of the Soviet-style of socialist management in Eastern Europe and its variants in a number of developing countries.

The ongoing process of globalization of national economies has produced a number of losers, mostly poor developing countries, and a small number of winners (although there are also large segments of losers and some winners within individual countries). This has led to an independent world commission—the World Commission on Social Dimension of Globalization—making a plea for "a fair globalization" that should be "creating opportunities for all" (WCSDG, 2004) and is experienced through work and employment.[1] Those developing countries

1. "People are most directly affected by globalization through their work and employment. That is how people experience the opportunities and advantages, as well as the risks and exclusions. For the gains from globalization to be widely shared, countries, enterprises and people have to be able to convert global opportunities into jobs and incomes. A major goal is to reduce unemployment, which has huge costs for people and society in industrialized and developing countries alike. But this alone is not enough. There are many people who are fully employed in unacceptable jobs—often in appalling working conditions, at low productivity or subject to coercion. Employment must be freely chosen and provide an income sufficient to satisfy basic economic and family needs. Rights and representation must be respected, basic security attained through one form or another of social protection, and adequate conditions of work assured. Taken together, these different elements make up what has come to be known as "decent work". This includes not only employment, but a wider set of goals which reflects the broader aspirations of women and men" (WCSDG, 2004: 64).

that have successfully coped with the challenge of globalization are mostly in Asia, and the most recent example is that of India. From the perspective of overall economic growth and related macroeconomic performance indicators, India has no doubt done remarkably well. However, the link between growth in income and what is called "decent employment" in ILO parlance is a problematic one. This has given rise to a lively debate on the nature of growth—"jobless growth" as it is often described—and its impact on the welfare of the majority of the people.

It is needless to emphasize that the linkage between growth and employment generation has not only economic significance, but also wider social and political ramifications. This is especially so in a country such as India, where emerging economic and social inequalities may well reinforce the pre-existing inequalities and inequities. The majority of the people live on less than, say, US$2 a day while the economy is attaining unprecedented rates of high growth (culminating around 9 per cent for the past three years). In order to obtain a comparative view of the links between growth, investment and employment during and before economic reforms, we have taken a period of two decades and divided them more or less equally. The precise choice of years has been dictated by the availability of comparable data on employment. The pre-reform period refers to 1983/84 to 1993/94 and the post-reform period refers to 1993/94 to 2004/05.

The high growth rate of the Indian economy raised its real per capita income by 67 per cent during the post-reform period, compared with 31 per cent during the pre-reform period. The macroeconomic fundamentals of the economy have turned around remarkably during the period of economic reforms but this has not perceptibly improved conditions for the vast mass of the population in general and workers in particular (see Appendix A-3.1). The current macroeconomic strengths of the economy are:

- a continuing high rate of growth and the expectation of its continuance if not acceleration;
- rising rates of saving and investment;

- high rates of growth of exports, although accompanied by a somewhat higher growth of imports;
- stability of the exchange rate under a system of managed float;
- a comfortable foreign exchange reserve position; and
- a low external debt burden.

However, from an employment point of view, not only is the picture somewhat grim, it could also be worrying. This relates both to the declining capacity of the growth process to generate employment and to the persistence of low quality of employment. The attendant consequences on human development could affect growth in the long term, with adverse consequences on improving quality of life, which is, or should be, the ultimate objective of economic development.

3.2 Growth, investment and employment

The macro view of growth, investment and employment is given in Figure 3.1. First of all, growth was secular during the whole period of 21 years but it picked up momentum during the last four years or so. Growth in investment has been faster than growth in national income in the recent past, given the increasing marginal propensity to save. Since well over 96 per cent of investment comes from domestic savings, such a trend underlines the capacity of the Indian economy to sustain the growth process without critical dependence on foreign investment.[2] However, the graph also depicts the low rate of growth of employment, using a broad measurement consisting of both "principal" and "subsidiary" workers.[3] This calls for further probing of the link between growth and employment in terms of employment elasticity.

The overall employment elasticity in the Indian economy (Table 3.1) declined by 26 per cent during the post-reform period. In fact, it declined sharply between 1993/94 and 1999/2000 and then recovered

2. In some years, the rate of gross domestic saving exceeded that of gross domestic investment, see Government of India (2007: 9)

3. The meanings of the various measures of employment are given later in this chapter.

Figure 3.1

Growth in national income, gross domestic investment and employment, 1984/84–2004/05

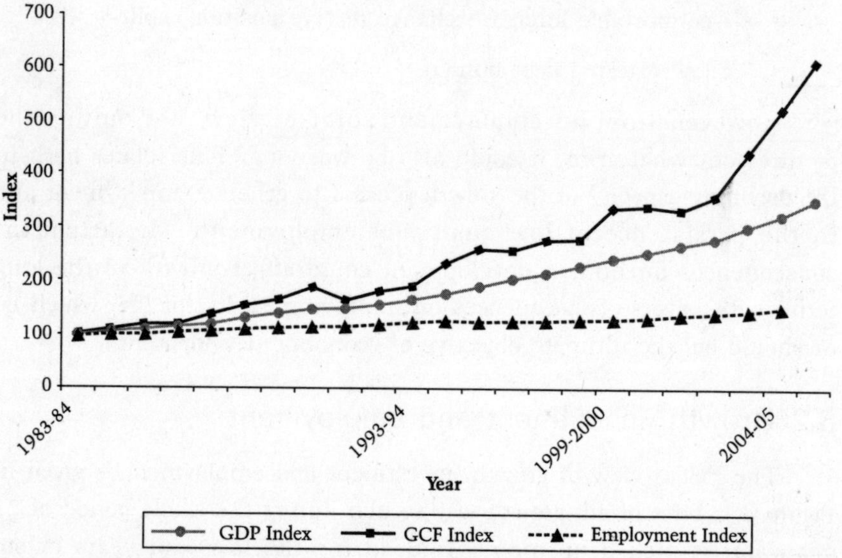

Note: National income is indicated by gross domestic product, gross domestic investment by gross capital formation and employment by workers in the principal and subsidiary statuses.

during the last five years. This led to a debate on jobless growth, especially in the organized sector of the economy. A decline in employment elasticity *per se* need not be undesirable if there is a compensating increase in growth. Such compensation has occurred, but not fully. While the income growth rate increased by 22 per cent only during the post-reform period compared with the pre-reform period, growth in employment declined by 8 per cent. During the pre-reform period, the employment growth was marginally lower than labour force growth (by 4 per cent) whereas during the reform period, the employment growth was lower by 12 per cent.

Some further probing of the linkage between growth and employment is called for as we are including all types of employment here without referring to the nature of such employment. A rough indicator of the quality of employment growth can be discerned by examining the employment elasticities with respect to the three main employment status characteristics: regular (including salaried), casual and self-employed. These employment elasticities are ranked in Table 3.2.

Table 3.1

Employment elasticity (UPSS), 1983–2004/05

Period	*GDP growth*	*Employment growth*	*Employment elasticity*
		Agriculture (primary)	
1983 to 1993/94	2.86	1.35	0.47
1993/94 to 2004/05	2.40	0.60	0.25
		Industry (secondary)	
1983 to 1993/94	5.96	2.78	0.47
1993/94 to 2004/05	6.58	3.60	0.55
		Services (tertiary)	
1983 to 1993/94	6.73	3.72	0.55
1993/94 to 2004/05	8.28	3.96	0.48
		Total	
1983 to 1993/94	5.18	2.01	0.39
1993/94 to 2004/05	6.30	1.85	0.29

Note: UPSS = usual principal and subsidiary status.

Source: Computations are based on GDP data of the Central Statistical Organisation at 1993/94 prices and employment data as per the 38th, 50th and 61st Rounds of the National Sample Survey (NSS).

Table 3.2

Ranking of employment elasticity by employment status

Period	*Agriculture*		*Non-agriculture*		*Total*	
Pre-reform	Casual	0.95	Casual	0.61	Casual	0.57
	Self-employment	0.29	Self-employment	0.53	Regular	0.36
	Regular	-2.29	Regular	0.47	Self-employment	0.29
Post-reform	Self-employment	0.55	Self-employment	0.51	Regular	0.45
	Casual	-0.09	Casual	0.47	Self-employment	0.34
	Regular	-0.72	Regular	0.40	Casual	0.12

What these results show could also reveal the changing nature of labour market demand in the era of economic reforms. During the pre-reform period, casual employment registered the highest elasticity, followed by regular employment and self-employment. This has given way to regular employment, followed by self-employment and casual employment. Agriculture has ceased to absorb any wage labour, casual or regular. In fact, there has been a shift of labour. However, the casual workers leaving agriculture would have found it very hard to find "regular" work in non-agriculture given their very low capabilities, whether in education, modern skills or related endowments. These workers first ended up as casual non-agricultural workers (1993–2000). But the more recent evidence (1999–2005) could well be a sign of a tightening of the casual labour market and hence, an increase in self-employment. The increase in regular employment elasticity could be interpreted as a sign of better quality of work, but its level is quite low. However, this indicates the demand for educated and skilled people. The facts that between 1999 and 2005, the increase in wage rates of casual workers slowed down and the 2.89 per cent annual growth rate in employment was accompanied by an increase of 2.3 per cent in labour force (supply) point to a distressing situation for the livelihoods of poor workers. As we shall see later, there are also other manifestations of distress (e.g. persistence of poverty) as far as employment in the informal economy is concerned.

3.3 Growth and decent work

The focus of this chapter is on the nexus of growth, investment and decent work. This calls for a definition of "decent work" (or "decent employment"), a recent concept introduced by the International Labour Organization to overcome its focus on workers in the formal economy. As an objective, the concept of decent employment is helpful in that it focuses attention on the need to create conditions for workers that are socially and morally acceptable. From an empirical investigation point of view, the concept of decent work should be amenable to measurement so that policy instruments can be designed and advocated for its extension. However, establishing such an operational definition has not been easy. What the ILO has provided is a formulation that makes decent work a converging focus of its four strategic objectives: the promotion of rights at work, employment, social protection and social dialogue.[4]

4. See ILO (1999: 3).

With a view to measuring decent work in the Indian context in an approximate way, what we attempt here is a rough translation of the above mentioned four strategic objectives constitutive of decent work. The first objective—promotion of rights at work—may be interpreted as the constitutional right to form associations, minimum wages and conditions of work.[5] The second may be interpreted as access to gainful employment. The third may be interpreted as minimum social security to meet such contingencies as sickness and old age. The last one could refer to the existence of institutional arrangements (such as tripartite bodies) for resolution of disputes or any major issues affecting the workers.

Keeping these in mind, we attempt a tentative measurement of decent work in India. This is carried out in several steps, ranging from a broad measure of employment (including both decent and not-so-decent types of work) to a more rigorous measurement that might satisfy the four strategic objectives of decent work. These are discussed below.

Using these minimal benchmarks, we attempt a measurement of decent work in India. This calls for some elaboration of the second decent-work objective—employment. Employment in India is measured by broadly dividing workers into principal and subsidiary workers. There is no precise measurement of duration of work largely due to the structural features of the economy and the combining of wage work with self-employment. Employment is measured in terms of people identified as workers from among all those who are in the labour force. There are three measurement categories for workers. The first includes those (in the labour force) who work the majority of days in a year, called "principal" workers, and also those who work for some part of the year, called "subsidiary" workers; these are categorized as Usual Principal and Subsidiary Status (UPSS). The second category, Usual Principal Status (UPS), refers only to principal workers; it is a subset of UPSS because it leaves out those who are identified as subsidiary (or marginal) workers.

5. The ILO has special concerns about child and forced labour, which it wants eliminated. In India, these are taken into account by national legislations that prohibit bonded labour and certain forms of child labour. These are the Bonded Labour System (Abolition) Act (1976) and the Child Labour (Prohibition and Regulation) Act (1986). The incidence of child labour per se has been on the decline, the latest figure being around 4 per cent as per the 61st Round of the National Sample Survey (2004/05).

The third category is Current Weekly Status (CWS), which includes both principal and subsidiary workers but is measured with reference to a short (weekly) reference period.

These measurements indicate access to work. A major deficiency in all these measurements is that they conceal a great deal of underemployment because there is no way to measure the average time worked in a year precisely. Further, underemployment in the income sense (disguised unemployment) could be much higher because the incidence of working poor (as measured against the official poverty line) is more than three times that of the unemployed measured on a daily status.

UPSS is used in many policy exercises and discussions. However, this broad measure of employment satisfies only one condition of the concept of decent work: access to employment. Only a small share of the workers in this classification are anywhere near the other strategic objectives.

We therefore move to a second approximation, which involves examining regular employment in the Indian economy. This excludes all those who are self-employed (who may also be regular but mostly stretch their working hours to earn livelihoods and are not always in a position to enjoy the other strategic objectives, especially the one relating to social security). Regular workers are often employed by employers and work in the formal sector of the economy. That also usually, if not always, entitles them to social security, unlike self-employed and casual workers. More often than not, they exercise their constitutional right to form trade unions and other associational bodies and have recourse to social dialogue. While this measurement is a much better indicator of decent work than the broad employment measures (i.e., UPSS, UPS or CWS), it may still include those without employment or social security and conditions for realizing the other two strategic objectives. We therefore move to a third approximation.

This third approximation is the measurement of workers in the formal economy (often referred to as "organized sector" in India). The official data on employment in the organized sector[6] are deducted from

6. As per the figures published by the Directorate General of Employment and Training (DGET), Ministry of Labour and Employment.

the total employment figures to arrive at the number of workers in the informal (unorganized) sector through a residual method. This has given an estimate of 7 per cent employment in the formal economy and 93 per cent in the informal economy, which has gained wide currency. However, we now have precise definitions of "formal economy" and "informal economy" as formulated by the National Commission for Enterprises in the Unorganized Sector (NCEUS), and their application to the employment data of 1999/2000 gave a figure of nearly 14 per cent of total workers in the formal economy. This is quite close to the share of regular workers.

However, the NCEUS also formulated precise definitions of "formal employment" and "informal employment" (as opposed to formal and informal economy) to find out the quality (whether decent) of employment. Here, formal employment refers to employment in the formal or informal economy but which enjoys some social security provided by the employer, which is usually given to those who are regularly employed. This gave a figure close to 9 per cent of total workers who are enjoying formal employment in the Indian economy. This measurement satisfies to a great extent the four strategic objectives. It refers to those who enjoy:

- minimum rights at work, such as the rights to form associations, reasonable conditions of work and above minimum wages;
- access to regular work;
- some legally backed social security benefits provided by the employer; and
- access to tripartite or similar social dialogue mechanisms.

By using the direct estimates of employment in the formal economy and formal employment, and also the employment figures of the Directorate General of Employment and Training (DGET) for 1999/2000, we have estimated formal employment for the previous two time points (1993/94 and 1983) to get an idea of the direction of change of formal employment that we call decent work. These estimates of decent work are given in Table 3.3.

Table 3.3

Estimates of decent work in India, 1983–2004/05

Category	*1983*	*1993/94*	*1999/2000*	*2004/05*
1. Total workforce (UPSS) (in million)	303.77	374.27	396.78	457.46
2. Work participation rate (UPSS) (%)	42.00	42.00	39.70	42.00
3. Work participation rate (UPS) (%)	37.40	37.50	36.60	38.00
4. Work participation rate (CWS) (%)	35.80	38.60	37.00	38.80
5. Regular (as % of 1)	13.82	13.66	14.88	15.20
6. Employment in formal sector (as % of 1)	15.90	14.60	14.22	14.71
7. Formal employment (as % of 1) (Decent work1)	11.00	8.90	8.74	7.54
8. Self-employed who are better off than (5) (as % of 1)	n.a.	n.a.	4.00	n.a.
9. Decent work2 (7) + (8) (as % of 1)	n.a.	n.a.	12.74	n.a.

Note: Figures in brackets refer to our indirect estimates as explained in Appendix A-3.2; n.a. = data not available.

Source: Items 1 to 7 computed from 38th, 50th, 55th and 61st Rounds of National Sample Survey (NSS). Item 8 from Glinskaya and Jalan, 2006.

However, these economy-wide averages conceal the variations between urban and rural areas and between men and women. By examining the disaggregated picture for the last two time points (Table 3.4), we find that urban males have the highest share of decent work (formal employment), followed by urban women, rural men and rural women. In fact, decent work is largely an urban phenomenon. Decent work, however, is only two-thirds of employment in the formal economy, or less than half of regular work for both men and women, even in urban areas. But the disturbing aspect is that there was some marginal decline during the last five years, when the economy was growing at well above 6 per cent annually.

However, there is also a case for a somewhat broader conceptualization of decent work in the Indian context. This is because a high proportion of the Indian workforce is classed as self-employed. This category can, however, cover a wide range of workers, from those whose conditions are no different from those of unskilled casual workers (e.g. street vendors) to those whose conditions may be equivalent to, or better than, those of formal workers (e.g. those who own some minimum level of capital assets and may hire a few workers, including independent professionals such as doctors, lawyers and

Table 3.4

Estimates of decent work in urban and rural India

Item	Year	Rural			Urban		
		Male	Female	Total	Male	Female	Total
1. Total workforce (UPSS) (in millions)	1999/2000	196.74	104.03	300.77	77.05	18.96	96.01
	2004/05	219.04	124.03	343.07	90.40	24.00	114.40
2. Regular (as % of (1))	1999/2000	8.85	3.09	6.86	41.70	33.23	40.03
	2004/05	8.98	3.72	7.08	40.62	35.58	39.57
3. Employment in formal sector (as % of (1))	1999/2000	9.59	5.04	8.02	35.01	28.26	33.67
	2004/05	10.56	5.75	8.82	33.65	26.73	32.20
4. Formal employment (decent work) (as % of (1))	1999/2000	5.39	1.95	4.20	24.29	17.53	22.96
	2004/05	4.71	2.00	3.73	21.08	15.08	19.82

Source: Same as Table 3.3.

architects). The existing category of self-employed is therefore, a catch-all one. This means that any analysis of the earnings of such workers and comparison with regular workers' earnings must be carried out carefully. Since the data on the self-employed give only the gross value added, it is not possible to get comparable data. Glinskaya and Jalan (2006), in a detailed study, examined the consumer expenditure data for the self-employed along with data for regular workers and reported that 50 per cent of the urban non-agricultural self-employed were in an equivalent or better position than regular workers. No such equivalence was found in respect of the rural self-employed. In fact, they concluded: "It is better to be regular/salaried worker [in rural areas] rather than being self-employed if working in the manufacturing sector" (ibid.: 271). Fifty per cent of the urban non-agricultural self-employed is equivalent to 4 per cent of the total number of workers in the economy or 17 per cent of urban employment. Therefore, if we combine the share of formal employment (Decent Work1) with this 4 per cent, we get a broader measure of decent work (Decent Work2) of around 13 per cent for the whole economy and around 40 per cent for the urban economy in 2000.

3.4 The disconnect between growth and decent work

The earlier discussion shows that the disconnect between growth and decent work in India is quite wide. This disconnect first appeared between growth and employment in general. Despite having a lower growth rate, the pre-reform period witnessed higher employment growth: at 2.1 per cent per annum with a growth rate of above 5 per cent. However, during the post-reform period, employment growth declined to 1.85 per annum despite a higher growth rate of well over 6 per cent (see Table 3.1). This disconnect was quite sharp during 1993–2000, when the employment elasticity declined to 0.15 resulting in an employment growth rate of just 1.02 per cent per annum. This period also witnessed an absolute decline in formal employment in the formal economy, contributed largely by the public sector.[7] When we consider the quality of employment we find that the disconnect between growth and decent work is quite robust over a long period of time. For example, the share of regular employment has remained more or less the same during both the pre- and post-reform periods. The marginal increase in the share between 2000 and 2005 may be due to the increased demand for educated labour during the post-reform period. However, if we take a long-term view, the share of regular employment at 15.2 per cent in 2004/05 is essentially the same as the 15.3 per cent in 1972/73! This should be a matter of serious concern to policy-makers because the unchanging proportion of regular workers has to be seen in the context of the transforming nature of the Indian economy, not only in the income sense but also in terms of employment (Figures 3.2 and 3.3). Although a slow process, the employment structure has started shifting away from agriculture; from a 74 per cent share in 1972 to a 57 per cent in 2005, a decline of 26 per cent. The corresponding decline in income share has been 50 per cent.

The recent evidence on the distribution of additional employment shows that only 5 per cent of the addition to the workforce secured formal employment. Between 1999/2000 and 2004/05, the economy added 60.7 million workers (principal and subsidiary). Out of this, the formal economy employed 10.7 million workers or 17 per cent. However, only 3.4 million of these were absorbed with some job and social security—the remaining 7.3 million were employed as informal workers.

---

7. As per DGET figures, the total employment in public sector declined from 19.4 million in 1993/94 to 18.5 million in 2002/03. The overall decline (i.e., public and private) was limited to 0.2 million, from 27.2 to 27.0 million.

Figure 3.2

Employment share by employment category, 1972/73–2004/05

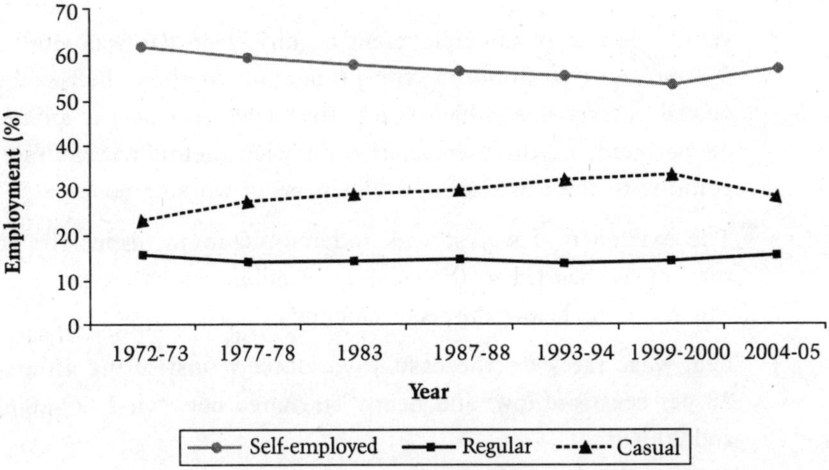

Figure 3.3

Employment share by sector, 1972/73–2004/05

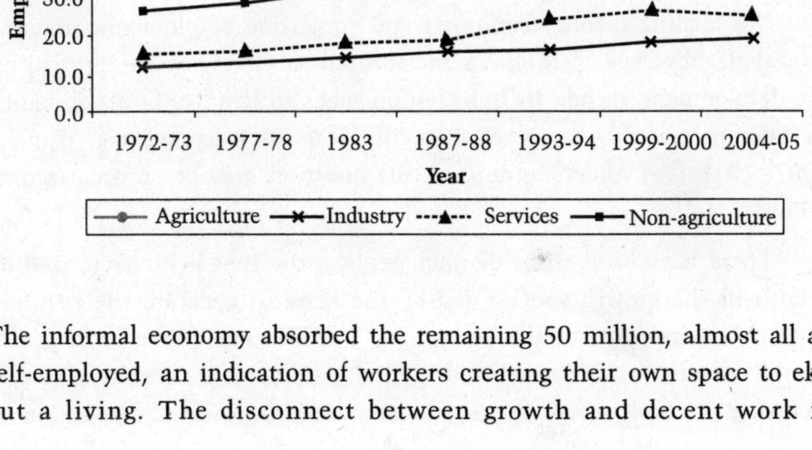

The informal economy absorbed the remaining 50 million, almost all as self-employed, an indication of workers creating their own space to eke out a living. The disconnect between growth and decent work is exacerbated by the absence of productive employment for significant sections of the workforce. The important outcomes of this lack of productive employment are as follows:

- While the rate of unemployment on any given day was around 8.3 per cent in 2004/05, the proportion of those below the official poverty line (which is less than US$1 per day) is around 28 per cent, or three-and-half times the unemployment rate, pointing to the existence of a vast mass of working poor.
- The existence of widespread underemployment, especially in rural areas, has led to the creation of public works programmes which are far below the requirements.
- Real wage rates for the casual workforce (constituting around 28 per cent) are low, and nearly stagnated between 1999/2000 and 2004/05.
- A vast mass of self-employed (marginal farmers, women homeworkers, street vendors, rickshaw pullers and so on) have conditions of work and earnings no different from those of casual unskilled workers.

3.5 Decent work and macroeconomic policy

This leads us to the question: to what extent is decent employment central to macroeconomic policy?

This question has been analysed in some detail by Papola (2006, 2007), a leading labour economist and sometime employment planner. As Papola observed, "employment featured as an important priority in the development agenda in India. Approaches to it have, however, varied in different periods over more than fifty years of independence" (Papola, 2007: 131). Our understanding of this question may be summarized as follows.

There have been three distinct periods: the first is characterized by a faith in the growth process led by the state to generate the required additional employment; the second, by a realization that growth per se would not create additional and quality employment, resulting in the factoring of employment in macroeconomic policy and the adoption of an "adjunct" policy with respect to employment creation; and third, by a return to the faith in the growth process, but led by the market, with the retreat of the state from the "commanding heights" of the economy as well as from public investment. During none of the periods was employment a central objective in planning and macroeconomic policy, although it has been a continuing concern.

The first period occurred between the early 1950s and the early 1970s. The objective of maximizing employment in a poor economy during this period rested on the classical wisdom of development economics. The growth process, with emphasis on the development of the modern sector (industry), was expected to lead to a structural transformation through the shift of labour from the traditional sector (agriculture). The state played an active role in promoting the modern sector by creating infrastructure and investing in both directly productive activities and social overhead capital, especially in basic capital and the intermediate goods industries and in higher technical education. The problem of employment of the peasants and artisans was expected to be taken care of by agriculture and small-scale artisanal and industrial activities. However, the expected growth rate (5 per cent) was not realized and there was an increase in underemployment and unemployment. The situation became grim, with continuing high population growth, widespread poverty, unemployment and a shortage of wage goods, especially food. Consequently, electoral politics focused attention to these emerging problems. This shifted the emphasis to employment.

The second period, from the early 1970s to the late 1980s, witnessed more concerted attention to the question of employment creation, if not its quality. The Fifth and Sixth Five Year Plans (1974–1985)[8] put much more emphasis on the employment-intensive sectors. The main instruments of macroeconomic policy were:

- reservation of a number of products for production in the small-scale sector;

8. The Fifth Plan was terminated in its fourth year due to a change of government. The Sixth Plan started in 1980. Two Annual Plans filled the interregnum.

- creation of development banks, such as the National Bank for Agriculture and Rural Development, to increase both long-term and short-term credit to agriculture, and the Small Industries Development Bank of India, for dedicated lending to small-scale industries;
- provision of subsidized credit and raw materials to agriculture and small-scale industries; and
- initiation of a number of development programmes for the small-scale sector.

At the same time, there was an attempt to advance employment generation as an "adjunct" to macroeconomic policy and planning. This was because of the realization that the growth process, even with factoring of the employment objective, might not create the required additional employment in the economy and could slow down the process of poverty alleviation, especially in the rural areas. Therefore, employment creation as an adjunct policy was actively promoted through programmes for generating self-employment and wage employment through public works.

The start of the third period coincided with the crisis in the external sector of the economy during 1990–91, which arose largely out of exogenous shocks for which the economy was not prepared. This gave rise to the discontinuation of the incremental policy reforms of the 1980s to a paradigmatic shift to economic reforms in tune with liberalization, privatization and globalization. The employment objective ceased to be a factor in macroeconomic policy and planning. In fact, many of the earlier policies had to be abandoned or considerably scaled down to be consistent with the logic of the economic reforms:

- the reservations for the small-scale sector were scaled down considerably and many of the concessions and subsidies were withdrawn;
- credit became more costly;
- the share of credit to agriculture and the small-scale sector declined sharply; and

- the question of choice of technology was left to the entrepreneurs.

Entrepreneurs also found that access to finance capital became cheaper due to a reduction in interest rates, increase in credit availability, greater access to foreign exchange for import of technology and so on. However, alarm bells began ringing on the employment front when the results of the 55th Round of the National Sample Survey (1999/2000) were published. The data indicated a sharp decline in employment growth despite a higher rate of growth in national income and consequent decline in employment elasticity. Two committees were set up (Planning Commission, 2001a and 2002a) and their recommendations—to increase the outlay on special employment programmes—were accepted. In effect, employment remained as an adjunct policy, albeit a scaled-down version, even during economic reforms undergoing some emphasis in recent periods.

That high growth per se was no panacea for increasing employment, let alone decent employment and access to income, was realized during the course of the Tenth Five Year Plan. The result (following a change of government) was a political commitment to launch a rights-based public employment programme in rural areas, known as the National Rural Employment Guarantee (NREG). Following from this, it was expected that the 11th Five Year Plan would give greater emphasis to employment in general, and to decent employment in particular. In fact, the Approach Paper to the 11th Plan set not merely growth but inclusive growth as the overarching objective (see Planning Commission, 2006). However, employment did not figure as a central objective. Instead, it was assumed that a higher rate of growth would take care of employment, thus compensating for any likely decline in employment elasticity. Employment programmes continued as part of the continuing adjunct policy. In effect, the employment dimension continues to be subordinated to the growth objective despite the visible and increasing disconnect between the two and the disparity in the quality of employment between the formal and informal economy. The informal economy has emerged as the reserve for absorbing the underemployed as well as the disguisedly unemployed going beyond the agricultural sector.

3.6 Potential trade-offs between employment and other macroeconomic policy objectives

One of the important questions relevant to our investigative research in this context is: if employment is not central to macroeconomic policy, what are the trade-offs with other potential policy objectives (such as price stability and balance of payments equilibrium)? This important question calls for a deep analysis that is much beyond the scope of this chapter. However, brief comments on the trade-offs between three important objectives—price stability, trade and fiscal consolidation—are offered here to give an idea of the degree of freedom available within the current paradigm of economic liberalization.

Inflation and employment

Price stability or inflation is an important concern and therefore, a target of macroeconomic policy in India. The political sensitivity of the issue has ensured that it gets prompt attention in policy. But the issue is usually viewed in terms of inflation *versus* growth. Both fiscal and monetary instruments are deployed to keep inflation at an "acceptable" level: around 5 per cent. However, from a long-term developmental point of view, employment has also been a concern for, if not central to, macroeconomic policy. The concern for keeping inflation at an acceptable level suggests that it has an indirect trade-off with the objective of employment generation. Except for a few public works programmes (which provide some relief to the working poor by way of limited additional employment), it is growth policies that by and large determine employment arising out of the derived demand. Generation of decent employment—regular work with reasonable wages and some social security—to the vast mass of the working poor in India demands enhanced public investment, especially in rural areas. Some of this could be linked to the additional investment required for developing physical infrastructure. During the 11th Five Year Plan, the investment required for infrastructure development has been estimated at US$350 billion over a period of five years, which demands an almost doubling of the current rate of investment from 4.6 per cent of gross domestic product to 8 per cent in the coming five years, as estimated by the

Planning Commission (2006: 4). There is an expectation that half the projected increase in investment will come from the private sector (including farming households and small-scale enterprises) (ibid.) and the rest will have to come from public investment. But employment generation in this way will have to be supplemented by innovative programmes for direct employment generation for unskilled workers, including women, as well as those engaged in so called self-employment. Such investments will have to come through enhanced public investment. This would lead to a rise in demand for wage goods that may not immediately be matched by supply due to certain rigidities and time lags, as in the case of agriculture. However, there is a view that the comfortable foreign exchange position of the country gives it an option to import such wage goods so as not to add to inflation. This calls for balancing an employment generation policy with the objective of targeted inflation and the use of foreign exchange reserves. Therefore, the apparent limitation imposed by the objective of price stability could be overcome by an explicit focus on policy coherence and planning. But the prevailing orthodoxy governing the agenda of economic reforms may not favour such an expansionary role for the state, however imperative the reality on the ground may be. This is linked to the overarching objective of fiscal consolidation (read reducing fiscal deficit) under the current economic reform process.

Trade and employment

The relationship between trade and employment has received considerable attention in the discussion on globalization because of the *a priori* reasoning that increased openness leads to increased trade and thereby, increased employment. The degree of openness in world trade is still an area of contention between developing and developed countries. Market access is still limited by both tariff and non-tariff barriers, and the rich industrialized countries have shown very little enthusiasm for removing the barriers faced by the developing countries. A major share of trade and investment is still conducted within developed countries, although the developing countries' share has increased during the past two decades. In a survey of the issues in the relationship between trade and employment, a recent ILO–WTO study brought out the complexities in the real world. The main message of the study is that:

> There are no simple generalizations possible on the relationship between trade and employment. The standard trade model focusing on inter-sectoral trade among very different countries proves to be a rather inadequate guide. There is a growing literature pointing to the importance of new factors influencing the trade-employment relationship such as the impact of FDI, the nature of trade (e.g. different types of intra-industry trade among similar countries versus North–South trade, the role of technological change and the impact of greater openness on the elasticity of demand for labour. Differences in the initial conditions of countries, in the nature of institutions and in how trade policies are implemented also affect the relationship between trade and employment. It is important to understand the role of these new factors in forming an overall judgement on the relationship between trade and employment as well as in the formulation of policy.
>
> (ILO–WTO, 2007: 86).

The record of India in terms of the impact of trade openness on decent work seems to be not very encouraging. A recent report by the Research and Information System for Developing Countries (RISDC, 2006) has painstakingly examined some of the issues related to trade and employment and provided some useful insights. While labour-intensive manufacturing offers the biggest scope for increasing employment, its share in total merchandise exports has in fact declined, from 65 per cent in mid-1990s to 49 per cent in 2003/04. But with the expiry of the Multi-Fibre Agreement, there is an expectation that textile products will provide further opportunities for increasing exports and thereby, employment. The increased openness seems to have worked in favour of relatively higher value exports, such as medium-technology exports and knowledge-intensive exports. The former increased its share from 12 to 20 per cent and the latter from 18 to 23 per cent during 1995/96 to 2003/04. Overall, export growth has been higher than growth of national income. Based on the increase in exports and its employment intensities, RISDC estimated a direct employment of 9 million and indirect employment of close to 7 million in 2004/05, which works out to 3.5 per cent of total employment. This excludes the emerging area of information technology and related services, which has witnessed a rapid increase in income and employment. According to one estimate, the employment in this sector is now close to 2 million. Based on the objective of doubling the export value in five years, it is expected that exports could create a total employment of close to 37 million. While these figures are impressive in absolute terms, their total impact on employment in general is still quite low. Furthermore, these figures need to be netted to account for the decline in import-competing activities arising out of the liberalization of trade.

The quality of employment is what determines whether work is decent work. It is here that the overall decline in decent employment in India causes some concern. Of course, India's success in exporting information technology and related services has gained wide attention. It is not only a skills/knowledge-intensive sector but also a high employment-intensive one. The growth in the exports of this sector has been matched by an impressive growth in employment. Given the educational and salary levels of the people employed in this sector compared with those of the regular workers in the Indian economy, there should not be much room for complaint, however questions have been raised about the conditions of work (Ramesh, 2004). In low-end labour-intensive manufacturing, the issue of employment quality—including such basic issues as job security, working conditions and wage rates—leaves much to be desired. Studies on industrial clusters and export-processing zones, such as garment making in Tiruppur, the export zone in Noida and leather goods making in Mumbai's urban slums, point to low earnings and the absence of decent working conditions (See for example Vijayabaskar, 2002; Neetha and Varma, 2004; Pais, 2006). These are examples of informal employment, even when the enterprises, such as those in Tiruppur and Noida, may belong to the formal economy.

Policy suggestions for using exports as a means of increasing employment in India have pointed out to the need for identification of employment-intensive as well export-intensive sectors (such as textiles and apparels, gems and jewellery, and leather goods) followed by promotion of low employment-intensive but high export intensity industries which are medium-technology intensive as well as the higher value added industries. What is conspicuously absent from these suggestions is the need to focus on the quality of employment. A generalized employment strategy without a focus on the quality of jobs is unlikely to promote decent employment under the present conditions to be found in the economy.

Labour laws and decent employment

There is an influential school of thought that believes the promotion of employment in the organized sector (often implicitly equated to decent employment) is hampered by existing labour laws in India. More often than not, the debate has focused on a clause in the Industrial Disputes Act that mandates manufacturing enterprises to seek prior government permission in the event of retrenchment of workers. This is applicable to all manufacturing enterprises employing 100 or more workers. While employers' organizations have argued vehemently for the removal of this clause, the trade unions have opposed this with equal vehemence. In practice, however, this clause has hardly come in the way of the employers' ability to restructure their enterprises: there is very little evidence of the Government having denied permission, and there is also a sub-clause that states that the permission shall be deemed to have been given in the event the Government does not communicate to the employer within 60 days of the receipt of the application for permission.[9] It is quite possible that the strongly held views of employers and trade unions reflect the underlying strategy of labour control: the former—in its pursuit for unhindered accumulation—wanting absolute control over labour by using the threat of dismissal as a powerful weapon for disciplining labour, and the latter being concerned for retaining membership and expanding worker solidarity in an age of the triumph of capitalism. The empirical reality, however, is one that does not strongly support the hypothesis that employment, especially in the organized sector, is hindered by this particular piece of labour legislation.

First of all, the above mentioned labour legislation is applicable only to manufacturing enterprises in the organized sector with an employment size of 100 or above. Here again, the real applicability is for the private sector. The employment in this group totalled 4.6 million in

9. Chapter VB of the Industrial Disputes Act (1947), Clause 25 (O) (3) states that: "Where an application has been made under sub-section (1) and the appropriate Government does not communicate the order granting or refusing to grant permission to the employer within a period of sixty days from the date on which such application is made, the permission applied for shall be deemed to have been granted on the expiration of the said period of sixty days."

2003/04, which works out to 1 per cent of the total employment in the economy or 6 per cent of employment in the industrial sector. One can therefore, imagine the area of impact of such a piece of legislation.

Second, the legislation should have resulted in a clustering of the employment size of enterprises at around, but less than, 100 workers. Table 3.5, however, shows that the average employment size of enterprises with less than 100 workers has remained almost unchanged, at a low figure of around 22–23 during the past two decades. The next size group, 100–499 workers, also changed little, with an average of 186 during the same period. It is in the larger enterprises that the average number of workers came down, from 1,213 to 829, but this average is still much higher than the ceiling of 100 workers. The decline in the average size of the large-sized enterprises could be explained by the restructuring of the labour-intensive large-scale factory enterprises in the textiles.

Table 3.5

Enterprises and employment by average number of workers in organized manufacturing in the private sector

Size class	*Year*	*Enterprises*		*Employment*		*Average employment*
		(thousands)	*(%)*	*(millions)*	*(%)*	*(number of workers)*
0–99	1981/82	74.92	89.2	1.74	33.6	23
	2003/04	106.19	87.6	2.37	34.2	22
100–499	1981/82	7.34	8.7	1.36	26.2	185
	2003/04	12.18	10.1	2.27	32.7	186
500 and above	1981/82	1.72	2.1	2.09	40.2	1213
	2003/04	2.78	2.3	2.30	33.2	829
Total	**1981/82**	**83.98**	**100.0**	**5.19**	**100.0**	**62**
	2003/04	**121.15**	**100.0**	**6.94**	**100.0**	**57**

Source: Compiled from unit level data of the Annual Survey of Industries, 1981/82 and 2003/04, made available by the Central Statistical Organisation, Government of India.

Despite the limited area of impact of this clause, it could be argued that the relaxation or removal of the clause is warranted on the ground that the technical aspects of production should determine the level of employment in an enterprise and that technological change is an imperative in a competitive environment. If such a view is accepted, then the question is one of how to protect the labour that would be rendered jobless, because labour cannot be treated merely as a "factor" of production in an economy. The ultimate concern here is one of protection and the issue at stake would then be the trade-off between income security and job security. Existing practices indicate that some countries, especially in Europe, have preferred to provide income security rather than job security so that the competitive capability of the enterprises is not hindered. In some other countries, a higher job security is provided with less income security (for example, see Garibaldi, 2007). This calls for a social model that has to be mediated by the state.

Indeed, the relationship between labour legislation and employment goes beyond the specific issue of "freedom to hire and fire". In the Indian context, there is considerable scope for labour law reforms that would create a better enabling environment for enterprises to function and grow and possibly contribute to employment. Some of these relate to streamlining inspections and filing of returns to make these hassle-free tasks, consolidation of labour laws, harmonization of definitions pertaining to "worker", "industry", and so on. There is also an urgent need to create minimum conditions of work, wages and social security in the informal economy, on which little attention has focused to date.

Fiscal consolidation and employment

As we discussed earlier, fiscal policy and fiscal instruments are crucial to the achievement of the goal—if any exists—of decent employment. Is there then a trade-off between fiscal consolidation and decent employment generation? If fiscal consolidation leads to a compression in government expenditure, then it could affect the goal of employment in general and decent employment in particular in an economy such as India, which is characterized by a large proportion of the workforce without adequate human capabilities and an overwhelming proportion of enterprises (mostly small and micro) without access to quality infrastructure and critical inputs such as credit.

The goal of reducing fiscal deficits in the name of fiscal consolidation can lead to different routes with different ramifications. In India, reducing fiscal deficit has not been adequately matched by a reduction in revenue deficits. In fact, revenue deficits have shown a tendency to persist or even to rise. This then affects the capital expenditure of the Government, which often adversely affects the goal of decent employment. If reduction in fiscal deficits is sought by a greater mobilization of taxes and other revenues, then the degree of freedom for the Government to spend increases and this could well lead to increased capital expenditure (public investment) if the objective of decent employment finds a place in macroeconomic policy. This often warrants—in addition to increased efficiency in revenue collection—taxing the rich and the corporate sector. The current orthodoxy would resist such a strategy, arguing that it would lead to a decline in private investment in the economy. However, the "crowding out" thesis behind this argument has to confront the "crowding in" argument, whereby public and private investments in a developing country context are often seen as complementary.[10] This is especially so for investment in such sectors as physical infrastructure and human development (leading to higher human capabilities through better health, education, social

---

10. Amaresh Bagchi, a prominent expert on public finance in India, has articulated the dilemma between fiscal consolidation and the developmental role of public investment. "The optimum level of fiscal deficit or debt for a country in a given situation is a contentious issue in public finance. One view is that given the requirement of investment in infrastructure and the social sectors, which is unlikely to come from the private sector in adequate measure, cutting down govt expenditure indiscriminately as happened under fiscal consolidation in the wake of the reforms would be counterproductive. While financing by non-distortionary taxation would be preferable, public investment in infrastructure even if financed by seignorage, it is argued, will help to accelerate growth by crowding in private investment potential of the economy, which in turn will help to narrow, if not close, the budget gap (Rakshit, 2001). The other more moderate view, while recognizing the positive role of fiscal policy in inducing growth, stresses the need to keep in view the possible short-term impact of deficit financing on prices and balance of payments (Chelliah, 2001). ... Given the requirements of public investment in infrastructure and the social sectors, an optimal debt policy would be to strike a balance among the options available for financing government expenditure, namely non-distortionary taxation, borrowing, and seignorage. A balanced strategy rather than blind adherence to irrational rules in the face of patent output gap would be conducive to both growth as well as fiscal correction" (Bagchi, 2007: 186–187).

security, etc.), where private investment would be shy to come in given the absence of private returns (or the limited scope for user charges). In this context, the East and South-East Asian experiences could provide useful lessons for India. The experience of China shows that a high level and rate of public investment has gone hand in hand with a high level of private investment, including foreign direct investment. It has been reported that China invests nearly 10 per cent of its national income in infrastructure, mostly through public investment, which is double the rate for India (Planning Commission, 2006: 3).

Since the beginning of economic reforms, there has been a significant decline in the share of public investment. From the Second Five Year Plan until the end of the Seventh Plan (from 1956 to 1990), the share of public investment in total investment was around 44 per cent; it declined to 33 per cent during the Eighth Plan (1992–1997) (Planning Commission, 2001b: 5) and was projected to decline to 31 per cent during the Tenth Plan (2002–2007). The 11th Plan also does not envisage a share of more than 30 per cent for public investment (ibid.: 14). A new instrument for investment in infrastructure has therefore been proposed: public–private partnership. While this would seem to be an attractive option, it does not easily lend itself to long-term planning because the expected private investment cannot be predicted. Furthermore, commitment of such private investment may not come without conditionality, especially in avenues where the private sector may not see any quick returns. Fears have also been expressed that such a model could go against the public interest. However, there is no case for abandoning this option, especially when the expectations about the long-term growth of the economy are high and such investments are likely to produce a win–win situation for both the Government and the private sector. There are some good examples of public–private partnerships in India in infrastructure, such as the development of airports and information technology parks and the movement of cargo through the railway system.

There is certainly a case for examining policy coherence between fiscal consolidation and decent employment creation in India. Such an exercise would have to take into account the room for expansionary policies—through enhancing public investment—within the acceptable limits of inflation, taxation and the degree of freedom available for imports of wage goods in order to smoothen the short-term supply constraints. This would open up the potentialities and possibilities for achieving decent employment within the current macroeconomic policy framework and identify the departures required, if any, from such a framework from a long-term developmental point of view.

Need for policy coherence

We would therefore, emphasize that there is not only a need for policy coherence within the existing macroeconomic policy framework, but that macroeconomic policy must also be firmly anchored within the larger framework of development policy and planning. The perceived disconnect is not only between macroeconomic policy and decent employment but between macroeconomic policy and the development agenda in general. In India, this often manifests as adjunct policies for employment, poverty alleviation, backward-area development, protection of small-scale sector, etc., responding to the exigencies of immediate political and social conditions. When the orthodox wisdoms in liberalization and privatization inform macroeconomic policy-making, development planning becomes an instrument to advance these goals, based on the trickle-down hypothesis, rather than the other way round.

This ties up with the issue of generating not just employment, as in the past, but decent employment. However, the reality on the ground in India, as we have seen earlier, is one where several steps have to be taken simultaneously to realize the goal of decent employment. First of all, the measures of employment conceal significant underemployment and disguised unemployment. This is manifested not only in the difference between principal and subsidiary workers, but also within the principal workers themselves. An indirect measure of underemployment is the ratio between unemployment rate (nearly 8 per cent by the daily status) and the incidence of poverty, which is around 28 per cent. Therefore, the problem of income poverty is an indicator of the extent of underemployment in the economy.

The extent of underemployment and the high proportion of low-income self-employment and casual employment in the economy call for enhancing the earnings of workers. For the underemployed, it is a question of securing adequate employment. As far as the self-employed are concerned, the problem is increasing their productivity. For the casual workers, apart from the problem of underemployment, they also face considerable obstacles in obtaining reasonable wages. An overwhelming proportion of these workers also do not have any social security to take care of contingencies such as health problems and old-age protection (see for example, NCEUS, 2006).

Does this mean that these issues cannot be tackled within the current framework of macroeconomic policy? If such concerns are not central to policy, they are addressed in the form of adjunct policies and programmes. There are several such policies and programmes, but the crucial test is whether they add up to a meaningful whole.

The problem of underemployment has been addressed in India through public works programmes. However, the quantum of employment provided on a per capita basis was way below the requirement. A major step forward was taken when a rights-based employment guarantee scheme, the National Rural Employment Guarantee (NREG), was introduced in 2006 to meet the demand for employment from unskilled rural labourers. However, the potential of such a historic initiative has been limited by several factors, including the ceiling on employment provisioning (100 days per rural household), slow coverage (beginning with one-third of districts, now raised to just over one-half), inadequate financial allocation[11] and slow pace of implementation (for an assessment of the state-wise performance, see Chakraborty, 2007). Despite all these, recent evaluations suggest that the scheme has had a positive impact.

However, such pro-employment and pro-income initiatives need to be evaluated against other initiatives, which might neutralize their positive outcomes. For example, the special protection enjoyed by the small-scale sector has been considerably reduced (e.g. by the dereservation of products and the withdrawal of many concessions) but

11. Beginning from April 2007, i.e., the second year of the NREG, the number of districts covered was raised from 200 to 330, i.e., 55 per cent of the total. However, financial allocation was raised from Rs. 113 billion to Rs. 120 billion, representing an increase of 6 per cent in nominal terms but hardly any increase in real terms.

the impacts have hardly been assessed. When protective measures are withdrawn, in the name of a creating a "level playing field", there is a case for instituting promotional measures so as to strengthen their competitive capacity. Similarly, a major policy initiative, such as the setting up of Special Economic Zones, should also be assessed in terms of its net contribution to employment and its impacts on the livelihood situations of those who are likely to be displaced, either directly or indirectly. In the case of the Special Economic Zones, the level playing field might have taken a reverse turn in that it confers an extra-level playing field to the prospective large corporate enterprises/ establishments by way of cheap land, often acquired by the Government, tax exemptions, relaxation of labour laws and a host of other concessions in the name of expected additional contribution to exports and growth. The same logic could then be applied with much stronger justification, on grounds of employment generation and inclusive growth, for creating special zones for the micro- and small enterprises in existing clusters across the country. Such a proposal, called Growth Poles, could be elevated to a strategy whereby a convergence of investments in physical and social infrastructure and common facilities could be brought about in existing clusters, many of which may have linkages with rural areas.[12] Given the reality of the existence of a very large number of small units in the Indian economy, a policy shift in favour of the small is an imperative for the realization of the agenda of inclusive growth and its concomitant productive employment generation.

Surveys have pointed out that the biggest problem faced by micro- and small enterprises is the availability of credit. The share of credit going to the small-scale sector has declined by more than half (from 18 to 7 per cent) between 1991 and 2005. The share of credit flowing to micro-enterprises is an abysmal 1.8 per cent of the net bank credit (as of

---

12. NCEUS has recommended the idea of Growth Poles to the Central government as a strategy to strengthen and develop micro- and small enterprises in existing clusters in the country (see NCEUS, 2005). Given the current impasse in Special Economic Zones (SEZ) policy, a case can be made to confer SEZ benefits and status to the proposed Growth Poles in existing clusters that will largely, if not only, benefit micro- and small enterprises and generate productive employment far in excess of that could be created by large-scale enterprises.

2005). At least 13 funds that have been set up to ensure that micro- and small enterprises have better access credit and that cheaper credit is available. But the combined capital of these funds pales into insignificance against the demand for credit by the micro- and small enterprises. In fact, the cost of credit for the micro- and small enterprises is much higher than for their bigger counterparts. The size of the unit and the cost of credit seems to be inversely related. The microcredit segment reports interest rates ranging from 12 to 48 per cent, depending on the source of such credit. In fact, the average amount of microcredit has been so small (less than Rs. 3,000) that it cannot but be a consumption-smoothing mechanism for the very small self-employed.

The biggest segment in the small-scale sector comprises the micro-enterprises with an average fixed capital of less than Rs. 2 lakh[13] (whereas the definition of a "micro-enterprise" is one with fixed capital of up to Rs. 25 lakh). Most policies devised for the small-scale sector often benefit the bigger rather than the small. There is therefore, a strong case for a focused approach to the problems of the micro-enterprises, which account for more than 98 per cent of the total units and around 85 per cent of workers in non-agriculture (Government of India, 2006).

The problems of the agricultural and related sector call for separate treatment. Enhancing productivity is the key here, to enable the surplus workers to move to the non-agricultural sector instead of the distress migration due to the slow pace of growth of agriculture. Here again, a regionally differentiated approach is called for, in which the dry-land regions (where much of the distress is concentrated due to the vagaries of nature and low productivity) need special treatment from several points of view, including food security and inclusive growth (see Kannan, 2007). The rationale for a strategy focused on dry-land farming has been well articulated (see for example, Vijayashankar, 2006; Shah *et al.*, 1998).

In terms of policy priority, two important areas are the development of physical infrastructure for rural areas (such as water control,

13. Rs. 1 lakh = Rs. 100,000.

transport, communications and electrification) and the development of social infrastructure to enhance human capabilities (education, health and sanitation, skill development and social security). Some of these areas have started receiving attention in macroeconomic policy-making, and the recent decision to enhance plan allocations to education and health is a case in point. But there is a long way to go. One of the crucial decisions here would hinge on the need for enhanced public investment and the ways to mobilize the required resources. A balancing of the roles of state and market is an imperative in a country such as India, given the enormity of the problem of underdevelopment and its concomitant inequities in a whole range of factors, including economic and social assets and human capabilities.

The agenda of decent employment therefore, provides an opportunity to re-examine the macroeconomic policies followed so far. From an employment point of view, the first approximation of decent employment—regular work—should become a macroeconomic indicator. The fact that the share of regular work has remained almost unchanged during the past three-and-a-half decades despite an acceleration in growth, a shift in employment away from agriculture and an impressive increase in saving and investment is something that calls for deeper analysis and, more importantly, for a policy rethink on the quality of growth. This could pave the way for widening the macroeconomic policy concerns and a balancing of macroeconomic policies with macro social policies. The latter often link economic dimensions with social dimensions. These concerns ultimately advance the objectives of decent employments.

Broadly speaking, there is need for a macro monitor to track the quality of growth being achieved—whether there is a disconnect between economic growth and social welfare. Employment is a crucial link between these two objectives. The concept of decent work may therefore, be broadly interpreted in this sense. This chapter suggests three possible, though not exhaustive, approaches for the policy-makers to be alert to in order to ensure that a preoccupation with economic growth *per se* does not distract from social concerns. Appropriate policies and measurement yardsticks are important in this context.

First, a concern with aggregate growth should be accompanied by a monitoring of the pattern of growth in the formal and informal economies separately. If there were a divergence between the two, this would then call attention to the constraints faced by the latter. Such a divergent growth should be seen as a warning of increasing inequality.

Second, an overriding policy concern with inflation may lead to measures such as a credit squeeze and/or a check on public spending to contain fiscal deficit. Such measures can compress investment, producing a negative impact on employment. A balance of concern is therefore, necessary between price stability and employment, both regular employment in the economy in general and the rural areas in particular. A major focus here should be the availability of wage goods to insulate the poor from the negative impact of inflation.

Finally, it should be recognized that, in the Indian context, income poverty is mainly, if not only, due to the existence of working poor. Two areas of policy concern here are: (a) the payment of minimum wages and the availability of social security, and (b) the improvement in human development. Legislation on a minimum wage would become more effective if attention were to be paid to enhancing the reserve price of labour. This could be done by improving the human development of the working poor. The policy concern here should be to focus on such areas as infant mortality, supplementary nutrition for children and pregnant mothers, school enrolment, and strengthening the public health care delivery system.

There could be many others that should be kept on the watch list. Evolving a detailed agenda for such checks and balances would be a useful exercise in policy coherence; a step for future studies.

Appendix A-3.1

Performance indicators for India

Table A-3.1

India's macroeconomic performance, employment and selected human development indicators

Indicator	*Pre-reform (1983/84 to 1993/94)*	*Post-reform (1993/94 to 2004/05)*
Macroeconomic indicators		
Growth in GDP	5.07	6.25
Percentage increase in per capita income during the period	31	67
Gross domestic savings at the end of the period (% of GDP)	22.5	31.1
Gross investment at the end of the period (% of GDP)	21.4	31.5
Annual growth rate in exports during the period (value in US$)	16.53	19.12
Annual growth rate in imports during the period	21.72	16.53
Current account deficit at the end of the period (% of GDP)	–0.47	–0.40
Foreign exchange reserve at the end of the period (US$bn)	19.25	141.51
Rate of inflation (wholesale price index)	8.19	5.87
Debt service ratio	n.a.	15.9
Employment indicators		
Growth rate in employment as % of labour force growth	96	88
Percentage of regular workers at the end of the period	13.66	15.20
Share of workers in agriculture at the end of the period	60.64	56.60
Growth rate in rural casual wage rate during the period	42.00	35.00
Human development indicators		
Value of HDI at the end of the period[1]	0.38	0.47
Incidence of poverty at the end of the period	36.6	28.4
Annual rate of reduction in poverty during the period	–0.88	–0.74

Note: [1] Refers to 1991 and 2001 respectively; n.a. = data not available.

Source: Government of India, *Economic Survey*, annual publication, issues for the years 1984/85 up to 2005/06; Planning Commission, 1993, 2001a,b, 2002b and 2006.

Appendix A-3.2

Estimating formal employment (decent work) in India

Our attempt to estimate formal employment (interpreted as decent work) calls for some explanation. Given the fact that the estimation of formal employment is possible only for the 55th (1999–2000) and 61st (2004–05) rounds of the National Sample Survey (NSS), there is a case for indirectly estimating formal employment for previous rounds. These are explained below.

The National Commission for Enterprises in the Unorganized Sector (NCEUS, 2006) defined the informal (unorganized) sector as well as informal (unorganized) employment in the Indian economy. The informal economy was defined as:

> All unincorporated enterprises owned by individuals or households engaged in the production and sale of goods and services and operated on a proprietary or a partnership basis and employing less than 10 persons.

The informal employment was defined as:

> Unorganised [informal] workers are all those who are working in the Unorganised Sector defined earlier and the workers in the formal sector without any employment security and social security provided by the employer.

The first definition of informality (sector concept) is based on two criteria: an enterprise does not have a legal personality distinct from its owner's; and employment size is small. The second definition is based on the criterion of workers not able to enjoy any legally binding security with respect to employment and social security. These two definitions are in accordance with the international definition accepted by the ILO.

The concept of formal employment therefore, takes into account those who have employment/social security provided by the employer. They may belong to both the formal (organized) sector and the informal (unorganized) sector. Such employment has been estimated for 1999/2000 and for 2004/05 from the 55th and 61st rounds of the NSS.

In order to estimate formal employment in previous rounds, we took the estimate of employment in the organized sector provided by the Directorate General of Employment and Training (DGET), Ministry of Labour and Employment. The employment figures reported by the DGET are based on the reports filed by enterprises in the organized sector, whether in agriculture or non-agriculture, rural or urban. Under the Employment Reporting Scheme, it is mandatory for all enterprises employing 25, or more workers to file their reports. For those employing between 10 and 25, it is voluntary. Due to practical reasons, the cities of Mumbai and Kolkata do not cover the latter category. Therefore, the reporting system may be said to suffer from two inadequacies. One is the non-reporting of the 10–25 workers category in two major metropolitan cities and the other is the voluntary nature of reporting for this category in other places. However, discussions with officials of the DGET revealed that the enterprises usually report those on their regular payrolls enjoying some social security. It is understandable that establishments may not be willing to report those employed on a regular or contract basis especially when they do not give any legally binding social security protection. We therefore, feel that the employment figures reported by the DGET could be closer to the estimates of formal employment in the economy. This is tested in Table A-3.2

Table A-3.2

Estimates of formal employment

Category		*Total employment (UPSS) (millions)*	*NSS estimates of formal employment (millions)*	*DGET figures (millions)*	*NSS (as % of DGET)*
Formal employment	2004/05	457.46	34.68 (7.6)	26.44	131
	1999/2000	396.76	34.47 (8.7)	28.11	122
Employment in the formal sector	2004/05	457.46	67.29 (14.8)	26.44	255
	1999/2000	396.76	56.45 (14.2)	28.11	201
Estimated formal employment	1993/94	374.28	33.43 (8.9)	27.18	123
	1987/88	301.38	31.23 (10.0)	25.39	123
	1983	303.77	33.43 (11.0)	24.01	139
Estimated employment in the formal sector	1993/94	374.28	54.63 (14.6)	27.18	201
	1987/88	301.38	51.03 (16.0)	25.39	204
	1983	303.77	48.26 (15.9)	24.01	201

Note: The figures in parentheses indicate National Sample Survey (NSS) estimates as percentages of total employment in the previous column.

What we find here is that the NSS-based estimates of formal employment were 23 per cent higher than the DGET's in 1999/2000 and 30 per cent higher in 2004/05. We took the ratio for 1999/2000 to estimate formal employment in the previous time points of 1993/94, 1987/88 and 1983 so as not to overestimate. For estimating employment in the formal economy, we used the ratio for the same year, i.e., 1999/2000.

4 Labour markets outcomes and policy challenges in India

Ahmad Ahsan, Dipak Dasgupta
and Ashish Narain

4.1 Introduction

The emergence of India on the global economic stage has been one of the big stories of the past two decades. India's growth rate has jumped from an entrenched 3.5 per cent in the 1970s, and has been averaging 9 per cent over the past two years. Today it is the fourth largest economy in the world in terms of purchasing power, and has made substantial inroads into reducing poverty.

The functioning of labour markets is central to understanding how the benefits of India's growth flow down to the population. This is because labour is the principal asset for most Indians, especially the poor and marginalized groups. The tight relationship between wage earnings, income and household expenditures across India's different regions (Figure 4.1) suggests that labour markets are the main channel through which growth is distributed across regions and people.

An important question is whether economic growth by itself is enough. This chapter points out that although faster growth has lead to better labour market outcomes, some serious concerns remain. Not enough jobs are being created as are required, even at relatively high growth rates. And a large number of the jobs that are created are often of poor quality in that they cannot guarantee workers a minimum standard of living. This does not portend well for a nation where the working-age population is expected to keep on increasing—by more than 12 million people over the next decade—and where the possibility of raising the growth rate to levels significantly higher than has been achieved so far is debatable. Again, while the Government's successful drive to

Figure 4.1

Real per capita expenditures against real weekly earnings for NSS regions, estimated from four surveys from 1983 to 2000

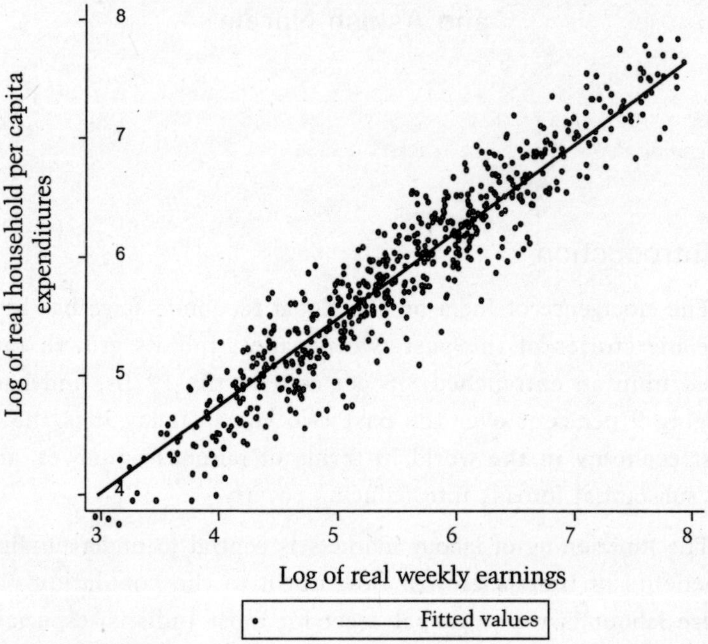

Source: World Bank, 2006b.

universalize primary education has raised workers' educational attainments, and also their expectations, this has not been matched by a commensurate increase in suitable employment opportunities. Youth unemployment, especially among the educated, is a serious concern. This suggests the need to look again at existing government policies, which are constraining labour markets, and at what could be done to achieve better outcomes.

This chapter analyses the available evidence on India's labour market developments. It assesses the major developments over the 1990s, identifies some key challenges and makes recommendations on how to improve labour market outcomes. The analysis is based primarily on the quinquennial household labour surveys conducted by the National Sample Survey Organisation (NSSO). Data from the

Annual Survey of Industries, the Labour Bureau, Government of India, and the Informal Sector Modules of the National Sample Survey (NSS) have also been used for the analysis in this chapter. The chapter draws heavily from a recent World Bank report, *India's employment challenge: Creating jobs, helping workers* (World Bank, 2006b).

The rest of the chapter is organized as follows: the following section (4.2) documents the changing economic and labour market structure in India. Section 4.3 discusses the pace of job creation in the economy and the effect it had on the overall employment situation. It also discusses how the benefits of growth were distributed unequally across regions and across worker classes. Section 4.4 examines the changes in productivity, wages and job quality and what they portend for the future. The importance of education and skills is increasing in a globalizing market. Section 4.5 describes the existing formal institutions in India for education and skills development and discusses the effectiveness of these provisions. Section 4.6 discusses labour regulation in India, with special focus on the Industrial Disputes Act, 1948.

4.2 Pattern of economic growth and labour market

Despite the acceleration of economic growth in India since the mid-1980s, the structural transformation of the economy has been relatively slow, compared to the fast growing East Asian economies, and is somewhat atypical of the experiences of most developing countries. Most surprising is the observation that since the 1950s, the contribution of industry to gross domestic product (GDP) has increased from 13 per cent to only around a quarter of GDP. Within industry, manufacturing's contribution has increased only minimally, to less than 15 per cent of GDP, which is much lower than in other developing countries. The contributions of industry and manufacturing remained largely unchanged through the 1990s, despite the reforms in the early years of the decade which were supposed to unshackle industry.[1]

The structure of employment has changed even more modestly than has been the case for the GDP. There has been little shift of

1. World Bank macroeconomic data set.

employment away from agriculture, and the sector still accounts for most employment (58.7 per cent in 1999/2000). The relatively small shift of workers away from agriculture has been mainly directed to the service sectors (Figure 4.2). The share of manufacturing employment more or less matched the share of manufacturing GDP and remained less than 15 per cent of all employment. Between 1978 and 2000, the creeping increase in the share of industry in total employment for India is in stark contrast to the rapid rises seen in Korea, China and Thailand (Ghose, 2004).

Figure 4.2

Distribution of India's workforce, 1983–2000

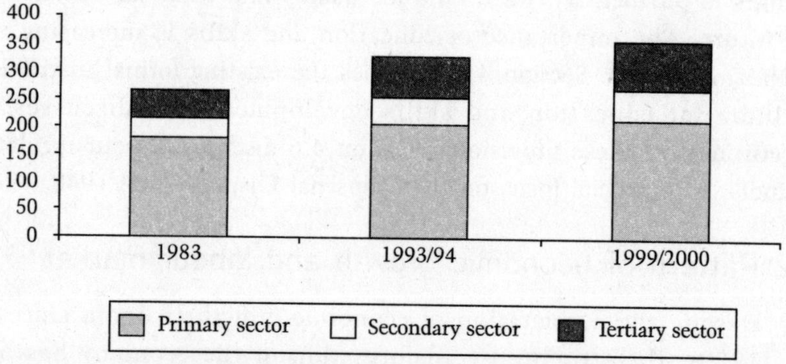

Note: Primary sector includes agriculture and allied activities and minerals, secondary sector includes industries and construction and tertiary sector includes services.
The vertical axis shows workforce in terms of million (numbers).

Source: Sundaram and Tendulkar, 2006.

The decline in agricultural employment growth in the 1990s was driven both by a decline in labour force growth and by the migration of labour from agriculture to non-farm jobs. It is arguable that this migration was mostly a result of pull factors, and was not distress driven. This is suggested by the observation that although both agricultural and non-farm rural casual wages grew steadily in real terms, non-farm rural casual wages consistently exceeded farm wages. This indicates that greater non-farm opportunities were drawing labour away from agriculture, which was in keeping with the structural transformation going on in the economy. However, district level studies show that some of the movement may also have been distress-induced.

Marginal farmers may have been pushed out of agriculture by the slowdown in agricultural growth and by falling productivity, the uncertainty of crop yields in rain-fed areas and the lack of insurance against the vagaries of the monsoons, depletion of water resources and land degradation.

The major player in the absorption of labour outside agriculture in the 1990s was not manufacturing, but the tertiary sector. It absorbed 55 per cent of the increase in the labour force between 1983 and 2000. A key question is whether labour was being pulled into the sector by better incomes, or whether it was being pushed into it for lack of alternative opportunities. Household data from the NSSO show that labour absorption was proportionately larger in the first and the fifth income quintiles of the distribution, with relatively less absorption of labour in the middle range. This suggests that the tertiary sector was absorbing labour disproportionately at the lower and the upper ends of the earnings distribution. At the same time, there was an outward shift of the earnings distribution in the tertiary sector at all levels, and particularly in the first and fifth quintiles. The suggestion is, therefore, that pull factors were more important than push factors in increasing employment in the tertiary sector.

The manufacturing sector in India is characterized by strong dualism when compared with other developing countries (World Bank, 2006b). In 2000/01, there were 14.8 million enterprises in the manufacturing sector, employing 45.7 million workers. Of these, only 1 per cent of enterprises and 26 per cent of workers were in the organized sector.[2] Two-thirds of the workforce in the unorganized sector worked in own-account enterprises based primarily on family labour. In rural areas, unorganized employment was even more strongly dominated by own-account enterprises (79 per cent), while in urban areas the picture was more balanced. Over the 1990s, the structure of unorganized

2. The data on the organized sector are obtained from the Annual Survey of Industries (ASI). The ASI collects two separate sets of data: the "census sector", which refers to a census of enterprises with more than 100 workers; and the "factory sector", which refers to a sample survey of enterprises with 10–100 workers. We use both sets to show the structure of the industry, but in the latter, for limited analysis of organized sector data we only use the census sector data.

manufacturing remained more or less stable, with only a slight decline in the share of own-account enterprises. At the other end of the spectrum, there was another clustering of workers at the 1000 and above employment size. The two extreme ends had large productivity differentials, which did not significantly lessen over the 1990s (Figure 4.3).

Figure 4.3

Distribution of employment and productivity by size groups

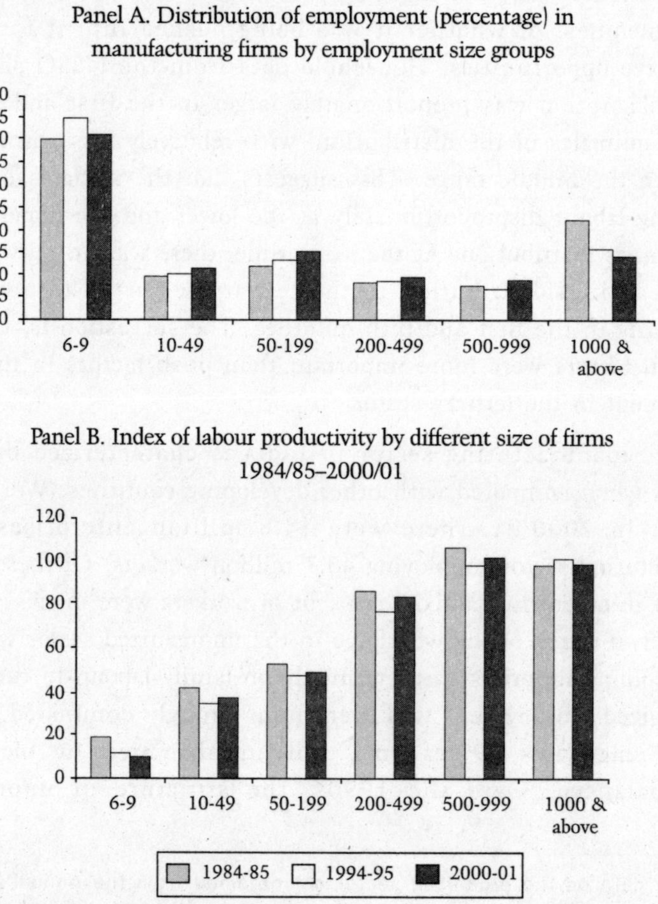

Note: Horizontal axes measure size group of firms.
Source: Mazumdar and Sarkar (2006).

An important distinction stands out. In the organized sector, growth in value added was passed on to workers primarily in the form of wage growth, while employment growth was virtually stagnant. Although likely to be underestimates, official estimates show that employment in organized or formal manufacturing grew minimally from 6.3 million in 1991 to 6.6 million in 2000 and then declined to 6 million in 2003.[3] This meant that the benefits of growth flowed primarily to "insiders" who were lucky enough to hold jobs in the sector. In the unorganized sector, however, the benefits of growth were transferred to workers in the form of both higher wages and increased employment. Employment in informal manufacturing grew by 2.1 per cent per annum over the 1990s. The average annual rate of growth of wage earnings in the unorganized sector, 5.1 per cent, was much higher than the 1.2 per cent wage growth in the organized sector (Unni, 2006). Despite the faster growth in labour productivity and earnings in the unorganized manufacturing sector, however, the gap between the organized and the unorganized sectors remained large.

4.3 Productivity, wage growth and job quality

In a developing country such as India, simply looking at employment rates can be misleading because most workers, especially males, have no option but to take up any work in order to survive. Employment numbers thus conceal significant underemployment and distress-driven employment in low-wage, low-productivity jobs in the informal economy (Table 4.1). The informal economy employs some 90 per cent of prime aged workers in the Indian labour force. Some received low wages, and most faced uncertain incomes and could afford little protection from health or other shocks. An indication of how large the problem is comes from the huge number of working poor—some 102 million people—or more than a quarter of all workers in 2000. Thus, employment figures need to be supplemented by information on changes in labour productivity and on job quality. We think of job quality as encompassing not only the wages, but also the security that a job affords to a worker.

---

3. *Economic Survey, 2005-06* (New Delhi, Government of India).

Table 4.1

Actual wages in comparison with poverty-line wages, 1999/2000

(wage/salary per day, rupees)

Categories	*Actual wage*		*Estimated*
	Average	*Lowest*	*Poverty line*
Rural male			
Regular employees	127.3	44.5	32.6
Casual labourers	45.5	39.3	46.6
Rural female			
Regular employees	113.9	28.2	32.6
Casual labourers	29.4	28.2	48.7
Urban male			
Regular employees	169.5	60.2	43.9
Casual labourers	63.3	49.7	62.7
Urban female			
Regular employees	140.2	33.9	43.9
Casual labourers	38.2	29	65.5

Note: Workers in age group 15–59 years. In rural areas, the lowest wage is found in cultivation; in urban areas, it is found in household service. The assumptions used to estimate poverty-line wages are as follows: poverty-line expenditure per capita in 1999/2000 is Rs. 335.46 in rural areas and Rs. 451.19 in urban areas; the average number of dependants is 1.5 for regular employees and 1.8 for casual labourers; each worker gets paid only for the days actually worked; a male casual labourer finds work for 4.7 days per week while a female casual labourer finds work for 4.3 days per week; regular employees, male or female, work six days per week.

Source: Ghose, 2004.

As mentioned earlier, labour productivity increased rapidly in the 1990s. This happened both as productivity rose in each major industry group and as labour was progressively redistributed to middle-productivity sectors. Figure 4.4 compares the deployment of annual increments to the workforce between the two periods 1983–1993/94 and 1993/94–1999/2002. In terms of new employment generated in the 1990s relative to the 1980s, there was a beneficial shift away from low-productivity sectors and towards the middle-productivity sectors. These sectors, such as construction, trade, hotels and restaurants, and transport, had labour productivity that was 2.5–3.5 times higher than in agriculture. At the very top end, employment declined in high-productivity sectors such as mining and quarrying, and in the electricity, gas and water supply sectors. These are dominated by the public sector, and were believed to be overstaffed even at the start of the decade (Planning Commission, 2001a).

Figure 4.4

Deployment of incremental workforce (millions) and productivity growth (percentage) by industry

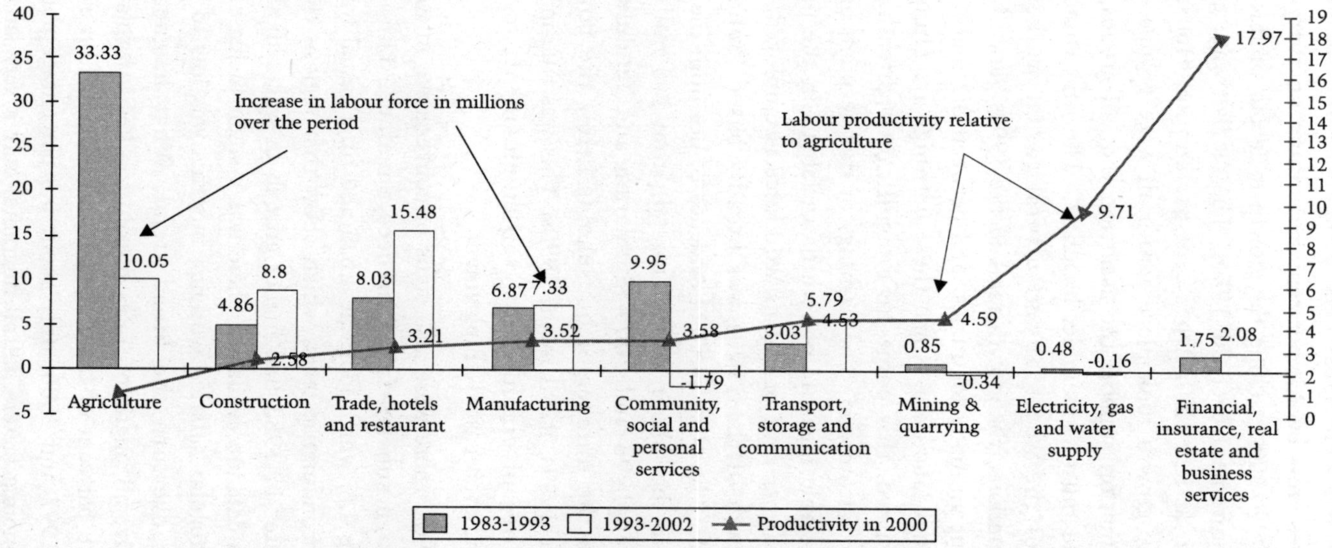

Note: Index values are relative to agriculture.

Source: World Bank, 2006b.

Real wages also grew across most occupations over the same period. Mean real wages grew by 3.4 per cent per annum on average between 1993/94 and 1999/2000, tracking the growth in labour productivity. This marked an improvement over the 1980s. The median wage growth was, however, lower, at less than 2 per cent per annum. Household data show that wage growth took place across all wage groups. Two other pieces of information support the assertion that all groups, including the poorest and most vulnerable, benefited. The first comes from an examination of the wages of agricultural casual workers. Across agricultural operations, the growth rates in the 1990s varied between 2.4 and 4.3 per cent annually for males, and between 3.2 and 5.5 per cent for female casual labourers. Since these earnings are almost entirely demand determined, this points to a significant tightening of labour markets at the bottom end. The earnings of this segment also provide the closest available measure of returns to labour in the unorganized sector, where 90 per cent of India's workforce is employed, suggesting that wage growth of the 1990s was broadly based (Sundaram and Tendulkar, 2006). The other piece of evidence comes from the number of working poor in the labour force. This fell from 115 million to 102 million between 1993 and 2000 (Sundaram and Tendulkar, 2004). Overall, while the number of households below the poverty level increased in the 1980s, it fell in the 1990s. This was true in rural areas for all categories of employment: self-employment, regular wage employment and even casual employment.

In the 1990s, there were also signs of convergence in wages across regions, although substantial differences remained. This comes out clearly in Figure 4.5, which looks at urban and rural casual wages, and is confirmed by econometric tests, which show that regions that had the lowest wage rates in 1983 had higher growth in wages in the next 17 years for which data are available. There was a slight increase in regional inequality for regular salaried workers, but this was low to begin with and does not overturn the broad trend. What has lead to this convergence? Overall migration rates remain too low to explain all of it. While about 1.8 per cent of India's population migrated on average each year between 1997 and 2000, only about 0.3 percentage points of this was due to economic factors. Of all migrants, only a very small part, 0.3

Figure 4.5

Convergence of casual wages: growth over 1983–2000 against real wages in 1983

A. Rural wages

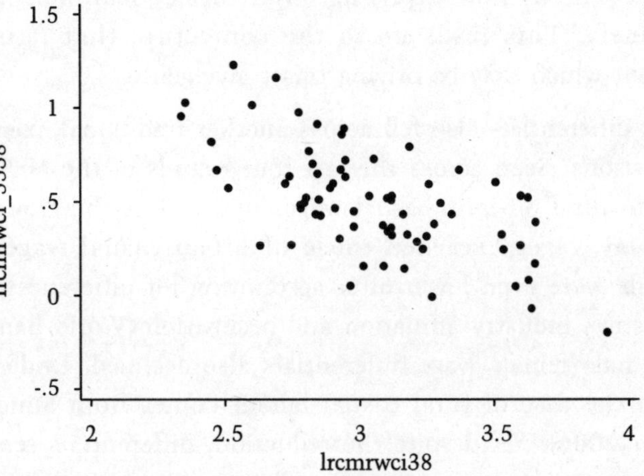

B. Urban wages

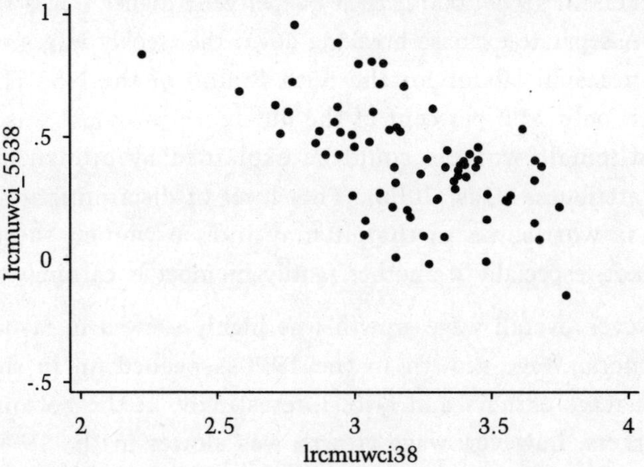

Note: The horizontal axis measures log of average regional wage in 38th round (1983) and the vertical axis measures the growth in log of average regional wage between 38th (1983) and 55th round (1999–2000).

Source: World Bank, 2006b.

per cent, migrated outside their districts or states. In comparison, some 5.5 per cent of the population of the United States of America migrated across the county or a state in the similar period.[4] This suggests that it may be labour demand which is playing the significant role. Significantly, the convergence is least for wages in agricultural operations. This is not surprising given that agricultural productivity varies widely. This leads us to the conjecture that it is off-farm employment which may be driving this convergence.

Wage differentials also fell across another traditional axis: rural and urban locations. Seen across the last four rounds of the NSS, the ratio of urban to rural off-farm casual wages declined as the growth rates of rural casual wages exceeded those of urban casual wages. Indeed, differentials were even lower after accounting for differences in worker characteristics, industry affiliation and occupation (World Bank, 2006b). Similarly male–female wage differentials also declined. Evidence of this decline in the case of rural casual labour comes from Sundaram and Tendulkar (2006). Yet despite the reduction, differentials remain large. In most occupations, especially manual ones, women's wages are about half as much as men's. The gap cannot be explained by individual, occupation or industry characteristics: even after accounting for these, male workers in 1999/2000 earned 64 per cent higher wages than female workers. A separate exercise breaking down the weekly wages of men and women in casual labour for the 55th Round of the NSS (1999-2000) found that only 27.5 per cent of the difference in casual wages between male and female workers could be explained by human capital and location attributes (Das, 2006). This level of discrimination in labour markets is worrisome in that it may induce women to stay out of employment, especially if another family member is earning.

However, overall wage growth was highly skewed in favour of high-wage earners. Wage growth in the 1990s speeded up in the top two deciles of wage earners and also, interestingly, at the bottom end. For most workers, however, wage growth was slower in the 1990s than in the previous decade (figure 4.6). The top wage earner among the deciles

4. US Census Bureau, *Geographic Mobility: March 2000 to March 2001*, *http://www.census.gov/population/www/socdemo/migrate/cps2001.html* (accessed 31 January 2008).

Figure 4.6

Real wage growth by deciles, 1983–1999/2000

A. Average real daily wage (1993/94 Rs)

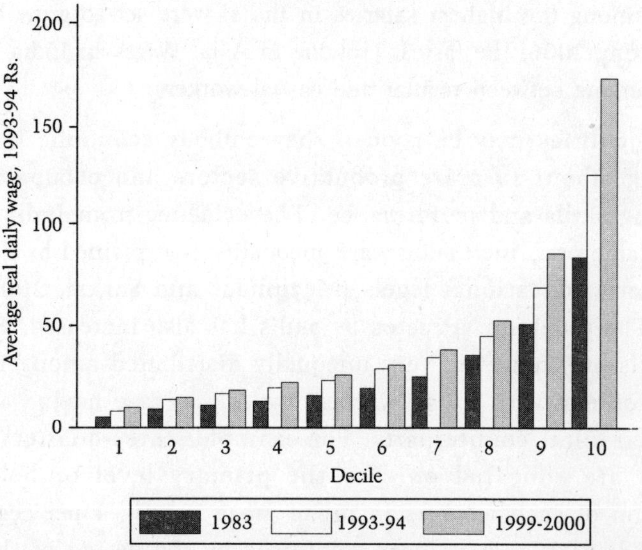

B. Percentage rate

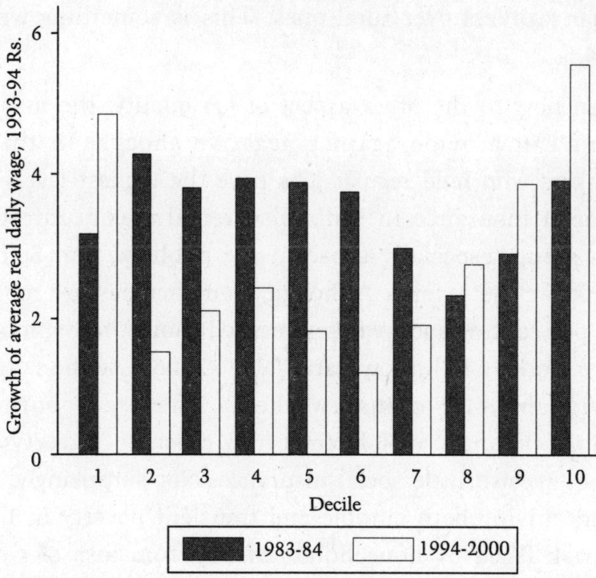

Source: World Bank, 2006b.

earned an average wage 15 times that of the lowest wage earner in 1983. By 1999/2000, the top wage had increased to almost 17 times the lowest wage. These inequalities are set to rise even more: the Hewitt Annual Salary Increase Survey for 2005–06 shows that Indian executive salaries, already among the highest salaries in India, were set to grow by 13 per cent during 2006, the fastest growing in Asia. Wages in India have also been diverging between regular and casual workers.

Inequalities may be good if they embody economic incentives, directing labour to more productive sectors and occupations and rewarding skills and performance. The evidence from India suggests that in large part, increasing wage inequality is explained by differences in workers' educational levels (Mazumdar and Sarkar, 2006; Unni, 2006). The premium attracted by skills has also increased. Education and skills are, however, very unequally distributed among rural and urban workers, with urban workers on the average having a big lead over their rural counterparts. For example, three-quarters of rural workers are educated only to the primary level or below. The proportion of such workers in urban areas is only 4 per cent. These existing disparities have been reinforced by the design of the formal government's technical and vocational education system, which favours urban workers over rural ones. This is something we return to in section 4.5.

We turn now to the other aspect of job quality, the insurance that employment can provide against negative shocks. In this respect, salaried workers who hold regular jobs have the highest levels of income security. Social insurance in India also remains concentrated mostly among this group, especially those in the public sector. Self-employed workers rank a close second. Although their incomes are more volatile, the top 30 per cent of such workers earned more than similarly placed regular wage workers (Glinskaya and Jalan, 2006). At the bottom of the scale, unarguably, lie casual workers. They face both low and unpredictable incomes which are often close to poverty levels. In addition, they receive little social insurance. Not surprisingly, one of the major factors driving both chronic and transient poverty in India is the uninsured risk faced by households arising from loss of work due to unemployment, poor health or injury.[5] In turn, such uninsured risk and associated credit and insurance market failures may contribute to workers remaining in low-productivity employment in the unorganized sector[6] and make poverty more persistent.

To track changes in job quality, therefore, a good proxy is to look at the compositional mix of workers. The mix changed somewhat over the 1990s. During this time, growth in regular wage employment among prime age workers was among the fastest in all employment categories, and was faster than it had been in the 1980s. At the end of the period, therefore, regular workers accounted for 16 per cent of the total workforce, marginally higher than the 15 per cent in 1983 (Table 4.2). Declines were, however, observed for the self-employed; these were matched by corresponding increases in the shares of casual workers.

Table 4.2

Distribution of workers by status, 1983–2002 (UPSS, 15–59)

Categories	*1983*	*1993/94*	*1999/2000*
Self-employed (%)	55	53	51
Regular workers (%)	15	15	16
Casual workers (%)	30	32	33
Total (millions)	**265**	**328.5**	**360.1**

Source: Sundaram and Tendulkar, 2006.

But did this imply deterioration in job quality? We argue that the evidence needs to be interpreted with caution. First, as noted earlier, real earnings rose for all categories of workers in the 1990s. In that sense, job quality improved for all categories. Second, the increasing share of casual workers was driven largely by trends in a few industries—agriculture, mining and construction—and was mainly a rural phenomenon. The overall trend may thus, reflect a change in technology in these industries rather than being a broad economy-wide trend. For

5. See Duflo *et al.* (2004) regarding health shocks.

6. See World Bank (2006b); see also Munshi and Rosenzweig (2005) for empirical evidence of credit and insurance market failures leading to limited mobility in rural areas.

example, in agriculture, growing casualization may possibly have been a reflection of increasing commercialization. In addition, the growing share of male casual workers itself may be a reflection of a life-cycle pattern that such workers display, moving from casual jobs to self-employment or salaried jobs as they move from youth to middle age, and their incomes increase.

It may be argued therefore that, overall, the 1990s marked some improvement in job quality for most workers. The rapid increase in productivity and, to a lesser extent, in wages, and the decline in the number of working poor were all positive developments. At the same time, serious challenges remained. Wages at the bottom end were still below that which would ensure that workers rise above the poverty line. The inequalities in earnings across individuals, regions, gender and caste groups are some of the other challenges facing India that need to be overcome to improve labour market outcomes. For example, in 1999/2000 the real weekly rural earnings in one region were less than one-tenth the weekly earnings in another. Also, while wages have been rising, they are also becoming more unequal, driven in large part by growing premiums on education and skill. Returns to secondary education are particularly high. At the same time, fewer than 10 per cent of the workers in India have completed secondary or post-secondary education. Access to these remains unequal across urban and rural locations, and across income groups.

4.4 Is there a trade-off between productivity and employment growth?

Labour demand did not grow as rapidly as desired in the 1990s. As mentioned above, this was in large part because demand from agriculture fell sharply. Agricultural employment—still accounting for 59 per cent of the labour force—stagnated as agricultural value added growth decelerated sharply in the second half of the 1990s. Employment in the formal economy was also stagnant because while the public sector shed labour, adverse relative price changes and regulatory policies encouraged private producers to invest in more skill-intensive techniques, which increased productivity rather than raised employment.

But was economic growth in the 1990s really "jobless"? Studying differences in labour market outcomes and growth experiences across regions provides a good handle for addressing the employment–output relationship. This analysis reveals that over the period, a 1 per cent increase in gross state domestic product (GSDP) led to a 0.4 per cent increase in male employment levels on average. The effect is much weaker, though still significant, in rural areas, where the elasticity is 0.2. The effect is stronger in the case of female workers: the same increase in GSDP leads to a 0.7 per cent increase in employment levels, a 1 per cent increase in urban employment and a 0.4 per cent increase in rural employment levels. Thus, economic growth was not jobless, although the employment elasticity was low (Ahsan and Pagés, 2006).

Low employment elasticity is not necessarily always a problem. The converse to low elasticity is rising labour productivity. This is important for a country such as India, where productivity levels in many sectors are low and cannot afford workers a minimum standard of living. Indeed, a panel of NSS regions across the last four NSS rounds shows that labour productivity increased at a very high rate, above 4 per cent a year, in 12 out of 17 states. At the same time, employment rates typically fell less (or increased more) in states that had the lowest gains in productivity (Figure 4.7). This might suggest a trade-off between productivity growth and employment. A careful analysis, however, suggests that the two are related in a more complex manner. In the short run, with low supply and demand elasticity, an increase in productivity will often result in lower employment elasticity. This may happen as technological improvements allow firms to produce more using the same resources. In the medium term, however, firms can decide either to maintain previous production levels with fewer workers, or to produce more with the same or more workers. Their decision depends on how much more output they can put into the market, and on whether they gain from substituting away from labour.

Figure 4.7

Growth of employment and labour productivity by regions

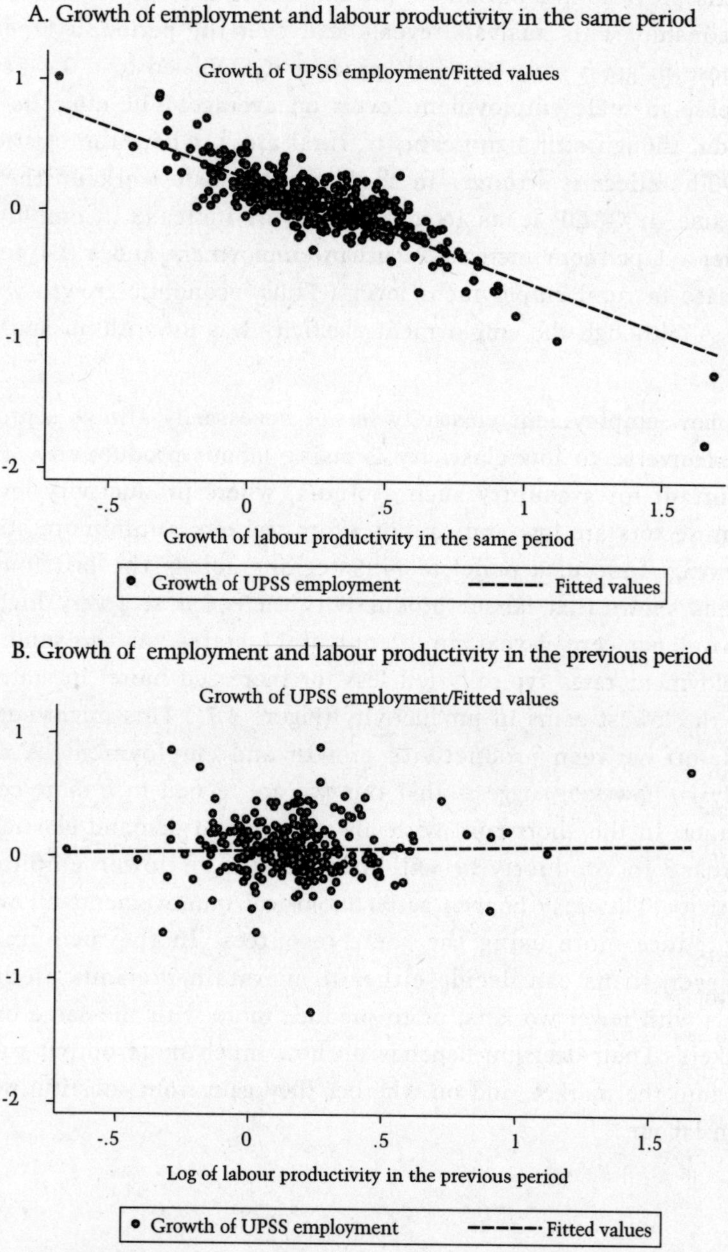

Source: World Bank, 2006b.

Thus, another look at the regional data, this time relating lagged productivity growth and current employment, shows that the relationship between the two is positive and significant. This shows that regions that had relatively high productivity growth in the past period can—after a period of adjustment—generate relatively high employment growth compared with regions which had relatively low productivity growth in the past. The productivity-led growth in the 1990s may thus, presage higher employment growth in the following decade, and India may be able to achieve the twin objectives of increasing employment and raising productivity simultaneously.

At the same time, more focus needs to be put on addressing the large differences in labour market outcomes across India's 32 states to ensure that all of these participate fully in sharing the benefits of rapid economic growth. The differences can be dramatic: for instance, male employment rates can vary from 65 per cent to 83 per cent. One of the main drivers of regional differences in labour market outcomes is level of economic activity (as measured by the GSDP). Over the long run, regions with higher economic growth rates show higher employment rates and earnings and lower unemployment rates. Therefore, ensuring that growth spreads to the states and regions that are currently lagging will be important.

Improving labour market outcomes for all will also require action along another important axis of social exclusion in India: caste. Caste has a significant impact on participation rates, occupational choice and mobility. Labour force participation rates for both Scheduled Castes (SC)[7] and Scheduled Tribes (ST)[8] are higher than for the non-SC/ST counterparts, even after controlling for other characteristics. SCs are typically landless labourers, while STs are historically forest dwellers whose mainstay is subsistence agriculture. Analysis of occupational groups indicates that SCs have remained restricted to caste-based occupations, and this also plays out within the public sector. Thus, SCs

7. Caste is a category in the endogenous system of hierarchical social stratification in India. Scheduled Castes (SCs) are lower castes in this system and have been scheduled (enlisted) by the Government of India for upliftment.

8. Scheduled Tribes (STs) are Indian tribes who are socially backward and have been listed (scheduled) by the Government for social upliftment.

dominate the manual jobs of sweeping and cleaning—historically assigned to them in the caste hierarchy. Other occupations, notably non-agricultural semi-skilled jobs, also tend to be caste-based. STs are less beset by this demarcation, since they were traditionally assigned roles outside the limits of the caste system. Since they for the most part own some land for subsistence agriculture, they also have a higher likelihood of being agriculturists (Das, 2006). Recent evidence on low occupational mobility in the Indian labour market also finds that caste has a significant effect (Munshi and Rosenzweig, 2005). Controlling for other characteristics, the effect of caste is an increased likelihood of being in casual labour and a reduced chance of being in non-farm self-employment. As noted before, rural casual workers are the most vulnerable section of the workforce, holding jobs which provide low wages and little security.

Thus, the 1990s demonstrate that while economic growth does have a positive effect on labour market outcomes, by itself this is unlikely to be enough. Other measures may be necessary to spread the benefits of economic growth to the sections of society that are being left behind. A key step towards achieving such a goal is to increase productivity and enable workers to move towards higher productivity jobs. We turn now to this issue.

4.5 How can government policies help?

The developments in the 1990s indicate that the informal economy will continue to dominate India's labour markets in the medium term. In this regard, the agriculture sector will be key, both because of its large size and because it continues to have potential for increasing productive employment. There is considerable potential for stimulating productivity and demand for labour through diversifying into horticulture, livestock and other high-value products. The spread of sustainable irrigation is another priority. Irrigated farms can use 50 per cent more hired labour than rain-fed farms. Growth in the farm sector has also been negatively affected by the Indian Government's current pricing and subsidy policies, which bias incentives against labour-intensive crops and cropping practices, and prevent the formation of efficient agricultural supply chains.

The tertiary sector is also likely to remain an important source of new jobs. Maintaining its dynamism is therefore, important. At the same time, however, it is unclear whether India's human capital and infrastructure are adequately developed to allow India to leapfrog the labour-intensive manufacturing stage and follow the growth path of an upper-middle income or even an OECD-type economy, based on skills-intensive services and manufacturing. A second issue is whether such a pattern of growth would have only a muted impact on poverty due to being unable to provide good jobs to the 90 per cent of workers who have not even completed secondary education. This would exacerbate inequality among India's regions by concentrating growth in the relatively better developed areas that already have more skilled labour and better infrastructure.

Thus, promoting employment growth in the manufacturing sector should be the main focus. As discussed above, small and medium enterprises have tremendous potential in this respect. They are well placed to receive workers transitioning out of agriculture. Currently, however, the incentive structure in the Indian manufacturing sector favours micro- and small industries, while the dualism in the capital markets gives advantages to large firms. The middle-sized firms are caught out in a disadvantaged no-man's-land. This is problematic for two reasons. First, the average productivity in micro- and small enterprises is one-eighth that in larger firms. It is also difficult to regulate these firms effectively. The welfare consequences of having such low-productivity employment are large in terms of lower output and wages, poorer working conditions, insecurity, lost tax revenues and constraints on financial development. Second, international experience shows that this missing "middle" group is the most dynamic in terms of employment generation and entrepreneurship development. By introducing more competition, this group also promotes efficient manufacturing growth. The absence of such firms is therefore, worrying.

At the other end of the scale, increasing the share of India's formal economy in employment is another urgent priority. This has remained virtually at a standstill, even a decade after liberalization. At the same time, organized manufacturing is best placed to provide good-quality employment to workers. Progress on this front requires certain reforms.

First, reforms are needed to improve the investment climate factors that currently dampen investment, productivity growth and job creation. These include providing law and order, protecting property rights, controlling corruption, improving policy and tax administration, investing in infrastructure in a sustainable manner, and increasing access to finance. Indian manufacturers have often identified infrastructure as the biggest constraint (World Bank, 2004c). For example, the cost of most infrastructure services is estimated to be 50–100 per cent higher in India than in China. Second, manufacturing and tertiary sector regulations that constrain factor mobility through raising barriers against entry, exit and trade (such as the product reservation policies) serve to dampen investment and competition. These need to be reappraised. India's generous depreciation rate of 25 per cent for investments in machinery and equipment for tax purposes, compared with 10 per cent in OECD countries, encourages firms to be capital-intensive.

Macroeconomic policies also matter. Adverse movements of producer prices in relation to consumer prices contribute significantly in lowering manufacturing elasticity (Mazumdar and Sarkar, 2006). This relative movement of prices, however, depends not only on labour market conditions, but also on overall macroeconomic factors, such as the real effective exchange rates. Econometric estimates show that after controlling for time trends, there is a robust relationship between real exchange rate appreciation and adverse movements in the domestic real exchange rates (World Bank, 2006b). Thus, keeping exchange rates competitive through guarding against inflation, especially for consumer goods, could increase labour absorption in manufacturing. This in turn has implications for fiscal policy. Higher deficits, government borrowing and inflation all tend to increase real exchange rates. Raising food prices thus, could lower manufacturing elasticity.

However, even after accounting for all these elements, analysis suggests that reforming specific labour market regulations and policies that currently have an anti-labour bias and making active labour market policies more effective remain priorities for growth and job creation. This is explored further in Section 4.6.

The Government can also help on the supply side. The increasing premium on education and skills in India highlights the potential gains to workers and to the economy through increasing their availability. Education may facilitate the "learning-by-doing" kind of skills acquisition. Similarly, developing skilled workers is likely to enhance the efficiency and flexibility of the labour market and reduce skills bottlenecks. Skilled workers are also more easily absorbed into the economy and their job mobility is improved. This is especially important in a country such as India, where a large part of the workforce remains stuck in agriculture and does not possess the skills to transfer to more productive employment in other sectors.

Starting from a low base, the labour force became more educated in the 1990s. This increase was in part due to the concerted efforts of the Government to increase the reach of primary education and eradicate adult illiteracy. The number of workers with less than five years of education came down from 80 per cent of the total labour force in 1983 to 65.5 per cent at the end of the century. Most new entrants to the workforce in the 1990s had completed primary education but were lower than graduate level. The total number of graduates in the workforce also increased, from 7.4 million to 21.4 million. Both the urban and rural workforce became more educated, although urban workers were better educated. Despite these improvements, however, the Indian labour force remained relatively unskilled compared with other emerging economies (Table 4.3), and addressing this is one of India's most important challenges. Only 17 per cent of the adult population have some secondary education, much lower than their income levels would have predicted. Contrast this with China, where the number was almost double this figure. Outcomes were even worse for females. This points to the need for India to catch up with other countries, especially at a time when the demand for skills is increasing through liberalization and globalization. At the same time, there is tremendous scope for doing so. There are 200 million children in the elementary school age group of 6–14 years, and 87 million 15–18-year-olds currently in secondary schools (Wu, 2005).

Table 4.3

India and the world: Educational attainment of adult population aged 25 and above (in 2000)

(percentage)

Region	Average years of schooling	No schooling	Highest level attained: Primary		Secondary		Tertiary	
			Total	Complete	Total	Complete	Total	Complete
India	3.6	44.5	33.2	12.4	17.4	6.5	4.8	3.3
China	5.7	20.9	40.7	15.3	35.7	14.1	2.7	2.3
Developing	4.9	37.2	35.9	12.8	19.7	8.8	7.2	4.9
Developed	9.8	4.1	27.4	14.4	39.4	18.4	29.1	16.8
Transitional	10.0	1.5	33.0	20.5	49.1	19.3	16.4	14.1
Latin America	5.7	17.7	50.6	14.4	19.9	8.4	11.8	7.7
Middle East and North Africa	5.4	32.0	29.6	10.2	29.5	10.2	8.8	3.4
East Asia	6.5	22.8	37.7	19.3	27.4	15.6	12.1	8.1
South Asia	4.2	48.4	30.6	11.0	16.7	6.5	4.3	3.0
Sub-Saharan Africa	3.8	43.5	34.2	7.7	19.2	6.6	3.0	2.4
Female population								
India	3.3	58.9	26.4	9.0	11.7	3.7	2.9	1.9
China	4.5	33.1	40.3	16.3	25.1	10.1	1.4	1.3

Source: Barro and Lee, 2000.

Education will also give rural workers greater flexibility to move to better paying occupations. This is suggested by the high concentration of illiterate rural workers in traditional primary occupations that involve on-the-job acquired low-level skills and have lower than average productivity, and the sharp decline of this concentration with increasing level of educational attainment (Sundaram and Tendulkar, 2006). This flexibility is also important in a country such as India, as it would allow a large part of the workforce stuck in agriculture to move to more productive employment in other sectors.

At the same time, close to 5 million school children drop out of school between class 6 and class 10 in India. Another 3 million students drop out between class 10 and class 12. For these student groups, the Government of India supports vocational education and training programmes across the country. The vocational education system is supposed to facilitate the effective transition between school and work for children and may improve their employment prospects and lifetime earnings. In addition, the Government also supports certificate-level crafts institutes. Programmes here are operated by the Industrial Training Institutes and the Industrial Training Centres. Finally, there are about 150,000 apprentices employed in various industries. Students who complete crafts are certified when they pass an All India Trades Test, conducted under the aegis of the National Council for Vocational Training (NCVT) but administered by the individual states. The states also administer tests for state-approved trades that are not affiliated with the NCVT.

These programmes have, however, met with only limited success so far. Student enthusiasm, especially for the vocational education programmes, has been low—as evidenced by the 40 per cent or so of places which remain vacant—and employers have also not rated these programmes very highly. International experience suggests that a good secondary education is more worthwhile at this stage than vocational education. The vocational training programmes are not much better. A comprehensive study of vocational training programmes was conducted by the ILO in 2002/03. The study found that in none of the states did more than 50 per cent of the graduates find wage employment or become self-employed, or even work in a family business. At the same time, employers in those states reported experiencing problems finding employees with the right skills, implying that graduates did not meet employers' needs. A survey by the Federation of Indian Chambers of Commerce and Industry in late 2001 also reported that close to 60 per cent of industry respondents felt that these institutions were not geared up to meet the challenges of the global economy, over 43 per cent felt that academic institutions were not aligned to the needs of industry, and 87 per cent felt that institutions should have greater exposure to industrial practices. NSSO surveys also show that, surprisingly, unemployment is highest among holders of technical diplomas. Since by design these programmes are meant to cater to identified labour market needs, the strong indication is that there is a mismatch between labour market requirements and the training provided (Figure 4.8).

Figure 4.8

Education-specific unemployment rates, 1999/2000

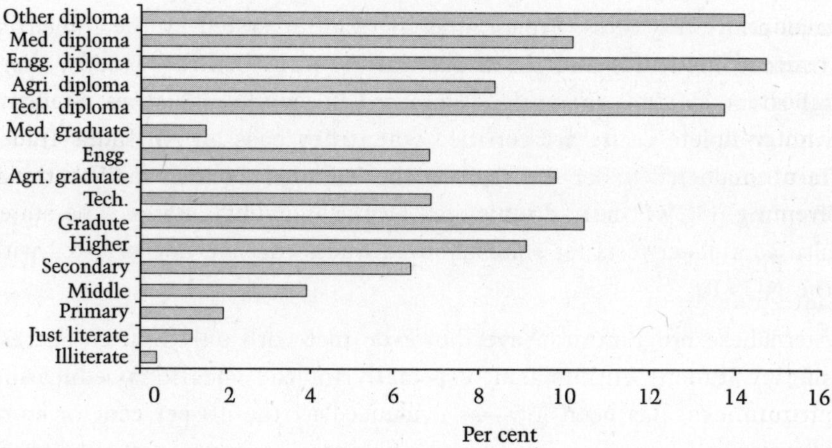

Source: Mathur and Mamgain, 2004.

A bigger failing of the system has been that current programmes have been quite inadequate for meeting the training needs of the large workforce in rural areas, arguably the group which should have been the main target. The formal training system, because of its entry requirements and geographical mapping, is not designed to offer skills to people with a low level of education, and particularly not to those in the rural non-farm sector.[9] But there are no other providers to fill the gap. Most workers continue to learn trades on the job, through informal apprenticeships at their place of work from other low-skilled crafts people. These apprenticeships are based on traditional technologies and on ideas from previous generations. The quality of training is thus, only as good as the skills of the master and his willingness and ability to pass them on. The theoretical aspects of training are weak or absent; only the simplest skills are learned, resulting in low-quality products.

What needs to be done to make these programmes more effective at helping workers and meeting labour market needs? International experience on vocational education suggests that policy-makers should

9. While one of the mandates of Industrial Training Institutes is to train workers for the informal economy, evidence shows this is rarely the case (Dar, 2006).

focus more on strengthening general secondary education. Similarly, major design and managerial reforms are needed in the vocational and technical education system. For example, significant involvement of employers in the decision-making processes of these bodies is critical to ensure that the system is responsive to market demands. Another important reform would be to create incentives within the system, through giving institutions greater autonomy in terms of deciding on training programmes, hiring and firing of teachers, and generating revenues by selling goods and services.

Finding the right role for the public sector in training is critical. State-provided training may be used to address market failures (e.g. externalities from training in general) and equity issues (e.g. provision of training for the informal economy), but it may be less necessary in an environment where private capacity exists. As a rule, unplanned public provision should not crowd out private supply. It is also not necessary for government intervention to be restricted to the provision of training. Indeed, government may have a more important role to play in activities that the non-government sector cannot undertake, such as developing policies and standards, preparing teaching materials, providing services of training instructors and even contracting training to the private sector. For example, reorienting public training institutions to meet the needs of the informal economy would not seem to be the solution. Public institutions would find it difficult to make the changes and serve both the formal and informal economy with the same skill and experience. Some innovative solutions are needed, for which international experiences could serve as a basis (World Bank, 2006b).

4.6 Labour regulation and reforms

Like all countries, India has enacted certain labour market regulations to address important market failures and to protect workers. Labour market regulations were first introduced in India in 1880 when the Factory Act was legislated. Driven in part by British manufacturers' concern to even the competition between the growing Indian textiles industry and their competitors in the United Kingdom, and in part by a nationalist desire to protect the interests of Indian labour, regulations from early on placed more emphasis on employment protection and less on efficiency of labour markets and dispute settlement (Pagés and Roy, 2006). Historically, the principle of employment protection was subsumed under the pursuit of "social justice": employment security was enhanced in the formal sector, not only by a whole range of new laws, but also by cases where judges referred to social justice to interpret laws. Removing or changing laws became politically difficult, with the result that demand for new laws led to proliferation.

The result of this proliferation is that India's labour regulations today suffer from unusual complexity. There are currently 47 central laws and 157 state regulations that directly affect labour markets. These laws—a few dating back to the nineteenth century—regulate minimum wages, hours of work, benefits, safety, security, conditions of employment, dismissal, trade unions and other aspects of industrial relations. These numerous laws have created unusual complexity in labour markets through overlapping and sometimes contradictory mandates and inconsistencies in basic definitions and concepts used (such as factory, worker, workmen, employees and employer). These complexities have been further compounded by a long trail of judicial decisions that have interpreted these laws, sometimes in an inconsistent manner. This in turn not only creates difficulties in enforcement, but also provides opportunities for discretionary behaviour, rent seeking and corruption. Specifically, it creates conditions for the "Inspector Raj"[10] to operate and extract rents from industry, with particularly bad effects for small and medium-scale industries, for whom these costs are disproportionately high, while large firms can pay to avoid inspections.

We focus particular attention on the Industrial Disputes Act (IDA) of 1948, probably the most important law governing labour markets. Two of its provisions have had particularly pernicious effects on the growth of manufacturing and formal sector jobs in India. The first concerns the dispute resolution mechanisms, while the second deals

10. "Inspector Raj" is the term used in India to refer to the "kingdom of the inspectors", which implies tyranny of the inspectors and a sense of their abuse of authority.

with laws restricting redundancy and layoff of workers, including those arising from the closure of the firm.

The IDA specifies a multi-tier conciliation-cum-adjudication system, created and maintained by the state governments. Although the system remains invariant in principle, its working changes from state to state. The lowest and the immediate tier consists of Conciliation Officers and Boards appointed by the state government. The Conciliation Officer either settles the dispute or sends a "failure report". The emphasis in the Act, however, is less on encouraging conciliation, and more on adjudication. The dispute then goes to Labour Courts, and further to Industrial Tribunals. The Labour Courts deal with disputes that affect workers. The Industrial Tribunals, apart from working as appellate bodies, deal with cases that affect all workers within an industry. Thus, cases dealing with wages usually go to a Tribunal. In rarer cases, disputes go to National Tribunals, which are centrally administered bodies empowered to deal with cases that have potentially national significance. There is some uncertainty on the status of the court orders. Although government can in principle suspend the order, in practice this option is seldom used.

The design of labour dispute settlement processes in the IDA creates incentives to adjudicate disputes rather than reconcile them. This happens for two reasons. First, at the mediation stage, which involves voluntary communication between the disputants, the Act makes provisions for the constitution of Works Committees. These are bodies internal to the firm. However, if a trade union has a significant representation of outsiders (the Indian Trade Unions Act allows for this), it would have little incentive in reconciling, as this would marginalize the union and the outside political actors. Second, and more important, the majority of cases of dispute concern discharge, dismissal and retrenchment. The legal provisions under the IDA are so protective that the worker expects to gain more from the courtroom than from conciliation efforts. As result, the number of court cases relating to labour disputes stood at around 533,000 towards the end of 2000 (Table 4.4).

Table 4.4

Numbers of dispute cases pending in labour courts, by state (October 2000)

Major states	*No. of cases pending*	*No. of cases pending for more than 10 years*
Assam	189	138
Bihar	5200	566
Delhi	28 837	2342
Gujarat	133 916	8616
Kerala	3450	63
Karnataka	17 457	2924
Maharashtra	142 345	11 508
Madhya Pradesh	89 341	0
Punjab	14 784	110
Rajasthan	20 066	775
Tamil Nadu	21 713	150
Uttar Pradesh	22 539	10 303
West Bengal	2225	283
Total (all states and UTs)	**533 038**	**28 864**

Source: Ministry of Labour, Government of India.

In addition to setting up adjudication systems, the IDA imposes significant restrictions on employers regarding retrenchment and exit. Units employing more than 100 workers require authorization from government (Chapter VB) for retrenchment and layoff. In practice, such authorization is rarely granted. Retrenched workers also receive priority in case of new recruitment. Closure of a unit will also require prior authorization (under Section 25-0 of the IDA). Employers in all establishments are required to provide one month's advance notice and severance pay equivalent to 15 days of work per year of completed service to retrench workers who have completed more than one year at the firm. These clauses impose inordinately high administrative costs of retrenching or laying off workers and of closing firms. These administrative costs are among the highest in the world (World Bank, 2006d).

In general, the numerous court decisions on labour disputes have increased uncertainty about the interpretation of these laws. For instance, Section 25-0 has been in the eye of a legal storm for nearly 50 years due to the barriers it creates for failed firms wishing to close their operations. This has raised transactions costs, created large rents in enforcing these laws, and lowered investors' confidence (Debroy, 2005; Pagés and Roy, 2006). Furthermore, enforcing the IDA has grown more unwieldy and complex, with the state governments and courts intervening more in enterprise-level disputes, raising costs and rents to regulators. This uncertainty results in the excessively long time taken to resolve labour disputes: where labour termination disputes are expected to be decided within three months, in practice many of these have been pending for as long as 10 years, with 2,000 pages of reported materials submitted for review (Khan, 2005: 90). Disputes referred to the High Courts can also lie pending for as long as 10 years (Table 4.4).

An important consequence of the costs imposed by the IDA is that firms are encouraged to remain small to stay outside the purview of the law. Interviews suggest that the medium and small-scale firms are threatened by permanent loss of business and clientele if there is a prolonged dispute. In the same vein, a recent McKinsey report on India's textile industry pointed out that Indian manufacturers often set up multiple small plants instead of a single large one to take advantage of the less demanding labour laws. As a result, Indian clothing plants typically have 10–20 per cent of the capacity of Chinese plants, and work at lower levels of efficiency (*Business Standard*, 19 February 2005). The costs also have a direct effect on employment. Chapter VB and Section 25-0 make labour effectively a fixed factor. Employers become averse to hiring more labour in their permanent complement and prefer using contract labour or casual labour. This also creates incentives for employers to choose more capital-intensive techniques, and so increasing wages instead of employment.

Restrictive labour regulations emanating from the IDA constrain production and job growth in formal manufacturing, promote the informal economy and deepen dualism. The growing empirical research on the impact of labour regulations in India highlights the costs of rigid labour regulations and reduced mobility. In one of the early works on the impact of labour regulations in India, Fallon and Lucas (1991) showed how labour demand fell significantly due to amendments to the

IDA in 1976 that made it binding on firms to seek government permission for retrenching regular workers. More recently, research focusing on the differences in labour laws between Indian states showed how states that increased the stringency of the IDA experienced a decline in formal economy manufacturing value added and employment (Besley and Burgess, 2004). In addition, Hasan *et al.* (2003) found that states with more stringent labour regulations (measured as in Besley and Burgess, 2004) have lower demand elasticities, and that these elasticities are less affected by trade reforms. A study analysing plant-level data in 40 of India's major cities (Lall and Mengistae, 2005) suggested that an inadequate investment climate—principally inadequate power supply and rigid labour laws—results in lower productivity at the plant level and lower manufacturing development in the states most affected by these laws.

A recent World Bank study (Ahsan and Pagés, 2007) also shows that manufacturing value added, employment and the number of factories are all adversely affected in states with the most restrictive labour laws. The study suggests that, overall, India has lost out on as many as 2.8 million jobs in the formal manufacturing sector as a result of the IDA *per se*. This is about 45 per cent in terms of the 6.4 millions jobs that currently exist in the formal manufacturing sector. The costs in terms of jobs were caused almost equally by the disputes part of the Act and by the retrenchment barriers clauses. However, the disputes-related regulations costs more jobs in capital-intensive industries, while the retrenchment-related regulations costs more in labour-intensive industries. States such as West Bengal, Maharashtra, Gujarat and Rajasthan have also paid a high price in terms of thousands of factories that do not exist because of IDA regulations. This is because these states have more stringent labour regulations relative to the rest of the states.

Restrictive regulations and labour laws also contribute to inequality by perpetuating dualism between the formal and informal economy. With the exception of Chapter VB of the IDA, most regulations, including labour regulations, become binding for manufacturing firms with more than 10 or 20 workers (if they do not have power) registered under the Factories Act, 1948. The impact of this is seen starkly in the fact that the overwhelming share of employment (about 75 per cent) is in firms with plant sizes below 10 workers. The bulk of the employment is therefore, in firms that remain unregistered and in the informal economy, where workers receive low wages and little protection. In contrast, fewer than 20 per cent of workers in a sample of fast-growing East Asian countries work in such small firms. More generally, Indian manufacturing-sector firms continue to show a highly bimodal size structure: the bulk of the firms are low-productivity small enterprises, while most of the others are relatively large firms with high productivity.

An important finding of the research was that, on the whole, restrictive regulations do not make formal-sector workers better off. While restrictive regulations on employment do lead to higher wages, workers are hurt by the decline in formal jobs. As a consequence, total payments to formal workers decline and the labour share (that is, the share of value added that goes to workers) does not increase. Dispute-related laws are even more costly for formal-sector workers as they reduce both employment and wages, and therefore total payments to workers (Ahsan and Pagés, 2007). Any gains in wages and working conditions are quickly eroded in a context of lack of job creation and growing labour supply. Moreover, the scarcity of formal jobs fuels income insecurity, as the event of a formal job loss is associated with a very low probability of re-employment in a similar type of job. Better regulation would enable more job creation and higher income gains for workers.

Therefore, reforms are needed. Reforming India's labour market regulations should have two main goals: first, to simplify regulations, with special emphasis on improving industrial relations, smoothing dispute resolutions and removing ambiguities and uncertainties; and second, to reduce the rigidities in labour markets. Specifically, four main types of reforms are called for:

- consolidating and simplifying labour laws, from the current 47 central laws to about four, covering the main areas of: (1) dispute resolution, (2) conditions of work and welfare, (3) wages and benefits and (4) social security;

- modernizing the IDA to reduce the bias towards adjudication in disputes and to increase flexibility for employers to hire and fire, but in a way that also protects workers' rights;
- resolving ambiguities concerning the Contract Labour (Regulation and Abolition) Act to introduce greater flexibility; and
- improving the labour law enforcement and inspection system.

4.7 Conclusions: India's employment challenges

This chapter has reviewed the developments in India's labour markets and highlighted the key employment challenges facing India. It has pointed out that the composition of employment in India has been slow to change, even while economic growth has accelerated and the economy has seen relatively significant structural changes. While the share of agricultural employment has declined, it has not been accompanied by an increase in the share of manufacturing employment. Most new jobs have been created in the informal service sector. As a result, the overwhelming majority of workers—about 90 per cent—remain in the informal economy.

The experience of the 1990s, however, suggests that wide concerns about "jobless" growth are not fully warranted. GSDP growth had significant effects on female employment in rural areas and on male earnings. A part of the decline in employment growth was clearly based on a deceleration in the supply of labour and a decline in participation. An important part of the decline in participation was voluntary; this was a result of schooling and higher household and spouse income, which enabled workers—especially female workers—to opt for housework and leisure instead of employment. Further, job growth was accompanied by productivity growth and an increase in wages. These trends and changes in the household per capita expenditures of workers, including in the self-employed sector, suggest that job quality has improved on average. Consistently, both mean and median wages grew across most sectors and states.

The experience of the 1990s and recent years, however, also points to important challenges facing India. Specifically, four important challenges lie ahead. The first, and the overarching, challenge will be to meet the demand for jobs by new entrants to the labour force. Given that 60 per cent India's population is younger than 30, India could enjoy a "demographic dividend" of some 123 million people entering the prime working age over the next decade, lowering the dependency ratio and raising growth prospects. However, such prospects will be realized only if the economy can provide productive jobs for the 80 million people—8 million per year—who are expected to seek jobs over the coming decade. Against this, the economy produced fewer than 6 million jobs per year between 1993 and 2000.

The second challenge is to improve the quality of jobs more rapidly, with a focus on improving the earnings of workers through higher productivity and lower underemployment. At present, the earnings of 102 million workers are inadequate to raise their families out of poverty. Added to this, good jobs have to be created for the new entrants to the labour force to avoid an increase in the ranks of the working poor. Especially important is the need to create good non-agricultural jobs for relatively unskilled workers in rural and urban areas. In the medium term, the focus has to be to facilitate the growth of informal-sector enterprises through facilitating credit, technology and marketing assistance. Alongside this, regulatory barriers and policies that discourage these firms from becoming formal need to be addressed so that firms can enter and benefit from the formal economy.

In particular, stimulating formal-sector employment in manufacturing has to be a key priority. Formal-sector employment growth in general has been at a standstill as relative prices and regulatory laws concerning employment raise transactions costs for producers, encouraging firms to opt for more capital- and skills-intensive products and technologies. While relative prices are likely to be self-correcting in line with changes in international and domestic economic conditions and as economic liberalization proceeds, particular attention needs to be given to addressing labour regulations that research suggests discourage job growth.

The third major challenge will thus, be to reform India's complex labour laws, whose costs are significant in terms of missed job opportunities. Conservative estimates, based on studying both *de jure* and *de facto* differences between labour regulations across states, suggest that India failed to create about 2.8 million formal manufacturing jobs due to IDA-related costs. Put another way, the two significant clauses of the Act alone cost about 45 per cent of all formal manufacturing jobs. Reforming India's labour market regulations needs to proceed along two directions. The first direction will be to simplify regulation, with special emphasis on improving industrial relations, smoothing dispute resolutions and removing ambiguities concerning labour laws. The second direction will be to reduce the rigidities in labour markets that currently discourage small- and medium-sized firms—for whom the transaction costs of rigid labour markets are onerous—from growing and increasing regular employment.

The fourth major challenge will be on the supply side, to improve education and skills of new and existing workers. At one level lies the more fundamental issue of expanding and improving secondary education and higher education so that producers can find the required skills in job seekers. Another task will be to improve vocational education and vocational training programmes for existing workers and the large number of school dropouts to give them skills that would make them attractive to producers. We have discussed some of the issues concerning this in detail in this chapter.

5 Nepal: A critical assessment of experience

Dilli Raj Khanal

5.1 Introduction

In Nepal, intensive macroeconomic policy reforms—begun in the early 1990s—have been ushered in by drastic poverty reduction goals.[1] Implicitly, economic growth has been assumed to be the main channel through which poverty reduction targets could be accomplished. High levels of investment, in turn, are regarded as being crucial for achieving higher growth rates. Although the current Tenth Plan (2002–2007), which also happens to be the Poverty Reduction Strategy Paper (PRSP) for Nepal, focuses on broad-based sustained growth, it does not include an explicit role for employment in enhancing growth or reducing poverty, despite the inclusion of various employment-related programmes.[2] Hence, poverty reduction is primarily sought through the higher investment and growth induced by macroeconomic policy reform.

In the quest for higher growth rates, since the beginning of the 1990s, Nepal has expedited economic reforms with the highest priority on policies to open up and liberalize the economy. The liberalization

1. Poverty reduction was one of the main goals of the Eighth Plan (1992–1997). Poverty reduction has been the only goal of the current Tenth Plan (2002–2007) and the Ninth Plan (1997–2002); see NPC (1992, 1997 and 2002).

2. In the plans and programmes, employment implications are projected based on estimated elasticities following an *ex-post* approach, and hence in the absence of *ex-ante* built-in analysis, they undermine the role of employment in poverty reduction. Even the spillover effect of employment on poverty reduction is hardly assessed. Also, any directly employment-related programmes that are incorporated in the plans are kept in isolation. For the Nepalese context, see ibid.

drive in India in 1991[3] and the Enhanced Structural Adjustment Facility (ESAF) programme of the International Monetary Fund (IMF) introduced in Nepal in 1992 have been instrumental for the rapid move towards economic liberalization. Now, the Poverty Reduction Growth Facility of the IMF and the Poverty Reduction Support Credit of the World Bank under the PRSP also exert influence on the nature and direction of reforms. The World Trade Organization's (WTO) commitments to fulfil the membership obligations are also pushing Nepal to pursue more "open-up" and liberalization policies.

Continuous pursuance of reform has enabled Nepal to become one of the most liberalized countries in the South Asia region (HMGN, 2004; Khanal, 2006a). The average tariff rate is now below 10 per cent. The Nepalese currency is fully convertible in the current account. In the large and medium industries, 100 per cent foreign equity participation is permissible, with no restrictions on repatriation of invested funds. There is no entry barrier to foreign investors in the financial sector. Almost all forms of subsidy have been abolished. Despite a fixed exchange rate with India, hard currency exchange rates are market determined. This is also true for interest rates. An important feature of the ongoing reforms in Nepal is that deregulation and macroeconomic stabilization have the highest priority.[4]

The rapid reforms were accompanied by fast growth in the Nepalese economy, especially during the first half of the 1990s. The growth rate was about 5 per cent on average during the Ninth Plan (1992–1997) period (NPC, 2002). There was a commensurate change in the structure of the economy, resulting in a sharp fall in the share of agricultural value added. Simultaneously, a big change in the employment structure took place in the economy. But such a momentum of growth could not be sustained for long. Some studies have tried to find out the underlying

---

3. Nepal maintains special trade relations with India in which primary products are traded freely. The applied tariff rates for manufactured products are also low compared with tariff rates for similar products from third countries. Indian currency is freely convertible in the Nepalese market. There are also no border restrictions and hence, people can move freely. As a result of all these, Nepal's macroeconomic policies are highly influenced by the policies pursued by India.

4. For features and sequencing of reforms, see UNDP (2004a) and Khanal *et al.* (2005).

reasons for this. A study examining Nepal's reforms from political economy and institutional perspectives concluded that policy coordination and proper sequencing were major problems in the course of the reforms.[5]

On the one hand, the major macroeconomic policies were implemented based on multilateral donors' policy conditions and hence, stakeholders were hardly consulted in the reform process. This was particularly true in case of voiceless and unorganized people or stakeholders. Major policy decisions were never discussed, even in Parliament, on a priority basis. Absence of policy coordination had a direct effect on the sequencing of policy reforms. The priority given to deregulation through subsidy withdrawal or abolition of administered prices and rapid opening-up policies became possible in the absence of strong resistance or opposing voices.

On the other hand, less priority was given to the structural and institutional reform aspects as a result of a growing nexus between the rulers at the highest political level and unethical segments in the business community. This was the reason for delay in the reforms in those areas which were perceived to be hurting these parties' interests. A deepening crisis in the financial sector and unprecedented rises in the costs of public utilities and infrastructure services were outcomes of this. A few commodity concentrated exports,[6] asymmetry in the deregulation policies in the agriculture sector,[7] low or declining productivity and competitiveness of trade and industry[8] and low or decreased access to the credit are some of the additional reasons pointed out by the studies. Similarly, the policy of perpetuating low levels of macro equilibrium through fiscal and monetary tightening[9] has also

5. These issues are discussed at length in Khanal *et al.* (2005).

6. Some partial analysis on those lines is found in UNDP (2004a) and Khanal *et al.* (2005).

7. See Khanal (2004) for detailed arguments.

8. A study carried out by the World Bank to assess the technical assistance requirement in the process of accession to WTO indicates that because of many macro policy gaps, these problems have either persisted or aggravated. For this, see HMGN (2004).

9. These issues are discussed in Khanal *et al.* (2005).

been found to have been detrimental to sustained growth and development. To maintain macroeconomic stability, as a part of donor conditions, the level of government expenditure was contained by curtailing the amount of development expenditure rather than by controlling recurring expenses. This resulted in small savings as well as low investment at the aggregate level.

The deceleration in the growth rate that started in the late 1990s led to a negative growth rate being registered in 2002. Recovery from such a downturn has yet to take place, with the growth rate still hovering around 2 per cent (MoF, 2006a). As would be expected, this has had a very adverse effect on the employment structure. The available information shows that both unemployment and underemployment remain major problems in Nepal.[10] There are two worrying phenomena in the Nepalese labour market. First, out of the total unemployment the proportions of youth unemployment in general and educated unemployment in particular are relatively high.[11] Second, the existing structural problem in the labour market has become aggravated as a result of a predominance of informal employment in the total employment. The share of informal employment is estimated to be as high as 94 per cent (UNDP, 2004a).

One of the positive aspects of the ongoing reforms is that poverty reduced considerably in Nepal during the period 1996–2004. The level of poverty was 42 per cent in 1995/96 but went down to 31 per cent in 2003/04; an 11 per cent decline in less than a decade (CBS, 2004a). A

10. However, in terms of definition and estimates, a large variation is found: very low unemployment rates have been reported by the Nepal Labour Force Survey (CBS, 1999) and the Nepal Living Standard Surveys (CBS, 1996b and 2004b). Periodic plans have therefore, attempted to make relatively more realistic estimates. Accordingly, estimates in the Ninth Plan show that unemployment and underemployment were about 5 and 47 per cent respectively in 1992. The Tenth Plan, after adjusting for underemployment, has derived an unemployment rate at 17.4 per cent for the year 2002.

11. A comparison of unemployment figures by age and education level indicates that against the average unemployment of 4.9 per cent in 1996, the unemployment among the age group of 15–24 was 14.7 per cent. For 2004, these figures were 3.8 and 12.1 per cent respectively. More importantly, the unemployment rate among the educated (above class 10) was 9 per cent in 1996 and went up to reach 9.4 per cent in 2004 (CBS, 1996b and 2004b).

drastically reduced poverty rate amidst the stagnating employment pattern and worsening employment in some sectors in recent years apparently shows there is no strong link between the two. However, an estimation based on Nepal Living Standard Survey (NLSS) panel data shows that poverty would have declined by 4.8 per cent instead of 11 per cent had remittances remained unchanged between the period 1996–2004 (CBS, 2006). This means that the massive expansion in foreign employment during the period 1996–2004 made the poverty reduction possible (ibid.). The ratio of income from remittances to total gross domestic product (GDP) has since gone up to 16–17 per cent (MoF, 2006a). A study shows that as a result of the rapid increase in the share of remittances income in private consumption and goods imports (14.6 and 41.8 per cent respectively[12]), the shocks-led deceleration in economic growth rate was to a greater extent halted (Khanal and Kanel, 2005). Conversely, the investment to GDP ratio indicates that no perceptible increase in the level of investment took place during the period 1996–2004. The investment to GDP ratio reached 26.4 per cent in 2004 from 25.2 per cent in 1995, with some downward oscillation in the intervening period (MoF, 2006a).

In summary, there are four discernible trends that may be regarded to be less conducive from the standpoint of sustaining poverty reduction. First, despite reduction in the level of poverty, the incidence of poverty among disadvantaged and marginalized people has remained very high, and more so among the people living in the remote areas or underdeveloped regions. Second, income inequality increased markedly during the same period. The Gini-coefficient, which was 0.34 in 1996, increased to 0.41 in 2004 (CBS, 2006). In view of the inequality coefficient reflecting, among other things, the inequitable distribution of benefits and opportunities during the process of intensive reforms, this trend is a major cause of concern from a policy point of view. Third, the decreased poverty has been found to be mainly associated with massive inflow of remittances income rather than with reform-induced growth or income-earning opportunities, as pointed out above. Fourth, despite

12. For 2005/06, the shares of remittances income in consumption and goods imports are 19 and 56 per cent respectively (NRB, 2006a).

foreign employment playing a decisive role in the reduction of poverty, the remittances income was primarily used for consumption purposes and hence, contributed very little to expanding investment or enhancing productive employment internally, preconditions for sustained growth and poverty reduction.

Against this background, this chapter tries to assess the macro policy induced linkages between growth, investment and employment in the Nepalese economy. Closer examination of the relationships between macroeconomic policies and growth, investment and decent employment is extremely important in view of growing evidence of "jobless" growth in many developing countries. There is also growing apprehension about the effectiveness of PRSPs and the Millennium Development Goals (MDGs) in reducing poverty, especially in view of the lack of explicit employment-enhancing policies in these programmes. These aspects have also been dealt with. In the following section, growth and employment trends are examined by comparing the pre- and post-liberalization periods. In the same section, employment elasticities and labour productivity trends are also presented and analysed to assess the likely effects of macro policy reforms. The third section critically examines the main features of macroeconomic policies in general, and trade, financial and investment policies in particular, from the standpoint of their role in enhancing employment opportunities. The final section is devoted to deriving major conclusions and policy implications.

5.2 Growth performance and employment patterns

Overall and sectoral growth performance

A trend analysis of the growth rate shows a marked difference between the pre- and post-liberalization periods. During the second half of 1980s, when the structural adjustment programme was implemented, GDP grew at a rate of 4.6 per cent on average, with 4.1 per cent agricultural and 5.0 per cent non-agricultural growth rates. Good monsoons and expansion of cultivated area were major contributors to the relatively high growth rate in the agriculture sector. Among the non-agriculture sectors, electricity supply grew at a high rate of 8.6 per cent owing to completion of a new power plant. Construction and manufacturing were the next fastest growing sectors (5.4 per cent).

During the first five years of intensive liberalization, the average growth rate was high, at 4.9 per cent. Growth in the non-agriculture sector was remarkable, with the growth rate reaching 10 per cent on average. Over this period, the growth in the agriculture sector was negative, primarily due to adverse weather conditions (Table 5.1). This means that had there been positive growth in the agriculture sector, the average growth rate would have been even higher. During this period, growth in the electricity and manufacturing sectors in particular was very high. The rest of the non-agriculture sectors also grew at a relatively rapid rate. A rapid expansion in the private sector activities taking place in the manufacturing, trade, transport, finance and real estate sectors in the aftermath of market-oriented reforms enabled accelerated growth in the non-agriculture sector.

Table 5.1

Sectoral growth rates, 1985–2005

(percentage)

Sectors	*1985–1990*	*1990–1995*	*1995–2000*	*2000–2005*
Agriculture	4.1	-0.2	2.8	2.8
Mining	4.2	7.9	3.4	1.6
Manufacturing	5.4	13.0	5.6	-1.3
Electricity	8.6	23.0	9.0	7.9
Construction	5.4	8.5	4.6	1.8
Trade	4.9	6.6	6.1	-1.4
Transport	3.6	7.5	9.2	4.6
Finance and real estate	5.1	5.8	6.4	3.7
Community and social services	3.0	7.3	6.1	3.0
Non-agriculture	5.0	10.0	6.3	2.5
GDP	4.6	4.9	4.5	2.7

Source: MOF (2000, 2001, 2002, 2003, 2004 and 2005a).

However, such a growth momentum could not continue for long. Aside from the worsening security situation and the triggering of political instability, the reforms were far from adequate to ensure sustainability of the growth rate (Khanal *et al.*, 2005). Although subsidies were withdrawn, structural and institutional reforms were not carried out in the agriculture sector, a sector key for maintaining high growth in the Nepalese economy. Financial sector liberalization was not accompanied by policies that could help to enhance the institutional or regulatory capacity of the financial institutions. Structural impediments hurting the interest of small businesses or enterprises were not priority areas of reforms. There was negligence in the institutional or governance-related reforms in the public utility and infrastructure sectors. In these areas, the policy thrust was on the intensification of deregulation, including frequent raising of administered prices. In the absence of broad-based reforms and with the exclusion of many areas from the orbit of reforms, the growth rate decelerated sharply during the period 2000-2005. The decelerating effect was particularly severe in the manufacturing and trade sectors. Some deceleration in growth took place in the finance and real estate sectors as well. Interestingly, the potential sharp downturn in the average growth rate was halted by the agriculture sector, which grew moderately as a result of good weather conditions. The fluctuating trend in the growth rate also had some effect on the speed of structural change in the economy.

During the period 1985–1990, only marginal changes in the structure of the economy took place (Table 5.2). The contribution of agriculture to the total GDP fell to 50.6 per cent in 1990, from 51.2 per cent in 1985. Correspondingly, a minor change occurred within the non-agriculture sector. The manufacturing sector's contribution increased to 6 per cent from 5.7 per cent during the same period. Almost a similar pattern is observed in the trade and construction sectors. During the initial years of the intensive reforms, structural shifts were very rapid. The share of agriculture in total GDP dropped by almost 10 percentage points during the period 1990–1995. There was a big surge in the contribution of the manufacturing sector, as its share reached 9.3 per cent from 6 per cent in 1990. Some increase in the contribution of the construction, trade, transport, community and personal services sectors also took place during this period. The better export opportunities enjoyed by the export-oriented industries until the mid-1990s had very positive effects on the structural shift. This momentum could not, however, be maintained for long due to a number of reasons, as described above.

Table 5.2

Sectoral contributions to GDP, 1985–2005

(percentage)

S.N.	*Descriptions*	*1985*	*1990*	*1995*	*2000*	*2005*
1	Agriculture	51.21	50.62	40.75	39.62	38.21
2	Mining	0.43	0.45	0.53	0.49	0.49
3	Manufacturing	5.65	5.97	9.31	9.16	7.72
4	Electricity	0.41	0.52	1.36	1.62	2.33
5	Construction	8.46	8.96	10.99	10.20	10.40
6	Trade	10.26	10.53	11.58	11.71	9.86
7	Transport	6.02	5.74	6.66	8.01	9.57
8	Finance and real estate	8.97	9.29	9.77	10.08	11.46
9	Community and social services	8.55	7.88	9.01	9.08	9.91
10	Non-agriculture GDP	48.78	49.37	59.24	60.37	61.78
11	Agriculture GDP	51.21	50.62	40.75	39.62	38.21
12	**Total GDP at factor cost**	**100.00**	**100.00**	**100.00**	**100.00**	**100.00**

Source: Same as Table 5.1.

After 1995, the shift away from agriculture toward non-agriculture was negligible, and even the shift within the non-agriculture sector was not as expected. The share of the manufacturing sector in total GDP reduced more sharply after 2000, and reached 7.7 per cent in 2005 from 9.3 per cent in 1995. Slightly a different trend is observed in the trade sector. The share of trade in GDP started declining only after 2000, and fell to 9.9 per cent in 2005 from 11.7 per cent in 2000. Interestingly, the share of finance and real estate has continuously increased, reaching 11.5 per cent in 2005 from about 9 per cent in 1985.

The sectoral growth trends reveal some possible ramifications from employment and poverty perspectives. First, during the period of intensive reforms, the agriculture sector was relatively neglected. As will be explained later, the agriculture sector's share of government development expenditure has reduced drastically in recent years. Such a reduction was in contrast to the Government's commitments to implement a long-term agriculture sector perspective plan. The plan emphasized the need to formulate and implement an integrated investment plan by incorporating road, electricity, irrigation, inputs and technology components as part and parcel of the plan. In the Nepalese context, the agriculture sector is considered to be a sector that has big potential for ensuring a sustained high growth rate, generating more employment opportunities and thereby, reducing poverty.[13] Even within the non-agriculture sector, capital-intensive sectors such as electricity and transport[14] grew at a faster rate, as evident from the Tables 5.1 and 5.2. Despite trade and industry being the engines of growth in the liberalized regime, both these sectors, after some pick up in the initial phase of intensive reforms, either sharply decelerated or stagnated.[15]

Growth and pattern of employment

Both aggregate and sectoral growth patterns had strong effects on the level and structure of employment. Along with the rapid change in the economic structure, a shift in the employment pattern also took place in the country (Table 5.3). In 1981 as much as 91.1 per cent of the active population was engaged in agriculture and related activities. This gradually decreased to 81.2 per cent in 1991. Changes in the employment structure were phenomenal during the period 1991–2001. During this period, employment in the agriculture sector reduced to 65.7 per cent. This was due in particular to the high rate of labour absorption by the manufacturing and trade sectors. A limited number of people were absorbed by these sectors in 1981. In 1991 the employment in these sectors increased to 2.1 and 3.5 per cent respectively. There was high rate of labour absorption between 1991 and 2001 in these sectors.

13. The Agriculture Sector Perspective Plan prepared under the guidance of Professor John Mellor shows that there is rich bio-diversity and a lot of potential for commercialization of farms, through crop diversification in *terai*, and development of horticulture in hills. These will have some spillover effects on agro- and forestry-based industries, and will not only lead to enhanced growth and productive employment in agriculture, but will also contribute to pushing the non-agriculture sector growth rate by more than 1.5 per cent. For details, see HMGN (1997).

14. Incremental capital output ratios for electricity and transport are 16.4:1 and 8.8:1, compared with 2.6:1 and 2.1:1 for industry and trade respectively (NPC, 2002). Likewise, if sectors such as trade and industry are expanded or grow rapidly, they would have more wide-ranging spillover effects on the economy. Therefore, these sectors are often said to be engines of growth. At the same time, they are employment enhancing in comparison with electricity and transport.

15. The underlying reasons are discussed at length in the policy review section (Section 5.3).

In 2001, they absorbed 9 and 9.9 per cent of the economically active population respectively. A gradual expansion of employment also took place in the finance and business services sectors over this period. In 1981, only 0.1 per cent of the economically active population was engaged in this sector. The contribution of this sector to total employment reached 0.8 per cent in 2001.

Table 5.3

Employment by industry, 1981–2001

Industrial group	*1981*	*Share in total*	*1991*	*Share in total*	*2001*	*Share in total*
Total	6 850 886	100.0	7 339 586	100.0	9 900 198	100.0
Agriculture.	6 244 289	91.1	5 961 788	81.2	6 504 689	65.7
Mining and manufacturing	971	0.0	152 418	2.1	888 301	9.0
Electricity, gas and water	33 029	0.5	11 734	0.2	148 218	1.5
Construction	3013	0.0	35 658	0.5	286 418	2.9
Commerce	2022	0.0	256 012	3.5	984 662	9.9
Transport and communication	109 446	1.6	50 808	0.7	161 638	1.6
Finance and business services	7424	0.1	20 847	0.3	76 687	0.8
Personal and community services	9850	0.1	752 019	10.2	663 737	6.7
Others	31 3570	4.6	28 004	0.4	163 412	1.7
Industry not stated	127 272	1.9	70 298	1.0	22 395	0.2

Source: CBS, Population Census 1971, 1981, 1991 and 2001.

Despite the big shift in the employment structure, the pattern conceals some serious structural problems persisting in the Nepalese labour market. It neither shows the actual employment phenomenon nor reveals the severity of problems in the labour market in terms of gainful employment opportunities. Although the ratio of self-employed to total employed reduced to 62.7 per cent in 2001 from 85.5 per cent in 1981, this was possible due to a jump in the share of "employees". Their share rose to 24.6 per cent from 9.1 per cent during the same period (Table 5.4). Had the increase in the share of employees taken place as a result of a reduction in the share of informal employment, this would have helped to enhance gainful employment opportunities and minimize the structural problems in the labour market to a greater extent. This did not happen. Thus, the shift in the employment structure did not reduce decent work deficits, since it was unaccompanied by a perceptible reduction in the share of informal employment.

Table 5.4

Economically active population 10 years of age and over, by employment status

Area, sex and age groups	*Total economically active*	*Employment status*				
		Employer	*Employee*	*Self-employed*	*Unpaid family workers*	*Not stated*
1981	6 850 886	46 968	621 432	5 860 419	172 789	149 278
Share in total		0.7	9.1	85.5	2.5	2.2
1991	7 339 586	41 455	1 571 300	5 522 827	171 631	32 373
Share in total		0.56	21.41	75.25	2.34	0.44
2001	9 900 198	376 349	2 438 328	6 210 841	874 678	
Share in total		3.80	24.63	62.73	8.83	0.00

Source: Same as Table 5.3.

As revealed by the Labour Force Survey (CBS, 1999), the above numbers conceal various dimensions of the structural problems perpetuating in this area (Table 5.5). First of all, out of the total self-employed, 78 per cent were engaged in agriculture-related work. Among them, 43.3 per cent were engaged in own-family work without any pay. This is persisting at a time when underemployment in the agriculture sector is still very high, at about 32.3 per cent. The Labour Force Survey of 1998/99 further revealed that out of the total labour force, 76.1 per cent[16] were still engaged in the agriculture sector. Similarly, of the 23.9 per cent labour force in the non-agriculture sector, 73.3 per cent were engaged in the informal economy. Assuming that the entire agriculture sector is in the informal economy, the job ratio in the formal economy works out at a mere 6.4 per cent. In the informal non-agriculture sector also, the ratio of rural labour force is as high as 77.4 per cent.

16. Unlike the population census, the Labour Force Survey shows a higher dependency on the agriculture sector. This is because the survey is based on labour-force criteria as opposed to the economically active population criteria used in the population census.

Table 5.5

Workers aged 15 years and above employed in agriculture and non-agriculture sectors (both formal and informal)

(thousands)

Formal/Informal	*Total*	*Legislative, senior officials*	*Professional*	*Technical*	*Clerks*	*Services work*	*Agriculture work*	*Craft and related trade work*	*Plant and machine operators*	*Elementary occupations*[1]	*Armed forces*
Total	**9463**										
Agriculture	7203										
Share of agriculture in total (%)	76.1										
Non-agricultural sector	2260	12	37	203	106	487	13	556	102	739	5
Share of non-agricultural in total (%)	23.9										
Share in non-agricultural sector (%)	100	0.5	1.6	9	4.7	21.5	0.6	24.6	4.5	32.7	0.2
Formal sector jobs	603	7	33	163	102	30	2	59	42	161	5
Share of formal sector jobs (%)	26.7	0.3	1.5	7.2	4.5	1.3	0.1	2.6	1.9	7.1	0.2
Informal sector jobs	1657	5	4	40	4	457	11	497	60	578	0
Share of informal sector jobs (%)	73.3	44.7	10.8	19.9	3.9	93.7	86.3	89.3	59.5	78.2	0
Urban	375	4	3	16	3	0	1	103	14	72	0
Urban (%)	22.6	80	75	40	75	0	9.1	20.7	23.3	12.5	0
Rural	1282	1	1	24	2	4	5	394	46	506	0
Rural (%)	77.4	20	25	60	50	0.9	45.5	79.3	76.7	87.5	0

Note: [1] Elementary occupations include street vendors, shoe cleaning, cleaners, building caretakers, porters, garbage collectors, fetching water, collecting firewood etc.

Source: CBS, 1999.

Some studies show that the situation in the informal labour market is worse. About two-thirds of the workers in the informal economy do not receive any kind of training whatsoever from any organization. The ownership pattern in the informal economy is dominated by male proprietorship (87 per cent). About 70 per cent of informal sector workers work 12 hours a day and earn in the range of Rs. 1,000–3,000 per month (Mainali *et al.*, 2002). This sector neither guarantees job security nor allows any collective bargaining power to the workers when fixing wage rates. At the same time, wage differentials between the male and female workers are high (ILO, 2002). Although improvements in wage levels have been reported by the latest survey, the deeper analysis of survey findings indicates widening wage differentials between the skilled and unskilled workers, including reduced wages of the urban non-agriculture unskilled workers. Real wages of the non-agriculture unskilled workers reduced by 6 per cent against a more than two-fold increase in the real wages of skilled workers during the period 1996–2004. In informal agriculture also, the share of wage income of the poor workers reduced considerably during the same period despite increases in average real wages (CBS, 2006).

Employment elasticity and labour productivity

To examine the changing pattern of employment elasticities, especially in the post-liberalization period, employment elasticities were estimated for the periods 1981–1990 (pre-liberalization period), 1990–2005 (a period of intensive liberalization) and 1981–2005. The results are reported in Table 5.6.

Table 5.6

Employment elasticities, 1981–2005

Sector	*1981–2005*	*1981–1990*	*1990–2005*
Agriculture	0.056	–0.075	0.124
Industry (manufacturing)	1.380	1.197	1.778
Services	0.561	0.626	0.538
Total[1]	**0.228**	**0.081**	**0.363**

Note: [1] Total = changes in employment to changes in total value added together in percentage terms.
Source: Author's estimates.

The coefficients reveal that only in the manufacturing sector has employment elasticity increased considerably, and more significantly that the increase mainly occurred during the period of intensive liberalization. There was also an incremental trend in the agriculture sector; despite a negative coefficient for the period 1981–1990, a positive coefficient was obtained for the period 1990–2005, although the coefficient was still very low.[17] More worryingly, not only was the elasticity for the service sector low for the entire period under consideration, it has also gone down steadily in recent years. Above all, despite some incremental increase, the overall elasticity is still very low. If the elasticity is any indication, this shows that growth in employment is not commensurate with growth in the economy.[18]

A very interesting trend is shown by the labour productivity figures (Table 5.7). A noteworthy aspect is that both elasticity and productivity in the agriculture sector went up simultaneously after 1990, indicating no trade-off problems between the two in this sector.[19] Conversely, productivity in the manufacturing and service sectors shows a different trend. In manufacturing, labour productivity decreased continuously after 1981 in contrast to increasing employment elasticity. In services, reduction in employment elasticity was accompanied by an increase in labour productivity, but only up to 2000. Thereafter, the productivity also started declining.

17. These are only indicative trends. The average coefficients of the relatively long periods cannot adequately represent more recent decreases in the employment pattern. Since the Ordinary Least Square (OLS) technique was used for the analysis, the estimates might include some upward bias and so may need further verification using more advanced techniques.

18. Conversely, increased workforce participation and decreased unemployment rates over time indicate that there might not be any jobless growth in Nepal. This would, however, need substantiation. It would be necessary to take into account the structural problems of the Nepalese labour market and give due consideration to the massive outflow of workers and the informalization of the labour market, including the shift of the workforce toward self-employment in both the agriculture and services sectors. At the same time, there is also a growing tendency towards policy-induced capital intensification in enterprises and firms. These various factors together with employment elasticities suggest the possibility of a weak linkage between economic growth and employment in Nepal.

19. The positive elasticity in agriculture after 1990 has made this possible. At the same time, it should not be forgotten that the agriculture sector growth performance is largely influenced by the weather or monsoon conditions.

Table 5.7

Labour productivity (value added per worker), 1981–2005

(at 1980 prices in Nepalese rupees)

Sector	*1981*	*1990*	*2000*	*2005*
Agriculture	2484	4202	8089	9621
Industry (manufacturing)	29 919	21 566	14 117	6094
Services	12 429	18 117	40 191	32 335
Total[1]	**3458**	**6716**	**14 512**	**14 309**

Note: [1] Total = labour value added at the aggregate level.

Source: Author's calculations.

Differences in labour force participation rates between males and females, rural and urban areas and various age groups reveal some underlying reasons for such a state of affairs. As shown in Table 5.8, the labour force participation rate has increased considerably during the period 1996–2004 among all age groups. This is true among both literate and illiterate people. The NLSS further shows that participation rate among males is higher (80.4 per cent) than among females (74.4 per cent). Likewise, the participation rate in rural areas is very high (80.2 per cent) compared with the urban areas (62.4 per cent) (CBS, 2004a). The increased labour force participation rate together with a marginal decline in the unemployment rate during the period 1996–2004 and the predominance of informal employment had an adverse effect on labour productivity in both the industry and service sectors.

Although available data do not help much when examining the relationship between labour productivity and wage earnings, the NLSS gives some idea on this. In 1996, the share of agriculture in wage employment was 53 per cent, and it went down to 37 per cent in 2004. Conversely, the share of manufacturing, construction and personal services increased to 24, 35 and 26 per cent respectively in 2004, from 21, 30 and 25 per cent in 1996. During the same period, the nominal daily wages in the agriculture and non-agriculture sectors increased to Rs. 75 and Rs. 133 respectively, from Rs. 40 and Rs. 74. However, when the wage levels for males and females are examined, a large gap is observed. In the agriculture sector, the female wage level was Rs. 65 as opposed to the male wage level of Rs. 85. In the urban areas, the wage gap was even higher, Rs. 137 for males and Rs. 101 for females (CBS,

Table 5.8

Participation rate and employment by age group and educational level, 1996 and 2004

(percentage)

	Employed		*Unemployed*		*Participation rate*		*Unemployment rate*[1]	
	2004	*1996*	*2004*	*1996*	*2004*	*1996*	*2004*	*1996*
Age group								
10–14	50.1	35.5	1.8	3.1	51.8	38.6	3.4	7.9
15–19	67.7	61.2	4.1	4.5	71.8	65.7	5.7	6.9
20–24	77.8	73.2	5.3	6.2	83.1	79.4	6.4	7.8
25–44	88.3	85.4	3.3	3.5	91.6	88.9	3.6	4
45–59	86.3	80.5	1.6	2.4	87.9	82.9	1.9	2.9
60+	60.7	49.3	1.1	0.5	61.9	50	1.7	1.3
Educational attainment								
Illiterate	79.9	73.5	2.2	3.3	82.1	76.8	2.7	4.3
School-literate	71.5	54.9	2.0	1.5	73.5	56.4	2.7	2.6
Class 03–05	67.1	55.2	2.4	3.5	69.5	58.6	3.5	5.9
Class 06–10	69.9	60.8	3.4	4.4	73.3	65.2	4.6	6.8
Above class 10	72.4	68.4	7.5	6.8	79.9	75.2	9.4	9
Nepal	74.3	67.2	2.9	3.4	77.2	70.6	3.8	4.9

Note: [1] Unemployment rate is the ratio between unemployed and participation rate.

Source: CBS, 1996b, 2004b.

2004a). The low wage level together with the gap between the male and female levels amidst a declining trend in the real wage levels of unskilled workers might have contributed to the reduction in labour productivity in the non-agriculture sector.

When a comparison between real wages and labour productivity is made, a converging trend in the agriculture sector and a diverging trend in the non-agriculture sector are found. In the agriculture sector, both real wages and labour productivity have increased in recent years, in contrast to decline in labour productivity and increase in real wages in the manufacturing and service sectors (CBS, 2006). This means that in these sectors, the labour productivity declined while the labour costs increased.

An additional analysis based on the NLSS is an examination of the pattern of workers' wage share of value added together with trends in employment or employment status, labour productivity and real wage rates. This analysis indicates possible reasons for the weak linkages between employment and growth rates, and reasons for the rising income inequality. During the period 1996–2004, there was some shift in the pattern of employment. Both in urban and rural areas, unskilled agricultural workers moved to self-employment.[20] At the same time, despite some reduction in the share of unskilled non-agricultural workers in the urban areas followed by a marginal increase in the share of skilled workers, the unskilled non-agricultural workers' share in the rural areas remained unchanged (12.7 per cent) during the same period. Overall, in addition to further informalization in the labour market, there was also some reduction in the share of wage earners in the total average household income (ibid., 2006). The decrease in the real wages of the unskilled non-agricultural workers in the urban areas together with a drastic reduction in the share of agriculture workers in both areas contributed to this. These trends clearly indicate that expansion in formal jobs accompanied by an increased share of skilled workers in the labour market would have a growth-enhancing impact. The phenomenal rise in the real wages of skilled workers partly corroborates this.

In the absence of detailed information on the share of wages in total value added or national income, it is difficult to gauge the income distribution implications of employment and wage patterns. However, the NLSS and the manufacturing census results provide some insights. The NLSS shows that out of the total household average income, the share of agriculture wage income decreased to 5.4 per cent in 2004 from 9.3 per cent in 1996. Although the share of non-agriculture wage income increased to 18.6 per cent from 14.1 per cent during the same period, the average share of wage income almost stagnated (from 23.5 per cent in 1996 to 24 per cent in 2004) (ibid., 2006). Moreover, as the increment in the non-agriculture wage share was primarily due to sharp jump in the real wages of skilled workers, the trend indicates worsening income inequality among the vulnerable wage earners during the period of

20. From 13.8 per cent urban male and 42.7 per cent urban female workers in 1996 to 19.9 per cent male and 51.8 per cent female workers in 2004 and from 60.8 per cent rural male and 82.4 per cent rural female workers in 1996 to 64.9 and 85.4 per cent male and female workers respectively in 2004.

intensive reforms. The manufacturing census results further reveal that the share of wages and salaries in the total manufacturing value added reduced to 19.6 per cent in 2002, from 24.5 per cent in 2004 (CBS, 1992, 2002a). All these trends indicate that for enhancing growth with equity, employment policy should be a major constituent of macroeconomic policy reforms.

Thus, the information available from different sources, together with estimates made on employment elasticity as well as labour productivity, indicates that there are serious structural and other problems in the Nepalese labour market. The predominance of the informal market with increased informalization tendencies and declining labour productivity in modern sectors, coupled with increased labour costs in hiring skilled labour in the formal labour market, make the problem serious and challenging. Further, challenges are visualized when the labour market is considered from the perspective of decent employment. Although the Labour Law of 1992 has some provisions in relation to social protection and labour standards, these are only applicable to enterprises that hire 10 or more workers. Consequently, as much as 94 per cent of the labour force does not come within the ambit of the labour law. This means that social protection and labour standards, so critically important from a decent employment point of view, are a serious problem in the Nepalese labour market. Moreover, there is also a problem in the enforcement of labour law. Often, enterprises use different means to avoid compliance with labour law. There is also a competing voice from the organized sector saying that a rigid labour law restricting hiring and firing rights is hampering growth and the productivity of enterprises. Against this background, macro policies and their impact on decent employment becomes crucial for future policy perspectives.

5.3 Macroeconomic policies and decent employment in Nepal

Macroeconomic policies linkages: An overview

In general, macroeconomic policies are expected to enhance investment and growth. There is also an implicit assumption that higher growth would, in turn, have positive impacts on poverty. But the country experiences show that the relationships are not straightforward. The different channels or transmission mechanisms through which growth is accomplished have different impacts on poverty (Pasha and Palanivel, 2004). If productive employment is the principal source of income, expansion in gainful employment opportunities would have positive impacts on both growth and poverty reduction. This might be called the "employment nexus" between growth and poverty.[21] Productive employment, in turn, is influenced by the sectoral composition of investment and growth, the choice of technology and the degree of effective functioning of the labour market. If economic activities are concentrated in sectors in which most of the poor work, then this is likely to have a positive impact on broad-based growth and poverty reduction.

There is also a substantial body of literature that argues that it is not only the overall growth that matters for poverty reduction, but also that the pattern of growth matters equally (Ravallion, 2001). Similarly, the net impact of trade liberalization and openness on employment opportunities depends on how far in the process employment is gained or lost while shifting resources from the non-tradable to the tradable sectors. Although many studies show a strong positive link between growth, employment and poverty, the findings are still inconclusive.[22]

---

21. Unfortunately, the growth–employment–poverty linkage does not find much mention in the literature on the pro-poor debate; see Pasha and Palanivel (2004).

22. There is a growing body of literature (for instance Frenkel and Romer, 1999; Dollar and Kraay, 2001; Bhagwati and Srinivasan, 1999) which, based on empirical studies, argues that trade liberalization in addition to an accelerating growth rate brings about industrial transformation, changes in the structure of employment and a decline in poverty. However, some studies reveal that there is no conclusive evidence of trade-induced productivity gains, bigger intra-industry reallocation of resources among import-competing industries or even efficiency gains or spillover effects in developing countries. Although generally gains in skill intensity are apparent in developing countries, they have been outstripped by welfare losses owing to unskilled job losses and wage vulnerability (Epitaru, 2003). The wage gap and displacement of unskilled labour caused by trade liberalization has been a major area of concern in many countries. For an intensive study of Latin America on these lines, see Perry and Olearraga (2006). For an excellent review on trade and poverty linkages, see Winters *et al.* (2002).

Moreover, unless exchange rate policy is made sufficiently flexible to become compatible with trade liberalization, the positive impacts of trade liberalization may be outstripped by the negative effects emanating from a rigid exchange rate regime.[23]

In recent years, there has been increased emphasis on service sector liberalization as well. It is argued that in view of financial services being inputs in the production process, financial sector liberalization or reform is necessary for efficiency in production and sustained high growth. Following McKinnon (1975) and Shaw (1973), financial market liberalization is considered a prerequisite for efficient investment and higher economic growth. In this respect also, no conclusive evidence is found. If foreign participation merely substitutes for domestic factors and the sector does not expand (i.e., the degree of competition remains unchanged), then there may not be a positive growth impact on account of the scale effect. In general, the employment effect of financial sector liberalization is ambiguous. If foreign banks concentrate on serving larger companies, this may worsen access to credit for small and medium-sized companies and so have a very adverse employment effect.[24]

The investment policy of the Government is also critical in enhancing productive employment and promoting pro-poor growth. If public expenditure is simply cut to reduce a fiscal deficit or maintain macroeconomic stability, this may have strong negative impact on both growth and employment. The slowdown would be even more pervasive if private investment were also to be adversely affected, as demonstrated by the policies pursued by the East Asian countries in the aftermath of crisis (Pasha and Palanivel, 2004). Different country experiences based on different theoretical underpinnings and empirical findings reveal that country-specific macro policy design or directions and their coherence are critically important for making growth and decent employment mutually inclusive.

---

23. For such arguments based on empirical findings, see Gunter *et al.* (2005).

24. For such findings, see Clarke *et al.* (2001) and Mattoo *et al.* (2001).

Some specific macro polices and their roles in enhancing decent employment

In Nepal, some systematic policy initiatives in trade and other macroeconomic areas were started only after the inception of the planning system in 1956. As evident from plan documents and other government policy pronouncements,[25] both trade and industrial policy regimes were guided by the state-led development strategy. As an offshoot, import substitution policies formed the building block of the trade and industrial policies. The banking system was either run or controlled by the state. Apart from dictating the economic activities in the private sector, the state was also involved in establishing and running enterprises. Under the restrictive trade regime, smuggling, lobbying, evasion of tariffs and building of plants with excess capacity in order to obtain import licences became commonplace. In addition to diversion of resources to unproductive areas, the interventionist policies also led to enhanced anti-export biases.

The short-sighted policies guided by mobilization of resources through encouraging trade depletion for political expediency hindered development of both trade and industry. Such a policy regime also limited employment in the protected public sector. Only after the deepening of the foreign exchange crisis in the early 1980s was Nepal compelled to embark upon liberal policies. More opening-up and liberalization policies were introduced and intensified after the restoration of democracy in 1990. Relatively low tariff rates, removal of almost all types of non-tariff trade restrictions and barriers as well as elimination of trade-distorting interventionist policies and introduction of relatively flexible exchange rate policy have made Nepal one of the most highly liberalized countries in South Asia. On domestic fronts also most of the macroeconomic policies have been liberalized, with a focus on deregulation, market orientation and economic stabilization. With WTO membership in April 2004, Nepal is engaged in further liberalizing trade and in creating appropriate legal, institutional and other regulatory

25. A plan-wise review up to the Eighth Plan is found in Khanal (1993). An overall critical review of trade policies up to the 1970s, including constraints imposed by landlockedness and trade treaties with India, is found in ILO/ARTEP (1982).

frameworks. How trade and other macro policy reforms are contributing to decent employment is crucial for accomplishing MDGs in a low-income country such as Nepal.

Trade and exchange rate policy

Prior to 1983, there was no separate trade policy. Trade agreements with India and other third countries together with frequent government announcements were the main bases for external trade. Only in 1983 was the first new trade policy announced. De-licensing of exports (except those banned or put under quantitative restriction), waiving of income tax on export earnings and introduction of duty drawback systems, including a bonded warehouse facility, were some of the policies included in the new policy. Despite these new measures, direct controls and attempts to guide the market were highly inefficient, encouraging resources towards unproductive activities (Sharma and Bajracharya, 1996). The new policy also constrained increased labour absorption in the industrial sector (DSC, 1990). The rent-seeking practices worked very adversely in this regard (Maxwell Stamp Associates, 1990).[26] The structural rigidity, state-led distortions and widening fiscal deficit gradually started a deepening crisis on the foreign trade and payments fronts in the late 1970s. The foreign exchange crisis compelled Nepal to go into negotiations with first the IMF, for standby credit arrangements under the Economic Stabilization Program, and subsequently the IMF/World Bank, for a Structural Adjustment Program (SAP) loan, to which various conditions for reforming the policy were attached. With the implementation of SAP, some liberal policy measures were introduced on the trade front. The quota system for imports from third countries was replaced by the import licence auction system in July 1986. In the year 1986/87, a duty drawback scheme was also introduced in the ready-made garment industry along with simplification of export procedures. The first phase of reform under standby and SAP lasted up to 1989/90.

---

26. The main features of policy and their ramifications are exhaustively discussed in this report.

However, these initiatives were neither adequate nor effective in promoting market orientation and enhancing efficiency. Much of the focus was on limited simplification of rules and regulations aimed at some easing of them for business and trade. There was, however, still wide discretion in decisions, resulting in favouritism and corruption (Cohen, 1995). To get a business registered took almost six months. The legal system was too archaic, unpredictable and unreliable. Even in cases where rules and regulations existed, the administrative structure was highly inefficient and fragile, and rent-seeking was excessive (Dixit, 1995). The tariff and non-tariff barriers, including quantitative restrictions, were hindering exports and preventing efficiency and competitiveness (Maxwell Stamp Associates, 1990). This had adverse effects on, among other things, mobilization of resources required for augmenting investment and promoting employment.

In 1990, Nepal began to move rapidly from a largely controlled regime towards a more open and liberal economic regime. India's unprecedented move toward intensive liberalization in the early 1990s and a wave of liberalization worldwide were mainly instrumental for this. Apart from a compulsion to synchronize macro polices with India, due to the reasons already pointed out, an expectation that liberalization would help to augment economic growth also contributed to the more intensive pursuit of liberalization policies. The features and sequencing of reforms were guided by the ESAF programme of the IMF, which Nepal introduced in 1992.[27] In the process, trade reform became the essential part of the overall policy reform, in which tariff and non-tariff reforms were carried out simultaneously. Replacing the trade policy of 1983, Nepal announced a new trade policy in June 1992. Increased role of the private sector, diversification of trade, enhancement of backward linkages of trade to reduce trade imbalances and expand employment were some of the objectives laid down in the trade policy. By July 1993, the Government had brought all import items into an Open General Licence (OGL), except for a few prohibited or banned goods such as narcotics and

27. For details, see Khanal *et al.* (2005).

arms. In parallel, steps were taken to reform the tariff system through drastic reductions in tariff rates and rationalization of tariff structures. The tariff slabs at present are in the range of 5 to 80 per cent. Besides basic duties, additional duties charged on imports from third countries were also withdrawn in 1993/94.

However, one important additional feature of tariff rates is the preferential treatment for imports from India. Currently, there is a rebate of 20 per cent on ad valorem customs duties of the tariff rate up to 40 per cent and 10 per cent on rates of more than 40 per cent. Nepal's trade with India and the accompanying trade facilities, concessions and rebates are governed by trade treaties between Nepal and India. It is worth noting that unlike past treaties, the treaty of 1996 was a landmark from the point of view of facilitating more liberal trade with India and promoting Nepal's exports to that country. The non-reciprocity market facility to Nepalese manufacturing products was the most progressive clause included in the treaty. However, the Nepal–India trade treaty renewed in 2002 has many regressive clauses, in which both quantitative restrictions and value added clauses are reintroduced. The 2002 treaty also made Nepalese exports to India subject to countervailing duties to make the prices of Nepalese exports comparable with the Indian counterparts. A rebate of 10 per cent of the customs duty also applies to imports from other SAARC (South Asian Association for Regional Cooperation) countries and China.

Another feature that apparently contradicts the spirit of trade liberalization is that special levies and charges have existed for the past few years, raising nominal rates of protection from 14 per cent in 2000 to 18 per cent in 2004/05 (World Bank, 2004d). Although gradual reductions in these levies and charges has been started in order to fulfil WTO obligations,[28] they still discriminate against foreign trade similar to general tariffs. There are other problems in the tariff structure that are encouraging a cascading tariff system. Several rates and bands are imposed, depending upon the stages of production or the degree of

---

28. In 2004/05, the special charges at the rate of 0.5 per cent imposed on imports has been abolished. Similarly, the development levy on agricultural commodities has been reduced from 10 per cent to 8 per cent (MoF, 2005a).

fabrication. This usually means that the highest rates are levied on final goods, lower rates applied to intermediates goods, and the lowest rates to raw materials and capital goods. A recent study shows that despite the actual tariff rates on imports going down to 8 per cent on the average, there is a big diversity in the rate structure (Khanal, 2006b).

Although commitments made in the course of accession to the WTO will gradually lead to simplification or rationalization of the tariff structure, Nepal's average tariff rate is lower than the binding rates. Nepal has also already opened up trade in services beyond Nepal's commitments to the WTO. It is worth noting that there none of the special export support measures contradict WTO rules (SAWTEE, 2005). It is also noteworthy that there has been a nearly complete dismantling of quantitative restrictions in trade in Nepal (World Bank, 2004d). A major step that Nepal has to take is to abolish all additional duties and levies within 10 years. Similarly, Nepal is far behind in introducing various new rules for enhancing market institutions, which are critically important for the sustainability of reforms and for reaping intended benefits.

Reform of exchange rate policy has also been carried in parallel, to make the exchange rate system compatible with ongoing trade liberalization. A dual exchange rate system introduced in 1977 and modified in 1978 was replaced by a cash subsidy programme in 1981. Under this scheme, exporters were provided a certain percentage of export earnings as a cash subsidy, with the aim of boosting exports. This scheme also could not be continued for long due to the heavy fiscal burden and administrative problems. Hence, in 1983 a flexible exchange rate regime was introduced, based on a currency basket system. Such a system continued until February 1993. In between, Nepalese currency was devalued twice, first in 1985/86 and again in 1991/92. Following a step-by-step approach, the Nepalese rupee was made fully convertible in the current account in 1993. Now, exporters are allowed to retain up to 100 per cent of their export earnings in their convertible currency accounts in domestic banks. Similarly, other types of foreign exchange earners are also allowed to open foreign currency deposit account in local banks.

Provision of dollar payment for the import of specified products, mostly raw materials, from India is also being continued. Raw material imports from India against dollar payment are relatively cheaper, which has some positive impact on the increasing competitive strength of Nepali manufacturing. Commercial banks are also allowed to extend loans in foreign currency to borrowers who are engaged in specified businesses that earn foreign exchange. The Foreign Exchange Regulation Act, 1962 has been amended twice, in 1992 and 2002, after the initiation of reform to make it liberalization-friendly. Now, the hard currency exchange rate is market determined. However, the exchange rate of the Nepali rupee with the Indian currency still remains fixed.

Both total imports and exports increased markedly in the post-liberalization period, as their contribution to GDP indicates (Table 5.9). The growth in imports was particularly noticeable up to 1995. Although the growth in exports continued up to 2000, the share of total trade reduced after 1995. When trade with India and trade with third countries are examined separately, some interesting trends are observed. In the post-liberalization period, when both imports and exports were picking up, the trade with third countries went up markedly, leading to decline in the share of trade with India. This was particularly due to a sharp deceleration in exports to India. After 1995, however, India's share of both exports and imports increased gradually, with a declining or stagnating trend in trade with third countries. Such a trend coincides with the progressive trade treaty between Nepal and India in 1996. This means that the adverse effect of the exchange rate, among other things, was to some extent compensated by the treaty with India, which granted the market for Nepalese products in India on a non-reciprocity basis. Even after reversal of various concessionary clauses in the renewed treaty of 2002, the market facilities in India for industries with Nepali or Indian value added content has helped to boost exports to India to some extent. But it is worthwhile noting that the share of trade has not reached the 1995 level and there has not been commodity or country diversification in trade. Recently, only some directional change has taken place, showing that trade liberalization has had little effect on trade creation.

Table 5.9

Trends in exports, imports and trade gap, 1980–2005

(Nepali rupees, millions)

Items	*1980*	*1985*	*1990*	*1995*	*2000*	*2005*
Total imports	3480.1	7742.0	18 324.9	63 679.5	108 505.0	132 186.8
India	1786.4	3895.8	4674.5	19 615.9	47 791.4	85 836.2
Third country	1693.7	3846.2	13 650.4	44 063.6	60 713.6	46 350.6
Total exports	1150.5	2740.6	5156.2	17 639.2	49 822.7	58 236.2
India	520.9	1601.7	602.5	3124.3	21 220.7	39 448.4
Third country	629.6	1138.9	4553.7	14 514.9	28 602.0	18 787.8
Total trade balance	−2329.6	−5001.4	−13 168.7	−46 040.3	−58 682.3	−73 950.6
India	−1265.5	−2294.1	−4072.0	−16 491.6	−26 570.7	−46 387.8
Third country	−1064.1	−2707.3	−9096.7	−29 548.7	−32 111.6	−27 562.8
Total volume of trade	4631	10 483	23 481	81 319	158 328	190 423
India	2307	5498	5277	22 740	69 012	125 285
Third country	2323	4985	18 204	58 579	89 316	65 138
Total imports	15.9	17.4	18.4	30.3	29.6	26.2
India	8.2	8.8	4.7	9.3	13.0	17.0
Third country	7.7	8.7	13.7	21.0	16.6	9.2
Total exports	5.3	6.2	5.2	8.4	13.6	11.6
India	2.4	3.6	0.6	1.5	5.8	7.8
Third country	2.9	2.6	4.6	6.9	7.8	3.7
Trade balance	−10.7	−11.3	−13.2	−22.0	−16.1	−14.7
India	−5.8	−5.2	−4.1	−7.9	−7.3	−9.2
Third country	−4.9	−6.1	−9.1	−14.1	−8.8	−5.5

Source: MoF, 1991, 2005b and NRB, 2006a.

As a way to enhance trade liberalization, Nepal has also virtually abolished all types of subsidies. In 1998, subsidies for fertilizers, irrigation and credit were abruptly abolished. Only a limited subsidy is available for food supply for the remote areas. The main aim behind this move was to enhance supply and thereby, provide production incentives to the farmers. In parallel, administered pricing systems have been removed (except for petroleum products) by allowing government enterprises autonomy in setting prices.

Generally, all these measures would have short to long-term growth and employment effects through income (factor prices and employment), expenditure (prices and availability of goods) and investment/

productivity channels. There may also be some immediate effects due to domestic and external shocks. Given these broad ramifications, Nepal faces an uphill task in reaping the potential benefits and minimization of risk and uncertainty.

The decline in exports after 2000 has had wide-ranging adverse effects from both growth and employment perspectives. More particularly, the phasing out of the Multi-Fibre Agreement in 2006 has led to a marked reduction in garment exports, with very serious adverse employment effects (MoF, 2006a; NGA, 2006). This is happening at a time when only a few commodities, such as garments, carpets and *pashmina*, constitute the major share of total exports (Figure 5.1). With the abolition of the garment quota from 2006 and no alternative

Figure 5.1

Shares of major exports, 1980–2005 (percentage of total exports)

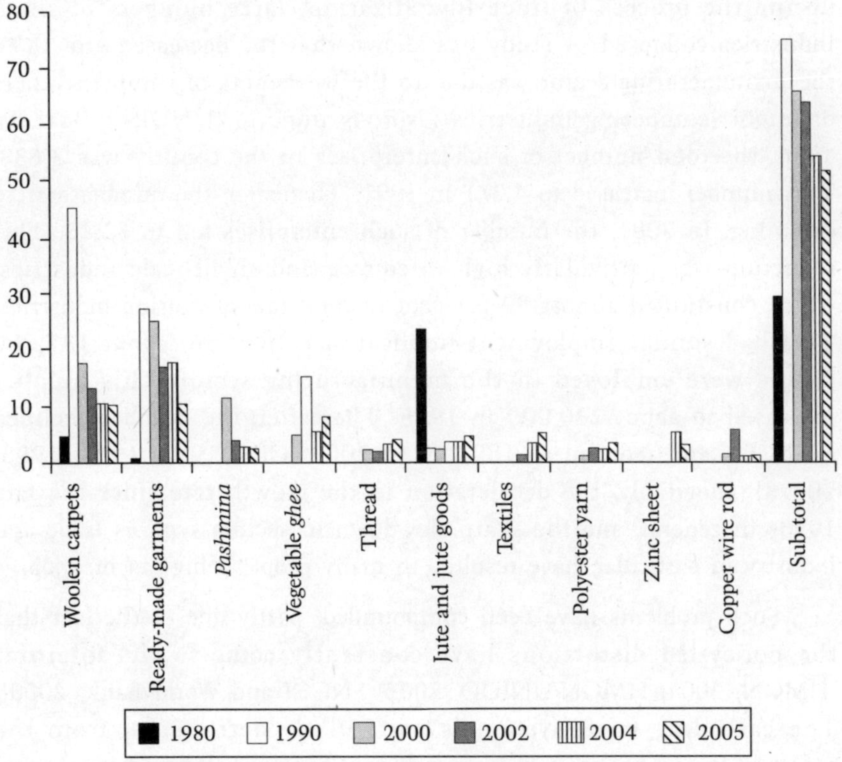

Source: Khanal (2006a).

exportable products in the offing, except some expansion in the exports of subsidiary-type products to India, the vulnerability of exports has increased markedly. At the same time, no significant changes in the structure of imports have occurred in Nepal for more than two decades. Manufactured products still constitute the largest share of Nepal's total imports. Intermediate goods constitute the second largest share of total imports, followed by food and then fuels. The almost stagnant structure of imports reflects the slow and narrow growth of the manufacturing industry during this period (Khanal *et al.*, 2005).

There are numerous interrelated problems associated with the existing trade pattern. First, almost all the few commodity-concentrated export industries rely heavily on imported raw materials and have virtually no backward linkages (HMGN/UNIDO 2002; HMGN, 2004). This is one of the principal reasons why linkages between the non-agriculture sector and the agriculture sector are very weak. Worryingly, during the process of trade liberalization, large numbers of small industries collapsed. A study has shown that the decreased growth in the manufacturing sector was due to the weakening of competitiveness of import-competing industries *vis-à-vis* imports (UNDP, 2004a). In 1986, the total number of such enterprises in the country was 3,633. This number increased to 4,271 in 1991. Thereafter, the number started declining. In 2001, the number of such enterprises fell to 3,213. This reduction was particularly high in cottage and small-scale industries, which constituted almost 90 per cent of total manufacturing industries. This had similar employment implications. In 1986, about 137,000 people were employed in the manufacturing sector. This number increased to about 230,000 in 1995. Thereafter, the number declined gradually, and reduced to 180,000 in 2001 (CBS, 1987, 1992, 1995, 2002a). Inevitably, the deceleration in the growth rate since the late 1990s in general, and the sharp slowdown in sectors such as trade and industry in particular, have resulted in many people being out of a job.

Such problems have been compounded, partly due to the fact that the policy-led distortions have constantly come to the forefront (HMGN, 2004; HMGN/UNIDO, 2002; FNCCI and World Bank, 2000). The cascading tariff system is particularly detrimental from the standpoint of encouraging high value added products and increasing employment opportunities. The existing tariff system imposes the highest rates on final goods, lower rates on intermediate goods, and the lowest rates on raw materials and capital goods. As an illustration, if such levels are combined with tariffs of 25 per cent on outputs and 10 per cent on inputs, effective rates of protection would vary from 28 per cent in agriculture up to 927 per cent in some assembly activities.

The bias inherent in this type of cascading tariff structure works in favour of low value added activities, such as assembly industries or production of intermediate goods (HMGN, 2004). As pointed earlier, most of Nepal's exportable industries rely heavily on imported raw materials, with both low value added and low employment intensities. Despite the immense potential for agro- and forestry-based industries using local raw materials, such a tariff structure has hindered the tapping of this potential, which could have helped promote forward and backward linkage industries (Khanal *et al.*, 2005).

Relatively stable exchange rates and hard currency alone could not provide adequate incentives for the Nepalese producers. This problem has become worse since 1998, after the abrupt abolition of subsidies in the agriculture sector. This is due in particular to the high level of subsidy in India in a situation where there is an open border, free trading arrangements for primary products and free convertibly of Indian currency in Nepalese market, as pointed out already.

Generally, policies providing price incentives to producers are expected to help them diversify commodity production for markets and thereby, generate both farm and off-farm employment. This is the major channel through which both production and farmers' incomes are expected to be boosted. This did not happen in Nepal. Relative movements in agricultural and non-agricultural prices for the period 1990–2003 show that the terms of trade in agriculture worsened, particularly since 2001 (Figure 5.2). As the figure shows, the increment in the index of the agriculture deflator was lower than the non-agriculture deflator in most of the years under consideration. Interestingly, at a time when the currency was devalued, there was almost convergence in the prices. Likewise, the short-term effect of deregulation in inputs and outputs had some positive effect. But since 2001, the terms of trade in agriculture have been deteriorating. This trend reconfirms that highly subsidized agricultural products from India dampened the prices of Nepali products, at a time when the input prices were rising massively after deregulation. Nepali farmers have therefore, been hit by high input and low output prices.

Figure 5.2

Ratio of agricultural to non-agricultural GDP deflator, 1990–2003

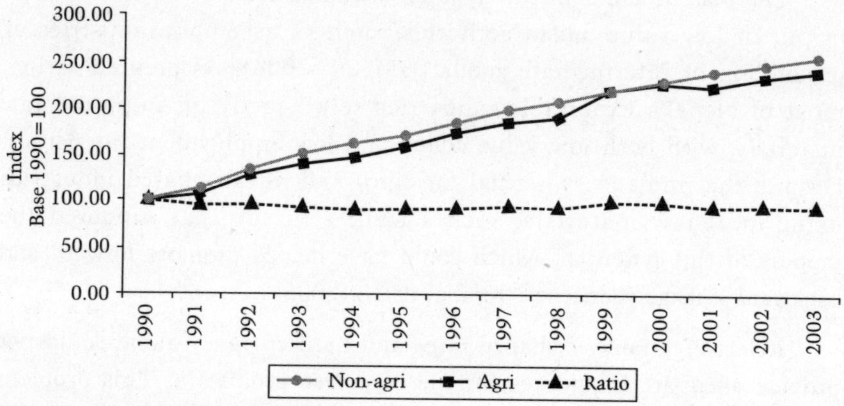

Source: Khanal and Kanel, 2005.

These findings are similar to other findings derived for Asian agriculture. These show that in many Asian countries, deregulation and market-oriented liberalization policies have helped very little in achieving positive results.[29] In many cases, price-induced liberal policies have failed to generate supply responses, either due to very low price elasticities or because of predominant role of non-price factors. Among the non-price factors, fixed land supply, lower initial input intensity and agroclimatic conditions (governing crop pattern) as well as demand conditions have been found to be decisive and important (see Desai and Nambodiri, 1997). As a result, new market-oriented policies have contributed very little to promoting growth and reducing poverty in many countries (see Vyas, 2002).

The fixed exchange rate system has been particularly detrimental in this regard. Under a fixed exchange rate system, increases in domestic costs-prices are transmitted to the prices of exports expressed in foreign

29. Effect of price induced policies on Asian agriculture has been thoroughly discussed in Vyas (2002).

currencies and hence, export becomes less competitive. In such a situation, there is an upsurge in imports and dampening of domestic production. Therefore, the exchange rate is the most powerful policy tool for influencing relative changes in the prices.[30] Despite the pegged exchange rate system with India, Nepal has tried to correct any mismatch through adjusting hard currency exchange rates based on cross-examination of rates between the Indian currency and hard currencies. However, the gap is widening after the deregulation of the input and output prices. Such a variation, together with the high rate of inflation in Nepal[31] *vis-à-vis* India, has led to the Nepalese currency to appreciate markedly. As shown in Figure 5.3, despite some fluctuations and gaps, there is continuous appreciation of the Nepali currency against the Indian currency. This means that by preventing depreciation of the Nepali currency, Nepal is subsidizing imports from India and is discouraging exports by decreasing the competitiveness of Nepali products *vis-à-vis* Indian commodities.

Figure 5.3

Movement in real exchange rate, 1985–2003

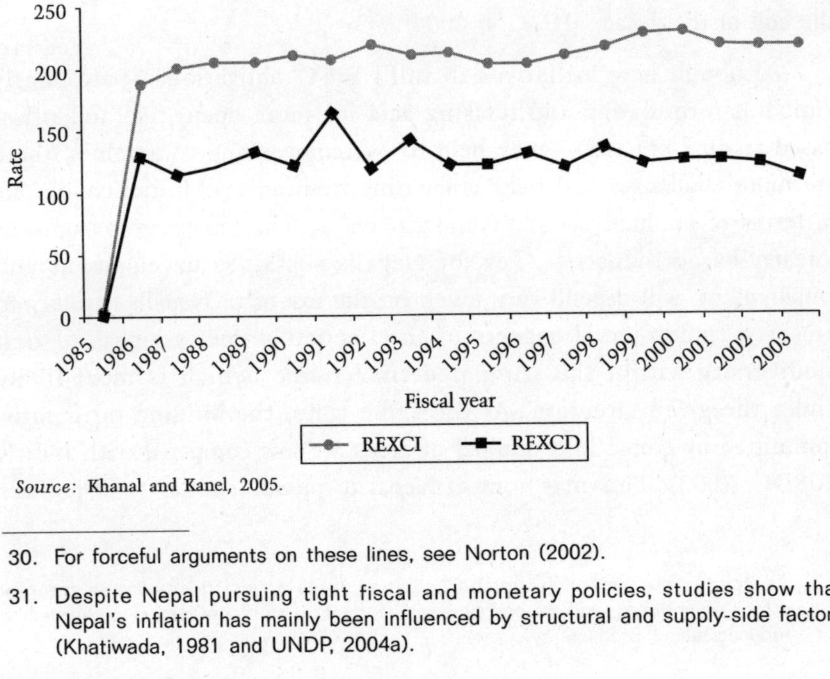

Source: Khanal and Kanel, 2005.

30. For forceful arguments on these lines, see Norton (2002).

31. Despite Nepal pursuing tight fiscal and monetary policies, studies show that Nepal's inflation has mainly been influenced by structural and supply-side factors (Khatiwada, 1981 and UNDP, 2004a).

The biggest impacts of such an exchange rate policy have been on the agriculture sector. The appreciation of the Nepalese currency in the context of higher subsidies to farmers in India has not only made the Indian agricultural goods cheaper in Nepalese markets, but also Nepali products have become less competitive. This has created disincentive to the Nepalese farmers. The appreciation of the Nepalese currency has also partly encouraged an inflow of workers from the neighbouring country.

The transaction cost, a major determinant of trade, is very high in Nepal (HMGN, 2004). High transaction cost and other distortions have continuously encouraged informal trade between Nepal and India (Taneja and Rohit, 2000). Despite Nepal being very rich in water resources, Nepal is one of the costliest countries in the world in terms of per unit electricity prices. These factors have also adversely affected inflow of foreign investment (IFC and World Bank, 1998; Dahal and Aryal, 2003). Although Nepal's lower wage costs provide an important competitive advantage, this is offset by the country's significantly lower labour productivity. While Nepal's productivity and competitiveness increased over the 1990s, these improvements could not be sustained to the end of the decade (HMGN, 2004).[32]

Although new initiatives to fulfil WTO obligations—particularly aimed at formulating and revising acts for more open, free and rules-based trading practices—may help to overcome many constraints, there are more challenges and risks emanating from adverse initial conditions in terms of productivity and competitiveness. The prospects for agro- or forestry-based industries, key for Nepal's sustained development and employment, will depend very much on the extent of Nepal's capacity to preserve trade-related aspects of intellectual property rights of rich biodiversity within the stipulated time frame, which is most likely under the given situation. At the same time, the binding tariff rates committed by Nepal in a number of areas are low compared with India's (RISDC, 2003). This may compel Nepal to pursue similar tariff policies

32. As pointed out earlier, higher participation rates amidst decreases in the real wages of unskilled workers and growing informalization of the labour market led to reduced labour productivity.

under the bilateral trade arrangements at a time when the free trading of primary products (in addition to, as pointed out earlier, growing asymmetry in agriculture and the exchange rate policy) is hurting the agriculture sector very badly. Also, subsidy limits set in the WTO agreement may prevent Nepal from providing required incentives to medium and small industries in the future (UNDP, 2004b). More dangerously, agreements on trade-related investment measures prevent member countries imposing conditions on foreign investors aimed at giving certain preference to local raw materials. Under these likely circumstances, local raw-material producers needing some incentive in the initial production phases may collapse, which may have high adjustment costs.[33] In view of all these issues and the deterioration in trade performance over recent years, it is clear that emphasis on trade openness and liberalization through removal of tariff or non-tariff barriers alone may not be sufficient to create benefits or unleash resources required for sustained growth and employment generation.

Over the past several years, vocational education, skills development and training, and medium-sized and micro-enterprises development programmes[34] have been emphasized from the point of view of augmenting employment opportunities. Most of these programmes have very limited coverage and are deficient and ineffective (ILO, 2002). The limited training programmes launched by many governments and other agencies over recent decades have not been effective due to their poor linkage with the changing demands of the labour market. A similar problem is found in trade schools, which produce lower or middle level technical workers in a limited number. The programmes to promote business or enterprise also have had very limited coverage. The low priority on technical education has further constrained the employability of the growing labour force.

---

33. One of the cigarette factories in Nepal that for a long time used local materials has started using imported raw materials. This has very adverse income and employment implications for the tobacco-growing farmers. Likewise, industries using local honey have started importing honey. Such a trend may intensify in future.

34. These are the programmes emphasized in both the Ninth Plan and the Tenth Plan (NPC, 1997, 2002) in which poverty reduction is the sole goal, as pointed out earlier.

Neither PRSPs nor the MDGs attach much importance on the role of employment-centric policies and programmes in reducing poverty. Lack of *ex-ante* poverty impact assessment practices for macroeconomic policies in general, and trade policies in particular, have led to the undermining of the importance of employment-centric policies or to an emphasis on growth without assessment of the broad ramifications. Despite some structural shift, compulsion to work mostly seasonally in low-productivity and low-income sectors, such as small-scale agriculture, rural non-farm trade and other activities as well as the urban informal services sector, has caused poor workers to remain poor despite engagement in a job. Gender biases, very low wage rates, concentration of the limited opportunities in a few accessible areas and erosion of employment opportunities due to the slowdown in trade and industry have further compounded the magnitude of unemployment problems.[35]

On the whole, contrary to expectations, the trade liberalization and exchange rate policies have been unable to enhance employment opportunities, as the trends in sectoral employment and structural problems in the labour market have indicated. Rigidity in labour laws has, in addition to encouraging informalization of the labour market, encouraged capital-intensive modes of production. In manufacturing, for instance, although there was some pickup in output growth, from 2 per cent in the pre-reform period to 8 per cent in the post-reform period, most of the increased growth resulted from factor accumulation rather than productivity improvement. Even in highly labour-intensive industries such as carpets, garments and other textiles, capital is estimated to have contributed significantly more than labour to output growth in the post-reform years.[36] Thus, neither the expenditure and

35. In the government bureaucracy, female employment is negligible. Until recently, foreign employment was prevented for the female workers. Although no data are available to link trade and employment, the phasing out of the garments quota together with more stringent rules against using child labour and the deceleration in the growth rate of the trade sector mean that employment in the trade sector has reduced in recent years.

36. Based on survey data (FNCCI and World Bank, 2000), a study of trade and competitiveness indicates that rigidity in labour laws was one of the problems for the more capital-intensive mode of production; for details see HMGN (2004).

income channel nor the productivity channel worked positively in the Nepalese context. Instead, the shocks emanating either from relative prices or from terms of trade have worked adversely. In the absence of effective institutional and governance-related reforms, the decontrol of prices and the subsidy withdrawal type deregulation-centric polices together encouraged inefficiency or cost in various sectors of the economy. This also worked adversely by increasing transaction costs in a big way. Despite Nepal having abundant water resources, the electricity tariff rate is one of the highest in the world. The frequent hikes in rates and little attention paid to efficiency aspects contributed for this. Due to low-quality and costly infrastructure, including business services, amidst cumbersome bureaucratic procedures, the transaction costs reach about 30 per cent of turnover (Taneja and Rohit, 2000). Above all, pro-poor growth and decent employment has been hindered by the insufficient attention given to addressing the structural or institutional constraints that prevent small farmers, small entrepreneurs and business people as well as vulnerable workers from reaping any benefits from the reforms.

Nepal's experience shows that the implementation of deregulation or other "big bang" liberalization policies in specific areas or sectors in isolation will be of little help for enhancing cost effectiveness or efficiency. In many instances, this actually induces a tendency for price hikes. The weak regulatory system, absence of anti-monopoly laws and effective implementation make the efficiency issue a major problem. This is happening in Nepal. Therefore, there is a need for a mix of policies and also for better sequencing. At first, a comprehensive reform approach that covers all the main sectors, including agriculture and infrastructure, is needed, with due care paid to policy synchronization. At the same time, institutional and governance-related reforms should be part and parcel of the overall reforms, of which management improvement and effective regulatory mechanisms should constitute a major component. Additionally, sufficient attention has to be given to small business and entrepreneurs in countries like Nepal, where structural impediments prevent them taking advantage of the liberal policy environment. Certain policy incentives together with specific institutional arrangements for credit or other facilities will be needed for this group.

Financial sector policy

A well-developed, healthy and competitive financial system is a prerequisite for enhancing efficiency in resource use, augmenting growth and ensuring access to financial services. All these will in the process expand and diversify opportunities, including employment opportunities. For these reasons, the financial sector policy constitutes an important component of macro policy reforms.

In Nepal, financial sector reform was started in the 1980s with steps to deregulate the interest rate structure (NRB, 1996). In 1984, opening-up policies were pursued by allowing joint venture banks to operate in Nepal. Similarly, the Finance Company Act was brought into effect in 1985 to meet the increasing demands of small borrowers. Removal of the statutory liquidity ratio and introduction of auctioning of treasury bills were other reform measures implemented during the 1980s. From 1989, Nepal Rastra Bank (NRB) began to fix capital adequacy ratios. In the same year, NRB also set an upper limit on the amount of loan to be provided to a single borrower or group of borrowers by a bank in order to minimize the risk of overconcentrating loans to few big borrowers. Similarly, the central bank also introduced an open-market operations policy as one of the monetary policy implementation tools in 1990.

A more intensive reform was started from the early 1990s. The Finance Company Act, 1985 was amended to allow promoters to hold 60 per cent of the total issued capital. The Development Bank Act, 1995 and Financial Intermediary Institutions Act, 1998 were introduced to attract the private sector and non-governmental organizations (NGOs) to establish financial institutions in the rural areas. In response, a large number of development banks, some of them as replicas of Grameen Bank, and financial NGOs and cooperatives came into operation during the post-reform period. Prudential norms were also gradually refined and strengthened. Similarly, in 1995 the limits on the amount of loans to a single borrower or group of borrowers were reduced to 35 and 50 per cent respectively. The regulation differentiating loan limits to fund and non-fund based loans was further revised in 2001 to 25 per cent of core capital in the case of fund-based loans and 50 per cent of core capital in case of non-fund based loans.

The mandatory priority-sector lending policy was introduced as early as 1974. The priority-lending policy was also continued in the post-liberalization period. The ratio was further raised to 12 per cent in 1990 from 8 per cent in 1984/85. In 1992, commercial banks were additionally directed to lend a certain percentage of priority sector lending to small borrowers. The purpose was to ensure that the agriculture sector and allied activities, including cottage and small-scale industries, were not deprived of funds. The implicit aim was to raise income and employment opportunities by providing certain incentives in these areas.

However, whatever reforms aimed at improving the financial health of the banking system were pursued, they were found to be highly inadequate (World Bank, 2002b). The financial system was found to be entering into deeper crisis. A study by KPMG Barents (2000) revealed that the two state-owned commercial banks were technically insolvent, with non-performing assets reaching as high as 60 per cent of total assets. As a result, a comprehensive Financial Sector Reform Program was introduced in 2002. The programme aims to create a competitive, market-friendly, well-diversified and prudently managed system capable of leading the healthy growth of the financial sector. As a part of the reform, the Nepal Rastra Bank Act, 2002 and the Debt Recovery Act, 2002 (with provisions for a Debt Recovery Tribunal) were introduced. The Nepal Rastra Bank Act, 2002 provides autonomy to the central bank. It also gives sufficient authority to the central bank to maintain financial discipline and perform its regulatory and supervisory roles more effectively. As a part of the ongoing reforms, the two state-owned commercial banks were contracted out to the foreigners. More recently, the Banking and Financial Act, 2006 (an umbrella Act covering all financial institutions) was enacted, with the aim of bringing about more reforms in the financial institutions in a more coordinated way.

The NRB classifies the institutions into "A", "B", "C" and "D" categories on the basis of minimum paid-up capital and provides the suitable licence to the bank or financial institution. At least 51 per cent ownership has to be held by the promoters in order to establish any bank or financial institution. Likewise, a 30 per cent share of total paid-up capital has to be allocated to the general public. There are no specific rules or regulations for domestic banks on employment. In the case of joint venture banks, they have to make separate Technical Service Agreements regarding the numbers and responsibilities of the expatriates (i.e., foreign investors).

In the aftermath of the reforms, the financial system has undergone rapid development. Before liberalization, the financial system consisted of only two commercial banks and few other financial institutions. In the post-liberalized regime, the financial system has rapidly developed and diversified. By mid-July 2005, the number of NRB-licensed bank and non-bank financial institutions totalled 181. Out of these, 17 were commercial banks, 26 were development banks and 60 were finance companies. The remaining 78 were microcredit development banks, saving and credit cooperatives and NGOs performing limited banking activities. Consequently, the total financial assets of the financial system reached 90 per cent of GDP in 2005, against 32 per cent in 1990. Similarly, in 2005 the deposit and credit ratios to GDP stood at 47.7 and 30.9 per cent respectively. While commercial banks dominate the financial system in terms of market share, a rapid change in share structure has also been taking place. In 2000, asset share of commercial banks was 92.9 per cent. Their asset share reduced to 86.7 per cent over a period of five years. Expansion in credit share of both development banks and finance companies has been rapid in recent years. Their combined credit share increased to 19.4 per cent in 2005 from just 6.5 per cent in 2000. A big change in market share is also taking place within the banking system. In 2000, the asset share of the two government-owned banks was 56.6 per cent. This reduced to 38.1 per cent in 2005. The share of the private banks increased over the same period, reaching 24.4 in 2005 from 8.2 per cent in 2000. The asset and credit expansion in the financial system has helped to enhance economic growth. But whether financial deepening has had a similar effect on employment is difficult to establish empirically.[37]

37. A study based on regression analysis showed a closer relationship between financial deepening and economic growth (Khanal, 2006a). Conversely, a production function estimated for the services sector surprisingly revealed a negative relationship between employment and growth (Khanal and Kanel, 2005). Either the predominance of informal employment or the decreased employment in this sector amidst the slowdown in the economy in recent years may be the principal reason for such findings. This is partly corroborated by another study, which indicated declining labour productivity since late 1990s (HMGN, 2004). Our estimates on employment elasticity and labour productivity further corroborate this.

The lending cost of capital and access to financial services trends may partly explain the underlying reasons for weak linkages between financial deepening and employment in the financial sector. During 1990–2005, there was a 14-fold increase in commercial bank credit. The main beneficiary was the industrial sector, followed by commerce. This may not be a cause for concern. But banks and financial institutions have, however, concentrated their activities in the urban areas in general, and in metropolitan Kathmandu in particular. The commercial banks, whether domestic or joint venture, have rather preferred to cater to the traditionally larger urban savers and to invest in safe and gilt-edged government securities and treasury bills. Thus, urban households enjoy a disproportionately larger access to organized sources of credit. This kind of investment involves no additional administrative cost and is easily convertible into ready cash in the secondary window operated by the central bank (Acharya, 2003). Out of the total listed companies, the financial institutions constitute more than 90 per cent (NSE, 2006). This additionally means that most of the lending activities have been confined to consumable products. As a result, lending in the agriculture sector has reduced considerably from year to year (MoF, 2006a).

Due to the inability to reduce the ratio of non-performing assets in the state-owned banks and an increasing gap between the deposit and lending rates (about 5 per cent), the cost of capital has remained constantly high. However, there are some persistent anomalies in this respect also. The lending rates applied to durable consumable goods are very low (ranging from 6.5 to 7 per cent) compared with the lending rates charged to the industrial sector (ranging from 12 to 18 per cent) (NRB, 2006b). The problem has now become aggravated in the rural areas, with very high interest rates being applied to rural areas in general, and to small and marginal farmers in particular. Although wholesale banking and microcredit have been popularized in recent years in the rural areas (in view of reduced credit outreach in the aftermath of financial sector reform), access to credit and affordability of interest rates have emerged as major problems. Despite a more than three-fold increase in per capita credit by the commercial banks in less than a decade, access to credit has not improved commensurately for the lower income strata and poor people. The Nepal Living Standard Surveys of

1995/96 and 2003/04 showed that borrowing households (from both the formal and informal financial system) had increased from 61 per cent in 1996 to 69 per cent in 2004. Of the borrowing households, only 15 per cent borrowed from the banking system in 2004 compared with 16 per cent in 1996 (Table 5.10). This means that the proportion of households having access to bank credit increased marginally, from less than 10 per cent in 1996 to just 10.4 per cent in 2004. Moneylenders and relatives account for more than 80 per cent of the lending. The poor have to resort much more to such sources. Only 8.3 per cent of the poorest consumption quintile had access to bank credit in 2004, almost the same as in 1996. The collateral-based lending practice of the banks had been a factor denying access to bank credit by the poor. Although lending free of collateral has increased considerably over time, to 28 per cent in 2004 from less than 12 per cent in 1996, it is yet to encompass most poor and vulnerable groups of society. In addition, households from the lower consumption quintile tend to borrow more for consumption. In 2004, 58 per cent of the borrowing of the poorest consumption quintile went on consumption. This means that these households had to meet their basic consumption needs by incurring debt (CBS, 1996a, 2004a). The expansion in consumption through increased indebtedness will not contribute to sustaining the well-being of poor households.

Table 5.10

Household borrowing and access to bank credit, 1995/96 and 2003/04

Item	*1995/96*	*2003/04*
Household borrowings (%)	61.3	68.8
Borrowings from banks (%)	16.1	15.1
Borrowings from relatives (%)	40.8	54.5
Borrowings from money lenders (%)	39.7	26
Proportion of the poorest quintile having access to bank borrowing	8.2	8.3
Proportion of the richest quintile having access to bank borrowing	21.8	26.8

Source: CBS, 1996b, 2004b.

More worryingly, when the direct employment effect of financial sector liberalization is examined, an unexpected trend is observed. At the time when the intensive liberalization was started, the two state-owned commercial banks were the major employers. In 1990, the two banks together employed about 15,000 people. But with the widening losses, these banks were compelled to streamline their employment policies. In particular, after the banks were contracted out, policies to reduce the number of employees were adopted. Consequently, a large number of employees were compelled to retire. This resulted in a sharp reduction in the level of employment in the banking system. In 2005, the number employed in these banks had been reduced to 6,000. When the employment patterns of the private domestic and joint venture banks are examined, a gradual expansion in employment by these banks is observed. But due to the drastic cuts in employees in the state-owned banks relative to the additional employment in the private banks, the overall employment in the commercial banks reduced to 10,005 in 2005 from 15,366 in 1990 (Khanal, 2006a).

Amidst all these unwarranted developments (from the standpoint of pro-poor growth and decent employment), the central bank has decided to phase out the priority sector-lending programme by 2007 without ensuring credit outreach in rural areas through credible alternative institutional arrangements. Moreover, Nepal has made commitments to the WTO in the course of negotiations to allow foreign joint venture banks to operate in Nepal by 2010. These clearly indicate further downside risks from both employment-induced growth and poverty reduction perspectives.

Investment policy

Nepal's investment policy[38] is also broadly guided by the ongoing reforms. The policy principally aims at promoting private investment, including foreign investment, and limiting the role of government in the economy by confining it to certain prioritized areas and activities. The Industrial Enterprises Act, 1992 and Foreign Investment and Technology Transfer Act, 1992 make specific provisions for easing the process of establishing industrial enterprises in Nepal and encouraging private sector investment. These acts also give certain incentives to labour-

38. No comprehensive investment policy has yet been formulated. Policy is broadly reflected in government plan documents, budgets, acts, and frequent policy announcements etc., in a scattered way.

intensive industries and industries using local raw materials. Similarly, foreign investors are allowed up to 100 per cent equity participation in large and medium-sized industries. A one-window system is also a part of the policies to promote private investment. The Nepal Stock Exchange Ltd., even allows portfolio investment not exceeding 25 per cent of total issued capital.

Monetary and fiscal policies have constantly been used for maintaining macroeconomic stability. The capital adequacy and open market operation policies are actively pursued by the central bank as a part of tight monetary policy. Also, with the implementation of the Nepal Rastra Bank Act, 2002, which provides autonomy to the central bank, the Government is fiscally more constrained in regard to its option to follow an expansionary policy. The Act has imposed certain restrictions on the Government in meeting budgetary deficits through overdrafts. Above all, in Nepal a tight fiscal balance has always been proactively pursued in the post-liberalization period. Unlike in many countries, the fiscal balance has been maintained by containing development-related expenditure on a massive scale, even in a period of economic slackness, or to accommodate massive expansion of security and other unproductive expenses. As a result, total expenditure has almost stagnated, from 19.7 per cent of GDP in 1990 to 20 per cent in 2005 (Table 5.11). Although there has been some steady expansion in revenue mobilization, the reduced budgetary deficit is the outcome of tightening the limits on internal borrowing.

In parallel, attempts were made to finance government expenditure through external aid. Fulfilment of ESAF conditions helped to mobilize external resources to a greater extent. However, unlike in the past, the share of the loan component increased markedly in the post-liberalization period. Only recently has this phenomenon slightly changed, with the foreign grant component again picking up, especially after the new aid strategy under the PRSP. Nonetheless, rapid expansion in the loan component has led to a massive rise in the total external debt outstanding. The total net debt outstanding to GDP ratio was 20.7 per cent in 1985, but had reached 49 per cent in 2004. Similarly, the debt servicing ratio rose to 1.6 per cent in 2004 from just 0.4 per cent in 1985 (MoF, 2006a). Despite Nepal getting concessionary loans, debt

Table 5.11

Trends in fiscal and budgetary deficits, 1975–2005

(million Nepalese rupees)

Item	*1975*	*1980*	*1985*	*1990*	*1995*	*2000*	*2005*
Total expenditure	1514	3471	8395	19 670	3 9060	66 273	100 937
Total revenue	1008	1880	3217	9288	24 605	42 894	71 322
Fiscal deficit	–505	–1591	–5178	–10 382	–14 455	–23 379	–29 615
Foreign grant	283	806	923	1975	3937	5712	11170
Budgetary deficit	–223	–785	–4255	–8407	–10 518	–17 667	–18 445
Foreign loan	104	535	1755	5960	7312	1 1812	8814
Share in GDP (%)							
Expenditure	9.5	15.9	18.9	19.7	18.6	18.1	20.0
Total revenue	6.3	8.6	7.2	9.3	11.7	11.7	14.1
Fiscal deficit	–3.2	–7.3	–11.7	–10.4	–6.9	–6.4	–5.9
Foreign grant	1.8	3.7	2.1	2.0	1.9	1.6	2.2
Budgetary deficit	–1.4	–3.6	–9.6	–8.4	–5.0	–4.8	–3.7
Foreign loan	0.7	2.4	3.9	6.0	3.5	3.2	1.7

Source: MoF, 1991, 2005b.

servicing is increasingly becoming a major problem. This has additionally constrained expansion of development programmes.

The squeezing of development expenditure in the quest for maintaining fiscal balance and containing the current account deficit has had very adverse effects on the sectors that either promote pro-poor growth or enhance off-farm employment. Potentially, this has also had a discouraging impact on private sector investment as a result of the deceased complementary public investment (Table 5.12). In 1990, the share of regular expenditure in GDP was 6.7 per cent, which reached 11.8 per cent in 2005. Conversely, the share of development expenditure reduced from 13.0 to 8.3 per cent during the same period. More distressingly, the share of agriculture and physical infrastructure declined to 0.47 and 2.33 per cent from 1.22 and 4 per cent respectively during the same period. There was some increase in social expenditure. However, primarily government revenue was overtaken by administrative and defence expenditure. This was happening at a time when under the PRSP, a medium-term expenditure framework (MTEF) had been formulated and implemented. From the table, it is clear that no inter or intra sectoral restructuring took place, even after the implementation of the MTEF, to make the sectoral allocation pattern compatible with poverty reduction targets. A more worrying phenomenon in recent years has been that the gap between budget allocation and actual spending on pro-poor programmes has remained high (UNDP, 2002). Despite increased evidence that access to both social services and infrastructure is a major problem among the low-income group (CBS, 2004a), investment policy lacks both comprehensiveness and coherence.

Table 5.12

Share of various expenditure components in GDP, 1990–2005

(percentage)

Year	Share in total	Regular[1]	Development	Social services	Economic services	Agriculture	Infrastructure	Administration and defence
1990	19.73	6.69	13.04	4.70	8.65	1.22	4.03	6.37
1995	18.60	9.17	9.43	5.08	6.65	1.29	3.25	6.87
2000	18.09	9.43	8.67	2.61	5.70	0.60	3.10	9.78
2001	20.26	10.85	9.41	6.03	5.77	0.62	3.20	8.46
2002	19.72	11.96	7.75	6.13	5.02	0.66	2.54	8.57
2003	19.20	12.56	6.64	5.93	4.29	0.45	2.25	8.98
2004	18.86	11.59	7.27	5.89	3.93	0.43	2.00	9.04
2005	20.02	11.76	8.26	6.21	4.00	0.47	2.33	9.81

Note: [1] Most regular administrative and recurring expenses come within this category, but the classification is not exhaustive.

Source: Same as Table 5.11.

All these factors created an adverse enabling environment for the private investment, including foreign investment (FNCCI and World Bank, 2000; HMGN and UNIDO, 2002; Khanal *et al.*, 2005). Trends in investment corroborate this. The ratio of total investment to GDP, which was 21.9 per cent in 1985, went up moderately and reached 26.1 per cent in 2005. At the same time, there was a wider fluctuation in the level of investment. The decreased government development expenditure together with the poor investment environment for the private sector have had adverse effects on the growth of investment. Likewise, during the period 1989–2003 total foreign investment was small, in the region of Rs. 8 billion, and the joint venture enterprises created employment opportunities for a mere 46,000 people (Dahal and Aryal, 2003). An equally worrisome phenomenon has been that even the slowly increasing investment could not be funded through internal saving mobilizations. The domestic saving–investment gap, which was 8.5 per cent of GDP in 1985, increased to, as high as, 13.8 per cent in 2005. Although part of the national saving–investment gap was filled by net factor income,[39] the gap remained fairly large at 11.8 per cent in 2005 (Table 5.13).

Table 5.13

Exports, imports, saving and investment gap (share of GDP), 1975–2005

(percentage)

Items	*1975*	*1980*	*1985*	*1990*	*1995*	*2000*	*2005*
Exports of goods and services	8.9	11.5	11.5	10.5	24.2	23.3	16.4
Imports of goods and services	13.4	18.7	20.0	21.1	34.6	32.4	30.2
Total investment	14.5	18.3	21.9	18.4	25.2	24.3	26.1
Domestic savings	10.0	11.1	13.4	7.9	14.8	15.2	12.3
Saving investment gap	4.5	7.2	8.5	10.5	10.4	9.1	13.8
Net factor income	1.6	2.1	1.4	1.9	2.2	3.5	2.0
Total national savings	11.6	13.2	14.8	9.7	17.0	18.6	14.2
Net resource gap	2.9	5.1	7.0	8.7	8.2	5.7	11.8

Source: MoF, *Economic Survey*, 1991, 2005b; NRB, 2003.

The adverse investment environment for both domestic and foreign investors and the low saving rate received little priority on the reform agenda. It was believed that the fiscal and monetary tightening would help to maintain macroeconomic stability, which would attract investors. It was additionally hoped that low inflation expectations, by raising the savings rate, would further contribute to the growth in investment. Despite increased evidence that a moderate rate of inflation is not harmful at the time of concerted efforts at socio-economic infrastructural development (Pasha and Palanivel, 2004), this aspect received little attention, primarily due to external influence. A quick look at the internal borrowing and the rate of inflation shows that no apparent one-to-one relationship is found between these two variables (Table 5.14).

39. There are problems in the estimation of net factor income due to some problems in the treatment of remittances income. Therefore, the net factor income estimation in the national accounts has to be interpreted more cautiously.

Table 5.14

Internal borrowing and rate of inflation

(percentage)

Year	*Internal borrowing as a share of GDP*	*Rate of inflation*
1985	3.86	–
1986	2.65	15.80
1987	2.42	12.30
1988	1.12	12.40
1989	3.23	7.50
1990	2.37	8.10
1991	3.65	9.70
1992	2.97	21.50
1993	2.94	8.60
1994	1.23	1.60
1995	1.48	7.50
1996	1.75	10.50
1997	1.90	8.30
1998	2.23	7.80
1999	1.79	18.80
2000	1.54	-0.40
2001	2.96	3.40
2002	3.61	2.90
2003	2.61	4.80

Source: MoF, 1991, 2005b; NRB (2000, 2001, 2002, 2003, 2004, 2005).

In the context of Nepal, policy effectiveness cannot be judged in isolation from more than a decade of insurgency. The security problems faced by enterprises, the disturbance to factor and product markets, increased recurring government expenses and the problem of enhancing access to credit and financial services worked adversely during the period under review. This adverse effect is quite visible on the growth, investment and employment fronts. Growth rate slowed down and became negative in 2002 as a result of a heightening of the violent conflict, especially since 2001. This adverse effect was sharpest in the non-agricultural sector in general, and on trade and the industrial sector in particular. The growth rate now hovers between 2.5 to 3 per cent. There was also a sharp deceleration in investment after 2000, which picked up gradually after 2002. This negative or low growth rate, coupled with an adverse investment environment, had serious adverse implications for employment. Employees in tourism suffered the most as a result of almost complete collapse of the tourist industry (MoF, 2006a).

At the same time, a close review of macroeconomic policies and their probable impact indicates that there were serious lapses on the policy front as well, especially from the point of view of decent employment. On the government expenditure front, other recurring expenses rose rapidly, along with security expenses, with an adverse effect on productive investment. This poor enabling environment, together with a disincentive structure to small enterprises, had a very adverse effect on the development of the private sector, a sector which could have generated employment in a sustainable way. In the course of financial sector reform, a probable adverse effect on access to credit among small enterprises hardly took priority. The main problem was that macroeconomic policies, particularly exchange rate and trade, financial and investment policies, were neither designed nor reformed from the standpoint of enhancing decent employment. Instead, many policy asymmetries in these areas became counterproductive from the point of view of employment in general and decent employment in particular. The Labour Act implemented during the early years of intensive reforms was continued without a parallel attempt to make it conducive to decent employment. This was due in part to negligence in making labour and employment policy one of the main ingredients of macroeconomic policy. Extreme positions, often taken either in favour of labour rigidity or complete flexibility, led to the sidelining of decent employment related issues to a great extent. If solutions had been explored instead within the broader context of employment promotion, social security, labour standards (including skill enhancement and labour productivity), the situation would have been more positive, even during the insurgency.

5.4 Major conclusions and policy implications

Conclusions

After pursuing intensive reforms for more than 15 years, Nepal has succeeded in becoming one of the most liberalized countries in the

South Asia region. This has enabled Nepal to diversify greatly both its economic and employment structures. Poverty has been reduced considerably, from 42 per cent in 1996 to 31 per cent in 2004. However, despite these outcomes, Nepal faces serious problems on many fronts. After an initial pick-up in the aftermath of reforms, growth has decelerated continuously and the rate is now below the population growth rate. This has halted, or even reversed, the changes to the growth and employment patterns. Similarly, while poverty intensity among deprived and vulnerable socio-economic groups continues, the income inequality has widened markedly in recent years. On average, the workforce participation rate has increased and the unemployment rate has decreased over time, however, the low employment elasticity shows that the rise in employment has not been commensurate with the growth in the economy. In addition, the trends in productivity reveal that labour productivity in both the manufacturing and services sectors has decreased in recent years. The predominance of unskilled workers among employees, the decreased real wages among urban unskilled non-agricultural workers and the large wage differentials between skilled and unskilled and between male and female workers all contributed to this. Further, informalization of the labour market and the decreased share of wage income in the post-liberalization period have had adverse growth and income distribution implications. These developments have generated apprehension regarding the ability of the ongoing reforms to enhance equal opportunities or to ensure benefits to all.

A closer examination of macroeconomic policies in general, and of trade, exchange rate, financial and investment policies in particular, shows that there are serious policy mismatches or asymmetries, particularly from employment-induced pro-poor growth perspectives central to poverty reduction and its sustainability. Similarly, despite continuous emphasis on employment and other related training, vocational education and business promotion programmes that promote labour-intensive modes of production, employment has never been at the centre of the development agenda. It is surprising that even PRSPs and the MDGs do not recognize employment as a major vehicle for poverty reduction. Their reflection is quite visible in policies and programmes.

A closer examination of the trade policy shows that deregulation and opening up of the sector was the predominant focus. In many instances, such policies were pursued without adequate rules and institutional frameworks. Only after accession to the WTO are many new rules being framed and implemented. At the same time, contradictory policies were pursued simultaneously, hurting pro-poor growth and employment.

Agricultural and forestry products, which have strong competitive advantages, never received prominence in the course of policy formulation. As a result, only a few commodities formed the cornerstone of export policy. These exports were in turn heavily dependent on raw material imports, and had almost no backward linkages. With a few exceptions, no major exportable industry had even forward linkages. At the same time, the increased sickness of import-competitive industries together with the stagnant import structure had additional adverse implications for growth and employment. Neglect of the cottage and small-scale industries amidst increased competition led to a drastic reduction in employment in the industrial sector.

The cascading tariff system has been particularly detrimental from the standpoint of encouraging high value added products and increasing employment opportunities. Such a system imposes the highest rates on final goods, lower rates on intermediate goods and the lowest rates on raw materials and capital goods. The bias inherent in this type of cascading tariff structure works in favour of low value added activities, whether they are assembly industries or production of intermediate goods. Thus, the trade policy regime pursued in the course of liberalization has been very harmful, particularly in terms of enhanced forward and backward linkages in the economy, which are essential for promoting broad-based growth and creating employment opportunities.

The problem has become worse since 1998, after the abrupt abolition of subsidy in the agriculture sector. This occurred despite the high levels of subsidy in India, a country with which Nepal has an open border and free-trading arrangements for primary products, and free convertibly of Indian rupees in the Nepalese market. The domestic terms of trade in agriculture worsened after 2001, with very adverse effects on the competitiveness of exports in general, and of agricultural products in particular.

The fixed exchange rate with India has also been detrimental to the export competitiveness of Nepalese products in general, and of agricultural products in particular, having strong prospects of equitable growth and high employment. In the liberalized trade regime, such a dual exchange rate regime is difficult to justify on any logical economic grounds. The fixed exchange rate with India transmits costs-prices to the prices of exports and hence, exports become increasingly less competitive. In such a situation, there is an upsurge in imports and domestic production is dampened. Despite the pegged exchange rate system with India, Nepal has tried to correct any mismatch through adjusting hard currency exchange rates based on cross-examination of the rates between Indian currency and the hard currencies. However, the gap is widening after the deregulation of the input and output prices. Such a variation, together with the high rate of inflation in Nepal *vis-à-vis* India, has led the Nepalese currency to appreciate markedly. This means that by preventing depreciation of Nepali currency, Nepal is subsidizing imports from India and discouraging exports by decreasing the competitiveness of Nepali products *vis-à-vis* Indian commodities. The biggest sufferer of such an exchange rate policy has been the agriculture sector. The appreciation has also helped to encourage an inflow of workers from the neighbouring country.

By ignoring efficiency issues, the deregulation-centric policies increased transaction costs markedly overtime, with adverse effects on trade. This has also continuously encouraged informal trade between Nepal and India. Despite Nepal being very rich in water resources, Nepal is one of the costliest countries in the world today in terms of per unit electricity prices. These factors have also adversely affected the inflow of foreign investment. Although Nepal's lower wage costs provide an important competitive advantage, this is offset by the country's significantly lower labour productivity. While Nepal's productivity and competitiveness increased over the 1990s, these improvements could not be sustained to the end of the decade. Although new initiatives to fulfil WTO obligations—particularly aimed at formulating and revising acts for more open, free and rules-based trading practices—may help to overcome many constraints, there are, however, more challenges and risks emanating from given adverse initial conditions in terms of productivity and competitiveness. The prospects for agro- or forestry-based industries, key for Nepal's sustained development and employment, will depend very much on the extent of Nepal's capacity to preserve patent right of rich biodiversity within the stipulated time frame, which under the given situation is most unlikely. More dangerously, the agreement on trade-related investment measures prevents the possibility of putting conditions on foreign investors to use local raw materials. Under such circumstances, the deterioration in trade performance over recent years indicates that the emphasis on trade openness and liberalization through removal of tariff and non-tariff barriers alone may not be sufficient to unleash the resources required for sustained growth and employment generation.

Despite phenomenal growth in the financial sector in the aftermath of macro policy reforms, the cost of capital and access to financial services still remain major problems. The weak linkages between financial deepening and employment in the financial sector are mainly due to these problems. The main beneficiaries of the increased lending of the commercial banks have been the industrial and commerce sectors in the urban areas. In this case also, more consumable products of big business houses are increasingly funded by siphoning off funds from small savers from both rural and urban areas.

The worrisome phenomenon is that investment in productive areas such as agriculture and industry has either stagnated or declined. This is a harmful trend from the perspective of long-term growth and employment. The inability to reduce the ratio of non-performing assets of the state-owned banks accompanied by an increasing gap between the deposit and lending rates (about 5 per cent) mean that the cost of capital has remained high. The problem has now become aggravated in the rural areas by very high interest rates applicable to the rural areas in general, and to small and marginal farmers in particular. Although wholesale banking and microcredit have been popularized in recent years (as a result of the reduced credit outreach in the rural areas in the aftermath of financial sector reform), access to credit and affordability of interest rates have emerged as major problems. Only 8.3 per cent of the poorest consumption quintile had access to bank credit in 2004, almost the same as in 1996. The direct adverse employment effect has been equally pervasive: compared with 1990, the level of employment in commercial banks had reduced by almost 60 per cent by 2005.

Amidst all these unwarranted developments, the central bank has decided to phase out the priority-sector lending programme by 2007 but without ensuring credit outreach in rural areas through credible alternative institutional arrangements. Moreover, Nepal has made commitments with the WTO in the course of negotiations to allow foreign joint venture banks to operate in Nepal by 2010. These clearly indicate further downside risks from both employment-induced growth and poverty reduction perspectives.

It is probable that in the absence of a separate, comprehensive investment policy, the scattered policies, which are inconsistent and lacking direction, have not been able to promote either foreign or domestic investment. On the contrary, they have discouraged investment in small industries and businesses. Despite the opening up of sectors, there has been no improvement in the investment climate. The deregulation-centric policies have not eased procedural matters or reduced transaction costs because they have neglected other changes and reforms required for efficiency enhancement. The weakness or non-existence of many market institutions and the oversensitivity of government fiscal or monetary policies for maintaining fiscal balance and limiting liquidity in the economy have also worked adversely in this direction. In the absence of supportive policies or institutional arrangements, small industries or businesses have been adversely affected. Above all, the Government's internal investment and expenditure policy seems to be inconsistent with its stated objectives and planned policies and programmes. Unlike in many countries, the fiscal balance has been maintained by squeezing development-related expenditure on a massive scale, even during the period of economic slackness, or by accommodating a massive expansion in security and other unproductive spending. The constraints on development expenditure in the quest of maintaining the fiscal balance and containing the current account deficit have had very adverse effects on the sectors such as agriculture and physical infrastructure which contribute to pro-poor growth and off-farm employment. Despite much attention on the PRSP and the MDGs, no intra or inter sectoral restructuring has taken place. The MTEF implemented within the PRSP has remained primarily ritualistic in this regard.

The contemporary policies overemphasize the reduction of government expenditure through fiscal or monetary tightening regardless of the nature of expenditure or type of investment. Against this backdrop, a quick look at internal borrowing and the rate of inflation shows that there is no direct one-to-one relationship between the two in the Nepalese context. This indicates the need for a review of the contemporary fiscal and monetary policies in order to allow a more balanced approach to be pursued, one that takes both supply-side bottlenecks and demand pull factors into account. Experience shows that inflation in Nepal has predominantly been affected by the supply-side factors.

Policy implications

To achieve better policy coherence and a more appropriate mix and sequencing of policies, it is first of all essential that a comprehensive approach is pursued in the course of macroeconomic policy reforms. This calls for adaptation of policies that are beyond deregulation or liberalization. It also calls for, unlike in the past, a priority on addressing structural and institutional problems. This will help to overcome the problems that impede the growth of small industries and businesses that have strong backward and forward linkages. Such a course of reform will also help to reduce transaction costs and enhance efficiency—key for raising the competitive strength of the economy. In the process, agriculture must be included in the orbit of reforms for equity-led sustained growth, expansion in productive off-farm employment and strengthening of linkages between the agriculture and non-agriculture sectors. The redistribution of land, focusing among landless and marginal farmers as well as other unskilled causal workers that always live in a vulnerable situation, will be critical in this regard. However, unlike the past, the land reform must be pursued in a way that is market-friendly. Above all, the comprehensive reforms must place employment in the centre of the policy agenda. More democratic processes and involvement of various stakeholders, including the voiceless, in the formulation of policies will enable this and will enhance employment and labour productivity simultaneously in the short term. Labour productivity in the agriculture sector corroborates this.

The mismatches or inconsistencies within macroeconomic policies have to be corrected through overhaul and harmonization. It is imperative in this context to pursue an *ex-ante* analysis of employment and poverty assessment of economic policies. Such an analysis would then allow decision-makers to identify the likely gainers and losers, and it would also serve as the basis for formulating complementary policies and programmes to compensate the potential losers, particularly those in the most vulnerable categories. The asymmetry persisting across macro, sectoral and micro policies *vis-à-vis* the development approaches being followed has to be corrected and rationalized, to make them coherent and consistent with sustained growth, decent employment and poverty reduction objectives. The ongoing trade liberalization based on a cascading tariff structure has to be changed in a way that could encourage local resource-based industries which are high value added and employment enhancing. For this, rationalization of the tariff structure will be needed. In the course of reforms, it is necessary that the agro- and forestry-based industries are duly encouraged, which in turn would help commercialization of the agriculture sector. Side by side, the asymmetry between the subsidies policies of Nepal and India needs to be harmonized and the present pegged exchange rate with India needs to be reconsidered to ensure elimination of any misalignment in relative prices, in order to reverse the worsening competitiveness of Nepal's agriculture, industry and trade. This will be essential, especially under the WTO trading arrangements, in order to reap the benefits from the new opportunities and to minimize the risks arising from the adverse initial conditions.

In the financial sector, the gap between the deposit and lending rates has to be narrowed substantially by augmenting structural and institutional reforms across the entire financial sector, with the focus on the effectiveness of ongoing reforms in the two state banks. In parallel, providing access to credit for the small industries and business in urban areas as well as availability of credit at affordable rates in the rural areas will be particularly important. For this, special financial institutional arrangements will be required. This will be urgent in view of the phasing out of priority-sector lending from 2007 and the beginning of banking operations by foreign wholesale banking by 2010.

A comprehensive investment policy also seems essential for providing a special incentives structure for both domestic and foreign investors. This will be necessary for the local producers. Investment policy should contribute towards the development of production clusters in different parts of the country, based on resource endowments and other potentialities; it should also give priority to the establishment of economic and export-processing zones in adjoining areas. This, in addition to attracting foreign investment, would boost labour-intensive local industries and businesses with employment opportunities.

Government needs to overhaul its internal investment and expenditure policy to bridge the gap between stated policy and programme goals and actual implementation. As well as a need for immediate steps to contain unproductive recurrent expenses, there is a need to restructure the investment programme, particularly for reversing the resource allocation trend. Diverting more and more resources toward agriculture and physical infrastructure will be particularly important for this purpose. The curtailment of rising security and other recurring expenses will help to unleash resources to a greater extent. At the same time, public–private partnerships, encouragement of the private sector to invest in infrastructure and increased access for the rural poor to financial services through cooperative schemes and microcredit programmes will ease the resource constraints considerably.

The overemphasis on fiscal and monetary policy tightening is unfounded, which has its roots in the Washington Consensus. The tightening must not disregard the link between the nature of spending or investment, its impact and its consequences in terms of income or employment generation in the short and long terms. While designing investment, income or wage policy, if a balanced approach is followed to maximize both short- and long-term returns, no serious short-term stability or long-term growth-related trade-offs are likely to emerge.

Labour policy reform should also be a part of overall reform. Some flexibility in labour policy will be necessary to check the informalization of the labour market. But this must be supplemented by policies that contributes to raise skills and enhance the productivity of workers. The low employment elasticity in general and the reduced labour productivity in industry and the services sector are major causes of concern. Therefore, various forms of structural bottlenecks in the labour market, including gender discrimination, have to be corrected for future growth potentials to be unleashed. Priority on vocational training and education along with a massive skills development programme are badly needed in Nepal in view of, among other factors, the displacement of Nepalese workers by foreign workers.[40] Drastic reform of the education policy or system is needed to make education more technical and vocational. After introducing a rights-based approach in the education system, at least up to the secondary level, the predominant emphasis should be on vocational and technical education. Similarly, initiation of special training programmes for unsuccessful high school graduates could be a better strategy to overcome the increasing unemployment problem among youths. In addition to helping to reduce the wage gap between skilled and unskilled workers, this could encourage self-employment.

The feudalistic practices that perpetuate discrimination against women and other disadvantaged people, including *dalits*, *madhesi*, deprived indigenous community and people living in remote areas, have to be abolished through initiating some affirmative actions by the state. Restructuring and reforms in the training and skills development programmes need to be consistent with the changing market demands. At the same time, access to training, technical and vocational education for disadvantaged including women is badly needed and could be provided through expansion of such facilities to inaccessible areas. This could also be improved through the encouragement of private sector involvement. Training and skills development facilities for workers seeking foreign jobs could greatly enhance the possibilities of decent

40. No comprehensive study on the encroachment in labour market by foreign workers is available. Some scanty information reveals that in construction works in Kathmandu, 80 per cent of workers are foreign.

employment abroad. Only recently, the discriminatory policy preventing women from going abroad for foreign employment has been corrected; although this requires effective enforcement. The practice of wage discrimination between males and females needs to be discouraged through an appropriate system of punishment and other means.

Lack of suitable coordinating, monitoring and policy feedback mechanisms also make the ongoing programmes less effective. A strong tripartite machinery plus institutions, involving, among others, the Government, employers and trade unions, would facilitate consensus-building processes through social dialogue in various contentious labour-related issues. A system in which labour market related information from the grass-roots level can regularly feed into it would be essential for such a machinery to function effectively.

To promote decent work, emphasis must be placed on productive work in which rights are protected and which generates adequate income with social protection. Today, the elderly, physically handicapped people and widows receive a limited allowance on a monthly basis from the Government. However, a more coherent social protection programme is yet to evolve. Similarly, more attention has to be given to improve the productivity of the informal economy. Given the large amount of informal activity, job creation in the formal economy alone cannot be expected to meet the need for productive employment in the economy. Introduction of less-stringent labour regulations for micro-enterprises in order to encourage their formalization and thereby facilitate access to credit and technical assistance, among other services, will be important in this respect.

The current debate on "hiring and firing" and labour market rigidities hardly makes any explicit reference to labour productivity issues. This important missing link creates obstacles in the consensus-building process through tripartite dialogue. Too much emphasis on hiring and firing in the canvassing for flexible labour laws without linking the argument to labour productivity related issues has led to polarization of attitudes among the contending parties and strong opposition from trade unions, human rights organizations and social activists.

Similarly, a reorientation of PRSPs and the MDGs is needed to keep employment at the centre of the policy and programme agenda. This calls for more accommodative as well as coordinating attitudes from the donors. More importantly, the opposite policy directions often found among multilateral or bilateral donors have to be resolved permanently. A technical-support approach from donors rather than a conditions-based approach would contribute greatly to internalizing the ownership of policies and programmes, which could really help bringing about policy coherence.

6 Pakistan: A tale of controlled market and weak governance

Nadeem Ul Haque

6.1 Introduction

Since its Independence, Pakistan has pursued policies that have been based on government-led development and industrialization through subsidies and incentives. As a result, government has been growing in size and has been engaged in expanding its role beyond the traditional functions of security and justice into the development projects market and market production.

Despite privatization and opening up of the economy, government continues to dominate the economy at the expense of market development. Moreover, policy remains path dependent, emphasizing production, especially industrial production, and continues to treat markets with suspicion. With opening out, a greater emphasis is placed on export promotion through the active involvement of government agencies such as the Export Development Board and the Ministry of Commerce. Conversely, imports still continue to have an import substitution bias in the engineering goods sector given that an Engineering Development Board comprising of owners of the protected industry has a large say in the protection of the sector.

Because of a continued emphasis on import substitution, policies to promote industrial growth primarily for export have developed an anti-consumer bias in the economy. The bias has been further reinforced by a view that domestic commerce, especially trade, is unproductive and does not create "value addition", to use a popular local term. This bias carries over into all levels of policy and government. Space and town planning treat commercialization almost as a sin, with restrictive building regulations and high fees.

The result is that the domestic commerce sector—trade retail and wholesale, construction, transport, warehousing, entertainment and leisure—remains seriously underdeveloped. This is also the sector that employs the most people and most of the poor people. If employment creation and poverty reduction are serious policy goals, policy thinking seriously needs to change from its current almost mercantilist approach, which is biased against domestic market development and the domestic consumer, to one where the domestic market is fully integrated into global markets and consumer welfare is maximized.

We take the view that a paradigm shift is now called for—a shift from the "planning model" to the free-market economy. The changeover is imperative for three reasons:

- the state machinery that has to put into effect the planning model is not competent to perform the task;
- globalization has made it difficult to pursue the planning model; and
- "new growth theory" does not support the model.

Rest of this chapter is organized as follows. Section 6.2 presents labour market outcomes in Pakistan. Section 6.3 describes the failure of the planning model, pursued to manage the economy. Section 6.4 describes the policy measures meant to provide an enabling environment, to achieve the transition to, and ensure smooth functioning of, the free-market economy. Section 6.5 highlights the need for a paradigm shift and new development thinking, which are followed by a set of recommendations in Section 6.6. Recommended sequencing of reform of the political economy has been discussed in Section 6.7. Section 6.8 concludes the chapter.

6.2 Pakistan's labour market

The growth rate of Pakistan's economy has shown improvement in recent years. However, the growth in employment has not only lagged behind the growth in gross domestic product (GDP), the growth in employment has remained more or less insensitive to the changes in the growth rate of the economy. Job growth is slower than the rate of growth of GDP—while GDP grew by 3.5 per cent per annum from 1993/94 to 2003/2004, employment grew by 2.4 per cent during the same period.

Figure 6.1

Pakistan: Growth trends in GDP, employment and labour force, 1984/85–1993/94 and 1993/94–2003/04

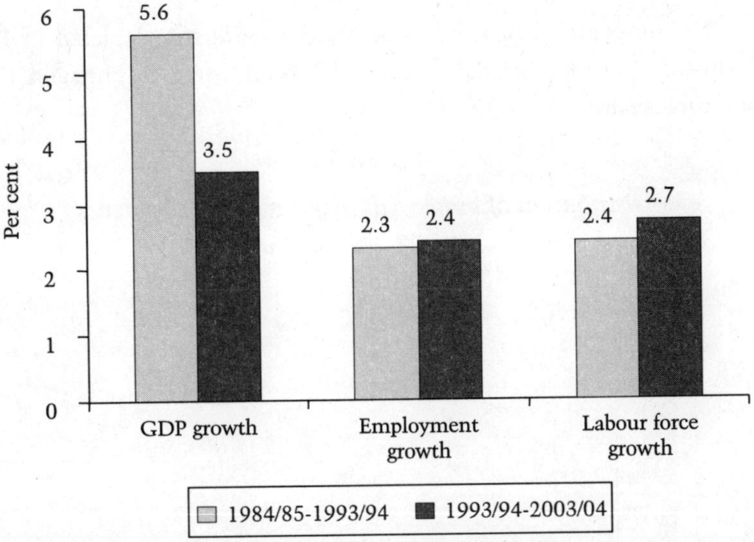

Source: Government of Pakistan, 1985, 1994, 2004; World Bank, 2004a.

It is evident from Figure 6.1 that while GDP grew at different rates during the periods considered, the employment growth remained static. The slow rate of job creation compounds the problem of low wages in existing jobs, which tend to have stagnated over the last decade. Besides, formal-sector jobs are rather scarce and the breakdown of labour force between the different sectors is not changing either.

Pakistan has a labour force of 45 million in a population of 150 million. This gives a crude activity rate of 30 per cent. The crude activity rate has stayed roughly constant since 1980, but it has registered some change in the ongoing decade as it went up from 29.6 per cent in 2001/02 to 32.7 per cent in second quarter of 2005/06. The "refined activity rate" has also registered an improvement of 4 percentage points (2001/02: 43 per cent; 2005/06(Q2): 47 per cent). Historically, the labour force has been growing at a higher rate than the total employment growth of 2.75 per annum, indicating that the incremental labour force is not being fully absorbed. The real unemployment problem is much larger than that implied by these numbers and comprises the seasonal unemployment of the informal and the agricultural workers, and a large but unknown numbers of "discouraged workers"' who have given up and cease to appear in the labour force.

The composition of the labour force by industry depicted in Figure 6.2 shows that the largest chunk of labour force is engaged in the agriculture sector.

Figure 6.2

Distribution of employed: Major industry divisions, 2001/02 and 2003/04

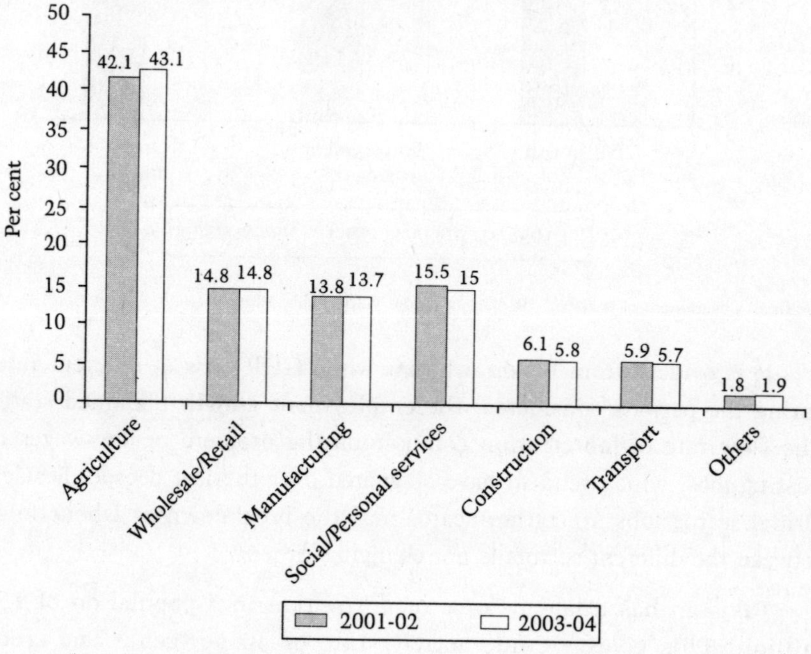

Source: Government of Pakistan, 2002, 2004.

The informal economy[1] employed 70 per cent of the non-agricultural labour force in 2003/04, thus registering an increase of 5 percentage points over 2001/02. The rather high percentage of the labour

1. Persons working in organizations that employ fewer than 10 people are included in the informal economy.

force engaged in the informal economy and its growth trend call for a further probe of employment in the informal economy. Figure 6.3 shows the composition by industry of the labour force engaged in the informal economy.

Figure 6.3

Informal economy workers: Composition by industry, 2003/04 (percentage)

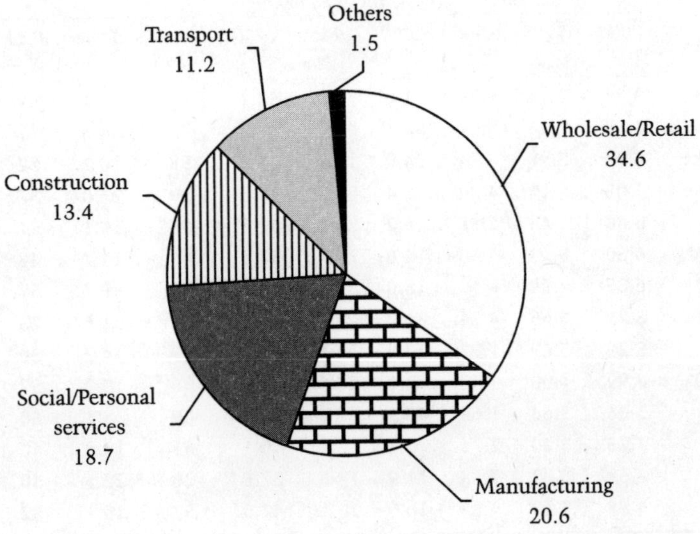

Source: Government of Pakistan, 2004.

Given that a sizeable chunk of the labour force is employed in the informal economy and that the informal labour is mostly labour-intensive, we feel that policies should be directed towards encouraging the sector rather than ensuring a forced transition from the informal to the formal economy.

The education level of the labour force in Pakistan presents a dismal picture. Table 6.1 shows that the average levels of schooling of the labour force in Pakistan have been consistently at the lower end of the world rankings. In addition, Pakistan's normalized scores on the Human Development Index and the literacy and enrolment rates (secondary and tertiary) fell between 1995 and 2004, indicating that gains made in basic education were less than those achieved in other developing countries of the world. It is no wonder that only about one-third of the manufacturing sector's workforce in Pakistan completed secondary education, as compared with a half for the rest of South Asia.

Table 6.1

Education and workers' skills

	Barro–Lee education index						*Harbison–Meyers skills index*			
	Average years of schooling			*% of population without schooling*			*1998*		*1995*	
	2000	*1985*	*1960*	*2000*	*1985*	*1960*	*Rank of 98*	*Score*	*Rank of 95*	*Score*
Pakistan	3.88	2.14	0.74	51.0	72.8	83.1	77	4.1	69	4.4
Bangladesh	2.58	2.06	0.61	50.1	63.0	87.0	76	4.3	72	3.9
Sri Lanka	6.87	5.88	3.94	14.0	11.9	37.1	58	10.1	52	9.1
Singapore	7.05	6.10	4.30	16.4	28.2	46.2	29	23.0	37	14.1
Malaysia	6.80	5.48	2.88	16.2	23.0	49.7	55	11.1	51	9.2
Thailand	6.50	5.18	4.30	12.6	15.7	36.9	45	14.7	48	10.7
China	6.35	4.94	–	18.0	31.5	–	59	9.7	67	5.1
Philippines	8.21	6.65	4.24	31.0	8.3	25.6	32	21.6	23	21.2
Turkey	5.29	3.69	1.92	20.8	39.1	59.2	49	14.7	50	9.8
Indonesia	4.99	4.00	1.55	32.1	23.6	68.0	56	10.3	57	8.3
India	5.06	3.64	1.68	43.9	61.6	72.2	69	8.1	60	7.1
Mexico	7.23	5.20	2.76	9.7	22.2	40.1	51	12.9	40	14.1
Peru	7.58	6.02	7.58	11.9	17.5	37.6	30	22.5	30	18.4
Brazil	4.88	3.48	4.88	16.0	26.1	47.5	57	10.1	52	9.1

Note: – = data not available.

Source: World Bank, 2006e.

6.3 Planning has not worked while quality of governance has declined

When Pakistan gained Independence in 1947, Keynesian activist policies prevailed in the West and communism had captured global attention as the economies of China and Russia apparently seemed to be doing well. Developing economies emerged to help countries like Pakistan to escape from poverty and promised rapid economic development based on planning and borrowing. It was natural in that era to view markets and private enterprise with suspicion. Moreover, since all rich countries were industrialized, the policy goal was clearly to industrialize at all costs.

The planning model adopted focused mainly on industrial development through protection and subsidies. Through direct subsidies, cheap land and credit, and protection through licensing and tariffs, industrial production has been encouraged throughout the past 60 years. Within industry, the policy tried to foster exports through licensing, subsidy regimes and an overvalued exchange rate and to protect import-substitution industry.

In this scheme, domestic consumption and commerce was discouraged. Quality goods and new products were considered to be luxuries and were taxed heavily. Subsidies and protection to domestic industry reduced the incentive for developing products of global quality. These enterprises did not produce goods of quality and they did not do any research and development.

However, the thinking in Islamabad continues to regard industrialization and production as the keys to growth. The view that "value addition" is to a large degree achieved through an industrial product remains firm. This view pervades policy at all levels. One important area is city planning, where domestic commerce does not receive adequate zoning (see Haque, 2006a).

Thus, given the Government's suspicion of the markets, the policy paradigm followed in Pakistan has been of a managed/planned economy. Government interventions are made on the presumption that markets fail. However, this assumption conveniently ignores the fact that the government may fail as well.[2]

There are still people who argue for more government intervention and less market intervention, even though international rating agencies continue to show that the quality of governance in Pakistan is poor. At the time of independence, Government was primarily concerned with providing law and order, security and maintaining and developing infrastructure. Over the planning era, Government has moved more towards a project management role and is in a continuous search for funding. Not only is the record on project development and management not good, but the record on governance may even have deteriorated

2. The main point in favour of the market economy is that the basis of the planned economy—"I know where your welfare lies"—is found wanting on many grounds.

during this period. This is clearly evidenced in the assessment of the Global Competitiveness Report, Transparency International and the World Bank, among others (Box 6.1).

Box 6.1

The state of governance in Pakistan

Transparency International

In the latest survey by Transparency International (2006), Pakistan is ranked 147 out of 163 (163 being the most corrupt).

Global Competitiveness Report (2006)

- In judicial independence, Pakistan's ranking is 77 out of 102.
- Irregular tax payments are quite large: Pakistan's ranking is 77 out of 102.
- Well-defined property rights are a key ingredient of economic growth: Pakistan's ranking of 71 out of 102 reflects a poor record on this count.
- On the Innovation Index, Pakistan's ranking is 94 out of 102. This reflects almost no innovation at all.

Value Chain Index

According to a World Bank survey, five sectors of Pakistan's economy—fisheries, mining, ready-made garments, light engineering and dairy—carry great potential but face serious constraints. The constraints include: high freight costs, electricity outages, delays in collecting rebates, bribes at the harbour and government involvement in cotton seed. All these constraints are directly traceable to poor governance.

6.4 A review of Pakistan's growth

The main periods of Pakistan's economic growth are summarized in Table 6.2. In Table 6.2, for each decade mentioned at the column heading, the rows show the important landmarks of the prevailing political-economic regime. There have been three episodes of economic growth during Pakistan's 59-year history: in the 1960s, the 1980s and the 2000s. None of the three periods lasted for more than 4–5 years. Each one was accompanied by external aid provided as a consequence of an external shock or war: the Cold War, the Soviet–Afghan war and the terrorist attack on 11 September 2001 (9/11), respectively. In the first two cases, the growth spurts ended when foreign aid tapered off. All the growth spurts were accompanied by growing disparities in personal and regional incomes[3] (Sheikh, 2006).

3. For review of Pakistan's economic/governance performance, we make liberal use of Sheikh (2006) and Zaidi (2005).

Table 6.2

The main phases of Pakistan's economic growth

1960s	*1970s*	*1980s*	*1990s*	*2000s*
6.97[1]	4.58	6.09	3.86	4.55
Aid-led growth	Aid stoppage	Afghan war, second aid episode	Afghan war ends, aid cut off	Third aid episode, aid rescheduling
Factor accumulation	Populism/ dictatorship	Remittance boom	Incomplete IMF programme, Fiscal Crisis Dock	Post 9/11 remittances
Growing disparities	Nationalization	Institutional deterioration	Return to sporadic democracy	Successful IMF programme, macro consolidation
Growing political polarization	Decline of institutions	Fundamentalism consolidates	Perception of misgovernance/ corruption	Growing disparities and polarization
War and civil disturbance	Rise of fundamentalism	Missed opportunities, reform postponed	Banking reform, privatization effort	Successful privatization
Planning		Expansion of public sector	Infrastructure and independent power	Unsettled politics, limited producer institutional reform

Note: [1] The figures in this row indicate average annual growth rate during the period (percentage).
The growth rates have been calculated from Economic Survey of various years published by the Government of Pakistan.

The aid bonanzas allowed Pakistan to avoid or delay structural reforms and the need to take the vested interests head-on. Getting away with an overvalued exchange rate,[4] high fiscal deficit and low tax to GDP ratio[5] for most of its history serves to support the assertion that correction of the structural imbalances was not undertaken, or at least was delayed. Some change has been observed in the structure of the economy from 1950 to 2005–06, with the share of agriculture in GDP declining to 21.6 per cent in 2005/06 from 53.2 per cent, and the share of service sector rising to 52.3 from 39 per cent during the same period.

4. The Pakistan rupee was devalued only twice between 1947 and January 1982, when Pakistan switched over to "managed float".

5. In 2005–06, Pakistan's tax-GDP ratio was much lower than even what was the average tax–GDP ratio of the countries with similar levels of per capita income in 1994.

However, the economy is still vulnerable to the vagaries of the weather, especially because Pakistan's exports are heavily dependent on one item: textiles (textiles comprised around 61 per cent of Pakistan's exports in 2005/06).

Until the 1970s, the private sector, especially the industrial sector, was allowed to flourish, under the infant industry argument, on the back of licenses and permits, high tariff protections and an overvalued exchange rate. The growth rate notwithstanding, this led to high income disparities that paved the way for the electoral success of Bhutto's socialist philosophy.

In step with Bhutto's electoral promises and the fashion at that time, the 1970s saw the nationalization of number of sectors, including insurance, banking, automobile manufacturing, vegetable oil, cement, chemical engineering and fertilizers. Unfortunately, but predictably, the performance of public enterprises (PEs) left much to be desired. Quite a few of them were in deficit and so a burden on the exchequer. Banks not only piled up huge non-performing loans but also facilitated the continued existence of an industrialist class that had, since Independence, thrived on concessions of one sort or another.

During 1980s, the public enterprises, at their peak, numbered more than 200 and their estimated share in the GDP reached 14 per cent (Sheikh, 2006). Due to the change in international opinion towards PEs in the 1980s, and the mounting fiscal burden of the Pakistani PEs and the lacklustre results of efforts to reform them, the privatization of Pakistan's PEs began—and continues to this day. The performance of the PEs had declined to the extent that the Government had to inject sizeable amounts of equity into some projects to make them viable for privatization—for example, United Bank Limited (Rs. 20.0 billion) and Habib Bank Limited (Rs. 7.0 billion)—while the liabilities of others were taken over by the Government.

Meanwhile, much of the 1990s was spent struggling with a balance of payments (BOP) crisis for which repeated IMF programmes were sought. Foreign exchange dependence increased and a large number of reforms were forced on the economy. The trade regime was substantially liberalized, except for the sectors that had the lobbies to protect themselves. A fair number of public sector enterprises were privatized. Perhaps the most significant reform was that of the financial sector.

Clearly, the most important conclusion to be drawn from all this is that the "planning/production/mercantilist model" has failed to deliver and that the growth strategy has to change. Unfortunately, however, there is a lack of research, and the academic community precludes a debate on this proposition; it does not educate the policy-makers or the public on lessons from the past either. The result is that the growth strategy continues to remain unchanged.[6]

6.5 Paradigm shift: The new development thinking

Are planned economies superior to market economies? Not necessarily (Box 6.2). Clearly, a paradigm shift in our policy thinking is required—the shift to a market- and consumer-oriented economy. To achieve this shift, political will and policy measures and a deeper understanding of economics and finance will be required.

Box 6.2

A planned economy: Good or bad?

The biggest argument against the market economy is the creation of concentration or monopolies in few sectors. However, under a "planned economy", the state sets up its own monopoly over the whole economy. Evidence shows that monopolies in market economies have been short lived and broken up by the introduction of substitutes; however, this is not the case in a planned economy.

Planned economies have not proved that they are even as stable as free-market economies, which has been accused of instability. A centralized plan is insensitive to the public's choices. Most collectivist economic planning is authoritarian in thinking; it assumes that the public are incapable of determining their own welfare and must have superior planners to do it for them. This concept is totally at variance with the democratic ideal, which presupposes that people have the right to direct their own welfare and to be free, even to be foolish if they so choose.

Imperialism and international unrest are relatively more evidenced in a planned economy. The reason is that the public are willing to make sacrifices in the event of national emergencies. The planners, being unable to give to the public what they could get under a free-market economy, must therefore foment international emergencies.

6. Of course, the rent-seeking lobbies that the earlier planning and control eras created work hard to keep the growth paradigm from shifting. Given that the Government is seen by many international observers not to be providing governance, there is an urgent need for all serious thinkers, especially the policy-makers, to consider the Government's role in the economy.

In thinking of a new strategy, we must draw on fresh developments in economic thinking around the world. Some lessons from the large amount of research that has been done internationally are as follows:[7]

- Important determinants of economic growth are knowledge, creativity and innovation. Societies that progress foster such activities.
- For economic growth to take place, institutions must be configured to foster security of life, property and contract, and to facilitate market development.
- Economic activity grows in open competitive markets. Economic activity and innovation is chaotic and cannot be planned by government and, hence, must be left to markets.[8]
- Growth takes place in creative cities, where individual liberty and economic freedom are maximized and community space developed to allow individuals to come together. Such cities are based on limited regulation since they encourage mixed use and commerce. Such cities foster knowledge clusters.
- The role of government is not to plan and attempt mercantilist sector and industry picking, but to provide the institutions that will foster the four activities outlined above.

The new economics defines very clearly the distinct roles of the government and the market place. By managing its role well, the government defines incentives within society for creativity and innovation. Social mobility is determined by creativity and knowledge creation and not by government policy. Instead of rewarding rent-seekers, policy seeks to reward talent and innovation.

---

7. In many developing countries, considerable inertia in thinking is displayed despite attempts at liberalization and advancing global communication. Indrajit Coomaraswamy of the Commonwealth Secretariat says: "We seem to have liberalised our economies but not our minds".

8. For evidence of benefits of globalization, see Bhagwati (2004) and Friedman (2000). Stiglitz (2003), whom many dirigiste thinkers quote, has some reservations on the international architecture but is quite accepting of most other aspects of globalization.

Clearly, "the early design" that has been adhered to—a domineering role for the Government, planning and mercantilism—is inimical to the new economics. One major flaw in the path-dependent growth policies that we have been following has been the neglect of institutions and governance.

6.6 What is to be done?

At least five areas need substantive rethinking if we accept the modern view of economics that we have laid out here.[9]

Accepting markets and globalization

The key point to note is that an acceptance of globalization means integrating into the global economy, and discarding the current approach of choosing areas in which to engage.[10] Globalization is the linkage of markets across national boundaries. Therefore, the benefits from globalization can only be realized through market development. The domineering role of government has stifled market development (Haque, 2006a).[11]

If this approach is accepted, current emphasis on production would be replaced by market development. With this emphasis, a whole host of new approaches to economic policy will need to be developed. For example, every planned government intervention in the marketplace, including revenue initiatives, would need careful scrutiny at the technical level by a broad group of professional economists, think tanks and universities so that their market implications can be understood before they are implemented. The yardstick for such an analysis and debate would have to be: "all government intervention must be market-neutral and minimal".

In market development, the issue of regulation would have to be faced. Two important points on regulation need to be recognized. First,

---

9. These areas should be widely debated, especially among the labour movement and civil society, if change is to happen. Remember, the powers that be and policy-makers benefit from the status quo. Only the poor need reform.
10. This will mean a change in the trade policy that seeks to protect favourites and to promote exports.
11. For example, agricultural procurement and storage currently remain dominated by government; subsidies to industry or exorbitant protection to some leads to distortion in the market place.

markets are self-organizing and self-regulating. Regulation only affects areas of market failure where self-regulation does not work.[12] Second, each market is specialized and needs specialists with the requisite skills to regulate the market. Generalists who are transferred from a government department most often will not do.[13]

Re-aligning government to the social contract

Public policy research has clarified the role of government to be one of correcting market failure and providing security to individuals and markets.[14] Government activity beyond the social contract needs to be carefully thought through. In this view, the role of government is to provide governance first. Development can only be done by a government that can provide governance. Even government activities within the social contract need to be conducted with as much transparency and accountability as possible. Government efficiency and output must always be monitored.[15]

Building institutions and governance

There is now widespread acceptance that institutions and governance need to be built for growth.[16] In reality, this has remained little more than wishful thinking. Most often, the effort of building institutions has relied on very expensive donor-funded projects driven by

---

12. Development is a chaotic and messy business best conducted through the market taking its own head. This is well-understood and has to be accepted. Policy must give this process space, but be ready to help clean up where it can in an informed manner.
13. The dictum that "every market needs government regulation" is convenient for rent-seeking but it ignores all economic theory and empirical evidence. Often, regulation is built on bureaucratic lines and run by generalist bureaucrats.
14. All tasks of government derive from this mandate of providing individual security and liberty and safeguarding the contracts and transactions conducted by sovereign individuals. Development projects and arranging for welfare and distribution are dimensions of improving welfare.
15. One important function of Parliament from its inception has been the monitoring of government. An important part of the new governance movement started by Margaret Thatcher and the New Zealand reform has been the measurement of the quality of government and the continuous reporting of such governance. Of course, this assumes an open and transparent government where citizens have a right to know.
16. See Acemoglu *et al.* (2005) for an analysis of the impact of institutions on growth.

costly consultants with little impact on the efficiency or the quality of governance or institutions. The focus of most of this work is the importing of "best practice", which the incumbents—with their current poor incentives—are supposed to implement.

Institutions are the rules and norms accepted by society as the ones under which it will operate. This sets up a huge agenda—from the constitution to the norms and culture in society. Constitutions define the checks and balances that incorporate the basic incentives under which the society functions. Economists such as Hayek (1978) contend that even this basic document needs to be aligned with economic efficiency, individual liberty and maximum welfare of all.[17]

Civilization is based on two very important principles—property rights and the rule of law—which need to be carefully developed and nurtured. The state guarantees property rights, the definition of which is continuously expanding with technology and population density. The former of these creates new goods and services as well as new uses for existing goods and services, leading to possible rights conflicts or redefinitions and reinterpretations. Related contracting mechanisms also seek to define property rights and claims that again require informed and appropriate state intervention.

Similarly, with increasing population density, individual property rights have to be traded off against community welfare as crowded urban spaces increase social externalities. Space and environment need to be shared so that individual freedom and privacy are maximized while increasing community welfare. Public goods infrastructure, such as roads, sewers and power distribution and communications like telephone wiring, will require the assertion of "eminent domain". Unless an informed and

---

17. Constitutional economics is an important subject and should be taken into account at moments of constitutional deliberations. One reason that Pakistan runs into a constitutional hiatuses is that in the framing of both the constitution and its amendments, no expert of this field was consulted; see Cooter (2000) and Hayek (1978). *The Federalist Papers* (Hamilton *et al.*, 1788) has a very good discussion of constitutional issues. Lord Acton's famous dictum "power corrupts" remains true, and hence, an important role of the constitution is to distribute power through checks and balances so that it does not concentrate anywhere.

thinking approach is used, eminent domain can convey too much power to the executive and be used for rent-seeking.[18]

An important ingredient for building governance is the establishment of the rule of law, which means an end of privilege and "network rent-seeking".[19] Experience of development in many countries has shown that ensuring justice and the rule of law leads to good market development and enhances growth. Establishing the rule of law and a good system of justice has now become a matter of priority.[20] A resource-constrained government must therefore use its resources wisely, and it must ensure that the key institutions of governance required for security and market development are properly developed.[21]

Developing creativity and social mobility: From rent-seeking to merit

Much recent research has emphasized that the key difference between the developing and the advanced countries is the creation and use of knowledge and creativity. In such an environment, merit must be rewarded at every level. This would happen if, as suggested earlier, the role of government is realigned, globalization is accepted and institutions are built. What sort of institutions would allow this creativity to be unleashed?

---

18. There is another interesting area for research and reform here. Currently, land development takes place under the Cooperative Societies Act (c. 1912 and its amendments) and the Land Acquisition Act (c. 1894 and its amendments). The former has no legal entity or any redistributive power of public resources while the latter should not be used for development of housing for the rich.

19. There is little sociological research in Pakistan, even though much work is required. One area that has important ramifications for the economy as well as polity is what we would term as "network rent-seeking". People are now working very hard to be a part of some important network so that they will be able to engage in rent-seeking. Not only is this a wasteful activity, it also destroys the socio-political fabric of the country and destroys the rule of law.

20. The principle of "equality before law" is maintained by an independent, competent and quality judiciary. The law must also show its responsiveness to changes in society. Hence, the legal system must also be capable of reform and innovation. The legal process must be fit for rapid enactment of needed laws and not always be dependent on a crisis or on an external donor forcing a change.

21. In building institutions on the principles required by modern economic and legal thinking, competent research needs to be conducted and widely debated to enable a consensus for well-understood reform.

Box 6.3

Civil service reforms

Monetization of perquisites

Salaries in the civil service are rather low and it is the perquisites/corruption that make up the shortage of cash income. The management of the economy yields the highest remuneration for civil servant in terms of rent-seeking, perquisites or outright corruption. Rent-seeking and perquisites range from securing government land at grossly subsidized rates to being on the board of a state-owned enterprise, thereby enjoying the attendant benefits. This class has a vested interest in maintaining the current system, which provides wealth transfer (Haque, 2006a). For this class, the benefits from rent-seeking and perquisites outweigh the benefits likely to accrue from reforms. The first and foremost reform would be to monetize all perquisites, including government housing. Other important reforms would include opening up all positions in the civil service to professionals.

Induction of professionals

Putting an end to rent-seeking requires professionals to be inducted in the civil service; people who could also find a job elsewhere. If these people are hit by the reforms they could opt to move out of the system, rather than have to attempt to maintain the rent-seeking/perquisites management regime. To achieve this objective, the current system of inducting civil servants only at a specified level (i.e., grade 17) needs to be replaced in favour of opening up all positions to outside professionals.

The entry of professionals into the civil service is essential for another reason. The shift from a managed economy to a market economy calls for a paradigm shift. The issue is therefore, who would facilitate the shift. The shift involves loosening the hold of the bureaucracy over the economy and whatever little role the state has, in terms of providing an "enabling environment", performing that role in a professional manner. The "generalists" that the civil service is stocked with are not suitable for the task. It is only the professionals, equipped with technical knowledge and relevant experience, who can facilitate "the shift".

Cost of job change and pension portability

To bring in efficiency, mobility into and out of civil service is to be encouraged. The cost of job change is currently too high. A civil servant who has served the Government for, say, 15 years and has a good offer from the private sector finds it difficult to move because he stands to lose the pension he has accrued to-date. The Government therefore ends up retaining a frustrated worker, who will be busy counting down the days to pension eligibility. The solution lies in making the pension portable, as is the case in the developed world. This may involve having pension funds. Whether or not pension funds would be an extra burden on the exchequer needs to be thoroughly worked out. Even if the pension funds pose some extra fiscal burdens, the benefits involved would outweigh the costs, especially when the issue of pension funds is already on the table, given their positive impact on savings and investment.

- *Shift to a consumer-oriented society.* Creativity can be built through change in policy stance and regulation that sees all activity—and not just production—as equally valuable. This will require a change in emphasis from the current focus of policy-makers on supporting producers through essentially mercantilist policies to an economy that allows consumers more choices and greater weight in the economy. Policy will then have to allow more space, both metaphorically and physically, to services, and especially to domestic commerce, which is currently stifled.[22]

- *Urban regulation for creative cities*. For this broader consumer-focused model, policy and regulation should accommodate the market development, even though at times it may not be as orderly as the planners may like. Most importantly, regulation for city and land development and utilization will have to be more accommodative of more city activities than are currently allowed. Currently, cities primarily allow for high-income, single-family housing, small retail and some industry. This approach also shuns urban density and values large open spaces with suburban housing. In the new model, much more density will have to be accommodated, including multiple-family dwellings (see Haque, 2006a).

Promoting markets and domestic commerce

Pakistan, with a population of 160 million, is a huge market in itself. Promotion of commercial activity within the country holds great promise for enhancing growth and for increasing the labour content of the growth. According to Haque (2006a): "Domestic commerce is the most pro-poor growth possibility in the country. Currently it employs about 40 per cent of the labour force and contributes about 52 per cent to the GDP. If provided with an enabling environment—estimates suggest that it can increase the growth rate by at least 2 percentage points." We discuss below some domestic commercial activities that, if undertaken, would significantly contribute to growth.

22. With better retail, warehousing and leisure activities, the markets, output and employment will expand. In an open economy, consumers will exert their preferences in the market through these activities. Economic activity will then take place according to the price signals conveyed by final consumer demand (Hayek, 1945). Products will be developed to satisfy consumer demand. Chances of high-quality products and brand names being developed will increase—and it is these products that will move overseas to increase domestic wealth.

Wholesale/retail trade

A substantial part of the labour force (35 per cent) from the informal economy is engaged in wholesale/retail trade. The fact that weekly sunday or friday makeshift markets established in some parts of the country do good business serves to indicate that retail trade requires more space than is allocated to it. Similarly the *khokhas* (kiosks) and *rehris* (barrows) selling vegetables and fruits etc., are seen in almost every nook and cranny of the country. Although these are doing business, most of them are considered as encroachers of state land. Looking at them as encroachers only increases the cost of doing business for these small-scale sellers.

To encourage retail trade, instead of looking upon *khokhas* and *rehris* as encroachers, the city authorities need to allocate enough space for them in commercial centres and different parts of the city (Haque, 2006a). In addition, the weekly sunday or friday markets could perhaps be allowed throughout the week. Retail trade is labour-intensive, therefore, an increase in the contribution of retail trade to GDP is likely to increase the job content of growth.

Branding, standardization and certification

Akerlof (1970) showed that asymmetry in information between buyers and sellers inhibits trade. Brands, by signalling the quality of a product, reduce the asymmetric information that Akerlof referred to. Thus, brands take care of the "lemons" that impede trade. Standardization of goods and third party certification also serve the same purpose. One can count easily, perhaps on one's fingertips, the small number of local brand names. The authorities need to encourage brands and certification.

The legal framework for registration of brands and protection of brand owners against imitation is rather weak. Given that the primary task of government in a free-market economy is to provide an enabling environment for businesses to flourish, the legal framework for registration of brands need strengthening. Another policy measure in this regard could be to introduce tax concessions for brand names; this could apply to almost every field, ranging from eatables to consumer durables, and even to schools.

Office and warehousing space

Another area for domestic development is fulfilment of the huge excess demand for office space and warehousing space. This would involve construction activity in the country and hence, reduce jobless growth. The fact that offices and shop-warehouses are located in residential houses in major urban centres serves to substantiate the huge excess demand in the country for extra space. Clearly, purpose-built offices and warehouses are better than converted residential houses, so why then are these not emerging? Hurdles include city zoning laws and high prices for real estate. Some cities have not allocated enough space for the activities, and where it is allocated the locations are not suitable. Height and density restrictions also constrain construction activity. Land development at too slow a pace by government has pushed up the prices to an unrealistic level. Finally, very old tenancy laws that favour the tenant to the detriment of the landowner are yet another impediment to commercial construction. Policy measures that remove these hurdles will certainly encourage construction activity and generate the associated benefits.

6.7 Sequencing of reform and political economy

With the deregulation and reorientation of the role of government, a huge growth dividend may be expected.[23] Yet there are opponents to this reform! Is there a critical reform that would unleash other reform? Obviously, those parties favoured by current policy would not favour reform.[24] One important point of entry could be to align the incentives for a key group with reform. One such group could be the public servants, for the following reasons.

Given the prevalence of rent-seeking and perk-management in government, the incumbents probably self-select themselves on the basis of their ability to play this game. To such individuals, gains from reform may

23. Reallocation of land resources within cities alone will open up many opportunities. New commercial activities, such as leisure, hotels and land development, will absorb large amounts of investment, which multinationals will hungrily provide.

24. Complete opening of the economy and a wholesale deregulation that develops strong competition will be one important approach to moving in the direction of the new strategy. But the two most powerful groups—current favoured industrialists and government machinery—will strongly resist such a move and will convert *de jure* liberalization into *de facto* closure.

not outweigh those from rent-seeking or perk-management. The approach should then be to change the rules so as to allow people who are more invested in reform to come into positions where reform can be made.

To break the current hold, incentives have to be changed to allow individuals who would choose reform over rent-seeking to enter key public positions. This can only happen if:

- the currently closed civil service is opened up at all levels, i.e., all positions face external competition;
- the generalist approach is discarded and appointments of professionals with the requisite skills are made;
- reasonable security of tenure is given, i.e., transfer is discarded as a weapon of control;
- mobility into and out of the public sector is encouraged;
- perquisites are abolished and all payments are in cash and totally transparent (performance-based bonuses are used and payments are competitive with the private sector); and
- reform is rewarded with honours and payment at market levels.

With this approach, government employees (judges, civil servants, public-service delivery employees) can all hope to invest in reform and gain from it. Over time, the incumbents engaged in rent-seeking will be outnumbered. Such a public service will be able to take on the vested interests and align society's incentives with economic efficiency and growth.

From a political economy standpoint, it seems that the critical measure to trigger wider and efficient economic reform would be to reform the public sector along the lines suggested here.[25]

---

25. A complementary reform would aim at catalyzing thinking and start debate on reform. This could best be done through a vibrant academia. Unfortunately, the Pakistani media cannot be counted on the side of reform and progress. Contrary to Sen's famous argument that the media is always an ally of reform and progress (Sen, 2001), the media in Pakistan has always been controlled by the Government to more or less freeze out any debate, especially debates on alternative strategies or reform. Throughout the country's history, the Government has found ways of controlling the media. Overt controls—licensing and direct censorship—were in place for many years. When these were given up, rationing of newsprint was used as a control device. When the media gained independence, the Government had also grown to be the largest advertiser and hence, retained control over the media. In Pakistan, academia, through its interface with globalization, will probably create the awareness and lead the media to promote reform.

6.8 Conclusions

There is an urgent need to shift the growth paradigm in Pakistan. Much has been learnt about the growth process in the world, and this knowledge needs to be applied in Pakistan. The earlier approach, based on government-centred planning, reliance on foreign resources and mercantilism, has not worked because the structure of incentives that resulted from this approach led to a neglect of governance and the development of rent-seeking. Talent and merit were disregarded by that system.

Economists are now emphasizing that for self-sustaining growth, such institutions need to be built that preserve individual freedom, provide security and facilitate market transactions; the Government merely provides these institutions, allowing markets to determine where economic activity goes. This is a meritocratic framework, where success is determined purely by the market place, and where government efficiency is judged by how well it develops the governance infrastructure that facilitates the market.

Given these new findings in economic research, Pakistan's growth strategy should be the subject of some debate. There may be a case for moving away from the current focus on government planning, production and mercantilism to a more market- and commerce-based approach. The new approach would be more aligned with globalization, creativity and innovation.

Obviously, vested interests would block such reform. However, one possible intervention identified could help to break the control of vested interests. The change has to take place at the level of acceptance of this new thinking, which can perhaps best happen through academic freedom and the development of a research culture. That will only come about when the education system, which currently is subservient to the government machinery, is granted complete autonomy and is professionalized.

For reform to take hold, the public service, which stands at the heart of the system, will need to be modernized in a manner that invests it in the reforms and takes it away from rent- and perk-management. The contention in this chapter has been that the crux of this reform of government will lie in the management of public service personnel—a management that would allow open competition of a professional kind to be established.

7 Sri Lanka: The role of strengthening policy coherence

Shyamali Ranaraja

7.1 Background

For most regions of the world today, a growing disconnect between economic growth and decent jobs is an empirical reality. The question of whether past policies are responsible for this mismatch, or indeed if policies have anything to do with this phenomenon, calls for explicit analysis. This is required to support or oppose the contention that the observed imbalance in the outcome is a reflection of a lack of coherence in policies, whether at the stage of formulation or implementation, or both.

Sri Lanka is no exception to this commonly observed disparity between economic growth and decent work. The achievements in human development made by Sri Lanka since Independence in 1948 are comparable with those of many developed nations. In several key areas, such as universal primary enrolment, gender equality and infant and maternal mortality, Sri Lanka is well placed to meet the Millennium Development Goals (MDGs) ahead of schedule. Despite those achievements, it is becoming increasingly clear that Sri Lanka has not performed as well in the distribution of the benefits of growth or in the reduction of poverty.

Recent development policy has therefore, accepted that poverty reduction must be made the focus of macroeconomic policy, rather than being considered a by-product of economic growth; the main strategy for achieving poverty reduction is increasingly acknowledged to be the expansion of employment and income opportunities, especially to the poor. However, Sri Lanka has recognized that it is not simply employment that provides a way out of poverty, but decent work: work that combines equity, efficiency and inclusion as means of empowering people to exit poverty.

At the 13th Asian Regional Meeting of the ILO constituents in 2001, the Government and workers' and employers' representatives from Sri Lanka made a commitment to develop a national policy and a national action plan for decent work. In keeping with that commitment, Sri Lanka is the first country in the South Asia region to develop a national policy and a national action plan on decent work. While this is a significant achievement, the adoption of the policy is but a small step in the process; much remains to be done to implement the strategies designed to ensure that economic growth creates the conditions for decent work.

In the context of decent work,[1] this chapter addresses the following issues:

- To what extent, if any, is there a disconnect between economic growth and growth of decent employment at the national level?
- To what extent is decent employment central to macroeconomic policy? If not, what are the ways and means of achieving this? What are the trade-offs with other potential policy objectives (such as price stability or balance of payments equilibrium)? How is decent employment reflected in financial, investment and commercial policy?
- Is there an apparent trade-off between labour productivity growth and decent employment growth? If so, is this trade-off essentially a short-term phenomenon?

The following section of this chapter (Section 7.2) sets out the nature of economic growth in Sri Lanka and its impact on employment and poverty reduction. The role of investment and its contribution to growth are also considered. The deficits that exist in the challenge of

1. Securing decent work for people everywhere is a primary ILO goal, a converging focus of all four of its strategic objectives: the promotion of rights at work, employment, social protection and social dialogue. It implies promoting opportunities for women and men to obtain decent and productive work, in conditions of freedom, equity, security and human dignity. The ILO's Report of the Director-General in the International Labour Conference, 87th session, 1999 (ILO, 1999), contains elaborate discussions on the theme of decent work, including a regional perspective.

achieving decent work at the national level are set out in Section 7.3, including the apparent trade-offs between decent work and labour productivity, balance of payments and economic stability. Section 7.4 briefly considers the extent to which current macroeconomic policy focuses on decent work. The chapter concludes by examining whether a better policy mix or better policy sequencing would strengthen the connections between growth, investment and decent employment to achieve the goals of decent jobs. It also makes recommendations for forging better links between policy and implementation, including a consideration of the necessity for coordination in the aid programmes or technical cooperation programmes of different multilateral agencies.

7.2 Growth, investment and employment in Sri Lanka

The economic and industrial policies of post-independent Sri Lanka varied according to the ideologies of successive governments. Economic policies that were adopted by one administration were abandoned by a succeeding administration, regardless of the success or failure of those policies. Economic policy was also decided on the basis of the ideology of the political party in power, and not on a pragmatic assessment of the requirements of the economy. Since Independence, general elections in 1956, 1960, 1965, 1971 and 1977 resulted in one of two major political parties, the United National Party and the Sri Lanka Freedom Party, alternatively forming governments. With the former being more market-focused in its orientation and the latter being more nationalist-socialist in outlook, the economic policies adopted by each successive government were diametrically opposed on many occasions. This created an ingrained disconnect between policies and implementation. It also gave rise to a lack of commitment and interest on the part of the public service in terms of putting policies into action; the likelihood that the next election would result in the change or abandonment of a difficult or unpopular policy created a disincentive for administrators to risk the consequences of implementation.

Macroeconomic overview

The annual gross domestic product (GDP) of Sri Lanka grew at an average of 4.3 per cent during the period 1981–1990, and at the rate of

5.2 per cent during 1991–2000. Post-Independence economic growth has been consistently positive, except in 2001 when a combination of factors resulted in negative growth. Despite this setback, economic growth in the period 2001–2005 averaged 5.18 per cent.[2] Rapid expansion of industry and services has led to growth, with the contribution of agriculture to the economy declining over time (Figure 7.1). This growth momentum is all the more remarkable given the outbreak of separatist civil war in 1983, which is estimated by the Central Bank of Sri Lanka to have reduced the country's GDP growth by 2–3 per cent per year over the 20 years of the conflict.

Figure 7.1

Growth rates of GDP and major economic sectors

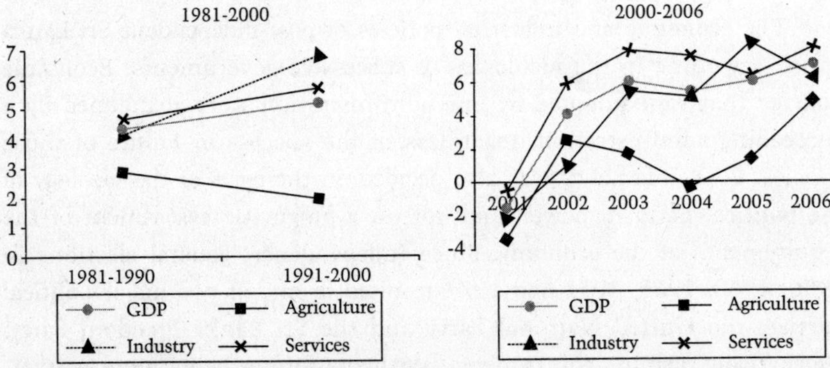

Source: Compiled from CBSL (1990, 2000, and 2006b)

Despite the positive growth, the volatility in the agriculture sector has been a matter for concern. Weather changes play a large part in the performance of this sector, and during times of drought or floods, agricultural output, especially paddy and tea, is adversely affected, resulting in substantive year-on-year changes. This volatility also affects

2. However, it has been argued that, as a result of the protracted civil war, the north and much of the east of the country are likely to have incurred negative economic growth due to the disruption of agricultural production and the destruction of economic, social and physical infrastructure. Since almost one-third of the country (the North-East Province) has been excluded from the national accounts since about 1990 due to the escalation of the civil conflict, if the possibly negative GDP growth in the north is taken into account, the average GDP growth rate of the country would have been much less than indicated by current official statistics (Sarvananthan, 2004).

employment, especially as most agricultural workers are in unstable employment relationships.

Trade, balance of payments and budget deficits

Sri Lanka has been highly trade-dependent, and both exports and imports have grown rapidly with the liberalization of the economy in 1978. However, the share of traditional agricultural exports (primarily tea, coconut, rubber and spices) has declined as industrial exports have increased at an average of about 15–17 per cent in dollar value annually (Figure 7.2). Apparel exports made up nearly two-thirds of all industrial exports, but other industrial products, such as leather, porcelain and wood, are gaining ground, especially due to several bilateral trade agreements, such as the Indo–Sri Lanka Free Trade Agreement which came into operation in 2000.

Figure 7.2

Industrial and agricultural exports (percentage of total exports)

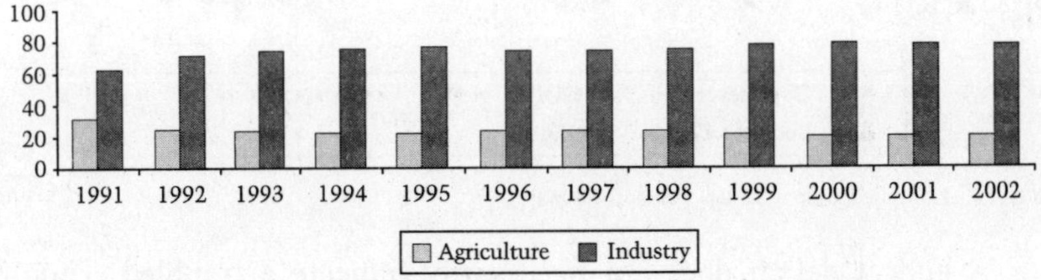

Source: Compiled from CBSL (1995 and 2005a)

Overall, imports grew at an annual average rate of about 11 per cent in dollar terms during 1990–1998, but imports increased more rapidly, especially due to the sharp rise in the cost of petroleum in the last three years. The pattern of trade has also altered, in that the largest parts of exports are to Europe and the United States of America while imports are mainly from India, China and other South-East Asian countries and territories such as Hong Kong, Indonesia, Korea, Malaysia, Singapore, Taiwan and Thailand. Therefore, Sri Lanka has trade surpluses with the United States of America, the United Kingdom and most European countries whilst having trade deficits with China, India and other Asian countries and territories.

Budget deficit

With the adoption of liberal economic policies in 1978, there was a rapid expansion of the budget deficit, partly caused by public investment in ambitious infrastructure projects, such as the construction of dams, power generation projects and irrigation channels. The single-digit budget deficit that had prevailed since Independence began to balloon, reaching 23 per cent in 1980 and remaining at double-digit levels into the 1990s (Figure 7.3). Since then, prudent fiscal policies have contained the deficit at single-digit levels, which appears to be a creditable achievement.

Figure 7.3

Budget deficit, 1991–2004

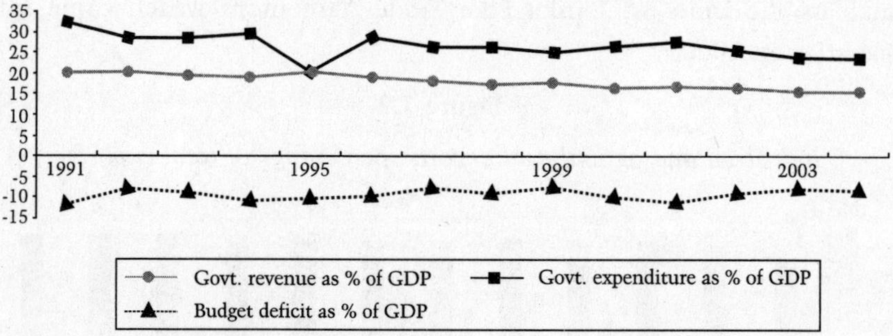

Source: Compiled from CBSL (1995 and 2005a) .

A budget deficit does not necessarily indicate a troubled economy, especially where a deficit is the result of productive public investments. However, if deficits are incurred mainly for public consumption, as is the case in Sri Lanka, then it could lead to negative impacts on the economy, such as high interest rates and inflation. Sarvananthan (2004) notes that public expenditure on defence since 1990 has been considerably more than the combined expenditure on education, health and poverty alleviation. Further, budget deficits also crowd out private investment, because of excessive government borrowing through the issue of treasury bills. This was the case in Sri Lanka in the early 1990s and brought about the need to reduce the deficit.

Growth and investment

Private and public investment together had risen to 28 per cent in 2000 (from 23 per cent in 1991), but then declined to 21 per cent in

2002 (Table 7.1). Part of the increase in public investment was due to investments in the defence sector, which cannot be considered development-oriented investment. More importantly, although the Government has acknowledged that the combined investment rate should be above 35 per cent of the GDP in order to attain a sustainable growth rate of 8 per cent or above, its policies have been unable to generate this level of investment.

Table 7.1

Public and private investment, 2000–2006

Categories	*2000*	*2001*	*2002*	*2003*	*2004*	*2005*	*2006*
GDP (million rupees at market prices)	1 257 636	1 407 398	1 581 885	1 761 161	2 029 365	2 365 593	2 801 828
Private investment	270 400	228 165	261 791	295 063	404 352	465 323	632 729
% of total investment	77	74	78	76	79	74	78
Public investment	82 232	81 519	73 013	93 693	104 591	162 211	179 637
% of total investment	23	26	22	24	21	26	22
Investment ratio[1]	28.0	22.0	21.2	22.1	25.0	26.5	28.7

Note: [1] Total investment as a percentage of the GDP.
Source: Compiled from the CBSL, 1995, 2005a.

The bank rate remained constant at 17 per cent from 1991 until 1998, declining to 16 per cent in 1999 but reaching a high of 25 per cent in 2000 amidst a deepening economic crisis in the country. Since then, it has declined to 18 per cent in 2001 and to 15 per cent in 2003, remaining at that level up to end-2006. High rates of interest have reduced the competitiveness of the domestic manufacturing sector *vis-à-vis* cheaper imported manufacturing products and as a result, a significant percentage of small and medium enterprises have closed down. The high rate of interest also acts as a disincentive for foreign investment.

Growth and employment

Employment creation has been one of the key focus areas of economic policy since the early 1970s, and more particularly after economic liberalization in 1978. However, the policies that have been followed have had mixed results. Although open unemployment has been reducing steadily, a marked disconnect between growth in employment and economic growth has emerged, especially since the 1990s.

While a decline in economic growth would also have contributed to this disconnect, other factors have had a bearing. Employment in the public sector declined steadily, from 15 per cent of the labour force in 1995 to about 13 per cent in 2005, and although the share of employment in the private sector increased by a comparable amount during the same period, unemployment also increased. A combination of factors therefore, led to a lower elasticity of employment over this period (Table 7.2).

Table 7.2

Employment: Output elasticity coefficients, 1990–1999 and 1999–2004

Period	*Elasticity of employment to total GDP*	*Average annual GDP growth*
1991–1995	0.1	5.6
1995–1999	0.8	4.8
1999–2003	0.2	3.4

Source: ILO, 2006a: 917.

Labour force participation

The labour force, defined as persons aged 10 years[3] and above who are able and willing to work, stood at 8.14 million in 2006. The labour force participation rate[4] has demonstrated a trend of decrease since 2002. The gender analysis of the labour force participation rate indicates that male participation has been over twice that of females throughout the recent past (Figure 7.4). This is particularly evident in the 25–49 age group, where the participation rate of males is in excess of 95 per cent while the comparable rate for females is less than 50 per cent. This is despite the majority of employment created in the Export Processing Zones and the Board of Investment of Sri Lanka sector throughout the 1980s and 1990s being predominantly for females. Policies for employment creation will therefore, have to be designed to encourage

3. Sri Lankan legislation prohibits the employment of any person below the age of 14 years, and this calculation of labour force data is inconsistent with that prohibition. This is one of the inconsistencies in data collection that will be brought in line with the concept of decent work.

4. The ratio of the labour force to the household population aged 10 years and above.

women in the most productive age group to join the labour force as male participation is unlikely to increase further.

Figure 7.4

Labour force participation rate, 1990–2005

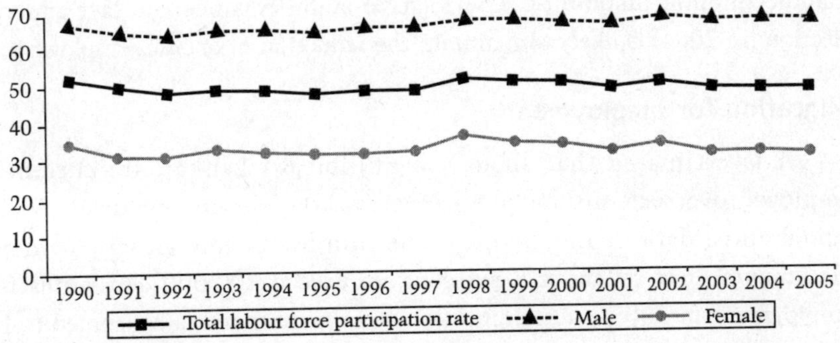

Source: CBSL (2005a)

Unemployment

During the 25 years after Independence, unemployment continued to rise steadily in Sri Lanka. In 1973, at the height of the era of import-substitution economic policy, nearly a quarter of the population was unemployed. With the liberalisation of the economy in 1978, combined with a decline in population growth, unemployment has decreased steadily to single-digit levels (Figure 7.5) (CBSL, 2005a).

Figure 7.5

Unemployment as a percentage of the labour force, 1995–2005

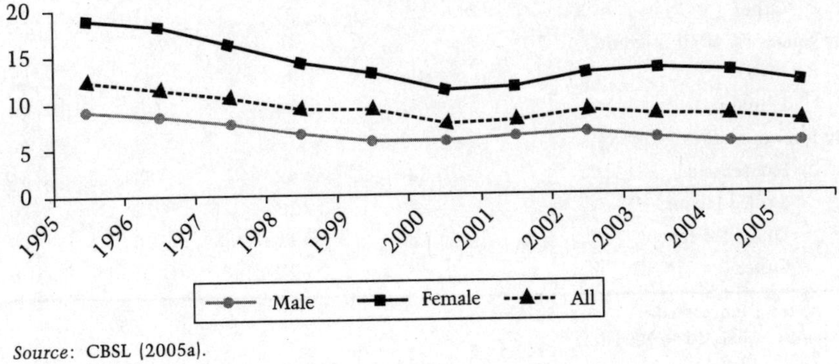

Source: CBSL (2005a).

After 2000, however, unemployment demonstrated a marginally increasing trend, but it has resumed a downward trend since 2004. Political and economic instability in the country since 1999, which saw three changes of administration at general elections, probably created upward pressure on unemployment due to closures of businesses resulting from policy and macroeconomic instability. The relative stability since the last general election (in 2004) is likely to maintain the reduction in open unemployment.

Migration for employment

It is estimated that about 1.2 million Sri Lankan are currently employed overseas, although migrant workers are not included in the labour force data of the country. The number of foreign employment placements grew by about 8 per cent, to exceed 200,000 departures for employment in 2005, and remittances by migrant workers continued to be a major source of foreign exchange for the Government. The majority of migrant workers in 2005 were female (59 per cent) as in past years, and over half were employed as housemaids (54 per cent), in the lowest income earning group (Table 7.3). Despite state initiatives to encourage skilled migration, 72 per cent of migrant workers were in the unskilled category, and this continues to be a serious issue for Sri Lanka.

Table 7.3

Profile of migrant workers, 2002–2005

Categories	*2002*	*2003*	*2004*	*2005*[1]
Employment placements (number)	203 773	208 808	213 453	230 953
By source (%)				
Licensed agents	75	74	73	72
Other	25	26	27	28
By gender (% of all migrants)				
Male	35	36	37	41
Female	65	64	63	59
By level of skill/category (%)				
Housemaid	53	49	52	54
Skilled labour	22	23	21	20
Unskilled labour	18	21	20	18
Other	7	7	7	8

Note: [1] Provisional.

Source: CBSL, 2000, 2005a.

Over the past few years, migration has not varied as a percentage of the labour force (Table 7.4), indicating that migration is unlikely to exert significant downward pressure on unemployment. Despite the active support for migration extended by the Government, migration does not appear to have risen significantly in relation to the growth in the labour force. One reason for this may be the perception of problems associated with employment overseas, and the relatively unstable conditions in the Middle East, which absorbs the majority of migrant workers from Sri Lanka.

Table 7.4

Migration for employment as a percentage of the labour force, 1999–2005

Year	*Annual migration for employment*	*Total labour force (thousands)*	*Annual migration as a % of labour force*
1999	179 735	6758	2.7
2000	182 188	6709	2.7
2001	184 007	6858	2.7
2002	203 773	7219	2.8
2003	208 808	7835	2.7
2004	213 453	7984	2.7
2005	230 953	8141	2.8

Source: Compiled from CBSL, 2002, 2005a.

Remittances by migrant workers also play a large part in the economy (Table 7.5), and currently stand at around 7 per cent of the GDP. They comprise the largest single net inflow of foreign currency into the country, even surpassing apparel exports (CBSL, 2005a). Income from migration therefore, supports a large part of government activity, in particular the financing of the budget deficit.

Table 7.5

Remittances by migrant workers

Year	*Private remittances (US$ million)*	*Gross official reserves (US$ million)*	*Remittances as a % of reserves*
1999	887	1639	54.1
2000	974	1049	92.9
2001	984	1338	73.5
2002	1097	1700	64.5
2003	1205	2329	51.7
2004	1350	2195	61.5
2005[1]	1736	2735	63.5

Note: [1] Provisional.

Source: Same as Table 7.3.

Although migrant work remains difficult to monitor and regulate, resulting in violations of rights at work and personal safety of these workers, it is clear that the Government will continue to rely on outward-bound employment to sustain the economy. Several policy initiatives have been proposed, in particular in the National Employment Policy (Ministry of Employment and Labour, 2002), to access opportunities for higher skilled overseas employment as such jobs are more likely to be better paid and in better situations. A disparity between policy and reality is self-evident in migration data. The Government in 2006 gazetted a regulation banning mothers with children aged 5 years and younger from seeking overseas employment, unless requirements as to providing for the care of such children were available and certified by the relevant village level authority. Although the stated intention was to reduce some of the social costs of migration, it was challenged by both migrants and activists alike, as it was likely to result in an increase in illegal migration and an increase in the cost of migration to workers due to additional certification being required. The regulation is therefore, not being enforced. Once again a disconnect is apparent: Government policy as stated in the National Policy for Decent Work and other documents is to improve the skill level of migrants and to increase the availability of more secure and better paying foreign employment, but implementation focuses on an increase in regulation which will be more likely to make the majority of migrant workers more vulnerable.

Some progress has been made in efforts to ensure decent working conditions in host countries as bilateral agreements have been negotiated by Sri Lanka with countries such as Italy, Korea and Malaysia. However, it is a continuous cause for concern that even for these jobs, Sri Lankan workers are paid less than migrant workers from other countries, for instance, workers from the Philippines.

Gender issues for decent work

In each of these areas, women face even greater barriers in relation to decent work. Data on labour force participation rates indicate that the participation rate for females has been lower that that for males and the unemployment rate for women still remains at more than double that for men. Therefore, efforts at creating employment must focus on creating more opportunities for women. Employment generation must become more "gender-friendly", with employers being encouraged to locate in rural areas, where more women live and work. This focus has been lacking in macro level policies, and policies for employment generation have not been based on this reality.

Women also face greater barriers in obtaining rights at work and in obtaining adequate representation. Although women in Sri Lanka have been traditionally active in the trade unions movement from its inception, they are conspicuously absent from the decision-making positions within the trade unions movement today. Even where trade unions have been formed in predominantly female occupations and workplaces, women have a very low level of representation at decision-making levels. One study found that a union with 74 per cent women in its membership had no women on its executive committee, while only a minority of other trade unions had a women's wing (Jayaweera *et al.*, 1998). The study concluded that this low representation for women at decision-making levels is the probable reason that gender-specific issues are seldom raised by trade unions with any degree of conviction.

Demographic data also indicate that women make up 70 per cent of all people currently not covered by formal pension schemes; however, women will constitute 70 per cent of the very old in the future. This leaves a large social security gap for women, both at present and increasingly in the coming years. Women are disadvantaged by the lack of social security schemes in the informal economy, such as for domestic workers and agricultural workers. Therefore, the needs of women must be addressed specifically when designing income transfer and social security schemes, which is not the case at present.

Part-time working opportunities, which are especially attractive to women as an effective way of combining work and family responsibilities, have been declining in Sri Lanka in the past two decades. Part-time work is important to women who wish to combine work with other responsibilities, such as caring for elders and the young, and so the scarcity of such work places women in precarious situations. Labour regulations that require more benefits and better terms for women (such as maternity, working hours and night work regulations) also serve as disincentives for employers to provide more flexible work arrangements for women.

Migration of women as unskilled workers in poorly paid jobs overseas, especially in the Middle East, has drawn considerable attention in the past few years due to poor working conditions and safety issues abroad. However, any attempt at bringing in legislative restrictions on such migration, as has been proposed in order to curb adverse social consequences for Sri Lanka, must necessarily require serious consideration in view of the enormous contribution made by these workers to the economy. The lack of opportunities for decent jobs in Sri Lanka is the main reason why these women accept such undesirable employment abroad.

The plantation sector

In the plantation sector, especially tea and rubber estates, 50–90 per cent of workers are resident in the estates. This has led to the creation of a "dependent-resident" labour situation, because due to the housing, schooling, health facilities, childcare etc., provided by the employer, the employee develops dependencies which ties him or her to that particular estate. Notwithstanding the frequently substandard nature of the facilities provided, due to this dependency labour mobility is not observed to any great extent between or from plantations, thus limiting the capacity of workers to obtain better paid employment. Women comprise 65 per cent of the labour force on tea estates and about 50 per cent of the labour force on all estates. On tea estates, women carry out 90 per cent of plucking activities, and women also work in factories on day and night shifts.

Although paid a wage calculated at a daily rate, plantation workers have traditionally enjoyed all the benefits attached to permanent employment. However, due to the higher rates of pay in off-plantation occupations, the reduction in labour reporting for work on plantations has shifted the nature of employment towards casual, informal arrangements. While this is a practical necessity due to the lower cost of employing such labour, there is a possibility that in the long term the employment security enjoyed by permanent employees may be eroded.

Low-cost labour has been a feature of plantations worldwide, and Sri Lanka is no exception. Wages remained stagnant until the enactment of the Minimum Wages Ordinance of 1927 and the Wages Boards Ordinance of 1941, whereby a minimum wage is prescribed and revised periodically for various categories of workers engaged in plantation work and in other types of agriculture. However, plantation wages still remain lower than those prevailing in other occupational categories.

Wages in the tea and rubber plantations have been determined in the recent past by collective agreements between the Employers' Federation of Ceylon and several plantation trade unions. A collective agreement entered into in December 2006 between employers and trade unions raised the basic daily wage to Rs. 170 (about US$1.70) supplemented by incentives to a daily rate of Rs. 260, but these wages are still well below daily wages outside the plantations. As a result, the rate of poverty in the plantation/estate sector is the highest in the country.

Growth in decent work

Sri Lanka has ratified 40 ILO Conventions, including the 8 core Conventions, and its national legal framework contains stringent measures in respect of these and other rights and freedoms at work. The Constitution of Sri Lanka guarantees the fundamental right to the freedom of association. In relation to the abolition of child labour, Sri Lanka is well ahead of its Asian neighbours. Sri Lanka is also the first country in South Asia to adopted a National Policy for Decent Work, which identifies existing gaps in providing decent work for all, and sets out strategies to bridge these gaps in a comprehensive action plan; at present, this action plan is being converted into specific projects and activities which will be implemented by the different ministries entrusted with the responsibility. This too is a step in the right direction, as the policy was developed under the guidance of a team of officials from these ministries, which have not traditionally interacted on policy development. However, despite a strong legal environment, there remain real challenges in giving practical effect to some rights at work.

Freedom of association and trade unions

A feature of trade unionism in Sri Lanka which has become more pronounced in recent times is the multiplicity of unions (Figure 7.6 and Table 7.6). Under the Trade Unions Ordinance No. 14 of 1935, a trade union can be registered with the Department of Labour under the signatures of seven members—this has resulted in a rapidly fluctuating trade union environment.

Figure 7.6

Membership and number of trade unions, 1990–2002

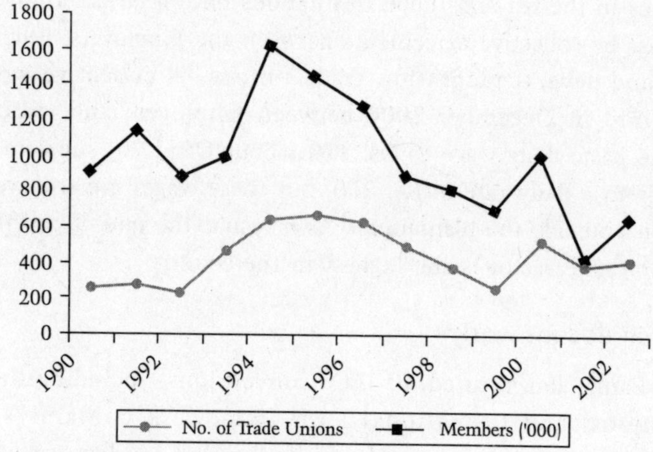

Source: Administrative Report, Department of Labour (2003).

Table 7.6

Rate of unionization of wage earners in the private sector

Year	*Private sector employees*	*Trade union membership*	*Unionized wage earners (%)*
1995	2 698 852	1 441 149	53
1996	2 865 078	1 264 641	44
1997	2 782 104	888 107	32
1998	2 737 260	799 821	29
1999	2 876 063	693 513	24
2000	2 928 783	1 000 104	34
2001	3 034 304	433 162	14
2002	3 179 525	640 673	20

Source: Calculated from CBSL, 2000 and 2005a.

This low minimum requirement for registration has led to a proliferation of smaller unions, although membership still tends to be concentrated in a few big unions and federations. At the end of 1991, 23 unions with individual memberships of over 5,000 accounted for 92.5 per cent of reported union membership (in relation only to those unions that have filed annual returns), but by the end of 2001 there were only 14 unions in that category, and their share of the reported membership had been reduced to 66 per cent. These unions operate mainly in the formal sector, and workers in the informal economy are largely without voice.

The lack of an apex body for trade unions, which could serve to focus attention on issues common to all workers—such as the need for revision of wages based on increases in the cost of living, restrictions on freedom of association etc.—has also prevented a coherent approach to ensuring workers rights. For instance, responses by trade unions to macroeconomic policy formulations by the Government at a national level has been inadequate; very often issues have been raised reactively and by individual trade unions, which has reduced the effectiveness of trade unions in compelling the Government to engage in social dialogue.

Social protection

Sri Lanka does not as yet have a single, universal system of social security. At present, social security consists of the Employees' Provident Fund (EPF) scheme for private sector employees, which is a contributory pension scheme (employers contribute a sum equivalent to 12 per cent of the employees' monthly earnings, while the employees contribute 8 per cent of monthly earnings). However, benefits are payable as a lump sum upon retirement or cessation of employment, and there is no provision to convert this amount into a periodic annuity for retirement.

The state pension scheme is a non-contributory pension scheme for public servants, where the expenditure is borne entirely by the state. In addition, there is an income transfer scheme, the Samurdhi Programme, for low-income families, which is also funded by the state. The disconnect in this area is that a large portion of the labour force, especially in the informal economy, is without any form of protection in the event of unemployment or other contingency. Sri Lanka has a rapidly ageing population, with the proportion of those aged over 55 years increasing rapidly in demographic data, and therefore, a crisis in social security is likely in the near future.

The above discussion on the impact of macroeconomic policy on the economy, investment and employment leads us to the next section, to consider whether economic growth has translated into opportunities for decent work at the national level, and if not, what are the possible reasons for this disconnect.

7.3 The disconnect between economic growth and decent work at the national level

The goal of decent work everywhere is to promote opportunities for women and men to obtain productive work in conditions of freedom, equity, security and human dignity. The key element underpinning this concept is the opportunity for work, meaning that all people who want work should be able to find work, since decent work is clearly not possible without work itself. The concept of "work" is not confined to wage employment, but can be any form of economic activity, including self-employment, unpaid family work and wage employment in both the formal and informal economy. Rights at work, or work in conditions of freedom, recognizes that work should be freely chosen and not forced on individuals, that access to work and the workplace itself should be free from discrimination and that certain forms of work, such as bonded or slave labour and child labour, are not acceptable and should be eliminated; it also means that workers are free to join workers' organizations. Social protection recognizes the obligation to safeguard health at work, and to provide financial and other protection in the event of ill health, old age and loss of work or livelihood, and other contingencies. Social dialogue requires that workers be treated with respect at work, and be able to voice concerns and participate in decision-making about working conditions; it also means that workers have the right to represent their interests collectively. The focus of these four dimensions is not just the creation of jobs, but also the creation of jobs of acceptable quality.

These four components—opportunity for work (employment creation), rights at work, social protection and the scope for social dialogue—must exist simultaneously for the realization of the goal of decent work. In the context of positive economic growth in the post-Independence period, can the concept of decent work be considered a reality in Sri Lanka?

There is no model for "perfect decent work", and every country must strive to overcome constraints unique to its situation in achieving that goal. In Sri Lanka, there are gaps or deficit areas in each of the four components of decent work, which persist despite a good record of economic growth. These problem areas are discussed further in this section.

Poverty and inequality

In the overall context, where decent work is a reality there should be freedom from want and deprivation. In Sri Lanka, economic growth has not reduced the levels of poverty in the country; on the contrary, poverty in some sectors has increased despite positive economic and social development. In 1969/70, around 18 per cent of the population was considered to be living below the poverty line; in the early 1990s, this had dramatically increased to more than a quarter of the population (Vidyaratne and Nigamuni, 2006), although it has shown a decreasing trend since the late 1990s, standing presently at around 22 per cent of the population. However, there has been no significant change in the pattern of distribution of wealth since Independence (see Figure 7.7); indeed, if anything the gap between the rich and the poor has become more marked. The poorest 20 per cent of the population (1st and 2nd deciles) receives less than 4 per cent of income, whilst the richest 20 per cent (9th and 10th deciles) receives 55 per cent of income. These levels of poverty and inequality prevail despite the per capita GDP having crossed the US$1,000 threshold in 2004.

Figure 7.7

Income shares by deciles of income receivers, 1953, 1978/79 and 2003/04 (percentage)

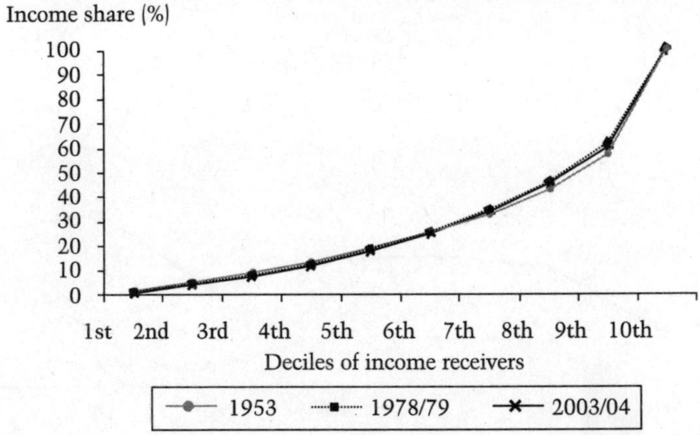

Source: CBSL (2005b).

This disparity, which is now recognized as being likely to prevent Sri Lanka from achieving its MDG of poverty reduction, is largely the result of the "trickle-down" theory of development followed by various governments since Independence, under which the state has engaged in a number of direct and indirect transfers to households for poverty alleviation. Free education and health services, land distribution and housing, income transfer and subsidies for production and social safety net programmes have been implemented to provide a basic standard of living to the poor. However, these programmes have not been successful in reducing the number of those in poverty, mainly as they lacked a component to assist the poor to exit poverty. Moreover, the poor are becoming increasingly concentrated in non-urban areas, as shown in Table 7.7. This suggests that the pace of structural change in the economy has not been sufficient to create adequate employment in urban

Table 7.7

National poverty headcount ratio, 1990–2002

(percentage)

Year	*Poverty headcount ratio*			
	National	*Urban*	*Rural*	*Estate*
1990/91	26.1	16.3	29.4	20.5
1995/96	28.8	14.0	30.9	38.4
2002	22.7	7.9	24.7	30.0

Source: Department of Census and Statistics, 2004.

Figure 7.8

Poverty (headcount) and share of GDP by province, 2002

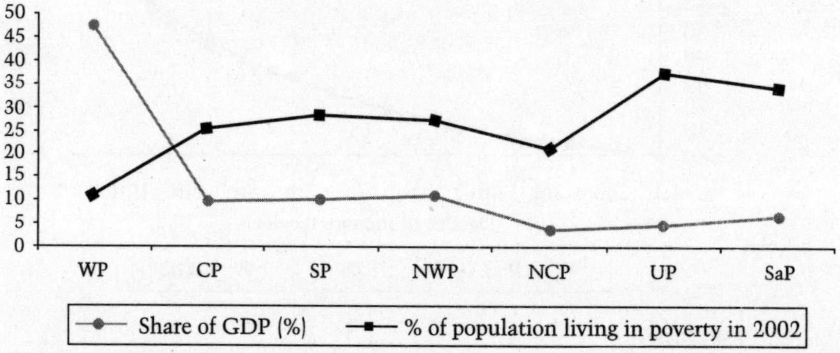

Notes: WP = Western; CP = Central; SP = Southern; NWP = North Western; NCP = North Central; UP = Uva; SaP = Sabaragamuwa. Northern and Eastern Provinces excluded.

Source: *Consumer Finance and Socio-economic Survey* (2003/04) and *Household Income and Expenditure Survey* (2002), Central Bank of Sri Lanka.

areas to absorb surplus rural labour, or to expand and diversify the rural economy to increase income-earning opportunities in the non-farm sectors. The inability of past policies to create sufficient regional growth to have a significant impact on poverty alleviation can be seen in Figure 7.8, where growth and poverty are inversely related.

Poverty alleviation in Sri Lanka therefore, needs to take a dual policy approach: an employment creation approach, to provide income generation opportunities for the poor rather than focusing solely on income transfer programmes; and a regional development approach, so that the poor can access employment opportunities where they reside. A disconnect between employment generation policy and implementation in the past has resulted in some imbalances in decent work, some of the more critical of which are discussed below.

Problems in employment creation

Many economic policies in the past have been designed to create employment, but the earlier discussion in this chapter has demonstrated that many of those policies, particularly investment, finance and trade policy, have not proceeded from a recognition of economic realities. For instance, there has been a steady movement of economic activity and employment from the formal to the informal economy, which is now estimated to account for nearly 70 per cent of employment in Sri Lanka. Although no independent assessment of the extent of the informal economy is available, the information in Table 7.8 on the unorganized sector, from the Consumer Finance and Socio-economic Survey, can be used as a proxy.

Table 7.8

Extent of the unorganized sector in Sri Lanka

(percentage)

Sectors	*1986/87*	*1996/97*	*2003/04*[1]
Central government	9.3	9.0	
Local government	0.7	1.4	13
Corporations and boards	13.6	2.8	
Co-operatives	0.9	0.7	
Private sector (organized)	8.8	16.2	17
Private sector (unorganized)	66.5	69.9	71
Total	**100**	**100**	**100**

Note: [1] Approximate.

Source: CBSL, 1988, 1998, 2005b.

Financial, credit and trade policy must focus on this aspect of informality in planning for growth. For instance, many micro- and small enterprises are not registered or licensed. This in turn limits their potential for development and expansion as they cannot borrow from banks or enter into legally binding contracts; it also reduces government revenue by making evasion easier. In this context, economic policy needs to focus on increasing registration and licensing based on its advantages rather than on penalties, as has happened in the past; registration, licensing and other bureaucratic procedures need to be computerized/networked, especially due to the decentralization of government, and officials at all levels concerned with implementing them need to be trained in effective service delivery.

The impact of the expansion in the informal economy on decent work can be seen in the increase in non-formal employment over the same period, and more than one-third of the labour force is now in casual, less secure forms of employment (CBSL, 2005a). This is because employers in the informal economy do not comply with formal procedures, such as registration, and workers are typically outside the scope of legislation and regulatory institutions. These same features make decent work more difficult to achieve in the informal economy.

Inefficient system of providing skills development

Other issues, such as the inefficiency in matching labour demand and supply, need to be approached from a different perspective than in the past. In Sri Lanka, youth unemployment is extremely high and appears to rise with education, being highest among those with post-secondary level qualifications. Especially among the more educated and relatively more affluent youth, a problem of "voluntary unemployment" exists, implying a conscious decision to wait for a job that matches personal preferences and career expectations instead of taking up an existing, and often well-paid, employment offer; 71 per cent of GCE (A/L) and above qualified people have searched for work for more than 12 months.

Negative perceptions towards certain kinds of jobs involving manual labour, gender stereotypes concerning vocations, a general rejection of entrepreneurship and self-employment, high aspirations created by access to higher education, and the perceived prestige and security of public sector employment, all artificially reduce available employment prospects. Among rural unemployed youth, nearly 14 per cent believed that no suitable work was available, and therefore, did not actively seek employment.

The "queuing hypothesis" linked to public sector employment and pay policies explains that in well-functioning labour markets, public sector workers have lower pay than their private sector counterparts in order to compensate for the greater stability, attractive benefits, lower work effort and prestige of their jobs (ILO, 2005b). In Sri Lanka, however, public servants are deemed to have, on average, higher pay as well as all of the above benefits. As a result, labour market entrants have an incentive to wait for job openings in the public sector, with most of them choosing to remain inactive instead of taking available jobs outside the public sector.

The Government's policy of reducing unrest among educated youths due to unemployment, especially among graduates of Sri Lankan universities, by providing them with employment in the public sector has exacerbated this "queuing" for public sector jobs. For instance, in 2005 the Government fulfilled a promise in its election manifesto to provide employment within the public sector for 42,000 graduates. Of that number of applicants, only 17,000 graduates stated that they were unemployed at the time of applying; the others were admittedly employed elsewhere, some in extremely lucrative and productive private sector jobs. However, the Government absorbed all applicants into the public sector, creating an expectation among those entering the university system of a privileged position within the public service upon graduation.

Although it is obvious that educational and skills development policy needs to be demand driven, Sri Lanka has not as yet succeeded in creating such a system. Despite the availability of free education up to and including university education and vocational training, there is no proper link between the supply and demand dimensions. The technical education and vocational training (TEVT) system is fragmented and uncoordinated, with no proper system of regulation of training providers. The absence of a national-level centralized body on higher education and TEVT has also hampered the development of an efficient system, with duplication of activities and no clear responsibilities between the various bodies. For instance, the Technical Education and Vocational Training Commission (TEVC), the Ministry of Labour and

Manpower, the Ministry of Skills Development, the Ministry of Vocational and Technical Training, the Ministry of Human Resource Development, the Ministry of Education and the Ministry of Foreign Employment and Welfare all function as training providers/regulators. The lack of cohesion between these institutions is largely responsible for the mismatch between skills demand and supply.

Current initiatives, such as JobsNet, a private–public partnership which functions as a job bank and a labour market information clearing house, and the National Vocational Qualification system of grading for training providers, are steps in the right direction. However, greater coordination between institutions and a more unified approach are essential to overcome this problem.

Rigidity in labour legislation

A global survey has indicated that Sri Lanka ranks as a country with a high level of employment "rigidity" (World Bank/ADB, 2005). The survey also found that countries with a high level of employment rigidity or regulation had fewer employment opportunities for women and youths, and that a larger portion of economic activity tended to shift to the informal economy, where decent work is inherently more difficult to ensure. The Termination of Employment of Workmen Act (TEWA) has been singled out as one of the most restrictive severance-pay systems in the world. Under this Act, no employer can terminate the employment of any worker without the prior consent of the worker in writing or prior written approval of the Commissioner. There are no set standards under the legislation with reference to which a dismissal can be justified. It is all left to the initiative of the employer. The TEWA covers an extensive range of industries, including shops, offices and factories. Workers under employment contract in any capacity—casual, probationary or fixed term—are covered under the Act. The exceptions are establishments with fewer than 15 workers and public servants or workers with less than six months' service.[5]

Although the Government has amended various legislative provisions from time to time on an ad hoc basis, a coordinated approach

---

5. ILO, 2007c.

to labour law reform has been missing. Even where reforms have been carried out, they have been ineffective or irrelevant. A forum where all stakeholders can discuss the reforms that are required, from the perspective of employment creation and investment promotion, has not been available. A more pragmatic and practical approach to reforms within a participatory framework would go a long way towards creating decent employment opportunities.

Lack of coverage and enforcement of legislation

Although Sri Lanka has a well-developed body of legislation relating to employment, much of this legislative protection is not available to large groups of workers. In the informal economy, large numbers of workers are not covered by labour laws, or such laws cannot be enforced for their benefit. For instance, agricultural workers, especially female agricultural workers, undergo much hardship due to the lack of enforcement of benefits such as EPF and Employees' Trust Fund (ETF) payments, maternity benefits and paid leave. In particular, the lack of access to any form of social security is a major cause for concern in this area, and the provisions of the TEWA become irrelevant in relation to work in the informal economy.

The main issues in this regard are the lack of capacity in the system of labour inspection to monitor all workplaces and ensure compliance, and the absence of any form of records or registrations by employers as many are in the informal economy. Although the Government has enacted many protective legislative provisions, it has not been willing to commit funds for enforcement. Since competition for resources is a key factor in the ability to increase the capacity of regulatory bodies, a transition towards a self-regulatory system, with the state providing supervisory services rather than enforcement, is what is likely to succeed.

Delays in judicial review of disputes

Workers have many avenues to follow if their rights are violated, but an overburdened system of justice makes it difficult to obtain redress, or inordinate delays make such redress pointless. For instance, the backlog of cases in the Labour Tribunals—to which a worker can appeal against the termination of his or her services by an employer—

stood at about 17,000 in 2005.[6] A typical case would take on average three years to reach a conclusion, making any challenge overly burdensome to the dismissed worker.

Although the Government has increased the number of Labour Tribunals and other bodies, the system cannot handle all the disputes that are directed through it. Further, a system of proceedings that is unnecessarily legalistic has developed through practice, although these Tribunals were not intended to function as courts of law. An evaluation of the fundamental constraints in the system, such as procedural and attitudinal limitations, with the participation of all stakeholders is required to overcome this problem. In instances where the relationship between employers and workers breaks down, the current system of legislation encourages recourse to litigation, which may ultimately disrupt, rather than restore, industrial harmony. There is a need to adopt alternative dispute resolution mechanisms in order to enable parties to resolve disputes without lasting damage to the workplace relationship.

Absence of a system of unemployment insurance

The system of social security in Sri Lanka combines several income transfer schemes with statutorily imposed "severance pay" schemes and superannuation systems. The missing element is a system of unemployment benefits or unemployment insurance, to bridge the gap between these two components. The absence of a comprehensive system of unemployment insurance may be seen as reducing the efficiency of the labour market as it restricts labour mobility; it is also a drawback in creating employment of quality within the formal economy, as employment tends to shift to the less secure informal economy to evade payment of statutory benefits.

Need for better protection in old age

The aged population, defined as those aged 65 years and above, is on the increase. Estimated as 7 per cent of the household population in 2001, this is projected to rise to 15 per cent of the population by 2016. Ten per cent of the elderly are also categorized as dependent. As life expectancy is also increasing, the social security scheme must provide

6. *www.justiceministry.gov.lk*

adequate benefits in old age; the current system of lump sum payment of benefits to workers in the private sector on retirement does not provide that income security.

Decent work and productivity growth

Sri Lanka has been able to achieve only modest growth in productivity (Table 7.9), and in the case of agriculture, productivity gains have been marginal (IPS, 2006). One of the most generous public holiday structures in the world, in addition to statutorily imposed paid leave for various categories of employees, have reduced the number of working days in a year; for instance, the public sector can have as few as 191 working days in a year. Low productivity is a serious concern for the private sector as well, especially with regard to the difficulty in introducing productivity-related wage schemes or performance appraisal systems. As a result, Sri Lanka has seen its competitiveness ratings slide, from being ranked 68th (out of 100 countries surveyed) in the world in 2003 to 98th in 2005. Current productivity growth, at about 2–3 per cent per annum, is also far below the corresponding levels attained by the newly industrialized countries, which have facilitated their elevated rates of real wage increase (5–10 per cent) in the relevant phases of economic growth (Rodrigo, 2006).

Table 7.9

Growth in productivity and real wages, 1980–2004

(percentage)

	1980s	*1990s*		*2000–04*	
Sector	*Productivity growth*[1]	*Productivity growth*	*Real wage growth*[2]	*Productivity growth*	*Real wage growth*
Overall economy	2.5	2.8	–	2.1	
Agriculture sector	2.8	3.0	–	0.2	–
Industry sector	–0.5	3.6	2.7	–0.3	–0.1
Services sector	2.3	2.6	3.0	3.8	0.4

Note: [1] Productivity growth between the two years of 1981 and 1986 has been used as a proxy for average productivity during 1980s. [2] Real wages are for 1992–1999 period. For the services sector and its sub-sectors, data available only from 1992 to 2004.

Source: Adapted from IPS, 2006.

The importance of raising productivity as a precondition for elevating wages and levels of living is recognized in domestic policy circles. The Vision 21 policy statement in 2000 recognized that "a wave of wage increases across the economy, without a corresponding increase in production, will stimulate inflation until such increases are nullified. The only way for wage increases to improve the quality of life is by increasing productivity, i.e., to increase output in relation to capital and labour employed" (Ministry of Finance and Planning, 2000).

From a perspective of ensuring that economic growth leads to poverty reduction, any achievement in productivity growth must be accompanied by growth in real wages. However, this has not been the case for all sectors during 1990–2004. In the 1990s, average growth of real wages in the manufacturing sector was much lower than the corresponding productivity growth (IPS, 2006).

The economic and social cost of the civil conflict

The two decades of civil war in Sri Lanka has cost the country dearly in terms of loss of life and destruction of infrastructure, as well as loss of income from tourism and the foregoing of foreign direct investment due to danger to civilian life and political instability. In addition, the opportunity cost of war has reduced in real terms investment in social and human development in the country. Sarvananthan (2004) compared defence expenditures with social expenditures as proportions of total public expenditures over a period in the late 1990s, and found that defence expenditure increased rapidly at the expense of expenditure on health, education, poverty alleviation and reconstruction and rehabilitation (R&R).

Table 7.10

Defence/social expenditure as a proportion of total public expenditure, 1991–2002

(percentage)

	1992	1993	1994	1995	1996	1997	1998	1999	2000	2001	2002
Defence expenditures	12	10.9	12.9	14.3	17.7	16.8	16.9	16.4	17.7	14.2	10.8
Social expenditures	13	9.9	12.8	12.7	13.5	12.6	12	12.7	9.8	11.7	9.6
(i) Education	5.4	4.3	4.5	3.5	4.2	4.2	4.7	5	3.8	4.2	3.3
(ii) Health	3.1	1.9	2.6	5.2	5	4.7	4	4.8	3.9	3.2	3.6
(iii) Poverty	4.5	3.7	5.7	2	3.2	3	2.5	2.6	2	3	2.2
(iv) R&R				2	1.1	0.7	0.8	0.3	0.1	1.3	0.5

Source: Sarvananthan, 2004.

In particular, in the year 2000 defence expenditure was very nearly double that of the aggregate expenditure on social aspects. However, a downward trend in defence expenditure can be observed since 2001 due to the Cease Fire Agreement entered into between the terrorists and the Government of Sri Lanka, but no reciprocal increase in social expenditure can be observed. Therefore, it is likely that the type of investment that would have resulted in improving decent work aspects has been foregone due to the impact of the civil conflict.

There are other, less direct, effects of the war on decent work, especially in relation to data collection and enforcement of legal rights and obligations. Much of the data collected in the last decade, especially the Labour Force Surveys, have excluded two out of the seven provinces, the northern and eastern provinces; given the large land area and the extent of economic activity and population contained in these provinces, the absence of data from these areas in the national data makes for a distorted picture. Enforcement of laws and regulations in these areas has also been affected adversely, and these provinces and others bordering the conflict have also suffered from the inability to mobilize resources for social development. It must therefore be noted that, despite the advances made in relation to decent work in the national context, the areas involved in the conflict are likely to be less privileged, and also to have more and bigger gaps in decent work.

Explaining the disconnect

The gaps in decent work discussed in the previous section arise from two distinct causes:

- an incorrect policy mix, which looks at investment, employment, economic growth and social growth as separate sectors and fails to address these issues from a broader perspective; and
- a lack of capacity and commitment within the administrative system to convert policies into action.

The incorrect policy mix is as much a problem of too many policies as the absence of a cohesive approach to policy formulation. Unusual perhaps for a developing country, Sri Lanka suffers from an excess of macroeconomic and development policies at the national level. For instance, the macroeconomic and development policies announced by the Ministry of Finance and Planning under different administrations since 2000 are shown in Table 7.11.

Table 7.11

Sri Lanka's major economic policies, 2000–2005

Policy	*Related area*	*Year*
Vision 21	The Path to Development – Investment Profile 2000–04	2000
Vision 2010	The Policy Framework of the Government of Sri Lanka	2001
Regaining Sri Lanka : Vision and Strategy for Accelerated Development	For the Poverty Reduction Strategy Program	December 2002
Creating our Future, Building Our Nation	The Economic Policy Framework of the Government of Sri Lanka	June 2004
Sri Lanka New Development Strategy: Framework for Economic Growth and Poverty Reduction. Creating Our Future – Building Our Nation	Interim Poverty Reduction Strategy Program paper	2005
Mahinda Chinthana: Vision for a New Sri Lanka[1]	Ten Year Horizon Development Framework 2006–16	October 2006
Budget speech	Economic policy of the Government	Annual

Note: [1] Mahinda Chinthana is the vision of Sri Lanka's President Mahinda Rajapaksa.
Source: IPS, 2006.

Each of these policies has been developed by the Department of National Planning under the guidance of the Ministry of Finance, in administrations where the Executive President has retained the portfolio of Minister of Finance, thus giving the highest possible validity to policy formulation. Nevertheless, each policy has been replaced by another policy, as a result of either a change in government after elections (2000, 2001 and 2004) or the election of a new Executive President (2005), without clear indications as to continuity or limits of implementation. For instance, the time frame incorporated in Vision 2010 is also covered in the current Ten Year Development Framework, but the latter makes no mention of how the previous policies and objectives will be incorporated in the new framework. Similarly, in some instances previous policy statements have been simply ignored in a newer policy, without regard for continuing budgetary allocations and administrative arrangements. The judicial reforms project undertaken with international donor assistance under the Regaining Sri Lanka policy is a case in point, as it continues to date but with no mention or inclusion in the current Ten Year Development Framework.

Effectiveness of policy implementation

The public administrative system in Sri Lanka, which plays a role in determining and defining policy and in its implementation, was based on the British Civil Service. Despite many changes after Independence, it continued to operate autonomously from the political system until the abolition of the independent Public Services Commission in 1972, when the Administrative Service was brought under the Cabinet, and the control of individual ministers. Thus, public administration became a political tool, with politicians having power to appoint, transfer or dismiss public servants at pleasure. Since that time, public sector employment has increased, although institutional capacity for governance has been substantially eroded. This has had enormous consequences for policy implementation, due to both politicization and the inefficient nature of the administrative structure.

Sri Lanka at present has one of the largest bureaucracies in the Asian region, with a ratio of 3.9 central and non-central Government employees per 100 people (as compared with 1.2 in India, 1.5 in Pakistan and a 2.6 average in Asia). Between 1990 and 2001, public sector employment grew at 3.6 per cent annually, outpacing the growth in the labour force (World Bank, 2004e). Overstaffing by as much as 30 per cent in the lower grades, administrative fragmentation, duplication, wastage (partly due to inefficient devolution of power to the provincial governments), perceived corruption and outdated processes and procedures have eroded the position of the public sector as the facilitator of the country's development programme (World Bank, 2004e).

The 13th amendment to the Constitution also added to the inefficiency by establishing provincial governments, which have not only become costly to maintain and administer, but have also created confusion in governance due to the overlap and duplication of functions between the centre and the provinces. Regular large-scale recruitment (usually as a result of electoral pledges) and the proliferation of government ministries, statutory bodies and public corporations due to the need to accommodate partners in coalition governments have raised the share of public sector employment to nearly 13 per cent of the labour force. In addition, central Government has not withdrawn from devolved functions as planned at the time of decentralization, and this has created ambiguity and confusion as to the duties and responsibilities of public officers. Coupled with outdated modes of management and the absence of a performance-based remuneration system, these factors have created a disconnect between policy and implementation.

Although a Department of National Planning has been created to facilitate the formulation and implementation of policy through budgetary allocations, the planning process itself and the conversion of policy into action has not occurred efficiently due to the inherent weaknesses in the system.

7.4 Linking macroeconomic policy and decent work

Having identified the degree of disconnect between macroeconomic policies and economic growth, investment, employment and decent work, this section examines the following questions. To what extent is decent work central to current economic policy? Can decent work policies be implemented given the existing budget constraints of the government? Will other policies (financial, commercial and investment) that are being pursued make it possible to achieve decent work goals in a reasonable time frame? Finally, do the financial, commercial and investment policies of the Government reflect decent work principles?

Decent work *versus* other policy objectives

The decent work concept may appear to conflict with other policy objectives, such as improving the international competitiveness of Sri Lankan industry or increasing the productivity levels of the workforce. Some of the key trade-offs are discussed below.

The type of employment created

Sri Lanka's approach to industrialization has been to focus on the apparel sector, with its main advantage being the low cost of labour (approximately US$2 per day). These jobs are manual/operative positions, with no career development or skills development involved. The majority of workers are females, who take up such employment for the short term due to the non-availability of other opportunities more in line with their aspirations. However, this disenchantment is becoming increasingly apparent as the apparel sector reported that in the period 2004-05, there were about 15,000 unfilled positions in this category (ILO, 2005b). The decent work dilemma is that while the concept calls for a fair wage, employers argue that to do so would result in Sri Lanka losing the competitive advantage of low production costs, and that the employers may be forced to reduce staff or close down operations, thus removing the basis of decent work.

The flexibility/security of employment trade-off

The perceived rigidity in the labour market in Sri Lanka has also resulted in employers attempting to protect themselves against the need to pay large amounts of compensation to workers where termination becomes necessary for operational reasons. They achieve this by adopting wider job descriptions and shifting to peripheral employment forms, such as subcontracting, casual employment and part-time employment. Workers remain in these types of employment for extended periods of time, and so are deprived of employment security, career progression and the ability to exercise their rights. Thus, by attempting to provide security through legislation, workers are being driven into less secure, uncertain forms of employment. The increase in the proportion of casual employees to over one-third of all employed indicates that workers are losing out in this trade-off.

Enforcing social protection mechanisms

Although the need for an unemployment protection scheme has been recognized, the method of funding has been the cause of much debate. Any attempt to increase contributions from employers is likely to result in a further shift of employment to the informal economy, where evasion of social security payments and other regulations is a common practice. For instance, the mandatory EPF and ETF contributions add 15 per cent to wage bills; 50 per cent of all employers are estimated to be evading such contributions.

Wage–productivity gap

Rodrigo (2006) found that despite productivity growth amounting to over 2.5 per cent per annum on average during the period 1990–1999, wage growth during that period was contained below productivity growth. Wage growth also lagged behind inflation, reducing the return for labour over time. Although decent work would appear to require an equitable wage structure geared to compensating workers both for productivity and for changes in the cost of living, in reality any attempt to ensure this is likely to reduce new employment opportunities. Rodrigo found that at the national level, part of the surplus accruing to the employer went into investment (and to the creation of new employment opportunities), rather than being used to raise incomes of those already in employment. Through past experience, attempts by the state to ensure that the private sector maintains a semblance of inflation parity has increased the rigidity of the labour market and has served to shift economic activity to the informal economy.

Sri Lanka is therefore, on the horns of a dilemma in relation to decent work and productivity: although employers have made productivity gains a precondition for wage increases, historically growth in productivity has not been translated into growth in real wages. This is a long-term phenomenon and therefore, it can reasonably be concluded that productivity enhancement would receive priority by both employers and the Government over any attempt to improve decent work.

In essence, for countries such as Sri Lanka any attempt to ensure that standards of decent work are met by employers is likely to result in the increase in the cost of such labour; either due to better wages, the provision of better working conditions and workers' rights or a comprehensive system of social protection. Although Sri Lankan wage levels lie substantially below those of the developed and newly industrialized countries, the country's ranking within the Asian region is in the middle order. Rodrigo (2006) notes that in the garments sector (for 1993), Bangladesh's hourly labour cost was less than half of Sri Lanka's, while that of China, India, Indonesia, Pakistan and Vietnam stood at between 71 and 80 per cent of the Sri Lankan figure. The prospect of multinational investors moving to lower labour cost locations is a phenomenon that countries competing for overseas capital have to contend with.

Lower competitiveness may well translate into a lower volume of exports, thus endangering the balance of payments position of the country. Even if there is an attempt to fund decent working conditions through a broader based scheme, such as special taxation of goods and services or income, the costs would be passed on to the consumer and would ultimately drive up inflation, adversely affecting workers once again.

7.5 Is decent work central to current economic policy?

Until recently, Sri Lanka's macroeconomic policy focused solely on fiscal and monetary policy and did not take into account, or provide for, social development objectives. However, the inability of economic polices alone to address the issues discussed in the previous section has led to a recognition that the drive for greater efficiency and higher productivity must be balanced with a respect for basic rights of workers.

In recent policy declarations, the Government has embraced the decent work concept as being a practical approach to combining economic growth with social progress and equity. Many issues that are important from a decent work perspective have also been addressed in the Draft National Employment Policy for Sri Lanka (Ministry of Employment and Labour, 2002) and the National Productivity Policy for Sri Lanka (Ministry of Employment and Labour, undated).

The National Policy for Decent Work in Sri Lanka (NPDWSL), drafted through broad stakeholder participation and sectoral task forces, was formally approved by the President and the Cabinet of Ministers of Sri Lanka in August 2006. The NPDWSL identifies weaknesses in the focus areas of decent work and sets out policies and strategies designed to overcome them. The National Action Plan for Decent Work, which is an integral part of the policy document, has also been developed with tripartite and regional participation to convert policy into action.

The Interim Poverty Reduction Strategy announced to the Sri Lanka Development Forum in 2005, in the aftermath of the devastating tsunami of December 2004, specifically recognized the need to promote decent work through economic policy:

> The development of a globally competitive economy requires a globally competitive workforce and the fostering of a highly favourable work-place environment. The establishment of strategic partnerships between Government, the private sector and unions and between employers and workers in the workplace can create a competitive advantage, since harmonious industrial relations attract quality investment and create higher value jobs. Such partnerships have to be based on trust and accountability arising from transparency and information. *A modern legal framework governing labour relations that promotes a sound business environment, job security and employment needs to be created to promote a decent work environment*, productivity growth and corporate governance [emphasis added].
>
> *Source*: Ministry of Finance and Planning (2005)

In addition to these macro level policies, there are other sectoral polices that focus on labour and employment and address various aspects of decent work:

- National Employment Policy for Sri Lanka (Draft)—Ministry of Employment and Labour (2002);
- National Productivity Policy for Sri Lanka—Ministry of Employment and Labour (c. 2003);
- Extension of Social Security to the Excluded and Poor: National Action Plan—National Task Force on Social Security (2004);
- National Policy on Disability for Sri Lanka—Ministry of Social Welfare (2003); and
- National Policy for Decent Work in Sri Lanka—Ministry of Labour Relations and Foreign Employment (2006).

The dilemma faced by Sri Lanka is that some policies have been issued under different administrations. During the period under consideration, Sri Lanka faced no fewer than three general elections (in 2000, 2001 and 2004) and on each occasion, the election resulted in a change of administration. Although each policy had been developed through national discussion and the input of relevant experts in each field, and though many had been debated in Parliament and approved thereafter, every new administration has distanced itself from the policies and plans of the previous administration and announced a new policy framework based on its own ideology. However, each of these policies remains valid and operates concurrently, creating more confusion for the public service, as well as for donors and the public, which relies on plans and goals set out in policy documents. Even where a party has been in power for some time, this expectation that policies are likely to change with changes in administration has lessened the impetus for implementation, with the agencies assigned to implement strategies sometimes adopting a "wait-and-see" approach.

The NPDWSL has now been incorporated into the Governments' Ten Year Development Framework (TYDF), in a chapter focused on building a flexible and globally employable workforce. The TYDF recognises many of the decent work deficits and adopts a policy approach coherent with the NPDWSL for overcoming those deficits. However, the chapter in the TYDF is not linked with other related sectors, such as the agriculture sector, the industrial sector or the livelihoods-development sector. This brings about an immediate disconnect, as the policies that are central to achieving decent work are sometimes in conflict with the other chapters. For instance, the chapter on industrial development proposes a paradigm shift in industrial development, to promoting "knowledge-based" and "technology-intensive" industries rather than existing "resource-based" and "labour-intensive" industries. However, this is in conflict with the employment generation focus of labour policies; furthermore, the proposed "knowledge-based" industrial focus would require a similar paradigm shift in the education and vocational/technical education chapter; such an approach is not reflected in that chapter. Similarly, although at the time the NPDWSL was formulated policy recommended that the public sector should not be used as a means of providing employment (which was endorsed by the government ministries concerned), the subsequently announced TYDF acknowledges public sector recruitment of undergraduates as being an important aspect of the Governments' efforts to provide youth employment.

Further examples could be given, and although it is clear that decent work is the focus of only one sector—the labour and employment sector—as has been the practice in the past, there is some indication that a change may be likely. For instance, infrastructure development is the priority area for the Government, both in order to attract investment and to make product and factor markets more efficient (CBSL, 2006a). Infrastructure development is also the priority in the NPDWSL as it has been identified as a major constraint on investment and consequently on employment generation. However, other measures identified in policy documents that appear to be in line with the decent work agenda are unlikely to be implemented due to financial constraints, lack of capacity and lack of political commitment. Therefore, it is clear that despite a national agenda on decent work and public avowals of support for the concept, macroeconomic policy does not sufficiently incorporate or recognise decent work principles.

However, many of the strategies for implementing the decent work agenda do not carry a huge financial commitment; they are more by-products of existing plans for which budgetary allocations have been made. Infrastructure development, as discussed, is a core policy for economic and investment growth, as well as for decent work, and budgetary allocations have therefore already been made; its inclusion in the decent work agenda as a means of attracting investment does not therefore require any additional funding. Many of the proposed actions can be implemented even within the current budgetary constraints.

7.6 Conclusions

Sri Lanka is in an enviable position from a perspective of progressing towards decent work, in that the concept has been endorsed by the Government at the highest level and has been incorporated in a specific and structured national policy together with a comprehensive plan of action. However, implementation of the national policy is likely to be a complex task, given the number of agencies and ministries involved. A degree of confusion is also likely due to the coexistence of several macroeconomic and development policies formulated by different administrations, which are in various stages of implementation and impact on current strategies for promoting decent work.

Several changes are recommended in order to increase policy coherence in relation to economic growth, investment and the decent work agenda:

- A different approach to the process by which macroeconomic and development policies are formulated is a necessity, to ensure that those policies incorporate other parallel, nationally accepted programmes of development. The current sectoral approach to development also adds to the complexity of the task of implementation as linkages between related sectors are not developed in a systematic way.

- Regional development has clearly emerged as a priority, both for economic growth and for promoting decent work. The Government needs to streamline the areas of responsibility of regional and central administrations in order to eliminate areas of duplication, ambiguity and waste of resources.
- A formal tripartite mechanism to coordinate and determine policy at the national level is essential, especially where labour and employment sectors are concerned, in order to facilitate necessary reforms and implementation of policy.
- The Department of National Planning, the government agency entrusted with the formulation of macroeconomic and development policies, must take an inclusive approach in carrying out that task. Planning must be coordinated within the Department by a body consisting of representatives of all line ministries involved in policy implementation, so that contradictions and internal inconsistencies in policies will be resolved at the very outset of the planning process.
- Another important aspect is the linking of policies and action plans to the budgetary allocation process, without which no government activity can proceed. A better coordination between linked agencies when requesting allocation of funds for common programmes would also utilize scarce resources better and ensure that the plan is implemented more efficiently. At present, the conversion of policies and plans of actions into components that can be supported in the national budget does not appear to be optimally efficient, at least insofar as the objective of achieving decent work is concerned.[7]

---

7. Based on discussions with the Department of National Planning and the Department of Labour of the Government of Sri Lanka.

Donor agencies, aid organizations and technical cooperation programmes of international organizations also have an important role to play in helping developing countries to implement policies more efficiently. Ensuring that resources are allocated to programmes based on a coherent development policy which has been converted to pragmatically budgeted plans and strategies for action would go a long way towards achieving proper implementation. This would also avoid programmes being implemented as isolated components, thus reducing the benefit of each programme, and would also prevent duplication of development efforts.

8 Afghanistan: Little space for decent work

Paula Kantor

8.1 Introduction

This chapter is one of a series which aims to assess the extent to which national-level policies to promote economic growth within the South Asia region are at odds with or complementary to the goal of achieving decent employment for all. The motivation behind the interest in developing a better understanding of the policy mix, sequencing and coherence necessary to support employment-intensive growth is the evidence of a disconnect between growth and employment generation in recent years—where growth increases but unemployment and underemployment remain unaffected and where many of the new jobs created do not provide incomes that can support basic needs. There is no question that growth is necessary for employment generation and poverty reduction; however, it is the quality of growth that makes it pro-poor[1] and employment-intensive and it is on this aspect that this chapter focuses. It assesses in the context of Afghanistan's reconstruction the extent to which nascent efforts to develop economic policy that promotes growth and investment consider employment, and more specifically decent employment for all, and it then makes recommendations on how to increase attention to this content within economic policy-making processes.[2] Afghanistan is at a unique juncture among South Asian nations, emerging from over two

1. Pro-poor growth is growth where the benefits flow more to the poor than to the non-poor; thus, distributional concerns are integrated within any discussion of pro-poor growth.
2. The term "decent work/employment" is used to mean the sufficiency and desirability of one's work—with "work" including wage employment, self-employment, home-based work and domestic activities (Rogers, 2001). The strategic objectives of decent work include: employment, security, rights at work and representation (Majid, 2001b).

decades of conflict and attempting to build a functioning state that is able to provide security, development and peace to its people. The challenges are huge, but so are the opportunities if more open debate is fostered around how to achieve these aims, and if action and policy in the economic sphere are not constrained by externally imposed mandates primarily informed by a neo-liberal pro-market orientation.

The next section provides a context for the chapter by assessing the constraints and opportunities the Afghan environment provides for achieving growth, investment and decent work. Section 8.3 briefly justifies the need for attention to decent work in Afghanistan, providing some evidence of decent work deficits drawn from the limited empirical data available, while Sections 8.4 and 8.5 provide the main analysis, reviewing key policy documents and donor reports to assess the extent to which national policy documents promoting growth, investment and macroeconomic stability integrate attention to decent work and how they might better do so. Section 8.6 summarizes and makes recommendations for how to move the rhetoric surrounding equitable development and pro-poor growth closer to reality in order to enable more employment-intensive outcomes in Afghanistan.

8.2 Setting the scene

The rule of the Taliban was ended in 2001, but Afghanistan still faces considerable challenges in relation to achieving security, rule of law, development and peace. These challenges, and the existing opportunities, are briefly reviewed here in light of how they affect prospects for formulating and implementing policy to foster growth, investment and decent work.

Security and the rule of law

The continued lack of security within Afghanistan is a clear and commonly recognized constraint on attracting investment (Goodhand and Pain, 2002; World Bank, 2005f), whether from non-resident Afghans or foreign sources. Insecurity also directly limits growth by constraining trade and business. Since growth is a recognized need in relation to employment generation, insecurity also limits the extent to which the Afghan economy has been able to generate employment. Thus, addressing security concerns is necessary for facilitating both economic development and the achievement of decent work. This has been an ongoing challenge, in part due to the continued inability or unwillingness of the state and other actors to address the conditions supporting insecurity. Of particular concern is the persistence of the conditions supporting the "war economy" and the continued benefits flowing to the powerful within this institutional set-up, such as commanders, drug traffickers and traders in other illegal or illicit goods (e.g. guns, gems, timber and fuel) (UNDP, 2004c); this means there is strong resistance to any institutional reform efforts that would strengthen the rule of law and the position of the central state relative to the provinces, potentially changing the distribution of benefits and increasing general security in the country.

Linked to insecurity and leading to slow growth and deterring investment is a lack of state enforcement capacity in relation to laws and regulations, new or existing (MoCI, 2006a; World Bank, 2005b; ADB, 2005, 2006). A legal and regulatory framework to draw in investment is in place and developing continuously (MoCI, 2006a), but a framework in and of itself is insufficient without enforcement capacity. Without increased state capacity, even the most investor-friendly regulatory framework will not sway investors to come to Afghanistan. This directly leads to the next challenge, that of weak institutional capacity.

Institutional capacity constraints

Due to the extended period of conflict and resulting exodus of many of its best trained citizens during that period, Afghanistan today faces a major capacity challenge within its state apparatus (ADB, 2005, 2006; World Bank, 2005b; IMF, 2004b; Afghanistan Government, 2005a). This constrains its ability to address security problems and also influences the state's ability to formulate and implement policy, whether in support of social development, economic development or other aims. Thus, this chapter must take into account the severity of these constraints in assessing both where Afghanistan is in relation to policy-making in support of growth, investment and decent work, as well as where it can go in the short, medium and long terms. One outcome of weak institutional capacity is perhaps over-reliance on external agencies and technical assistance personnel in guiding Afghanistan's policy direction. This dependence is evidenced in the 2005 Interim Afghanistan National Development Strategy (I-ANDS) where the macroeconomic policy and poverty diagnostic sections rely quite heavily on documents previously produced by the World Bank. Thus, the state's ability to evaluate the policy stances of other organizations and make independent decisions about where it wants to go may be hindered by a low capacity, as well as by its weak bargaining positions *vis-à-vis* these international agencies.

Another outcome of weak formal and informal institutions, which affects the poor most negatively, is the permeability of interests represented in existing institutions (Wood, 2004). Thus, state institutions may not support the public interest but instead the personal interests of state workers. Similarly, markets do not function freely with equal access for all but are embedded within the power structures put in place during the conflict (local commanders, traders in illicit goods such as opium and guns, small numbers of traders controlling licit markets) and regulated by informal institutions (gender norms, traditions, kin and tribal networks), affecting who has access and who benefits most (UNDP, 2004c; Lister and Pain, 2004). Thus, Afghanistan as a context of low formal institutional capacity, where both formal and informal institutions may not work in the favour of the poor, can be characterized as operating under an informal security regime (Gough, 2004; Wood, 2004): "a set of conditions where people cannot reasonably expect to meet their security needs via accessing services from the state or via participation in open labour markets. Thus they have to rely more heavily upon community and family relationships of various kinds" (Wood, 2004: 50). Thus, people depend on informal institutions, which may operate quite effectively, but again not necessarily transparently or in the interests of the poor.

Under informal security regimes, the dysfunction of states and markets, particularly from the perspective of the less powerful, including the poor, means that these groups have to develop alternative informal mechanisms through which to manage risk and create security, often becoming dependent on hierarchical relations of unequal power (i.e., commanders for personal security, patrons for credit or employment) (Wood, 2003, 2004). In such an environment, real attention to the needs and interests of the poor within policy circles may be non-existent, and one must go one step further to question what policy-making means in such a context. Is there really a policy-making process that can be assessed, contributed to or influenced, or do groups representing vested interests make decisions behind closed doors? This is still an open question. In the end, the existence of an informal security regime within Afghanistan affects interest in and commitment to pro-poor growth and hence, the potential to forge links between economic growth and decent employment outcomes, at least in the short term.

Neo-liberal economic policy influences

National policy documents such as *Securing Afghanistan's Future* (Afghanistan Government, 2004) and the reports from the 2005 Afghanistan Development Forum (2005a, 2005b) illustrate the strong influence that neo-liberal perspectives have on economic policy in Afghanistan. They clearly state that private sector development and reliance on the free market are the means of achieving national growth and development aims, with a more marginal and enabling role for the state. Other features that define a neo-liberal economic model include low trade barriers, reductions in state expenditure and minimization of state regulation of economic activity. Thus, when the "neo-liberal" approach is referred to in this chapter, it is to this complex array of characteristics that reference is being made.

There has been some discussion of the relevance and adequacy of this paradigm for Afghanistan (UNDP, 2004c; Pain, 2004), but more public debate is needed. Facilitating this debate is a role for those in the international community less committed to this economic policy approach, including the ILO with its Decent Work Agenda. The Afghan state also provides some indications that it is not wholly supportive of the approach through statements made in some documents backing pro-poor growth, equitable development and decent employment for Afghanistan's citizens (e.g. I-ANDS and the Afghanistan Compact).[3] These contradictions and the means of turning a stated interest in pro-poor growth into reality are discussed in more detail in Section 8.4.

3. I-ANDS, the Interim Afghanistan National Development Strategy, is Afghanistan's interim Poverty Reduction Strategy Paper (PRSP) document. It builds upon the Afghanistan Compact, an agreement reached in January 2006 between Afghanistan and the international community regarding priority benchmarks to be achieved over the next five years, linked to donor funding commitments.

Opium economy

One cannot discuss growth, investment and employment in Afghanistan without considering the opium economy since its proceeds amount to approximately 30–50 per cent of non-opium GDP. The opium economy is linked to insecurity and poor governance (World Bank, 2005c; ADB, 2005, 2006), and progress on these fronts is only possible if there is a shift in power away from those controlling the proceeds of opium production. This will be a long time coming, but commitment to generating decent work in rural Afghanistan can play a role in providing better alternatives than are currently available to those working in the fields (Afghanistan Government, 2004; UNDP, 2004c). Thus, calls for better conditions in and earnings from work in the non-opium rural economy can fit within the broader objectives of creating alternative risks and rewards to poppy growing or working in the fields, and is something to consider in raising the profile of decent work and employment generation in general in the Afghan context.

Dearth of labour market information

Another factor characterizing Afghanistan at present is a significant lack of empirical information, including data on the labour market. This clearly limits economic policy formulation processes and the effectiveness of skills development programmes, since there is no reliable information on labour demand, the characteristics of labour supply or its change over time.

The Central Statistical Office (CSO) has released data from 2002 on the sizes of the working-age, employed and unemployed populations, but the source is not provided (CSO, 2003). It appears as if the data are estimates based on 1979 population data, with the same "per cent employed" figure applied to later population data, again for which no source is provided. Hence, a major state-led initiative, and one of the Afghanistan Compact benchmarks, is to conduct a labour market survey. A unit in the Ministry of Labour, Social Affairs, Martyrs and Disabled (MoLSAMD) was created to compile secondary information and to begin preparing to collect primary labour-related data on a regular basis. This is a vital input for designing relevant skills-development programmes, drawing investment in sectors with available matching skills and developing a national employment policy.[4]

Informal economy

Another important contextual factor for South Asia as a whole when discussing growth, investment and decent work is the informal economy. It is estimated that in Afghanistan, 80–90 per cent of economic activity is informal (World Bank, 2005c). It would follow from this that most employment is also informal, apart from at least a portion of employment in the public sector and in formal firms (e.g. Roshan, Afghan Wireless Communication Company (AWCC), Coca-Cola plant and NGOs) that is likely to be formal (with contracts, benefits etc.).[5] In light of this, discussions on growth and investment policy must address the informal economy head on. They must move beyond existing discussions on formalizing informal economic activity (MoCI, 2006a), which seems destined to fail given the persistence of informality in a range of developing country contexts (Chen, 2004; Harriss-White, 2003), to discussions on how to improve conditions of work for informal workers. The latter is possible, but it has not been on the agenda in Afghanistan; it is an entrée for the Decent Work Agenda.

Different perspectives on the informal economy are evident in current documentation on growth, investment and development in Afghanistan, with the World Bank tending to view it as a constraint on development and a coping mechanism that will decline with growth[6];

---

4. The need for this information for developing a national employment strategy was recognized by Deputy Minister of Labor in an interview (February 11, 2007). A working group was established in late 2007 to begin discussing the development of a national employment strategy. A first step will be completing a labour market survey.

5. Due to the lack of labour market data in Afghanistan, accurate indicators of the share of formal and informal employment in general and by sector are not available. Nor are there data on share of Afghan *versus* imported labour and growth in employment. Note that investment in formal enterprises may generate only limited employment, and not all will be formal: the Coca-Cola plant generated only 350 jobs for an investment of US$25 million (BBC, 2006). In the public sector also, not all employment is formal. According to the 2006 *Afghanistan Statistical Yearbook*, 25 per cent of the 295,000 government workers were contract workers and not permanent (CSO, 2006).

6. Again, evidence of the persistence of informality across developing country contexts casts doubt on this perception of informality (Chen, 2004).

the World Bank perhaps focuses more on the illicit informal economy linked to opium and smuggling, under the control of warlords and commanders, and less on informal employment per se (World Bank, 2005b, 2005c). Conversely, the National Human Development Report (NHDR) (UNDP, 2004c) recognizes the importance of the informal economy to national income and livelihoods, perhaps focusing more on informal employment and lawful but untaxed activity. In the end, informality will not disappear quickly, either the licit or illicit, due to the many challenges of insecurity and weak institutions already described. The aim is to minimize the illicit by changing the social relations and economic incentives that motivate people to choose these activities, while also improving opportunities in the licit informal economy to increase the incomes and security of those dependent on it for income, as well as increasing the revenue it creates for the state. This is where the Decent Work Agenda can have considerable effect.

Human capital constraints

It is widely acknowledged that a key constraint on growth and development in Afghanistan is the shortage of skilled staff, resulting from the low levels of human capital investment possible during the 25 years of conflict in the country (World Bank, 2005f, 2005c; UNDP, 2004c; ADB, 2005, 2006). This is a major factor to be addressed when considering appropriate employment and investment policies for today and the future and the investments that need to be made to build capacity among the existing and future workforce. Reliance on imported skilled labour from Pakistan, Turkey and India, among others, is a short-term solution, which was put in place in part due to the hurry to make progress on reconstruction projects. The long-term outcomes of this rush to complete projects without building local capacity are unknown, but they are not likely to be positive. More long-term sequenced planning is required to link planned economic investments with skills building to ensure Afghans benefit from future growth. This is discussed in more depth in Section 8.4.

ANDS process

The final contextual factor is the soon to be completed process of developing Afghanistan's PRSP—the Afghanistan National Development Strategy (ANDS); the official deadline for completion is end March 2008.

This was an opportunity to integrate more than rhetoric on pro-poor growth into policy dialogue and bring attention to employment generation and the distribution of growth front and centre. As yet, there is very little focus on employment within existing related documents (Afghanistan Compact, I-ANDS) and what attention there is, places employment squarely under social protection and not under economic governance and private sector development, something consistent with the treatment of employment in some World Bank documents (Afghanistan Government, 2006; World Bank, 2005c). The sectoral nature of the ANDS process also may impede the holistic view needed to appropriately address the complex interactions between growth, investment and decent work. Thus, much could be done to take advantage of the opportunity the ANDS process provides. This offers an opening for the aid community committed to a more equitable distribution of growth to work with the ANDS Secretariat to ensure these issues gain more prominence in the document's preparation and in its implementation.

8.3 Decent work deficits in Afghanistan

The aim of this section is to briefly justify the attention given to decent work among the many other challenges facing Afghanistan. Some may say that employment and the quality of employment are lower order priorities; particularly issue of employment quality. However, others have disputed the ability to separate the two or the need to give attention to growth—and in Afghanistan's case, security and governance—first and rights issues second (Majid, 2001b; UNDP, 2004c; Rogers, 2001). In fact all are complementary, and excluding rights-based issues from the start may make integrating them later almost impossible (Rogers, 2001).[7] As argued later in this chapter, attention to employment itself, regardless of its quality, needs to be strengthened within discussions on investment and growth. This attention must be placed within longer term strategic thinking about what type of investment is required to provide "high

7. The relative neglect of rights-based issues in the economic and employment spheres has parallels in the neglect of human rights abuses and the admitted climate of impunity that exists in the political sphere (UNDP, 2004c), recently exhibited in the lower house of Parliament's passage of a resolution giving general impunity to those associated with illegal acts during Afghanistan's many years of conflict.

road" employment opportunities[8] given Afghanistan's human resource and institutional capacity constraints. Competing for the "low road", against the likes of China and India, does not seem in Afghanistan's favour, unless favourable trade agreements are reached and industries are protected—something in contravention of the current free-market approach to promoting economic growth.

A final justification for integrating decent work objectives with ongoing efforts to achieve security and growth is the relativity of the concept of decent work (Rogers, 2001; Majid, 2001b). While there should be a floor below which working conditions and labour standards should not go, this can be defined nationally, through an open process which sets realistic benchmarks based on what a country can achieve in a given period, in its current social, economic and political context. These benchmarks could then be adjusted upwards periodically as progress is made. Assisting in the process of setting and re-setting benchmarks is another way the aid community committed to rights-based approaches and decent work can support the Afghan Government to integrate decent work within its growth and investment aims.

But what is the situation in terms of decent work deficits in the Afghan context? The tables below provide data from a longitudinal study of urban livelihoods in three cities conducted by the Afghanistan Research and Evaluation Unit (AREU) and also data on rural incomes compiled from the National Risk and Vulnerability Assessment's (NRVA) 2003 data.[9]

Table 8.1 illustrates that for the poor urban workers studied, work tends to be insecure in regard to work days accessed and does not generate sufficient returns on average to meet expenditures, except among the Herat sample. Therefore, most families rely on borrowing to meet daily needs as well as to meet other expected and unexpected costs, such as ceremonies, marriages and ill health (Beall and Schutte, 2006). Of

8. Holmström (1999) defines "low road" employment policy as that dependent on low-cost labour and labour deregulation to foster profit, compared with "high road" employment policy which invests in increased efficiency through technology and innovation and passes the returns to workers through better wages and work conditions.

9. The AREU study covered 40 poor households in each of the three cities (Kabul, Herat, Jalalabad); the study used a longitudinal panel design, so each household was visited once a month for 12 months, starting in February 2005.

particular interest in Table 8.1 is the percentage of workers accessing less than 200 days of work per year and the median days of work accessed. Research on rural livelihoods has estimated that a base of 200 days of work per year is required for survival (Scoones, 1998). This base is likely to be too low for the more costly urban areas, but still few in the Afghan study sample achieved it. This indicates a high prevalence of underemployment in terms of access to work days among informal workers in urban Afghanistan.

Table 8.1

Data on earnings and work days among poor urban workers in three cities

Item	*Kabul*	*Herat*	*Jalalabad*
Median annual earnings per worker (US$)	344	340	514
Median days of work per year	131	96	120
Percentage working fewer than 200 days per year	72	69	74
Median per capita annual income (in HH) (US$)[1]	99	155	132
Median per capita annual expenditures (US$)	140	135	145

Note: [1] Median annual earning is a worker-level measure. Median per capita annual income is a household level measure, distributing household earned income across all members.

Source: Beall and Schutte, 2006; Kantor and Schutte, 2007.

Data on rural livelihoods are more limited, but show how a considerable share of workers interviewed in the 2003 NRVA were employed in daily wage work, among the most insecure work available in the informal economy (Table 8.2). Only 10 per cent of employment is salaried, which is likely to be the most closely associated with formal employment. Returns from work are also highly variable, being based on type of work and linked to skills level and season. The importance of skills to wages highlights the need to extend the outreach of the National Skills Development Programme (NSDP) and to make it more demand led.[10] The data in Table 8.2 also show how working in the opium economy is clearly a rational decision given the considerably higher wages on offer.

10. The NSDP is discussed in more detail later in the chapter, in the section on labour productivity growth and decent employment.

Table 8.2

NRVA data on rural employment

	Salaried	*Daily wage*	*Self-employed*	*Paid in kind*	*Unpaid*
Share of employment (%)	10	40	45	4	1
	Casual unskilled, mid season	Casual unskilled, high season	Regular labourer	Poppy worker, harvest	Semi-skilled informal
Average daily wage (US$)	1.69	2.92	3.65	11.53	5.51

Source: World Bank, 2005f.

AREU research on rural livelihoods found that uncertainty around income leads to reliance on diversification strategies, with families allocating labour across farm, off-farm and non-farm opportunities, as available. For the poor, these strategies do not lead to accumulation, but tend to be a coping mechanism (Grace and Pain, 2004).

These data from rural and urban Afghanistan clearly support the need to bring employment into the centre of the debate around poverty reduction, growth and investment; both how to generate more employment of good quality and how to improve prospects in existing sectors, particularly within the informal economy. The extent to which this is occurring is assessed in the next sections.

8.4 Growth, investment and decent work in policy and programmes

This section draws primarily upon evidence from reviews of existing documents to make conclusions about the place of decent employment in the discourse on growth and investment and in macroeconomic policy. Some of the documents reviewed represent national policy positions (Afghanistan Compact, I-ANDS and ANDS documents), others ministry and quasi-state institution positions (Ministry of Commerce and Industry (MoCI) and Afghanistan Investment Support Agency (AISA)), and still others, the position of multilateral aid agencies with a specific interest in growth and investment (World Bank, International Monetary Fund (IMF) and Asian Development Bank). There is little primary data to bolster arguments, and the quality of that which does exist tends to be questionable. Policy-making processes are in their infancy in Afghanistan, and while they are influenced by the previously mentioned informal systems and vested interests, this does not preclude efforts to use "opportunities" such as the ANDS process to change the current scenario and create a place for decent work within discussions of economic development programmes and policy.

Links between economic growth and growth in decent employment

> The economic vision of the government of Afghanistan is an economy that provides decent employment with sustainable and growing incomes for all Afghans.
>
> (ADF, 2005a: 1).

> The quality of growth is very important. What is needed is growth with improving social indicators and without a significant deterioration in income distribution.
>
> (Afghanistan Government, 2004: 7)

In the Afghan context, as the quotations above show, there is at least a rhetorical link between economic growth and decent employment, in that many national policy documents do not just claim economic growth as an objective, but want that growth to be pro-poor, broad-based and/or equitable (ADF, 2005b; Afghanistan Government, 2004, 2005b, 2006). These descriptive terms are what provide an entry for decent work into economic policy debates: interest in pro-poor growth should imply interest in the patterns and distribution of growth. As the NHDR notes, the main asset of the poor is their labour power, so if growth patterns are to benefit the poor, employment needs to have a central place in growth-promoting strategies (UNDP, 2004c). Therefore, there is definitely a place for decent work in discussions of growth, and of investment feeding growth. The question is to what extent this stated goal is more than rhetoric—do state policies and other documents important to policy-making in the country maintain a commitment to pro-poor growth through action and strategy, or does employment and its quality disappear from the agenda? As the quote below asserts, rhetoric is not sufficient to make progress on integrating human development concerns, such as decent work, into the growth discourse—there must be concerted state-led action.

> International experience confirms that the mutually reinforcing relationship between economic growth and human development does not arise automatically but has to be reinforced explicitly through Government-led pro-poor policies and programs.
>
> (ADF, 2005b: 1)

Evidence to date in Afghanistan points more often to the disappearance of the pro-poor dimension of growth from discussions of economic growth and investment, and to a lack of concern with employment generation in general, let alone the quality of that employment. This can be seen in the early stages of reconstruction through a willingness to support only emergency employment through the National Emergency Employment Program, which provided labour days in public works programmes for low wages, with the low wages supporting self-selection in recruitment by the poor (World Bank, 2005b). As the programme title implies, the employment created was short lived and not sustained. While it helped families get through a winter, it has done little to generate longer term growth or secure livelihoods through a more strategic approach to promote sustainable livelihoods.

Linked to this is the recognition that while high rates of economic growth have been achieved in recent years (from an admittedly low base),[11] the structure of the economy has remained unchanged—maintaining a heavy reliance on agriculture—and that the growth and the related employment creation have been of a temporary nature (World Bank, 2005f, 2005c). Growth has been driven largely by reconstruction-related sectors, which are likely to decline in time, by the aid industry, which again is not likely to sustain itself at current levels in the medium to long term, and by the illicit poppy economy, which the United Nations Office on Drugs and Crime estimates employed 2.3 million people in 2004 and 2.0 million in 2005 (UNODC, 2005). Declines in the latter reflect efforts at reducing cultivation, the success of which will vary in relation to a range of social, political and economic factors. In the end, though, these current growth and employment drivers are not sustainable and even if they were, there is little evidence that growth in these areas necessarily leads to increased employment or good quality employment for a large

11. The ADB estimates the average annual change in GDP from 2002–2004 to be 17.4 per cent and 14 per cent in 2005; adjusted for inflation, these become 3.1 per cent and 1.7 per cent real GDP growth rates (ADB, 2005, 2006).

proportion of the population. Construction tends to be dominated by foreign workers (Pakistani, Turkish and Egyptian); the NGO and aid sector draws mainly skilled workers, in some instances removing them from the occupations they have trained for (e.g. doctors who are programme managers or drivers etc.) and excludes the large number of unskilled and uneducated; the opium economy generates considerable employment, at high wages but also with considerable risk. Based on this, there is a call for new drivers of growth, with investment priorities ranked with significant attention to employment intensity and quality. To date, such criteria have not been included in investment strategies or approval processes. This is supported by a representative of AISA, who recognizes that in the global economy, placing restrictions on potential investors (e.g. employment *versus* capital intensity, or hiring of Afghan workers) may push them to invest in other countries.[12] Under this pressure, employment concerns seem to disappear from the agenda.

The rhetorical nature of pro-poor labels and the disappearing focus on employment and its quality in the Afghan context can be explained by the footloose nature of global capital and the influence of the neo-liberal model that guides economic policy, as supported by USAID, the World Bank and IMF. There are contradictions embedded within applying this model and using pro-poor and decent work descriptors in policy documents. Such contradictions are evidenced in one of the reports by the Afghanistan Development Forum (2005a), in a chapter on an enabling environment for private sector development. Following the quote used to open this section, the chapter goes on to state that the means to achieve pro-poor growth and decent employment are a dynamic, competitive private sector operating under free-market principles—basic tenets of the neo-liberal economic approach, along with an open economy and a reduced public sector (Heinz and Pollin, 2003). The sentiment around the potential equity in a free market system is echoed in documents on the MoCI's website. These documents, and hence the Ministry, support the efficient and equitable operation of the free market economy, and seek to create a regulatory framework to ensure that the benefits of the free market economy are realized—i.e., that the market is free to operate and not that a structure

12. Interview with AISA representative, 11 February 2007.

is in place to ensure its benefits are equitably distributed. In fact, the documents link equity to competition, stating that a competitive environment is needed to ensure equitable market operation, with no seeming acknowledgement of evidence of increasing poverty and inequality linked to structural reforms and the unregulated workings of the market in other contexts (UNDP, 2004c; Jolly *et al.*, 1987). All of this exemplifies how the focus of economic discourse is on the market and its freedom to operate, and less on Afghan citizens—their abilities to access markets and how benefits of economic growth and markets are distributed across individuals with different powers and capabilities. It is very much a market-centred view of economic development, where people—workers and non-workers alike—have very little place, as does the state. This bodes ill for the Decent Work Agenda and the ability to achieve pro-poor growth.

The 2004 NHDR takes quite a different stance on the role of the market in development in Afghanistan. It embeds itself more firmly in a contextual analysis of the reasons behind Afghanistan's decades of conflict and how reliance on the market may strengthen instead of mitigate these factors. It brings power and inequality directly into its analysis, something missing from many other policy-oriented documents, providing in many ways a more realistic portrayal of the context and the strategies needed to bring positive change to a broad representation of Afghans.

In particular, the NHDR recognizes how past power holders, who benefited from the war economy, still hold control over markets, often through access to political influence and through oligarchic power and the resulting ability to control access to markets by other producers, sellers or buyers and to control prices. Thus, relying on and strengthening markets in their current forms may only increase the power of local commanders and traders, as well as poverty and inequality (UNDP, 2004c; Lister and Pain, 2004), because the structures supporting the informal security regime are not addressed. The same results can be expected from following a free-market approach that presumes, at least in theory, that all have access to markets on equal terms; this conception of markets ignores the existence of power within markets, and ends up giving power holders with established links, a free hand to continue to accumulate wealth, often at others' expense (i.e., the state, labourers etc.).

> Yet experience shows in a number of developing or post-conflict countries around the world, a market approach to reconstruction and development policies [reduced role of the state; focus on user fees and cost recovery for basic services; private sector led growth] may inevitably have a number of negative externalities, which policy makers in Afghanistan must be aware of—widening inequalities, large pockets of poverty, limited provision of social and public goods and high levels of crime. For Afghanistan, a market approach to reconstruction may fail to incorporate the root causes of conflict: unequal distribution and competition over resources, lack of inclusion, poor political accountability and legitimacy, among others.
>
> (UNDP, 2004c: 174)

Admittedly, changing the structure of markets, who controls them and how their benefits are distributed is not going to be a simple process; it requires achievements in governance and rule of law which have been a long time coming. However, strengthening existing markets by relying so fully on them is not a step in the right direction for growth in general or for pro-poor growth and decent work since it might sustain existing insecurity given the continued capture of the benefits of growth by the powerful. There must be more institutionally integrated approaches to growth, informed by a human development perspective, which provide a greater role for the state in shaping in whose interests markets operate than is envisaged under the neo-liberal paradigm (UNDP, 2004c); this is not something necessarily supported by all agencies, particularly those more closely associated with an open market approach to development in the country.

Aid agencies supporting a greater state role need to support the state in the short, medium and long terms to increase its capacity to appropriately and constructively intervene in regulating processes of growth. If this does not happen with greater effectiveness than is currently the case, there is no reason to believe that the state will necessarily perform much better in promoting the needs of the poor, given the informal security regime currently in operation in Afghanistan, where personal interests often permeate all spheres, including the state.

Part of Afghanistan's economic growth strategy is to increase private investment from both domestic and foreign sources in support of the vision of the private sector as the engine of Afghanistan's growth (World Bank, 2005b; Afghanistan Government, 2004). To this end, a law on domestic and foreign private investment in Afghanistan was drafted and approved in December 2005 (MoCI, 2006b) in fulfilment of one of the Afghanistan Compact benchmarks under economic governance and private sector development. While one of the stated goals of the law is to expand the labour market and the standard of living of Afghans, the overall aim is to encourage and protect domestic and foreign private investment; there is no mention of protecting Afghan labour. The law is pro-business in terms of conditions for profit transfer and extent of foreign ownership, and the only mention of labour-related issues is that firms should employ and build the skills of Afghans whenever possible—the requirement is no more binding than that. This has definite repercussions for employment generation for Afghans in the country, as there is anecdotal evidence of the extent of foreign workers on payrolls to build roads, work in hotels and serve food in the cafeterias of aid agency compounds. Some of this reliance on foreign workers reflects the rush to get things done, which has led to decisions that do not take a longer term perspective on skills building and sustainability. However, the time has come for these considerations to come to centre stage, and for reliance on foreign semi-skilled and skilled labour to be reduced in favour of building capacity locally, for the long term pay-off involved.

To further facilitate private investment, AISA, a semi-autonomous institution, was established in 2003. While the promotion of investment does not necessarily have negative implications for decent employment, under a neo-liberal development model it often does due to the links between open markets, competition for foreign direct investment (FDI) and the resulting pressure on labour conditions, costs and worker representation flowing from this competition (Heinz and Pollin, 2003). Within AISA and the MoCI, there is less evidence of interest in protecting labour, which reflects the focus on the private sector and a pro-business environment. In fact, the MoCI website, in a section on strengthening the investment climate, states clearly that labour regulations need to support the concerns of the private sector; this coincides with statements in other documents supporting a pro-private sector regulatory environment, such as from the World Bank (World Bank, 2005f). Thus, Afghanistan's approach fits into the global move towards flexible employment regimes, aimed at attracting FDI but which may not serve a pro-poor growth and Decent Work Agenda.

There is evidence that some view such flexibility positively; for example, the World Bank report on the investment climate in Afghanistan (2005b) lists labour regulation as an area where Afghanistan has made progress, in that Afghan firms have more flexibility in hiring and firing workers and in setting working hours than neighbouring countries. There is less concern for workers' rights or conditions within this perspective, and instead there is an implicit support for increased informalization of labour (i.e., for increased informal labour relations within formal enterprises). This support for informal labour relations within firms is quite different from the more negative views of informality of firms; the latter is deemed to be a hindrance to growth by limiting sources of state revenue and, in some cases, by supporting insecurity and existing power relations (World Bank, 2005f, 2005c). Evidently, informalization of labour is a positive move, enhancing flexibility of firms and promoting growth, but at whose expense? This is not discussed. Instead, the acceptance of labour informalization shows a break in the link between promoting growth and achieving decent work objectives. Thus, growth in formal firms in Afghanistan (e.g. the Coca-Cola plant and in the telecommunications sector—Areeba, Roshan, AWCC) may increase employment, but the extent to which it will be decent work and for Afghans is less certain given support for flexibility in labour contracts and the lack of binding requirements to hire and train local workers. Establishing and regularly implementing a labour market survey that examines levels and quality of employment will assist in monitoring how employment is changing and who is benefiting.

One way forward in relation to labour informalization is presented by Heinz and Pollin (2003), who recognize that one cannot ignore the imperative of economic growth (an argument this chapter supports), but that growth alone is not sufficient to stop informalization, and may in fact increase it under a neo-liberal economic framework. Thus, what is needed is growth coupled with improved regulation of formal and informal labour markets. Regulations should be developed with the joint interests of business and labour in mind, and linked to mechanisms to increase capacities within the state to enforce the regulatory framework. Thus, in the Afghan context, the ILO's tripartite structure seems a way forward to develop a regulatory environment that is practical and supports economic growth, but with a clear pro-poor and decent work orientation, reflecting the Afghan capacity for enforcement and setting progressively higher targets as capacity develops. There is some evidence that this approach is already in use, as the Ministry of Labour, Social Affairs, Martyrs and Disabled (MoLSAMD) conferred with an employers' representative (Chamber of Commerce) and workers' representatives in developing the newly revised labour code. This is not without its challenges, particularly as workers' groups have not yet been federated, so there are issues to be resolved regarding who represents them and through what structure.[13]

An interesting assessment of the role of employment in poverty reduction provides an analysis that can be usefully applied to economic and employment policy development in Afghanistan (Osmani, 2005). It offers a proactive analytical framework to guide discussions around growth, investment and employment creation for pro-poor outcomes, instead of assuming that growth and private sector development will automatically bring employment (ADF, 2005b; Afghanistan Government, 2006), which tends to be the standard practice among many state and multi-lateral agencies, particularly the IFIs.

Osmani's article links employment generation to the achievement of the Millennium Development Goals (MDGs), and the most relevant part for this chapter is his analysis of the role of employment in achieving MDG 1 on poverty reduction. He makes the link between employment and poverty reduction through labour being the poor's most valuable and widely held asset. Osmani's analysis is relevant to the Afghan context in that the country aims to achieve Afghanized indicators of the MDGs by 2020; hence, more attention now to employment policy, and decent work within such policy, can contribute both to the stated aim of pro-poor growth and to achieving the poverty reduction MDG.

Osmani builds an argument that lack of employment, underemployment and low returns to employment are proximate causes of poverty, with low returns resulting from some combination of: a surplus labour environment, where high competition reduces wages; low productivity of labour, due to low skill and technology; and adverse terms

13. Interview with Deputy Minister in MoLSAMD. The CSO (2006) reports there are 622 unions in Afghanistan, which the MoLSAMD states are not federated, meaning representation at meetings is problematic.

of trade, due to low product prices or high input costs (Osmani, 2005). One key thing missing from this analysis of the causes of low returns, linked in part to terms of trade, is how people are included within labour markets. Many are included on poor terms, with little voice and power, due to who they are in the social and economic context (Wood, 2003, 2004). This is another factor, along with the three above, relevant to low access to and returns from employment in the Afghan context.

How can these constraints be addressed? Osmani (2005) relies very much on growth as the solution, but provides a more nuanced assessment of the quality of growth required than found in Afghan analyses to date. He describes three factors characterizing the growth necessary to break down the conditions supporting underemployment and low returns—leading to a more pro-poor growth, sensitive to the quality of work opportunities. The three factors are as follows:

- Growth factor: The rate at which growth occurs or the economy expands. An adequate rate of growth in and of itself is necessary but not sufficient to increase employment and reduce poverty.
- Elasticity factor: The extent to which the increase in growth enhances both the quantity and quality of employment. Is it employment-intensive growth or not? The aim is for the former if pro-poor growth linked to decent work is an aim.
- Integrability factor: The extent to which the poor can integrate into the economic processes where growth is happening, and on what terms. To what extent do the poor benefit from growth areas?

These factors provide criteria against which possibilities for investment can be assessed for the extent to which they will promote labour-intensive and pro-poor growth, and not just growth for the few. Thus, elasticity depends on the sectors within which investment and growth are proposed and their labour intensities (Osmani, 2005). In the Afghan context, sectors for growth and employment generation highlighted in the I-ANDS are: agriculture, agro-business, pastoral occupations and rural enterprise; productive use of state assets; mines and extractive industries; and transit and trade. Of these, the first has the greatest potential for enhancements in quantities of employment (if capital does not replace labour). Mines and mineral extraction and transit and trade may also create some employment, but perhaps not in large enough numbers to address the employment challenge Afghanistan faces. Finally, privatization of state-owned enterprises has been assessed as having a considerable negative effect on employment (Paterson and Blewett, 2006), putting more pressure on the other identified sectors to increase their employment generation capacity. In all cases where employment may be created, concerted effort will be needed to ensure its quality, within the capacity constraints of the state to enforce protective regulatory frameworks.

Assessing the integrability of growth opportunities is vital to ensuring that the poor benefit. Thus, "an element in the desired policy framework must be some real attempt at the inclusion of the working poor in the growth process itself as opposed to them just being second round beneficiaries of growth multipliers" (Majid, 2001b: 17). This takes considerable strategic thought and a commitment to lobby for the types of investment that provide opportunities to the poor, as well as holistic thinking about the skills development and other inputs required (information, finance etc.) to ensure that the poor benefit.[14] It means not necessarily settling for low value added opportunities for the poor, which might limit Afghanistan's and the poor's ability to move out of poverty in the medium to long term, but thinking through how to attract higher quality employment opportunities and build the labour force required to support them. This calls for inclusive development which does not prioritize economic growth over distribution of benefits, or security over employment generation, but recognizes interlinkages and the need for progress on all fronts (Majid, 2001b). Coordination, a stumbling block in many developing country contexts, is required. The ANDS process, both its development and implementation after March 2008, could provide the framework for this integrated thinking.

As a minimum, however, concerns for the employment intensity of growth and the inclusion of the poor within processes of growth must be better integrated into mainstream discourse on economic policy in Afghanistan, if the nexus between growth, investment and decent work is

14. The working group commissioned to develop a national employment strategy provides an opportunity for such integrated thinking.

to be realized. As yet this is not happening sufficiently, as evidenced by the World Bank's agenda for growth (2005c), which includes improved security, maintenance of macroeconomic stability, delivery of support services and an enabling environment for business. All are necessary components, but they are insufficient without the addition of elements explicitly related to what employment will be generated and who will benefit.

Macroeconomic policy and decent employment

The overarching guide to macroeconomic policy in Afghanistan, as in many other developing countries, is structural reform. Since March 2004, Afghanistan has applied an IMF Staff Monitored Program (SMP), the precursor to a full Structural Adjustment Program (SAP), which is used in contexts where weak administrative capacities require technical assistance for implementation of reform measures (IMF, 2004a; ADB, 2005). The SMP's aims are the same as a standard SAP and include civil service reform, liberal trade and exchange rate regimes, prudent monetary policy to manage currency in circulation and keep inflation low, and revenue generation strategies (taxes and fees) aimed at reducing reliance on external aid (IMF, 2004a). Afghanistan has received positive feedback on its implementation of the SMP—its macroeconomic policy has been labelled stable and prudent (World Bank, 2005f; ADB, 2005, 2006). The main negative remark has been related to legal system constraints; laws on financial management and investment have been only slowly developed.

The focus on structural reforms and the substantial attention within this on inflation control are part of a neo-liberal approach to economic management, according to Heinz and Pollin (2003). They state that inflation control tends to receive more attention under neo-liberal macroeconomic policy strategies, rather than fiscal and monetary policies that might support employment generation. In the Afghan case, little to no mention is made of employment generation in any of the documents directed at macroeconomic policy that were reviewed. In the one place where labour markets are mentioned (ADB, 2006), it is to note the negative influence of the donor and drug economies, which increase aggregate demand and affect labour markets by increasing wages unsustainably. While it is true that the aid and drug economies have had distortionary effects on labour markets (e.g. educated Afghans working as drivers for the aid agencies' high levels of pay), what also can be drawn from this statement is the need to avoid increasing wages as this could increase demand, and thus inflation. The overarching concern for inflation means efforts to increase wages as part of a decent work campaign would likely be discouraged for their potential inflationary effect, as well as due to concerns that higher wages might reduce FDI.

One can conclude from a review of documents on Afghanistan's macroeconomic approach (IMF, 2004a, 2004b, 2006; ADB, 2005, 2006) that there is little or no place for employment generation and decent work. This reflects the more general absence of direct engagement with employment-related issues throughout Afghanistan's economic policy documents and among the agencies contributing to them. Instead, employment tends to be placed within social protection discussions, and focused on "vulnerable groups" such as women, disabled people, youths and demobilized soldiers (Afghanistan Government, 2006, 2005b). While these groups do require employment policies specific to their needs and interests, employment is also an economic policy issue that needs discussion within both macro- and microeconomic policy debates. Employment problems do not only affect the vulnerable; employment generation and the quality of the opportunities created must form a core part of the strategy supporting Afghanistan's growth and development if the benefits of growth are to be more equitably shared. This implies a need to balance macroeconomic policy attention between inflation control, which is important and benefits the poor, and fiscal and monetary policies, which enable employment growth through fostering increased demand (Heinz and Pollin, 2003). In the end, what is needed is an approach to macroeconomic policy development in Afghanistan that does not completely abstract from the people it will affect; policies must be assessed against how they will affect workers economically and socially to bring social concerns into the IMF SMP process. This reflects the understanding developed in the 1990s that SAPs can have detrimental effects due to their lack of attention to social development implications (Rogers, 2001; UNDP, 2004c; Jolly *et al.*, 1987).

Labour productivity growth and decent employment

The World Bank's report on the investment climate in Afghanistan (2005b) provides data on labour productivity in the country. At a median output per worker of US$3,333, Afghanistan has similar labour productivity to that in other Central Asian countries, but falls far short of the levels found in India (US$9,146) and Pakistan (US$10,043). The World Bank explains this difference through variations in the capital intensity of industry (World Bank, 2005b). In terms of employment generation aims, Afghanistan's lower capital intensity can be a good thing since, as Osmani's elasticity factor would support, Afghanistan and other nations aiming to strengthen the employment potential of growth must seek employment-intensive sectors to drive that growth. The key challenge for Afghanistan will be increasing labour productivity without replacing labour with capital or in other ways causing downward pressure on overall employment levels or the quality of that employment.

The trade-off between productivity improvements and decreases in employment levels or quality is a real threat. The non-binding nature of the statement related to employing Afghans in the investment law is one indication of possible problems (MoCI, 2006b). The only mention of employment within the law is in relation to hiring Afghans when possible, with no reference to limits on capital to labour ratios; such limits could aid in ensuring the employment generation effects of investment, at least for the short to medium term. Such limits are likely not considered sufficiently pro-business, though they would be pro-development. Thus, although capital-intensive new investment could create highly productive employment, it would actually produce very little new employment. This again highlights the relevance of Osmani's elasticity factor in decisions about prioritizing investments.

Another possible threat is evidenced in the view that high levels of market competition are important to increasing labour productivity (World Bank, 2005f). Such competition forces out unproductive firms (potentially increasing unemployment) and pushes any remaining firms to increase performance. The question that is not asked is: at whose expense does this come? Often it is at the expense of the workers, who may be pushed to work longer hours, with less leave and at a higher pace. Hence, decency of work may decline. If productivity or pace of work was quite low, some added pressure to improve performance may not be a bad thing, but this can be taken too far in the global competition for FDI. This is what must be guarded against in the

Afghan context: Afghanistan must not take the low road of cutting costs and working conditions to increase productivity and profit, which then creates only poor-quality, low-paying jobs for its citizens (Holmström, 1999). There is another way to proceed, which addresses another widely acknowledged deterrent to growth and labour productivity in Afghanistan, and that is through building the skills of workers (World Bank, 2005f; ADB, 2005, 2006; Afghanistan Government, 2005b, 2006). This is a more positive strategy and may increase productivity and decency of work, albeit in the medium to long term.

This strategy views labour as a resource to be invested in and not a cost to be cut (Holmström, 1999). Investing in the capacities of Afghan workers will pay dividends in the future and seems to be a far more plausible strategy for sustained pro-poor growth than relying so fully on the market and competition to drive the economy and its outcomes. It probably does mean a more active role for the state than envisaged currently, which has implications for institutional capacities for implementation, but the benefits are worth the effort required to move Afghanistan in this direction. This approach takes on board Osmani's third factor, integrability. It emphasizes the need to bring together sectors of growth and investment, understandings of their related skills requirements, and skills development curricula to form a holistic employment strategy that will benefit both the poor and non-poor. Ideally, the effort to draft a national employment policy will have the political will and capacity to integrate all of these issues.

Skills development is a priority of the Afghan Government, as evidenced by its place as one of the Afghanistan Compact's high-level benchmarks under education, and one that has been fast-tracked for early achievement. The benchmark is composed of two primary outcomes: the completion of a human resource study by mid 2007[15] and that 150,000 men and women will be trained in marketable skills by end of 2010. Both are important objectives, with the first enabling monitoring of the second if the study becomes institutionalized and is repeated. The second objective fits well with what is called for here, but it may be too output focused (rather than outcome focused) in its current structure, and the

15. Initially to be completed by 2006, but this deadline was postponed to mid 2007 and amended to require only a review of secondary data on the labour market. The first labour market survey, collecting primary data, has yet to be done as of early 2008.

target set is beyond what the current capacities can attain, even by the end 2010. Those involved in the skills development technical working group as part of the ANDS process recognize the output focus of the benchmark and are monitoring the number of trainees in employment, instead of only numbers trained, as the final outcome of interest (SDWG, 2006). Still more can be done in relation to both aims to ensure decency of work is also tracked—on the one hand, in the labour market study by incorporating measures of work quality, and on the other for trainees to ensure that not only their access to employment after training is monitored, but also the quality of employment found.

The NSDP is currently being implemented through both state- and NGO-run vocational training programmes. The 1384 (March 2005 to March 2006) training programme had a target of training 1,935 people, of which 774 were to be women; the programme exceeded this target, training 2,170 people, of whom 910 were women (SDWG, 2006). The lack of labour market information is a hindrance to scaling up these training programmes, as there is little knowledge of what skills workers have and what skills employers desire. Funded agencies within the NSDP are required to collect local-level information about employment opportunities to feed into their training, but the effectiveness of such data collection and its use in designing training is as yet unknown. Thus, for women particularly, there is concern that training is in the usual activities acceptable for females (e.g. embroidery, carpet weaving and tailoring), which may not offer sufficient opportunities for decent incomes in many cases. Many income-generation and micro-enterprise development programmes for women also reflect this narrow focus on usual activities; this narrowness must be challenged and skills built among NGO staff in how to assess markets and evaluate potential opportunities for women, which must be in keeping with the cultural norms affecting women's mobility but also challenge them over time.

Another means to increase provision of skills training, and to ensure it fits demand for labour among firms, is to develop incentives for firms investing in Afghanistan to provide skills training to Afghan workers. Such incentives can be worth the cost (to the Government and/or the donors who fund them) relative to other types of incentives offered to foreign firms (tax holidays in particular) in that they foster investment in "Afghan assets".

The broad recognition of the need for investment in human capital in Afghanistan is extremely positive. However, one can also see a risk attached to the chance that discussions around these investments will remain within the social sectors and not be substantively debated within mainstream economic discourse. This can marginalize skills development and similar activities due to the priority generally given to the economic and political over the social in Afghanistan's reconstruction to date. Efforts to make economic policy debates more integrative of social issues would probably improve the relevance and developmental and pro-poor impacts of the outcomes of such discussions.

8.5 Aid community role in promoting growth, investment and decent work

Within Afghanistan there is considerable support for growth and investment objectives from many multilateral development agencies, but without concurrent attention to employment potential or particularly employment quality. What has been lacking are more efforts by national and international agencies less fully supportive of the current pro-market orientation of economic policy to enter into the debate and make achieving pro-poor growth, and with that decent work, more integral to the growth and investment strategies pursued. There are various ways that agencies have pursued and can pursue such a strategy.[16]

One way put forward by Heinz and Pollin (2003) in their paper on labour standards and informalization is by working with the Government to build interest and a better understanding of and ability to implement a regulatory environment that balances business and worker interests. This would be a counterpoint to current understanding of the state as enabler only and the existing pro-business stance, providing alternatives and assisting in weighing the pros and cons of different approaches. Supporting nascent efforts at establishing a tripartite structure led by the MoLSAMD can contribute to this.

16. Some agencies that have been active include ACBAR (Agency Coordinating Body for Afghan Relief) and its economic governance group and within this, as well as independently, Christian Aid and Oxfam.

One current example of this type of approach is the drafting of the revised labour code, which was approved by Presidential decree in February 2007. The code was drafted through a joint effort between the Government (led by the MOLSAMD), employers and workers, and is a document with a relatively pro-labour stance, in terms of rights to severance pay, holidays, paid maternity leave and a termination notice period of one month. Many challenges still exist, particularly in terms of enforcing it, since many of the articles require considerable capacity and personnel for enforcement (e.g. ensuring benefits guaranteed are actually provided, such as paid maternity leave, payments to staff in case of unexpected work stoppage and pensions). Another weakness is its lack of recognition of the informal economy and the challenges of implementing a labour law among informal enterprises and workers. The law will therefore, only apply to a narrow group of formal workers. However, it is a base from which to start to advocate for decent work for a broader group of workers, and a test for the emerging tripartite structure.

This raises another role for the aid community—as advocate for employment-related issues. Currently, most economic policy documents do not provide any in-depth discussion of employment generation in relation to growth and investment. There is a need to educate those involved in economic policy formulation as to why employment creation and decent work should be mainstreamed. This involves continued participation in the ANDS process by those agencies representing divergent views on the current economic approach of the state and its partners, so that different views are expressed and new approaches can be considered. Capacities can be a constraint, with advocacy experience weak among some national NGOs and knowledge of or comfort with economic issues often weak across both national and international agencies.

One gap in terms of advocacy on issues such as decent work is the lack of integration of economic rights within the agendas of rights-based organizations working in Afghanistan, such as the Afghanistan Independent Human Rights Commission and Global Rights. Expanding their work into this arena could greatly assist in bringing more attention to the Decent Work Agenda.

Finally, as noted in the NHDR (UNDP, 2004c), there is a need to focus less on sectoral approaches and to increase coordination in order to develop more integrated approaches to development problems, including employment promotion. The current structure of the ANDS tends to support sectoral perspectives, so there is scope for the various oversight groups (i.e., the donor External Advisory Group and the members of the Joint Coordination Monitoring Board) and independent agencies (i.e., AREU and ACBAR) to bring a more integrated view to the process.

8.6 Conclusions and recommendations

This review of the existing nexus between growth, investment and decent work in the Afghan context must conclude that the nexus does not yet exist, particularly not in a sustainable manner. In most mainstream documents laying out national policy positions or documents influencing economic policy, there is little to no substantive engagement with the employment challenge that Afghanistan faces, either in terms of numbers or quality of jobs. This may reflect both the influence of economic development models that emphasize the roles of the private sector and the market in growth, as well as the tendency in the past to give more attention to political processes over economic growth (World Bank, 2005f). The latter is now changing, so the challenge lies in bringing the rhetoric on pro-poor growth into reality through a movement away from a largely market-oriented approach toward one which integrates human development aims, including employment promotion and decent work.

Various elements are required to make this happen. First, there is a need for a realistic assessment of the drivers of war and conflict, and thus, of the required reforms and transformations to economic institutions that are needed to create sustained structural change providing a context for poverty reducing growth. Elements of the assessment exist and can be added to (Lister and Pain, 2004; Goodhand, 2004; Bhatia *et al.*, 2003; UNDP, 2004c), but fostering institutional change will be a medium to long term aim.

Second, one interest of this chapter was to determine whether it is policy mix or sequencing which plays the larger role in improving the nexus between growth and decent work. While both are relevant, for the

Afghan case, due to the tendency for employment to disappear from the economic policy agenda, policy integration is seemingly more important initially. It is needed to ensure that employment policy finds a place in mainstream economic discourse in the country. This should involve a discussion of the criteria by which to prioritize growth sectors and investment opportunities, which includes reference to employment generation and the beneficiaries of this employment. Osmani's work can contribute to ensure a pro-poor orientation to the integration of employment generation and decent work into economic growth debates.

While employment is clearly a concern of the Ministry of Labour, Social Affairs, Martyrs and Disabled, a range of other ministries also lay claim to employment-related aims for their target groups, or should be interested in employment due to their focus on the economy.[17] The range of ministries considering employment-related programmes is evident in the Afghanistan Compact benchmarks under social protection, where employment-related objectives are listed for demobilized soldiers, vulnerable women and youths, and are indirectly referred to in relation to returnees.[18] Therefore, there is a challenge to coordinate potentially divergent employment-related programmes and to develop a unified voice across ministries with which to advocate for employment promotion and decent work within the state apparatus. The ANDS process provides a possible way forward. While it is not necessarily positive that employment is segregated under social protection in the ANDS, the sector strategy for social protection provides an opportunity for these divergent ministries to come together to develop a coherent approach for promoting employment across their target groups, one not based only on the status quo in terms of market relations and power structures but

17. Those claiming interest for target groups include the Ministry of Women's Affairs, the Ministry of Culture and Youth and the Ministry of Refugees and Repatriation. The Ministry of Foreign Affairs shares an interest in overseas worker programmes with MoLSAMD, while the Ministry of Commerce and Industry and Ministry of Economy should integrate a greater focus on employment within their work.

18. Some programmes related to these objectives are in process. For example, employment service centres exist which cater in part to the needs of demobilized soldiers, youths and returnees, and women's income generation programmes exist (some with the limitations previously discussed). Some of these subgroups are also target beneficiaries of the NSDP.

one that aims at increasing equity in the distribution of resources. A strong leader is required from within the government or international community to drive this sector strategy development process.

If Afghanistan is to achieve its aims of increasing security and rule of law, and if it is to consider some movement away from its implementation of a primarily market-driven economic development strategy, building state institutions and their capacity is vital. It is vital to creating a state that is able to take on a wider role in economic and social development; one which protects the interests of the poor and vulnerable and takes action to develop and implement pro-poor oriented policy. Building state capacity, as well as improving public sector incentive structures, is also central to dismantling the informal security regime currently operating in the country, which serves as a barrier to having public and pro-poor interests win out over personal interests. Finally, improved state capacity is also important to ensuring that an institutional environment can be created that provides a supportive context for broad-based growth driven by employment-intensive development which creates secure livelihoods for both the poor and non-poor.

9 Iran: Decent work challenges

Hassan Taee

9.1 Introduction

Human labour and employment have been investigated for a long time. The various aspects of employment have been studied by economists and social scientists from their own perspectives. To quote Amartya K. Sen:

> At the risk of oversimplification we can distinguish between three different aspects of employment:
>
> (i) The income aspect: employment gives an income to the employed.
>
> (ii) The production aspect: employment yields an output.
>
> (iii) The recognition aspect: employment gives a person the recognition of being engaged in something worth while.
>
> (Sen, 1996: 445)

So, whether we look at employment from an individual or a societal point of view, we will find it to be particularly complex and important.

If we change our point of view and analyse employment and the labour market merely from an economic point of view, we could say that employment has been derived from production (labour demand is a derived function) and that the labour market has a subtle relationship with economic markets, such as goods and services, money and capital. These markets interact to form the economic cycle. Thus, employment has to be analysed within the framework of the market and enterprises (Borjas, 2005).

To improve the analysis of human labour and employment, especially the decent work aspect, we need to consider not only the economic cycle, but also the business environment and investment climate.

The expression "employment opportunity" can be interpreted differently from different points of view. Given human beings' capabilities over a lifetime, and the value added they can have for an enterprise, we can conclude that an employment opportunity is 30 person-years of work, which is created by the interactions of the economic life cycle within the labour market. It is from this point of view that we can say that labour demand is derived from production; in other words, interactions between the economic agent (e.g. household, enterprises, government and the foreign/external sector) within the common economic markets creates the supply and demand for labour.

It is important to note that all the interactions and economic transactions that occur in this process take place within an environment called "bio-space" (or "bio-sphere"), which in turn (though in a completely abstract way) consists of a series of subsets: knowledge space, political space, legal space and economic space. Each space, in turn, is composed of several components.

The knowledge space can be seen as comprising public literacy and/or skills levels, the level of information, knowledge, communications, experiences and values. It includes how society benefits from this knowledge, the educational institutes and processes, and also the position of knowledge in solving the problems that arise during transition to higher stages of development. The components of this space define the society's scientific capability and intelligence.

The political space of a society can be measured by the level of cooperation between the various elements within society, ranging from family units to private and public firms, and its interaction with the outside world. Moreover, it can be seen in the ability of the different branches of government, the executive, legislative and judicial, to work together. Understanding these different factors and the way they interplay allows one to know about the level of hope the society has for the future and gives economists the ability to correctly assess future policies.

The legal space of a society can be defined as the whole set of existing rules and regulations and how dynamic and stable they are. It includes the role of the people to monitor both institutions and the government on the implementation of the rules, and on how committed they are to the rules and regulations. This space defines and establishes the rights and the security of the economic agents. More importantly, when a transaction takes place in the market, even though it might be considered an economic event it also involves the transfer of a package of legal ownership-related rights from one person or entity to another.

The economic space of a society consists of the stock of financial, human, natural and physical resources available. It also includes the levels of technology and the methods of using the production factors, the degree of development of economic entities and the market, competitiveness, and the existence of a culture of work and risk-taking among the economic agents. Additionally, the existence of entrepreneurs, managers, consultants, innovators and theoreticians define the level of economic-cycle activities within this space.

The objective here is to show that many factors are needed for an enterprise to create jobs and that when these factors change, they affect supply and demand in the labour market. Thus, from a diagnostic point of view, achieving decent work is far more difficult than simply creating job opportunities. It is a multidimensional phenomenon which interacts with many factors affecting the level of production and the society's bio-space.

9.2 The trend of economic growth and formation of gross fixed capital

Iran ended an eight-year war with Iraq in 1989. Immediately after that, the planning and academic sectors[1] focused on the generation of stable economic growth, with regard to the changes in population and their effect on the labour market. Stable economic growth is one of the principal objectives of any economic system. Achieving this goal is dependent on the development of the foundations for growth, via mechanisms such as capital accumulation, human capital development and increase in the productivity of factors of production.

Since 1989, Iran has implemented three development plans, and is currently enacting the Fourth Plan. During the period 1989–2005, the role of the Government (via monetary and fiscal policies) and the currency income from oil exports have been the two most important factors affecting economic growth. Of course, in a country with one of the youngest

1. Planning academic sector means universities and research centres.

populations in the world, the Government had to have a significant role in this process (Central Bank of Islamic Republic of Iran, various years).

During the First Development Plan (1989–1993), the country witnessed the reconstruction of the economy and the end of the depression caused by the war. In this period, investment started to improve, and the use of spare production capacity along with the economic adjustment policy caused the current account balance to become positive and oil revenue to increase; the economy therefore, underwent favourable growth. The average rate of growth of output and investment increased to 7.4 and 9.2 per cent respectively, which in comparison with the negative rates of the wartime period shows the improvements in the economy. This also helped to reduce the unemployment rates.

Table 9.1

Population, active population and participation rate, 1989–2004

Year	*Total population (thousands)*	*Active population (thousands)*			*Participation rate (%)*		
		Total	*Male*	*Female*	*Total*	*Male*	*Female*
1989	53 187	13 942	12 450	1492	38.5	66.7	8.5
1990	54 496	14 330	12 772	1559	38.3	66.1	8.6
1991	55 837	14 737	13 107	1630	38.1	65.5	8.7
1992	56 656	15 035	13 279	1756	38.9	64.6	9.1
1993	57 488	15 345	13 453	1892	38.4	63.6	9.4
1994	58 331	15 668	13 630	2038	38.0	62.6	9.8
1995	59 187	16 005	13 809	2196	38.6	61.7	10.2
1996	60 055	16 365	13 990	2366	36.0	60.8	10.6
1997	60 936	17 040	14 540	2500	36.4	61.2	10.8
1998	61 830	17 732	15 094	2638	36.7	61.7	11.1
1999	62 736	18 428	15 650	2779	37.0	62.1	11.3
2000	63 664	19 118	16 197	2921	37.4	62.6	11.6
2001	64 528	19 804	16 725	3078	37.8	63.0	11.9
2002	65 540	20 419	17 188	3231	38.2	63.5	12.2
2003	66 700	21 006	17 624	3383	38.6	64.0	12.6
2004	67 700	21 568	18 034	3535	39.0	64.5	12.9

Source: Amini, 2006; Statistical Center of Iran, 1976, 1986, 1996.

After 1994, and the start of the Second Development Plan (1995–1999), severe inflation led the Government to implement economic

Figure 9.1

Gross national product (GNP), investment (INV) and savings (SAV), 1989–2003

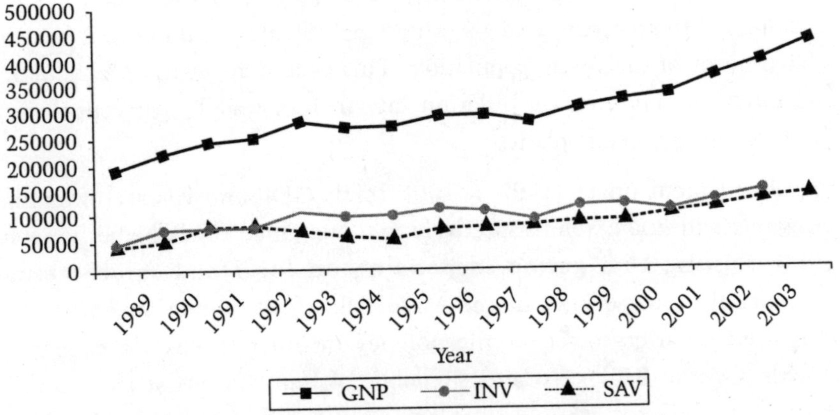

Note: Values in the vertical axis is in billion Rials (at 1977 prices).

stabilization (expenditure control) policies. During these years, OPEC increased oil production, which caused oil prices to decrease; thus, Iran's oil revenue was reduced and consequently both rates of growth of output and investment decreased, to 8 and 3.2 per cent respectively. This, of course, had adverse effects on the labour market.

The Third Development Plan, which was implemented during 2000–2004, was generally an attempt to reform the national economic structure. In this period, because of the existence of policies such as commercial decentralization, unification of the exchange rate, elimination of unnecessary regulations, development of infrastructure and increase in the oil revenue, the rate of investment growth was 11 per cent and the GDP growth rate was more than 5 per cent. Generally, in the post-war period the trends in growth rates in GDP and investment improved and led to stabilization in the country's economic conditions (Management and Planning Organization, 2000).

Over the course of the past three development plans, Iran's economy followed a policy of gradual deregulation in trade policy and efforts were made to improve the trade performance. Internally, many of government's non-governing responsibilities (such as managing big companies) were transferred to the private sector.

During the past three plans, expansionary monetary and especially fiscal policies were implemented in most of the years. This might have helped Iran in meeting the resource requirements during the post-war economic reconstruction, including development of the much needed economic infrastructure and meeting the cultural, training and health-related needs of the young population. This caused an increase in liquidity and inflation. The average inflation rate in Iran was 15 per cent during the three development plans.

At constant prices (1997 = 100), Iran's GDP and volume of annual investment in 2004 were respectively two and three times higher than in 1989. During this period, depending on local and international circumstances (especially in the Middle East), economic authorities in Iran used a variety of economic policies in order to sustain economic growth (Central Bank of Islamic Republic of Iran, various years).

The ratio of investment to gross domestic production is high in Iran. One reason for this high ratio is the high level of investment that takes place within the construction sector. Construction is divided into two categories: residential and non-residential. Investing in the residential sector is driven by the young nature of the population (married couples need independent homes or apartments), while investment in the non-residential sector reflects infrastructural development taking place within the economy.

Figure 9.2

Saving and investment ratio, 1989–2004

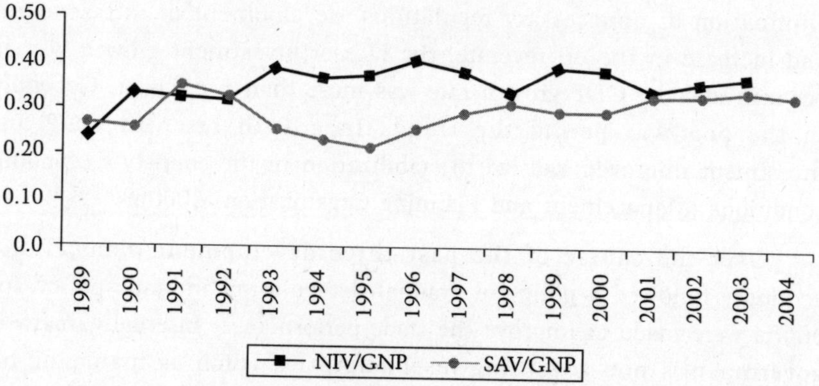

The rate of saving is outpacing the rate of investment; this is due to a number of significant reasons. A portion of the savings are used for making up the budget deficit and for covering the governmental costs that the Iranian economy usually encounters. A smaller portion of the savings are transferred outside the country.

9.3 Population and the labour market

According to 1996 data and information, the population of Iran was 60 million people. The recent demographic trend is characterized by a decrease in the percentage of the 0–14 year olds in the total population and an increase in the proportion of 15–64 year olds, and especially 15–24 year olds. The size of this latter group in 1986, 1996 and 2004 was 9.4, 12.4 and 17.4 million people respectively. The rapid increase in the population of this young group has put the labour market and the authorities under pressure to meet their social and economic demands (Statistical Center of Iran, 1976, 1986, 1996; Taee, 2002).

The HRDP project

In order to examine the future education and employment needs of Iranian youth, the Iranian Management and Planning Organization (MPO) in collaboration with the Institute for Research and Planning in Higher Education (IRPHE), within the framework of the Third and Fourth Socio-economic and Cultural Development Plans (2000–2004 and 2005–2009), has undertaken a comprehensive research project on Human Resource Development Planning and Policy Making (HRDP). The aim of the project was to assess the current status of the country's human resources and to study the possibilities for enhancing the existing capabilities, given the real needs of the society and especially, of the labour market.

As a precursor, a scientific committee was formed at IRPHE in 1998–1999. The committee included government officials and senior experts from universities, the MPO and the IRPHE. At the outset, the HRDP scientific committee specified the comprehensive model of this study and suggested the research areas of the knowledge-based economy and improving labour markets. The committee was of the opinion that the preparation and expansion of human capital can be regarded as a sound basis for establishing a learning society and the key to its achievement. It was also believed that gaining high-quality human capital should be considered as the main prerequisite for achieving human development (Taee, 2002).

Findings of the HRDP project

Youth employment: The existing situation

With an average annual population growth rate of 2.8 per cent, the total population of Iran increased form 25.8 million in 1966 to 60 million in 1996. Given the forecasted rate of 1.46 per cent, the population size was expected to increase to 70 million in 2006. One of the main issues affecting Iran's labour market is employment opportunities for young people and people who are entering the labour force for the first time. Iran has 36 million people under the age of 25, and if the fertility rate does not change much, this population will dominate all areas of the economy, society and politics over the next 20 years. Increased production and investment along with other economic policies have allowed the Iranian economy to produce new jobs in response to the employment demands of a growing young population.

Figure 9.3

Active population, 1989–2004 (thousand persons)

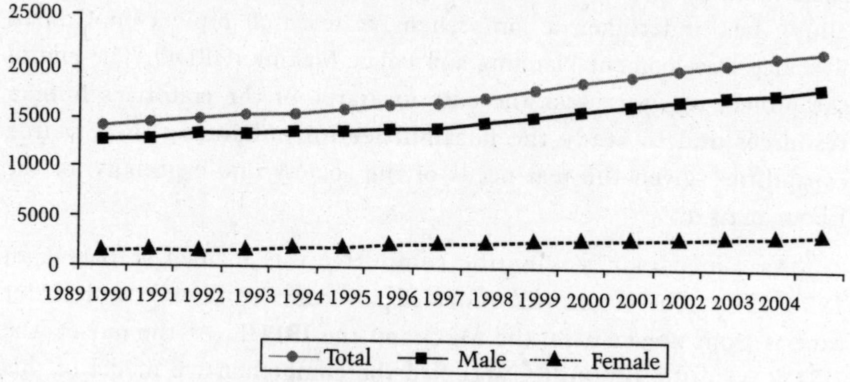

The evolving nature of demand

The demand for third level[2] educated labour increased from around 497,000 in 1986 to 1.4 million in 1996. The ratio of third-level educated labour employed to total employment increased from 4.5 per cent in 1986 to 9.6 per cent in 1996. The forecast for 2006 was 14 per cent.

Population transformation: Threats and opportunities

Iranian society is experiencing a demographic structural change that will affect the economy, society, culture and politics of Iran:

- Opportunities: Provision of high-quality education for youths and those less than 25 years of age could ensure the supply of human capital required for sustainable development.
- Threats: A recession in the labour market would endanger the educational investment in the population born in the past two decades, manifesting itself in economic and social backwardness (Taee, 2001).

Strategies for job creation

The recommendation of the scientific committee of the HRDP was to establish the High Council for Employment, the function of which would be to:

- coordinate the different ministries responsible for job creation;
- support entrepreneurs and investors;
- monitor the performance of the employment-related ministries;
- design the employment strategies;
- arrange policies for labour market regulation;
- design policies considering the funds allotment to sectors and regions in annual budgets;
- analyse the national labour market to design proper policies and to introduce relevant procedures.

2. The term "third level" refers to the segment of human resources that has successfully completed at least two years of higher education.

Policies for job creation

A number of policies were recommended by the scientific committee of the HRDP:

- Replace elderly employed labour with new jobseekers:
  - prohibit retired labour re-employment;
  - reduce the age of retirement;
  - encourage voluntary retirement;
  - enhance the welfare of the retired.
- New job creation:
  - encourage new labour employment instead of increasing working hours;
  - create new regional, national and international markets for firms;
  - control the smuggling of imported goods;
  - support investment scheme funds in different sectors;
  - support unemployed youths to use job-creating facilities;
  - improve vocational training for youth and women.
- Protect job creation:
  - provide self-employment assistance—education and financial and marketing facilities;
  - encourage employers to create new jobs;
  - decrease production costs through restricting transaction costs.
- Job creation credits and facilities:
  - direct financial credits to non-governmental agricultural, construction, manufacturing and mining activities;
  - financial aid to rural and deprived regions;
  - interest-free loans to rural youths and to women who head families to acquire tools and equipment;

- financial credit to private cooperative and self-employment projects;
- technical assistance to private, cooperative and self-employment;
- earmarked employment credits to regions;
- employment credit to charities and social protection organizations;
- development credit to underdeveloped regions;
- financial aid for debt-servicing to infrastructure projects;
- financial aid to state-owned enterprises;
- allot foreign exchange to ongoing projects;
- sponsor training courses for unemployed educated youths;
- financial and non-financial facilities to high-technology industries.

Suggestions

A range of other actions has also been suggested by the scientific committee of the HRDP:

- Improve the intake rate of various educational levels.
- Expand vocational education aiming at youth skills improvement.
- Expand higher education aiming at youth knowledge improvement.
- Establish governmental and non-government employment service centres.
- Prepare policies for enhancing labour market flexibility.
- Pay attention to modern industries as a basis for generating small firms.
- Encourage R&D and establish knowledge firms and knowledge-based firms.

- Encourage competitive markets and restrict monopolistic activities.
- Revise administrative, employment and tax laws and regulations affecting the labour market.
- Expand the tertiary sector and encourage social work.
- Expand the stock of social capital in parallel with physical, financial and human capital.
- Institutionalize "permanent learning" and moving toward a knowledge-based economy.
- Enhance youths' core competencies: self-autonomy, self-cognition, learning to learn and skills development.

Many of those policies, strategies and suggestions listed above were used in designing the Third and Fourth Socio-economic and Cultural Development Plans (2000–2004 and 2005–2009). After the end of the Third Plan, it can now be concluded that the country's most important achievement in regard to the labour market is that despite the growth of the active population, the unemployment rate has decreased and the general situation for employees has improved.

Some of the data and information mentioned earlier in this chapter were related to the findings of the MPO and IRPHE studies carried out before the Third and Fourth Development Plans, and other information was from the results of forecast studies on the labour market. What happened in reality is demonstrated in Tables 9.1, 9.2 and 9.3 and Figures 9.3, 9.4 and 9.5.

For example, the active population or the labour supply grew from 13.9 million people in 1989 to 21.6 million people in 2004. The total participation rate and participation of men and women changed from 38.5, 66.7 and 8.5 per cent to 39.0, 64.5 and 12.9 per cent respectively. As is clear in Table 9.1 and Figure 9.3, the number of women in the labour force has grown more than 100 per cent during this period (Taee, 2001, 2002).

Table 9.2

Employment by gender, 1989–2004

(thousand persons)

Year	Employment				
	Total	Male	Ratio(%)	Female	Ratio (%)
1989	11 972	10 875	90.8	1098	9.2
1990	12 494	11 334	90.7	1160	9.3
1991	13 097	11 865	90.6	1231	9.4
1992	13 311	11 955	89.8	1356	10.2
1993	13 560	12 063	89.0	1497	11.0
1994	13 913	12 249	88.0	1664	12.0
1995	14 354	12 493	87.0	1861	13.0
1996	14 909	12 815	86.0	2094	14.0
1997	15 089	12 944	85.8	2144	14.2
1998	15 486	13 259	85.6	2227	14.4
1999	16 006	13 677	85.5	2328	14.5
2000	16 444	14 024	85.3	2420	14.7
2001	16 884	14 372	85.1	2512	14.9
2002	17 596	14 949	85.0	2647	15.0
2003	18 287	15 506	84.8	2781	15.2
2004	18 906	15 999	84.6	2907	15.4

Source: Same as Table 9.1.

Table 9.3

Employment by activity, 1989–2003

(thousand persons)

Year	Agriculture	Ratio (%)	Industry	Ratio (%)	Services	Ratio (%)
1989	3199	0.27	3155	0.26	5574	0.47
1990	3211	0.26	3404	0.27	5930	0.47
1991	3220	0.25	3630	0.28	6246	0.48
1992	3256	0.24	3783	0.28	6453	0.48
1993	3294	0.24	3952	0.29	6314	0.47
1994	3354	0.24	4147	0.30	6409	0.46
1995	3519	0.25	4292	0.30	6543	0.46
1996	3569	0.24	4599	0.31	6742	0.45
1997	3599	0.24	4727	0.31	6763	0.45
1998	3676	0.24	4721	0.30	7089	0.46
1999	3724	0.23	4844	0.30	7438	0.46
2000	3657	0.22	5080	0.31	7707	0.47
2001	3705	0.22	5109	0.30	8070	0.48
2002	3863	0.22	5417	0.31	8316	0.47
2003	4009	0.22	5616	0.31	8662	0.47

Source: Same as Table 9.1.

Figure 9.4

Labour force participation rate, 1989–2004 (thousand persons)

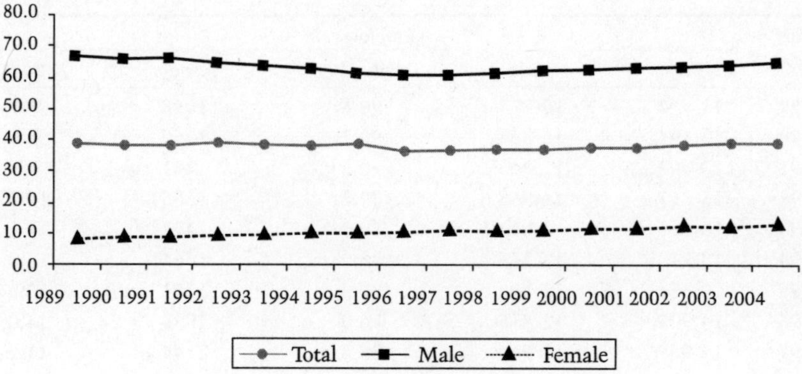

Figure 9.5

Employment, 1989–2004 (thousand persons)

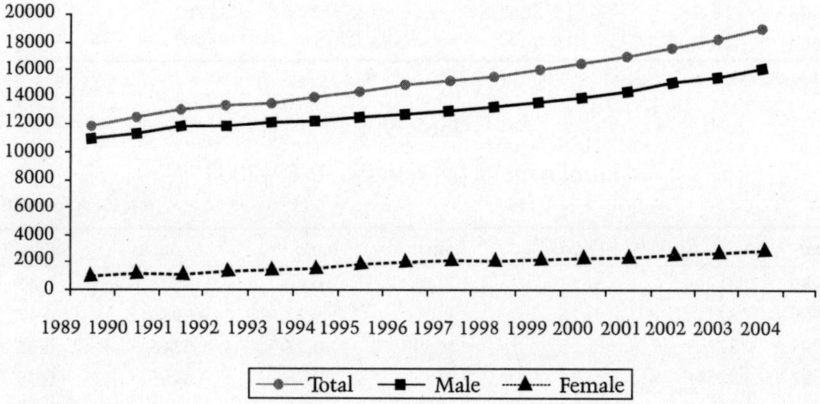

9.4 Labour market and employment policies

The policies, strategies and investments of Iran's three development plans increased the country's total employment from 11.9 million to 18.9 million people (see Table 9.2 and Figure 9.5). Achieving 7 million new jobs during a period of 15 years is a reasonably creditable achievement for Iran's economy. Despite the creation of new jobs, Iran had about 2.7 million unemployed people in 2004 (Table 9.4 and Figure 9.6). The need to create a dynamic labour market to accommodate the supply of the young labour force in the future and generate millions of new jobs are major concerns for policy-makers and analysts of the labour market (Amini, 2006; Statistical Center of Iran, 1976, 1986, 1996).

Table 9.4

Unemployment by gender, 1989–2004

(thousand persons)

	Unemployment					
Year	*Total*	*Rate (%)*	*Male*	*Male*	*Female*	*Rate (%)*
1989	1969	14.1	1576	12.7	394	26.4
1990	1836	12.8	1438	11.3	399	25.6
1991	1640	11.1	1242	9.5	398	24.4
1992	1724	11.5	1324	10.0	400	22.8
1993	1785	11.6	1390	10.3	395	20.9
1994	1755	11.2	1381	10.1	374	18.3
1995	1651	10.3	1316	9.5	335	15.3
1996	1456	8.9	1176	8.4	280	11.8
1997	1951	11.5	1596	11.0	356	14.2
1998	2246	12.7	1835	12.2	411	15.6
1999	2423	13.1	1972	12.6	450	16.2
2000	2673	14.0	2173	13.4	501	17.1
2001	2920	14.7	2353	14.1	566	18.4
2002	2823	13.8	2239	13.0	584	18.1
2003	2719	12.9	2117	12.0	602	17.8
2004	2662	12.3	2034	11.3	628	17.8

Source: Amini, 2006; Statistical Center of Iran, 1976, 1986, 1996; Economic Research Institute, 2005.

Figure 9.6

Unemployment rate, 1989–2004 (percentage)

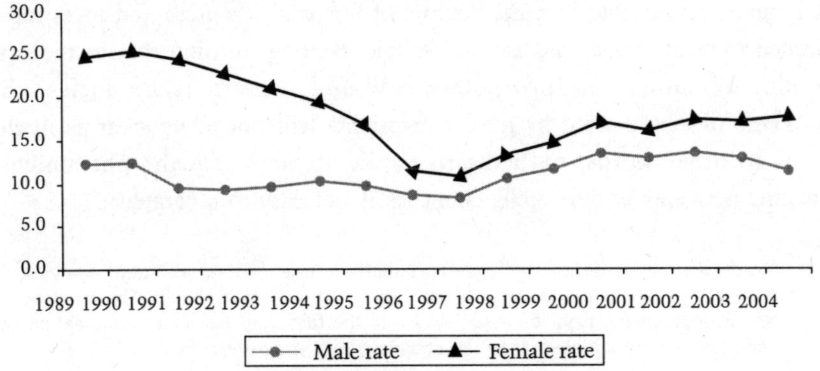

As explained earlier in this chapter, the Iranian economy experienced one of the highest rates of population growth during the 1976–1986 decade. The effects of this population boom were seen in the labour market of the 1990s. Moreover, educational policies following the end of the Iran–Iraq war caused a delay in the entrance of men into the labour market. Later on, this segment of the population also entered the labour force, though with a higher educational background.

Historically, Iranian women have continually been active within society, albeit their activities have usually been in the household sector rather than in the labour market setting. Thus, relative to international standards of employment, the rate of participation of Iranian women in the labour market has been low. The Islamic Revolution brought about a change in outlook regarding the education of girls. Today, women enjoy high levels of education and are actively seeking a greater share within the labour market. Interestingly, the number of females accepted into national universities is nearly equal to that of males. As Table 9.1 shows, women's rate of participation in the labour force increased under the three development plans (1989–2004) from 8.5 to 12.9 per cent.

As can be seen in Table 9.1, the proportion of women in the labour force has undergone a significant growth, and it will continue to grow more and more in the future. These women, who are more educated than before, will change the prospect of Iran's labour market, and if the upcoming new jobs of the future do not match their skills and expectations, there will be a major social challenge for the country.

In order to create more jobs, which is the first step for achieving decent work, Iran needs consistent monetary, financial and commercial policies. But it is necessary to note that the volume of financial resources and investment needed to create these jobs is considerable. Bearing in mind that in the new production processes incorporate new and modern technologies, the numbers of jobs created by new investments will not be as great as in the past. In other words, with regard to the "jobless growth" phenomena, creating new jobs in developing countries is not easy to accomplish.[3]

3. No detailed information on labour productivity is available, although analysts do believe that labour productivity in Iran has not grown as it should. The low level of labour productivity might be associated with the fact that the aim of job creation has been taken more seriously than the economic efficiency principle.

An analysis of the link between increased production and employment opportunities has been carried out by estimating the employment elasticity of growth for the period 1989–2004. This period was then split into two separate sub-periods, 1989–1996 and 1996–2004, and the employment elasticity measured for these two sub-periods separately (Table 9.5).

Table 9.5

Employment elasticity of growth, 1989–2004

Year	*Growth in output (%)*	*Growth in employment (%)*	*Employment elasticity*[1]
1989–1996	6.3	3.2	0.51
1996–2004	5.1	3.0	0.59
1989–2004	5.7	3.1	0.54

Note: [1] Percentage change in employment divided by percentage change in output.
Source: Same as Table 9.4.

It can be seen that the link between production and employment increased in the 1996–2004 sub-period compared with the 1989–1996 sub-period. In other words, a 1 per cent increase in production created more employment opportunities in the second sub-period than in the first. The reason behind a rise in the unemployment rate during 1996–2004 was that the rate of increase of labour supply outpaced that of labour demand. The rate of increase in labour supply was 50 per cent higher in the second sub-period than in the first.

The presence of an unofficial labour market is another feature of Iran's labour market. According to studies undertaken by the analysts, employment in the unofficial sector[4] was nearly 30 per cent of the total in 1996. Yet, with the creation of modern firms from the late 1990s onwards, it is likely that the size of the workforce active in the unofficial labour market has declined, or at the very least, has not increased. Moreover, during the Third Plan (2000–2004), active labour market policies were strongly implemented. Therefore, private sector firms that wished to enjoy the benefits of these policies had to move from being unofficial.

An important question is what the impact of globalization will be on employment. It is clear that globalization greatly impacts on

4. Unofficial sector means informal sector.

domestic labour markets, and as economies converge, countries are forced to take into account global economic activities when assessing their own policies and behaviours. However, since Iran's economy is not highly integrated into the global economy, it can be argued that the Iranian labour market is more affected by domestic policies than by global developments.

An important consideration is the role of the private sector in creating employment. As it can be seen from Table 9.6 and Figure 9.7, the private sector created about 5.8 million jobs during 1989–2003. The contributions of the public and private sectors to job creation in 1989 were 33 and 67 per cent respectively, which had changed to 24 and 76 per cent in 2003. Iran's labour market analysts forecast that the public sector's share in creating new jobs in the future cannot be more than its current share.

Table 9.6

Employment in the public and private sectors, 1989–2003

(thousands persons)

	Employment			
Year	*Public*	*Share (Per cent)*	*Private*	*Share (Per cent)*
1989	3872	0.32	8056	0.67
1990	4118	0.33	8430	0.67
1991	4346	0.33	8751	0.67
1992	4286	0.32	9025	0.68
1993	4237	0.31	9323	0.69
1994	4219	0.30	9694	0.70
1995	4224	0.29	10 129	0.71
1996	4258	0.29	10 651	0.71
1997	4222	0.28	10 866	0.72
1998	4246	0.27	11 240	0.73
1999	4300	0.27	11 706	0.73
2000	4329	0.26	12 116	0.74
2001	4348	0.26	12 536	0.74
2002	4417	0.25	13 180	0.75
2003	4474	0.24	13 813	0.76

Source: Same as Table 9.1.

Figure 9.7

Employment in the public and private sectors, 1989–2003 (thousand persons)

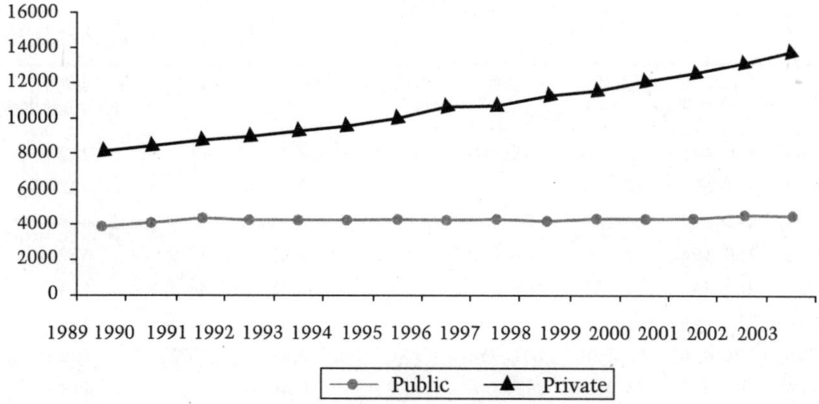

Another issue that is important here is the quality of the employment opportunities created. Since most of the jobs created were in the private sector of the official labour market, one can be assured of the relative usefulness of the jobs created. This is due to the fact that private sector firms will only employ an additional person if their value of marginal product is more than their wage. Naturally, as an employee's talents and skills improve, there will be a higher desire on the part of an employer to hire him or her.

Thus, as a matter of policy, there is much greater reliance on the private sector to be the engine of growth of future employment. The private sector has to grow to absorb millions of young educated people, through new enterprises and direct and indirect employment. Development of the private sector through allocation of financial resources in foreign and domestic currencies has been one of the major policies and goals of both the Third and Fourth Plans. To match the growing needs of job creation, the economy needs to increase saving and investment rates at a much higher level.

One of the employment creation oriented activities of the Third Plan was the granting of loans from the Foreign Exchange Currency Fund to private sector projects, both nationwide and state-wide. According to the Ministry of Economic Affairs, this policy will continue in the future.

Table 9.7

Gross national product (GNP), gross fixed capital formation (INV), gross national saving (SAV), consumer price index (CPI) and income per capita (INCP), 1989–2004

(billion Rials, 1977 = 100)

Year	*GNP*	*INV*	*SAV*	*INV/GNP*	*SAV/GNP*	*CPI*	*INCP (thousand Rials)*
1989	190 441	50 418	45 549	0.26	0.24	17.1	2728
1990	221 632	57 401	73 543	0.26	0.33	18.6	3223
1991	242 613	84 016	77 402	0.35	0.32	22.4	3483
1992	250 193	81 090	79 139	0.32	0.32	27.9	3526
1993	282 540	72 729	108 507	0.26	0.38	34.3	4148
1994	271 648	62 390	99 837	0.23	0.37	46.3	3922
1995	274 696	59 560	101 853	0.22	0.37	69.2	3922
1996	292 307	74 465	118 346	0.25	0.40	85.2	4111
1997	292 187	83 765	110 407	0.29	0.38	100	4018
1998	282 066	86 485	94 217	0.31	0.33	118.1	3790
1999	308 760	91 505	120 469	0.30	0.39	141.8	4132
2000	323 093	95 267	124 330	0.29	0.38	159.7	4269
2001	336 070	108 762	113 877	0.32	0.34	177.9	4375
2002	370 041	121 826	132 220	0.33	0.36	206	4819
2003	399 703	134 971	148 468	0.34	0.37	238.2	5115
2004	436 223	144 259	n.a.	0.33	n.a.	274.5	5518

Note: n.a. = data not available.

Source: Central Bank of Islamic Republic of Iran, *Economic Report and Balance Sheet* (various issues). Economic Research Institute, 2005.

The Foreign Exchange Currency Fund was created to protect investment and production from the ups and downs of the oil market and revenues accrued from the sale of oil. In the past years, since the high incomes derived from oil have exceeded governmental needs, the excess foreign currency has been deposited in the Fund. Many large private sector projects and public sector projects have been funded from this source; this has itself created some employment opportunities.

Another important issue for Iran's labour market is the share of agricultural, industrial and service activities in employment creation. Table 9.3 and Figure 9.8 show a decrease in the share of agricultural activities, from 27 per cent in 1989 to 22 per cent in 2003. The share of industrial activities grew, from 26 to 31 per cent, and the share of service activities remained constant during the period. Labour market analysts forecast that the agricultural sector's share of employment cannot increase in the future. Also, the share of industrial activities cannot grow as it did in the past. However, the service activities have to be started in new areas and should grow remarkably.

Figure 9.8

Sectoral shares in total employment, 1989–2003 (thousand persons)

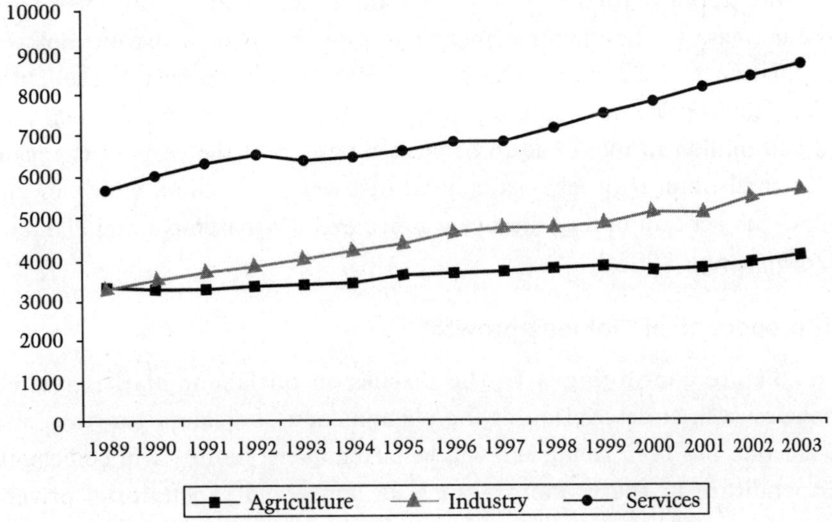

Based on the earliest available statistics on the distribution of job opportunities within the Iranian economy, which date back half a century, one can calculate that more than 50 per cent of employment was in agricultural activities. During the period since then, employment in this sector diminished. Yet, agriculture's contribution to GDP has continued to be significant, and has remained relatively steady in the past two or three decades. Investments and better use of resource allocation have together created a positive food security umbrella for Iran's population.

However, in the field of industry, especially manufacturing industry, Iran does not enjoy a favourable situation, despite nearly 100 years of experience in the field. Iran needs a great number of manufactured goods, and every year manufactured and semi-manufactured goods make up a high proportion of Iran's imports. Therefore, development plans pay a great deal of attention to industrial development and activities.

Many analysts in Iran forecast that industry's share of employment will also remain steady in the years to come, and that new service-oriented sectors will create the necessary new employment opportunities.

According to the Statistical Center of Iran, the unemployment rate varied between 1989 and 2004: it decreased from 14.1 per cent in 1989 to 8.9 per cent in 1996, but it again increased to 12.3 per cent in 2004 (Amini, 2006; Statistical Center of Iran, 1976, 1986, 1996). Even with the decrease in the unemployment rate over this period, the unemployed population was 2.7 million people in 2004. In the prospect of the Third Plan (2000–2004), 499,000, 684,000, 809,000, 872,000 and 962,000 jobs (3.826 million in total) had to be created in each of the years of the plan. The total number of jobs actually created was 2.9 million; which means that 75.8 per cent of the objective was achieved (Management and Planning Organization, 2005a).

The concept of "jobless growth"

Before continuing with the discussion on labour market related policies, a brief description of the phenomenon of "jobless growth"—and what Iran has been facing and will be facing in the future—will be helpful. Expenditure in the economy—such as household expenditure, private sector investment, current and civil expenses of the public sector and export expenses—has effects on the labour market and employment. Some of these resources just maintain the existing employment levels while others create new economic capacities and jobs. So spending in the economy has an effect on employment levels, but different forms of expenditure have different effects.

As can be seen in Appendix A-9.1, when credit resources, regardless of their origin, enter financial markets they can be used in different ways and they can cause an increase or a decrease in direct or indirect employment within an economic activity. Appendix A-9.1 shows the effects on employment creation of allocation of credit resources. As can be perceived, it is not easy to foresee what employment will be created by investment. This gets more complicated when economic growth and progress in technology are taken into consideration. Therefore, a decrease in employment even when investment and production grow in an economy would not be unexpected. This phenomenon is sometimes analysed as "jobless growth" in the framework of an output–employment lag, where employment grows much more slowly than production. Employment may decrease in the wake of modernization in the traditional sectors in developing countries. However, many developed countries are now facing unemployment due to changes in technology, which creates jobless growth.[5]

Jobless growth is another side of technology-induced unemployment. In other words, modernization of production processes can result in technology substituting human labour more than expectation. When this happens, growth will not create new jobs, and the number of existing jobs is also likely to decrease. In the 1970s and the 1980s, it was thought that technology growth would not decrease employment, but what happened in the 1990s and after made the experts and analysts reconsider this view (Rifkin, 1996). In the 1990s, new technology and knowledge-intensive production process greatly decreased employment.

Income policies: Pricing and wage determination

In order to achieve decent work, income policies have been seriously implemented in Iran since the period 2000–2004. These policies are used as tools to overcome the inflation pressure caused by demand increase. Income policy includes every action that a government takes about the pricing of goods and services and the determination of salaries. Such policies were introduced in the Third Plan.

In order to evaluate the major indices related to salaries during the years of the Third Plan, the quantity of "personnel services compensation" is used, consistent with Iran's national accounts. Personnel services compensation means the total cash and non-cash fees that an enterprise pays its employees to compensate for the work done in a certain

5 The issue of jobless growth is something that all countries must deal with during their economic development and is not limited to developing countries. It is not an issue that just one country faces, such as Iran. Rather, the process of innovation and the combination of new methods of production, especially using new technologies, reduce the need for labour.

accounting period. The share of personnel services compensation in gross domestic expenditure was 19.25 per cent at current cost in 2000. Personnel services compensation increased at an average rate of 28.81 per cent in each year of the Third Plan. Over the same period, the average rate of growth of gross domestic expenditure was 23.10 per cent annually (the personnel services compensation has grown 5.7 per cent more than gross domestic expenditure) (Management and Planning Organization, 2000, 2005b).

The labour market in Iran can also be evaluated using the index of construction workers' fees. This index increased from 142.3 in 2000 to 285.8 in 2004 (base year 1997 = 100).

A further index is the minimum wage, which is meant to be a measure of the minimum fees paid for unskilled labour. According to the labour law of Iran, this minimum is defined by the High Council of Labour. The nominal minimum fee in 2000 was 458,010 Rials per month, which increased to 1,066,020 Rials in 2004. The real amount of the minimum wage was 286,794 Rials in 2000, which grew to 388,350 Rials in 2004 (at constant price 1997 = 100). This shows an annual average growth rate of 7.87 per cent.

One of the objectives of these economic policies is to preserve the purchasing power. Given this, the Government has always been trying to increase real wages during the Third Plan.

Social welfare and income distribution

After the Islamic Revolution in 1979, social security has developed greatly in terms of the types of insurances, cash and non-cash aid and extent of population coverage. During the past years, the Government's policies and the financial resources allocated by the Government, entrepreneurs and employees have improved the situation considerably. Despite the improvements in this area, social support has not yet met the people's expectations. These needs are associated with, on the one hand, the decrease in social security's funds and on the other hand, an increase in the number of insured people and the new insurance coverage. In particular, since the beginning of the Third Plan, social security insurance has been implemented for rural areas and for urban households whose heads are self-employed.

Presently, the main problem that threatens the continuity of insurance coverage, both in quantity and quality, is the low level of savings (reserves) per head of the insured population. Thus, one of the major problems Iran is facing, which also is an obstacle to achieving decent work, is insufficient social protection. This issue can only be solved through tripartite cooperation between the Government, employers and employees, and evolution of the related institutions.

The Government and the employers have improved cooperation and the related institutions, but unfortunately the syndicate institutions for employees have not grown sufficiently. Insufficient growth of the worker institutions has been affected by the Iranian society's social and knowledge spaces, and also by the lack of workers' willingness to take part in syndicate associations. The need to develop tripartism to solve worker–employer issues and the importance of social security and social protection through social dialogue, therefore, are underscored.

In recent years, many non-governmental organizations have entered this area and started defending workers' rights. But in order to be able to utilize the tripartite framework to achieve decent work in Iran, we need more serious efforts to establish workers' institutions.

In the period 2000–2004, the index of social welfare increased due to an increase in income per head and relative improvements in income distribution. The Gini coefficients in the years 1999 to 2004 were respectively 0.401, 0.399, 0.399, 0.419, 0.416 and 0.399 (Central Bank of Islamic Republic of Iran, various years). The ratio of income of the higher deciles (the richest) to income of the lower deciles (the poorest) for the whole society decreased from 19.4 in 2000 to 15.8 in 2004, at an average annual rate of 4.9 per cent. This ratio also improved in urban regions, in which the ratio of income of the highest 20 per cent to the lowest 20 per cent of the population decreased from 10.1 in 2000 to 8.43 in 2004. In rural regions, this ratio decreased at an average annual rate of 5.3 per cent during the Third Plan, while the rate for the urban regions was 2.3 per cent (Management and Planning Organization, 2005b).

9.5 Decent work requirements

Amid the rapid changes in the labour market in the era of information and communication technologies, along with the needs for synergic interactions in international relations, flexibility in the labour market and protection of human and national resources against challenges, the threat of unemployment and its unwanted aftermath have become every country's national concern. Also, the retention of human pre-eminence, the establishment of social justice and the creation of harmony between the human and social aspects, in order to achieve a balance between economic and social development and consequently sustainable development, have become priorities in most countries. In this regard and according to the international regulations, the 101st article of Iran's Fourth Plan (2005–2009) has focused on preparing the so called Decent Work National Plan document (see Appendix A-9.2) (Management and Planning Organization, 2005a).

9.6 Concluding remarks

Iran's economy has experienced many major changes during the period 1989–2004. During the three development plans, initiatives on structural adjustment, economic stabilization and economic reform have been combined, on necessity, with appropriate policies for increasing production, investment and employment. The society is evolving from the special political and social conditions caused by war, to a civil society in which economic agents, political parties, syndicate associations and non-governmental organizations are taking advantage of the social rights they deserve. Removing the obstacles to youth employment and preparing decent work for young people is not an easy task. The success heavily depends on the ongoing situation in other markets. Any improvement in the labour market is subject to proper functioning of other markets, ranging from markets for goods and services to financial markets. Solving the problem in the labour market and addressing the complicated and multidimensional issue of decent work necessarily requires reorganizing and enhancing the performance of the three main institutions of society: the Government, firms and households.

Structural changes have occurred in government and Iran is now experiencing good governance. Even though it may in some years have moved away from this goal, such problems are temporary.

Structural changes have occurred within enterprises. The enterprises have understood that in order to survive in the present competitive environment, they have to utilize knowledge-based methods of production. They have also learned to see the human resources they have as valuable assets of the organization.

Structural changes have also occurred within households. They now know how to continuously learn and acquire more skills.

During the period 1989–2004, the gross national product (GNP) increased by 2.3 times, the gross fixed capital formation grew by 2.9 times and the gross national savings increased by 3.3 times (all based on fixed prices: 1977 = 100). The average gross fixed capital formation to GNP ratio was 29 per cent and the average gross national saving to GNP ratio was 35 per cent. Income per capita based on fixed prices (1977 = 100) increased by 2 times (Figure 9.9). The average inflation rate was 15 per cent.

Figure 9.9

Per capita income, 1989–2004

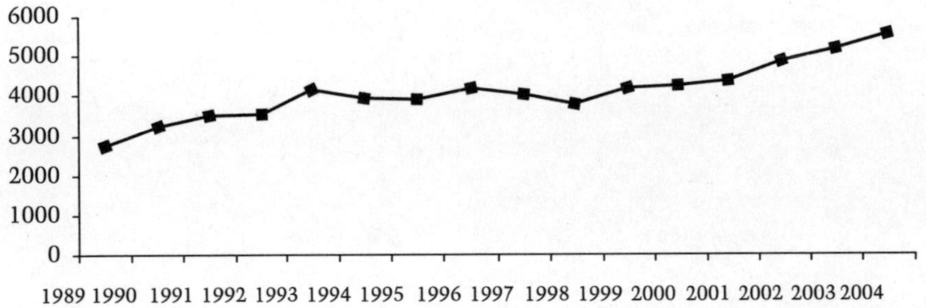

During this period, 7 million new jobs were created and the unemployment rate was preserved at 12.3 per cent. The role of the private sector in creating employment has become important. This sector created about 5.8 million jobs during 1989–2003. Development of the private sector through allocation of financial resources in foreign and domestic currencies has been one of the major policies and goals of both the Third and Fourth Plans.

Labour market analysts forecast that employment in the agricultural sector cannot increase its share in the future. Also, the share of industrial activities cannot grow as in the past. But the service activities have to be started in new fields and should grow remarkably.

Social, economic and political changes have been significant. But Iran's economy, which has a young population and needs a million new jobs each year that qualify as decent work, needs to make more efforts in economic and social areas. The first step is to create new jobs; the next step is to ensure that workers earn enough to meet the needs of both their present and future life. Important objectives such as social dialogue and protection are subsequent concerns.

Finally, we have to say that decent work is a multi-dimensional issue and a relative concept. In each stage of economic development, decent work will have a specific meaning. Undoubtedly, the requirements of decent work in societies with the income of more than US$30,000 per head are different from those for societies with less than US$10,000 income per head. These different levels of decent work are related, on the one hand, to the economic cycle and on the other hand, to the evolution of the society's bio-space, and to the development of the elements of the society's knowledge, legal and political spaces.

Appendix A-9.1

The impact of credit resources on employment creation

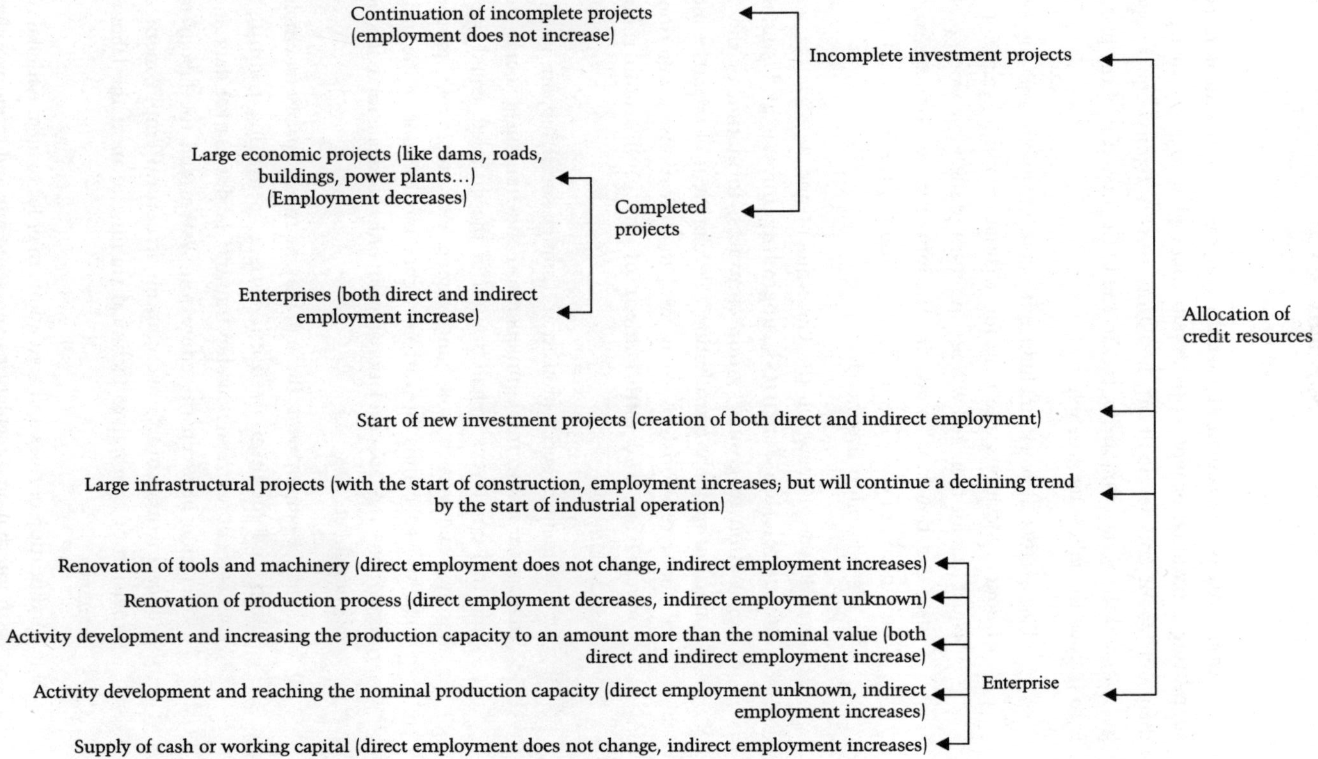

Appendix A-9.2

The Fourth Development Plan (2005 to 2009)

Article 101 of the Fourth Plan states that the Government is responsible for submitting a national decent work development plan to Parliament, as the new theory of labour and development, based on human dignity, equal opportunities, freedom and the security of labour, by the end of the first year of the plan. The plan is to include the following principles:

1) Basic rights at work, including freedom of unions and support for civil labour associations, the right for negotiation and organization in groups, equal fees for men and women in return of the same work, prohibition of discrimination in jobs, meeting the minimum working-age requirements, prohibition of child labour, determination of the minimum fees in regard to the minimum livelihood.

2) Social dialogue between the Government and its social associates (civil labour-relations entities), upgrading human and social capital, negotiation in groups, group contracts, formation of the "tripartite council of national consultation", development of tripartite mechanisms in labour relationships, structural modifications, promotion of social conversation and enforcement of the civil labour-relationships associations.

3) Development of social protection, through social support, unemployment insurance, enforcing compensation mechanisms, social support for informal employees, rehabilitation of the disabled, equal opportunities for men and women, supplying women with proper jobs, provision of the right for legal claims for workers' rights, modification of the social support regulations and labour relationships in order to create more flexibility in the labour market.

4) Productive employment, through making more capacity for employment in small and medium-sized enterprises, providing training aimed at employment, entrepreneurship training, labour market data analysis, full cooperation between the education system and the labour market (to reduce mismatching), overcoming structural employment obstacles, provision of appropriate technical training to meet the labour market's demands.

5) Modification of rules and regulations in order to align national regulations with international regulations and standards and recent worldwide labour

changes, and to remove discrimination from all arenas, especially the labour market.

General objectives:

1) Protection of human dignity and generosity
2) Enhancement of labour productivity
3) Growth and development of the national economy
4) Sustainable development, with emphasis on environment protection
5) Regulation of the labour market and reducing the unemployment rate
6) Development of the country's human and social capital
7) Regulation of labour relationships on a tripartite basis
8) Compliance with international labour regulations
9) Development of social protection
10) Enforcement of the labour institution
11) Enhancement of the contribution of women and youth

Guidelines and strategies

General strategies:

- Ensure centralized policies and systematic implementation
- Focus on domestic, regional and international cooperation
- Upgrade domestic capabilities and focus on use of the private sector
- Achieve decent work goals through cultural effort

Employment strategies:

- Balance labour wage and non-wage costs with labour productivity
- Support training and upgrade the labour force's skills and knowledge
- Ensure flexibility of the labour market
- Enhance matching between the educational system and the labour market's demands
- Support entrepreneurship and make provisions to create employment

Social support strategies:

- Provide health and security for the labour force
- Enforce and develop support systems for the labour force
- Improve the labour monitoring and inspection system

Basic labour rights policies:

- Increase women's cooperation and their work capabilities
- Ensure effective efforts to eliminate child labour
- Support the organization, rights and freedoms of worker–employer associations

Social conversation strategies:

- Promote social conversations within the labour environment
- Modify and balance the rules and regulations monitoring labour relationships.

Clearly, achieving the stated objectives of the Fourth Plan is beyond the activities of one or a few executive authorities. It needs full-scale cooperation between all of the country's regulatory and executive sectors, non-governmental sectors, worker–employer associations and every single person in the labour force (Labour and Social Security Institute, 2005).

References and selected reading

Acemoglu, D., S. Johnson and J.A. Robinson (2005). "Institutions as the fundamental cause of long-run growth", in P. Aghion and S. Durlauf (eds): *Handbook of economic growth* (Amsterdam, North-Holland), pp. 385–472.

Acharya, M. (2003). "Development of the financial system and its impact on poverty alleviation in Nepal, NRB", in *Journal of Economic Review of Occasional Paper* 15: 1–33, April.

Afghanistan Development Forum (ADF). (2005a). *Creating an enabling environment for the private sector* (Kabul).

———. (2005b). *From liability to asset: Ensuring pro-poor growth in Afghanistan* (Kabul).

Afghanistan Government (2004). *Securing Afghanistan's future: Accomplishments and strategic path forward*, report prepared for international conference, 31 Mar.–1 Apr. Available at: *http://www.adb.org/Documents/Reports/Afghanistan/securing-afghanistan-future-final.pdf* [accessed 28 Dec. 2007].

———. (2005a). *Millennium Development Goals, Islamic Republic of Afghanistan, Country Report 2005: Vision 2020*, report commissioned by the Islamic Republic of Afghanistan and sponsored by the United Nations Development Programme (UNDP). Available at: *http://www.ands.gov.af/src/src/MDGs_Reps/MDGR%202005.pdf* [accessed 28 Dec. 2007].

———. (2005b). *Afghanistan national development strategy: An interim strategy for security, governance, economic growth and poverty reduction*. Available at: *http://www.reliefweb.int/library/documents/2006/unama-afg-30jan2.pdf* [accessed 28 Dec. 2007].

———. (2006). *The Afghanistan Compact*, Building on Success, The London Conference on Afghanistan, London, 31 Jan.–1 Feb. Available at: *http://www.fco.gov.uk/Files/kfile/20060130%20Afghanistan%20Compact%20Final%20Final,0.doc* [accessed 28 Dec. 2007].

Ahmed, M. and A.H. Mondal (1993). "Structural adjustment, labour market reforms, industrial relations and productivity in Bangladesh", in ILO–ARTEP: *Social Dimensions of Economic Reforms in Bangladesh* (Geneva, ILO), pp. 35–70.

Ahsan, A. and C. Pagés (2006). "Some implications of regional differences in labor market outcomes in India", in *India: Meeting the employment challenge* (New Delhi, Institute for Human Development), pp. 92–109.

———. (2007). "Are all labor regulations equal? Assessing the effects of job security, labor dispute and contract labor laws in India", Policy Research *Working Paper* WPS 4259 (Washington DC, World Bank).

Akerlof, G.A. (1970). "The market for 'lemons': Quality uncertainty and the market mechanism", in *The Quarterly Journal of Economics* 84(3): 488–500, August.

Akyüz, Y. (Forthcoming). *Global rules and markets: Constraints over policy autonomy in developing countries* (Geneva, ILO).

Amini, A.R. (2006). *Labour market time series data* (Tehran, Management and Planning Organization, Office of Macroeconomics).

Arrow, K.J. (1962). "Economic welfare and the allocation of resources for invention", in R.R. Nelson (ed.): *The rate and direction of inventive activity* (Princeton, NJ, Princeton University Press), pp. 609–626.

———. (1963). *Social choice and individual values* (New York, John Wiley).

Ashoff, G. (1999). "The coherence of policies towards developing countries: The case of Germany", in J. Forster and O. Stokke (eds): *Policy coherence in development co-operation*, EADI Book Series 22 (London, Frank Cass), pp. 128–179.

Asian Development Bank (ADB). (2005). *Asian Development Outlook 2005. Afghanistan* (Manila). Available at: *http://www.adb.org/Documents/Books/ADO/2005/afg.asp* [accessed 28 Dec. 2007].

———. (2006). *Asian Development Outlook 2006. Afghanistan* (Manila). Available at: *http://www.adb.org/documents/books/ado/2006/afg.asp* [accessed 28 Dec. 2007].

———.; World Bank (2005). *Sri Lanka improving the rural and urban investment climate*. Available at: *http://www.worldbank.lk* [accessed 23 Sep. 2007].

Audretsch, D.B. and F.P. Maryann (1996). "R&D spillovers and the geography of innovation and production", in *American Economic Review* 86(3): 630-640, June.

———. and S.E. Paula (1996). "Company-scientist locational links: The case of biotechnology", in *American Economic Review* 86(3): 641–652, June.

———. and T.A. Roy (1997). "Sources of growth: The entrepreneurial versus the managed economy," CEPR *Discussion Papers* 1710 (London, Centre for Economic Policy Research (CEPR)).

Bagchi, A. (2007). "Fiscal deficit", in K. Basu (ed.): *The Oxford companion to economics in India* (New Delhi, Oxford University Press), pp. 183–187.

Bakht, Z. (2000). "Growth performance of the manufacturing sector: A review of the revised industrial GDP under SNA '93", in A. Abdullah (ed.): *Bangladesh economy 2000: Selected issues* (Dhaka, The Bangladesh Institute of Development Studies), pp. 117–36.

Bangladesh Bureau of Statistics (BBS). (2002). *Estimate of investment: Methods and data sources* (Dhaka).

———. (1987). *Statistical Yearbook of Bangladesh* (Dhaka).

———. (1999). *Statistical Yearbook of Bangladesh* (Dhaka).

———. (2000). *Statistical Yearbook of Bangladesh* (Dhaka).

———. (2005). *Statistical Yearbook of Bangladesh* (Dhaka).

———. (2006). *Statistical Yearbook of Bangladesh* (Dhaka).

———. (2007). *Statistical Yearbook of Bangladesh* (Dhaka).

Barro, R. and J.W. Lee (2000). "International data on educational attainment updates and implications," National Bureau of Economic Research (NBER) *Working Paper Series*, No. 7911 (Cambridge, MA, NBER).

Beall, J. and S. Schutte (2006). *Urban livelihoods in Afghanistan* (Kabul, Afghanistan Research and Evaluation Unit (AREU)).

Besley, T. and R. Burgess (2004). "Can labor regulation hinder economic performance? Evidence from India," in *The Quarterly Journal of Economics* 119(1): 91–134.

Bhagwati, J. (2004). *In defense of globalization* (New York, Oxford University Press).

———.; and T. Srinivasan (1999). *Outward orientation and development: Are revisionists right?* (New Haven, Yale University).

Bhatia, M. *et al.* (2003). "Profits and poverty: Aid, livelihoods and conflict in Afghanistan", in S. Collinson (ed.): *Power, livelihoods and conflict: Case studies in political economy analysis for humanitarian action*, Humanitarian Policy Group Report 13 (London, Overseas Development Institute), pp. 67–90.

Borjas, G. (2005). *Labor economics* (New York, McGraw-Hill).

Brezis, E.S. and F. Crouzet (2006). "The role of higher education institutions: Recruitment of elites and economic growth", in T.S. Eicher and C. Gracia-Penalosa (eds): *Institutions, development, and economic growth*, CESifo Seminar Series (Cambridge, MA, MIT Press), pp. 191–215.

British Broadcasting Company (BBC). (2006/09/11) "Coca Cola returns to Afghanistan", 9 Nov. Available at: *http://news.bbc.co.uk/go/pr/fr/-/2/hi/south_asia/5334120.stm* [accessed 28 Dec. 2007].

Central Bank of Islamic Republic of Iran (1989). *Economic report and balance sheet, 1988/89* (Tehran).

———. (1990). *Economic Report and Balance Sheet, 1989/90* (Tehran).

———. (1991). *Economic Report and Balance Sheet, 1990/91* (Tehran).

———. (1992). *Economic Report and Balance Sheet, 1991/92* (Tehran).

———. (1993). *Economic Report and Balance Sheet, 1992/93* (Tehran).

———. (1994). *Economic Report and Balance Sheet, 1993/94* (Tehran).

———. (1995). *Economic Report and Balance Sheet, 1994/95* (Tehran).

———. (1996). *Economic Report and Balance Sheet, 1995/96* (Tehran).

———. (1997). *Economic Report and Balance Sheet, 1996/97* (Tehran).

———. (1998). *Economic Report and Balance Sheet, 1997/98* (Tehran).

———. (1999). *Economic Report and Balance Sheet, 1998/99* (Tehran).

———. (2000). *Economic Report and Balance Sheet, 1999/2000* (Tehran).

———. (2001). *Economic Report and Balance Sheet 1379, 2000/01* (Tehran).

———. (2002). *Economic Report and Balance Sheet, 2001/02* (Tehran).

———. (2003). *Economic Report and Balance Sheet, 2002/03* (Tehran).

———. (2004). *Economic Report and Balance Sheet, 2003/04* (Tehran).

Central Bank of Sri Lanka (CBSL). (1988). *Consumer Finance and Socio-economic Survey, 1985/86* (Colombo).

———. (1990). *Annual Report 1989* (Colombo).

———. (1995). *Annual Report 1994* (Colombo).

———. (1998). *Consumer Finance and Socio-economic Survey, 1995/96* (Colombo).

———. (2000). *Annual Report 1999* (Colombo).

———. (2002). *Household Income and Expenditure Survey 2002* (Colombo).

———. (2002). *Annual Report 2001* (Colombo)

———. (2004). *Annual Report 2003* (Colombo).

———. (2005a). *Annual Report 2004* (Colombo).

———. (2005b). *Consumer Finance and Socio-economic Survey, 2003/04* (Colombo).

———. (2006a). *Recent economic developments: Highlights of 2006 and prospects for 2007* (Colombo, Ministry of Finance).

———. (2006b). *Annual Report 2005* (Colombo).

Central Bureau of Statistics (CBS). (1987). *Manufacturing Census* (Kathmandu, Government of Nepal).

———. (1992). *Manufacturing Census* (Kathmandu, Government of Nepal).

———. (1995). *Manufacturing Census* (Kathmandu, Government of Nepal).

———. (1996a). *Nepal Living Standard Survey Report* (Kathmandu, Government of Nepal).

———. (1996b). *Nepal Living Standard Survey (NLSS)* (Kathmandu, Government of Nepal).

———. (1999). *Nepal Labor Force Survey Report* (Kathmandu, Government of Nepal).

———. (2002a). *Census of Nepal 2001* (Kathmandu, Govt. of Nepal).

———. (2002b). *Manufacturing census* (Kathmandu, Government of Nepal).

———. (2004a). *Nepal Living Standard Survey (NLSS) report* (Kathmandu, Government of Nepal).

———. (2004b). *Nepal Living Standard Survey (NLSS)* (Kathmandu, Government of Nepal).

———. (2006). *Resilience amidst conflict: An assessment of poverty in Nepal (1996–96 and 2003–2004)* (Kathmandu, Government of Nepal).

Central Statistical Office (CSO). (2003). *Afghanistan Statistical Yearbook* (Kabul, Government of Afghanistan).

———. (2006). *Afghanistan Statistical Yearbook* (Kabul, Government of Afghanistan).

Centre for Policy Dialogue (CPD). (2001). *Developing a policy agenda for Bangladesh: Civil Society's Task Force Reports 2001* (Dhaka: CPD and The University Press Limited).

Cervellati, M.; P. Fortunato and S. Uwe (2006). "Growth and endogenous political institutions", in T.S. Eicher and C. Gracia-Penalosa (eds): *Institutions, development, and economic growth*, CESifo Seminar Series (Cambridge, MA, MIT Press), pp. 215–249.

Chakraborty, P. (2007). "Implementation of employment guarantee: A preliminary appraisal", in *Economic and Political Weekly*, 17 Feb., pp. 548–551.

Chandler, A.D. Jr. (1977). *The visible hand: The managerial revolution in American business* (Cambridge, MA, Harvard University Press).

Chandrasekhar, C.P. and J. Ghosh (2006). "Working more for less", in *Macroscan*, 28 Nov. 28. Available at: *http://macroscan.org* [accessed 11 Dec. 2007].

Chelliah, R.J. (2001). "The nature of fiscal crisis in the Indian Federation and calibrating fiscal policy", in *Money & Finance* 2(5): 52–75.

Chen, M.A. (2004). *Rethinking the informal economy: Linkages with the formal economy and the formal regulatory environment*, paper presented at the EGDI and UNU-WIDER Conference on Unlocking Human Potential: Linking the Informal and Formal Sectors, Helsinki, 17–18 September.

Clarke, G. *et al.* (2001). "Does foreign bank penetration reduce access to credit in developing countries? Evidence from asking borrowers," Policy Research *Working Paper* No. 2716 (Washington DC, World Bank).

Cohen, N.P. (1995). "Why does economic liberalization make sense", *EconNews*, June (Kathmandu, USAID).

Cohen, W.M. and S. Klepper (1992). "The tradeoff between firm size and diversity in the pursuit of technological progress", in *Small Business Economics* 4(1): 1–14.

Cooter, R. (2000). "Do good laws make good citizens? An economic analysis of internalized norms", *in Virginia Law Review* 86(8): 1577–1601.

Dahal, M.K. and S. Aryal (2003). *Improving Nepal–India economic relations: A study of the impact of foreign direct investment (FDI) and transfer of technology in Nepal* (Kathmandu, Institute for Integrated Development Studies).

Dar, A. (2006). "The vocational education and training system in India", in *India: Meeting the employment challenge* (New Delhi, Institute for Human Development), pp. 472–97.

Das, M. (2006). "Do traditional axes of exclusion affect labor market outcomes?", in *India: Meeting the employment challenge*, pp. 48–80.

Debroy, B. (2005). "Issues in labor law reform", in B. Debroy and P.D. Kaushik (ed.): *Reforming the labor market* (New Delhi, Academic Foundation).

Department of Census and Statistics (2004). *Official poverty line bulletin* (Colombo).

Department of Labour (2003). *Administrative Report* (Colombo).

Desai, B.M. and N.V. Nambodiri (1997). "Price and non-price determinates of agriculture supply", in B.M. Desai (ed.): *Agricultural development paradigm further Ninth Plan under new economic environment* (New Delhi, Oxford and IBH Publishing), pp. 570–590.

Development Study Consultants (DSC). (1990). *Policy planning models for the Nepalese economy with special reference to the industrial sector* (Kathmandu).

Dixit, P.M. (1995). *Economic policymaking: The Nepal experience* (Kathmandu, Patan Rotary Club).

Dollar, D. and A. Kraay (2001). "Trade, growth and poverty," Policy Research *Working Paper* No. 2615 (Washington DC, World Bank).

Duflo, E.; A. Banerjee and A. Deaton, (2004). "Health care delivery in rural Rajasthan", in *Economic and Political Weekly*, Vol. 39, pp. 944–949.

Duma, N. (2007). "Sri Lanka's sources of growth", *Working Paper* No. 07/225 (Washington DC, IMF)

Economic Research Institute (2005). *Economic Time Series Data 1974–2004* (Tehran).

Epitaru, P. (2003). *Trade liberalization, firm performance and labor markets outcomes in the developing world: What can we learn from macro level data?* (Parma, University of Parma and CESPRI-Boccori University).

European Commission (2005). *Policy coherence for development accelerating progress towards attaining the Millennium Development Goals*, Communication to the Council, the European Parliament and the European Economic and Social Committee, COM/2005/0134 final (Luxembourg).

European Centre for Development Policy Management (ECDPM); Instituto Complutense de Estudios Internationales (ICEI) (2005). *EU mechanisms that promote policy coherence for development: A scoping study*, Triple C Evaluations N2 (Amsterdam, Aksant Academic).

Fallon, P.R. and R.E.B. Lucas (1991). "The impact of changes in job security regulations in India and Zimbabwe", in *World Bank Economic Review* 5(3): 395–413.

Federation of Nepalese Chamber of Commerce and Industry (FNCCI); World Bank. (2000). *The business environment and manufacturing performance in Nepal* (Kathmandu).

———. (2002). *A study of financial sector of Nepal* (Kathmandu).

Frenkel, J. and D. Romer (1999). "Does trade cause growth?", in *American Economic Review* 89(3): 379–399.

Friedman, J. (2000). "Globalization, class and culture in global systems", in *Journal of World-Systems Research* VI(3): 636–656.

Fukusaku, K. and A. Hirata (1995). *OECD and the ASEAN economies: The challenge of policy coherence* (Paris, OECD).

Garibaldi, P. (2007). *Marginal labour market reforms in Europe*, paper presented at the Conference on Labour Regulation in Indian Industry, Institute for Studies in Industrial Development, New Delhi, 21–22 Nov. 2006.

Gaston, R.J. (1989). "The scale of informal capital markets", in *Small Business Economics* 1(3): 223–230.

Ghose, A.K. (2004). "The employment challenge in India," in *Economic and Political Weekly* 39(48): 1191–1195.

Glinskaya, E. and J. Jalan (2006). *Quality of informal jobs in India*, paper presented at the Conference on Labour and Employment Issues in India, Institute for Human Development and World Bank, New Delhi, 27–29 July.

Goodhand, J. (2004). "From war economy to peace economy? Reconstruction and state building in Afghanistan", in *Journal of International Affairs* 58(1): 155–173.

———. and A. Pain (2002). *Afghanistan: Current employment and socio-economic situation and prospects*, InFocus Programme on Crisis Response and Reconstruction *Working Paper* No. 8 (Geneva, ILO).

Gough, I. (2004). "Welfare regimes in development contexts: A global and regional analysis", in I. Gough and G. Wood (eds): *Insecurity and welfare regimes in Asia, Africa and Latin America: Social policy in development contexts* (Cambridge, Cambridge University Press), pp. 15–48.

Government of Bangladesh (2000). *Economic Review 1999* (Dhaka).

———. (2000). The Fifth Five Year Plan 1997–2002 (Dhaka).

———. (2005a). *Unlocking the potential: National strategy for accelerated poverty reduction* (Dhaka).

———. (2005b). *Economic Review 2004* (Dhaka).

———. (2006). *Economic Review 2005* (Dhaka).

———. (2007). *Economic Review 2006* (Dhaka).

Government of India (2006). *Fifth Economic Census 2005* (New Delhi, Central Statistical Organisation).

———. (2007). *Economic Survey, 2006–07* (New Delhi, Ministry of Finance).

———. (Various rounds). *National Sample Survey (NSS)* (Kolkata).

Government of Pakistan (1985). *Labour force survey, 1984/85* (Islamabad, Federal Board of Statistics).

———. (1994). *Labour force survey, 1993/94* (Islamabad, Federal Board of Statistics).

———. (2002). *Labour force survey, 2001/02* (Islamabad, Federal Board of Statistics).

———. (2004). *Labour force survey, 2003/04* (Islamabad, Federal Board of Statistics).

———. (2006). *Economic Survey, 2005–06* (Islamabad, Ministry of Finance).

Grace, J. and A. Pain (2004). *Rethinking rural livelihoods* (Kabul, AREU).

Griliches, Z. (1992). "The search for R&D spillovers", in *Scandinavian Journal of Economics* 94(0): S29–47.

Gunter, B.G.; Cohen, M.J. and H. Lofgren (2005). "Analyzing macro-poverty linkages: An overview", in *Development Policy Review* 23(3): 243–265.

Hamilton, J.; J. Madison and J. Jay (1788). *Federalist papers*, reprinted in C. Rossiter (ed.): *Federalist papers* (New York, New American Library, 1961).

Haque, N.U. (2006a). "Beyond planning and mercantilism: An evaluation of Pakistan's growth strategy", in *The Pakistan Development Review* 45(1): 3–22.

———. (2006b). "Why perks block reform", in N.U. Haque and M. Ud-Din (eds): *Public sector efficiency: Perspectives on civil service reform* (Islamabad, Pakistan Institute of Development Economics).

———. and N. Durre-e (2006). *Renew cities to be the engines of growth*, PIDE Policy Viewpoint No. 2 (Islamabad, Pakistan Institute of Development Economics).

———. and W. Izzah (eds). (2006). *Domestic commerce: The missing link* (Islamabad, Ministry of Commerce, Government of Pakistan).

Harriss-White, B. (2003). *India working: Essays on society and economy* (Cambridge, Cambridge University Press).

Hasan, R.; Mitra, D. and K.V. Ramaswamy (2003). "Trade reforms, labor regulations and labor-demand elasticities: Empirical evidence from India", National Bureau of Economic Research (NBER) *Working Paper*, No. 9879 (Cambridge, MA, NBER).

Hayek, F.A. (1945). "The use of knowledge in society", in *American Economic Review* 35(4): 519–530.

———. (1978). *Law, legislation, and liberty, Vol. 2: The mirage of social justice* (Chicago, IL, University of Chicago Press).

Heinz, J. and R. Pollin (2003). "Informalization, economic growth and the challenge of creating viable labor standards in developing countries," Political Economy Research Institute (PERI) *Working Paper* No. 60 (Amherst, MA, PERI).

Hilker, L.M. (2004). *A comparative analysis of institutional mechanism to promote policy coherence for development. Case study synthesis: The European Community, United States and Japan*, paper prepared for the OECD policy workshop Institutional Approaches to Policy Coherence for Development, 18–19 May. Available at: *http://www.eucoherence.org* [accessed 23 Sep. 2007].

His Majesty's Government of Nepal (HMGN). (1997). *Agriculture sector perspective plan* (Kathmandu).

———. (2004). *Nepal: Trade and competitiveness study – A study conducted with donor's assistance as a part of the integrated framework for trade related assistance for HMG of Nepal* (Kathmandu).

———.; United Nations Industrial Development Organization (UNIDO). (2002). *Industrial development perspective plan: Vision 2020* (Kathmandu).

Holmström, M. (1999). "A new map of Indian industrial society: The cartographer at sea", in *Oxford Development Studies* 27(2): 165–186.

Hussain, A. (2007). *Markets, the state and the poor*, paper presented at the 'Policy Coherence for Decent Work' conference, Labour Hall, Lahore, before representatives of various trade unions, 22 Feb.

Institute of Policy Studies (IPS). (2006). *Economic growth, employment and poverty reduction in Sri Lanka* (Colombo, ILO/UNDP), unpublished mimeograph.

International Finance Corporation (IFC); World Bank. (1998). *Nepal attracting foreign investment to Nepal's infrastructure* (Kathmandu).

International Labour Office (ILO). (1999). *Decent work*, Report of the Director-General, International Labour Conference, 87th Session, Geneva.

———. (2002). *Decent work for poverty reduction: An ILO contribution to the PRSP in Nepal* (Geneva).

———. (2003). *Review of the core elements of the Global Employment Agenda*, Committee on Employment and Social Policy, GB.286/ESP/1(Rev.)-2003-02-0278-2EN.Doc, Mar. (Geneva).

———. (2004a). *A fair globalization: Creating opportunities for all*, World Commission on the Social Dimension of Globalization (Geneva).

———. (2004b). *Decent work country programmes*, Director-General's announcement, Circular No. 599. Available at: *http://www.ilo.org* [accessed 11 Dec. 2007].

———. (2005a). *An employment strategy for the Islamic Republic of Iran* (New Delhi).

———. (2005b). *Labour market skills mismatch*, Jobsnet–ILO Project (Colombo).

———. (2005c). *World Employment Report 2004–05: Employment, productivity and poverty reduction* (Geneva).

———. (2006a). *Key indicators of the labour market (KILM)*, 4th ed. (Geneva).

———. (2006b). *Decent work in Asia: Reporting on results 2001–2005* (Geneva).

———. (2007a). *Global employment trends*, Brief, Jan. (Geneva).

———. (2007b). *Global employment trends*, Brief, Mar. (Geneva).

———. (2007c). "Sri Lanka", *Termination of Employment Legislation Digest*, DIALOGUE (Geneva). Available at: *http://www.ilo.org/ifpdial* [accessed 22 April 2008].

———.; Asian Regional Team for Employment Promotion (ILO/ARTEP). (1982). *Employment and development in Nepal* (Bangkok).

———.; World Trade Organization (WTO). (2007). *Trade and employment: Challenges for policy research* (Geneva).

International Monetary Fund (IMF). (2004a). *Islamic State of Afghanistan: Staff-monitored program*, Country Report No. 04/110 (Washington, DC).

———. (2004b). *Islamic State of Afghanistan: First review under the staff-monitored program*, Country Report No. 04/364 (Washington, DC).

———. (2005a). *Sri Lanka: 2005 Article IV Consultation – Staff report, staff statement; and public information notice on the executive board discussion* (Washington, DC).

———. (2005b). *Sri Lanka: Selected issues and statistical appendix* (Washington, DC).

———. (2006). *Islamic Republic of Afghanistan: 2005 Article IV Consultation and Sixth Review under the Staff Monitored Program*, Country Report No. 06/113 (Washington, DC).

Islam, R. (2006). "Employment poverty linkage: A cross-country analysis", in S. Ahmed and W. Mahmud (eds): *Growth and poverty: The development experience of Bangladesh* (Dhaka, The University Press Limited), pp. 47–67.

Jabbar, S.K.J. (2006). "Readymade garment sector in Bangladesh: A study from the employers' perspective", ILO: *RMG industry, post-MFA regime and decent work: The Bangladesh perspective*, papers and proceedings of the National Tripartite Meeting on Enhancing Employment, Global Competitiveness through Decent Work: Post-MFA Challenges and Opportunities, Dhaka, 24 Aug. 2005 (Dhaka, ILO), pp. 52–93.

Jansen, M. and E. Lee (2007). *Trade and employment: Challenges for policy research* (Geneva, ILO and WTO).

Jayaweera, S.; T. Sanmugam and J. Abeywardena (1998). *Women and trade unions* (Colombo, Centre for Women's Research).

Jenkins, H.; Lee, E. and G. Rodgers (2007). "The quest for a fair globalization three years on: Assessing the impact of the World Commission on the Social Dimension of Globalization", *Discussion paper* DP/175/2007 (Geneva, International Institute of Labour Studies).

Jolly, R.; A. Cornea, and F. Stewart, (1987). *Adjustment with a human face* (Oxford, Oxford University Press).

Joshi, P.K. *et al.* (2004). "Agriculture diversification in South Asia: Pattern, determinants and policy implications", in *Economic and Political Weekly* 39(24): 2457–2467.

Kannan, K.P. (2007). "Interrogating inclusive growth: Some reflections on exclusionary growth and the prospects for inclusive development in India", in *Indian Journal of Labour Economics* 50(1): 17–46.

Kantor, P. and S. Schutte (2007). *Create more quality jobs with better pay to improve livelihoods and political stability*, AREU Policy Note Series (Kabul, AREU).

Kaul, I.; I. Grunberg and M.A. Stern (1999). *Global public goods* (New York, UNDP and Oxford University Press).

Kelegama, S. and R. Epaarachchi (2003). "Garment industry in Sri Lanka", in G. Joshi (ed.): *Garment industry in South Asia: Rags or riches?* (New Delhi, ILO), pp. 187–231.

Khan, A.U. (2005). "Regulating labour markets", in B. Debroy and P.D. Kaushik (eds): *Reforming the labour market* (New Delhi, Academic Foundation Press).

Khanal, D.R. (1993). "Development planning in Nepal, in Somlakand", in S. Tambunlertchai and S.P. Gupta (eds): *Development Planning in Asia* (Kuala Lumpur: Asian and Pacific Development Center), pp. 133–48.

———. (2004). *Fiscal impact of Nepal's WTO membership from human development perspectives* (HMGN and UNDP).

———. (2006a). *Service sector liberalization in Nepal, Bangladesh and Malaysia: A comparative assessment of financial and insurance sectors of Nepal*, report submitted to United Nations Economic and Social Commission for Asia and the Pacific (ESCAP)/Asia-Pacific Research and Training Network (ARTNeT) (Bangkok, ESCAP).

———. (2006b) *Public finance implications of trade related policy reform in Nepal*, report submitted to UNDP Regional Center (Colombo, UNDPRC).

———.; Kanel, N.R. (2005). *Macroeconomic policy, shocks and poverty reduction in Nepal: A simulation-based quantitative analysis* (Kathmandu, Institute for Policy Research and Development).

———. *et al.* (2005). *Understanding reform in Nepal: Political economy and institutional perspectives* (Kathmandu, Institute for Policy Research and Development).

Khatiwada, Y.R. (1981). *An econometric analysis of the determinants of inflation in Nepal* (Kathmandu, Tribhuvan University).

Knight, F.H. (1921). *Risk, uncertainty and profit* (New York, Houghton Mifflin).

KPMG Barents (2000). *Final report on Nepal banking reform project*, Nepal Bank Ltd, Rastriya Banijya Bank (Kathmandu).

Labour and Social Security Institute (2005). *First draft of decent work national document* (Tehran).

Lall, S.V. and T. Mengistae (2005). *The impact of labor market regulations on firm level productivity and manufacturing growth* (Washington DC, World Bank).

Landes, R. and A. Gulati (2004). "Farm sector performance and reform agenda", in *Economic and Political Weekly* 39(32): 3611–3619.

Leff, N.H. (1979). "Entrepreneurship and economic development: The problem revisited", in *Journal of Economic Literature* 17: 46–64.

Lister, S. and A. Pain (2004). *Trading in power: The politics of "free" markets in Afghanistan* (Kabul, AREU).

Lizzeri, A. and N. Persico (2004). "Why did the elites extend the suffrage? Democracy and the scope of government, with an application to Britain's 'Age of Reform'", in *Quarterly Journal of Economics* 119(2): 707–765.

Lübker, M. (2007). "Labour shares", *Technical Brief* No. 01, Policy Integration Department (Geneva, ILO).

Mahmud, W. (1996). "Employment patterns and income formation in rural Bangladesh: The role of rural non-farm sector", in *The Bangladesh Development Studies* 24(3/4): 1–27.

———. *et al.* (2000). "Agricultural diversification: A strategic factor for growth", in R. Ahmed; S. Haggblade; T. Chowdhury (eds): *Out of the shadow of famine: Evolving food markets and food policy in Bangladesh* (Baltimore, MD, The Johns Hopkins University Press), pp. 232–60.

———. (2006). "Employment, incomes and poverty: Prospects of pro-poor growth in Bangladesh", in S. Ahmed and W. Mahmud (eds), pp. 21–45.

Mainali, M.P. *et al.* (2002). *Gender Dimension of Skill Development in Nepal* (Kathmandu, ILO).

Majid, N. (2001a). "The size of the working poor population in developing countries", *Employment Paper* No. 16 (Geneva, ILO).

———. (2001b). "Economic growth, social policy and decent work", *Employment Paper* No. 19 (Geneva, ILO).

Management and Planning Organization (MPO). (2000). *Third socio-economic and cultural development plan of Islamic Republic of Iran, 2000–2004* (Tehran).

———. (2005a). *Fourth Socio-economic and Cultural Development Plan of Islamic Republic of Iran (2005–2009)* (Tehran).

———. (2005b). *Economic Report: 2004–2005 and Five Year Performance Supervision Report of the 3rd Development Plan* (Tehran).

Mathur, A. and R.P. Mamgain (2004). "Human capital stocks: Their level of utilization and economic development in India", in *Indian Journal of Labor Economics* 47(4): 655–676.

Mattoo, A.; R. Rathindran and A. Subramanian (2001). "Measuring services trade liberalization and its impact on economic growth", Policy Research *Working Paper* No. 2655 (Washington DC, World Bank).

Maxwell Stamp Associates (1990). *Second industrial sector study Nepal* (Kathmandu, Maxwell Stamp Associates).

Mazumdar, D. and S. Sarkar (2004). "Reforms and employment elasticity in organised manufacturing", in *Economic and Political Weekly* 39(27): 3017–3029.

———. (2006). "Employment elasticity in organized manufacturing in India", in *India: Meeting the employment challenge* (New Delhi, Institute for Human Development), pp. 309–38.

McKinnon, R.I. (1975). *Money and capital in economic development* (Washington DC, The Brookings Institution).

Ministry of Commerce and Industry (MoCI). (2006a). Available at: *http://www.commerce.gov.af* [accessed 14 Dec. 2006].

———. (2006b). *Private investment law*, unofficial version. Available at: *http://www.commerce.gov.af/pdf/Private%20Investment%20Law.pdf* [accessed 14 Dec. 2006].

Ministry of Employment and Labour. (2002). *Draft national employment policy for Sri Lanka* (Colombo).

———. (n.d.) *National productivity policy for Sri Lanka* (Colombo).

Ministry of Finance (MoF). (1986). *Economic Survey* (Kathmandu, Government of Nepal).

———. (1991). *Economic Survey 1990/91* (Kathmandu, Government of Nepal).

———. (1998). *Economic Survey 1997/98* (Kathmandu, Government of Nepal).

———. (2000). *Economic Survey 1999/2000* (Kathmandu, Government of Nepal).

———. (2001). *Economic Survey, 2000/01* (Kathmandu, Government of Nepal).

———. (2002). *Economic Survey, 2001/02* (Kathmandu, Government of Nepal).

———. (2003). *Economic Survey 2002/03* (Kathmandu, Government of Nepal).

———. (2004). *Economic Survey 2003/04* (Kathmandu, Government of Nepal).

———. (2005a). *Budget Speech 2004/05* (Kathmandu, Government of Nepal).

———. (2005b). *Economic Survey 2004/05* (Kathmandu, Government of Nepal).

———. (2006a). *Economic Survey 2005/06* (Kathmandu, Government of Nepal).

———. (2006b). *Budget Speech 2005/06* (Kathmandu, Government of Nepal).

———. (2007). *Budget Speech 2006/07* (Kathmandu, Government of Nepal).

Ministry of Finance and Planning (2000). *Vision 21: The path to development – Investment profile 2000–2004* (Colombo).

———. (2005). *Sri Lanka new development strategy* (Colombo).

Ministry of Labour (2003). *Administrative Report* (Colombo).

Muqtada, M. (2003). *Promotion of employment and decent work in Bangladesh: Macroeconomic and labour policy considerations* (Geneva, ILO).

Munshi, K. and M.R. Rosenzweig (2005). "Why is mobility in India so low? Social insurance, inequality, and growth", Center for International Development (CID) *Working Paper* No. 121 (Cambridge, MA, Harvard University).

National Commission for Enterprises in the Unorganized Sector (NCEUS). (2005). *Pilot projects for growth poles for promoting development of the unorganised sector (mimeo)* (New Delhi).

———. (2006). *Report on social security for unorganised workers* (New Delhi, Government of India).

National Planning Commission (NPC). (1992). *Eighth Plan* (Kathmandu).

———. (1997). *Ninth Plan* (Kathmandu).

———. (2002). *Tenth Plan* (Kathmandu).

Neetha, N. and U.K. Varma (2004). *Labour, employment and gender issues in EPZs: The case of Noida EPZ*, NLI Research Studies Series No. 052 (Noida, VV Giri National Labour Institute).

Nepal Garment Association (NGA). (2006). *A report on the status of garment industry* (Kathmandu).

Nepal Rastra Bank (NRB). (1996). *Quarterly economic bulletin* (Kathmandu).

———. (2000). *Quarterly economic bulletin* (Kathmandu).

———. (2001). *Quarterly economic bulletin* (Kathmandu).

———. (2002). *Quarterly economic bulletin* (Kathmandu).

———. (2003). *Quarterly economic bulletin* (Kathmandu).

———. (2004). *Quarterly economic bulletin* (Kathmandu).

———. (2005). *Quarterly economic bulletin* (Kathmandu).

———. (2006a). *Monthly Economic Situation*, July (Kathmandu).

———. (2006b). *Monthly Economic Situation*: *Current macroeconomic situation* (annual) (Kathmandu).

Nepal Stock Exchange (NSE). (2006). *Annual report on Nepal stock exchange* (Kathmandu).

Nicod, M. (2004). *Institutional approaches to promote policy coherence for development: Findings and lessons from DAC peer reviews*, paper prepared for the OECD policy workshop Institutional Approaches to Policy Coherence for Development, 18–19 May, Paris (Paris, OECD).

North, D.C. (1990). "A transaction cost theory of politics", in *Journal of Theoretical Politics* 2(4): 355–367.

Norton, R.D. (2002). *Agricultural development policy: Concepts and experiences, Part I* (Rome, FAO).

Organisation for Economic Co-operation and Development (OECD). (1996). *Trade, employment and labour standards: A study of core workers' rights and international trade* (Paris).

———. (2003). *Policy coherence: Vital for global development*, OECD Observer Policy Brief, July (Paris).

Osmani, S.R. (2005). *The role of employment in promoting the Millennium Development Goals*, paper prepared under the joint ILO–UNDP programme on "Promoting Employment for Poverty Reduction" (New York and Geneva, UNDP and ILO).

———. *et al.* (2003). *Macroeconomics of poverty reduction: The case of Bangladesh*, paper presented at the Asia-Pacific Regional Programme on Macroeconomics of Poverty Reduction, Kathmandu, 4–6 Jan. (UNDP).

Pagés, C. and T. Roy (2006). "Regulation, enforcement and adjudication in Indian labor markets: Historical perspective, recent changes and way forward", in *India: Meeting the employment challenge*, pp. 361–90.

Pain, A. (2004). *On "Securing Afghanistan's future": The case for more and not less government* (London, Novib).

Pais, J. (2006). "Some features of migration and labour mobility in the leather accessories manufacturing in India: A study of the informal sector industry in Dharavi, Mumbai", *Working Paper* No. 2006/06 (New Delhi, Institute for Studies in Industrial Development).

Papola, T.S. (2006). *Employment in development agenda: Economic and social policies*, paper presented at the IILS-IGIDR conference on "A Development Agenda for Employment and Decent Work in India", Indira Gandhi Institute of Development Research, Mumbai, 10–11 Aug.

———. (2007). "Employment trends", in K. Basu (ed.), pp. 131–136.

Pasha, H.A. and T. Palanivel (2004). *Pro-poor growth and policies: The Asian experience*, Asia-Pacific Regional Programme on the Macroeconomics of Poverty Reduction (Kathmandu, UNDP).

Paterson, A. and J. Blewett (2006). *Putting the cart before the horse? Privatisation and economic reform in Afghanistan* (Kabul, AREU).

Paul-Majumder, P. (2002). "Organizing women garment workers: A means to address the challenges of integration of the Bangladesh garment industry in the global market", in M. Muqtada; A.M. Singh; M.A. Rashid (eds): *Bangladesh: Economic and social challenges of globalisation* (Dhaka, The University Press Limited), pp. 139–68.

Perry, G. and M. Olearraga (2006). *Trade liberalization, inequality and poverty in LAC*, paper presented to the ABCDE of World Bank, St Petersburg.

Picciotto, R. (2004). *Policy coherence and development evaluation: Concepts, issues and possible approaches*, background paper prepared for the OECD policy workshop Institutional Approaches to Policy Coherence for Development, 18–19 May (Paris, OECD).

Planning Commission (1993). *Report of the expert group on estimation of proportion and number of poor*, Perspective Planning Division (New Delhi, Government of India).

———. (2001a). *Report of the task force on employment opportunities* (New Delhi, Government of India).

———. (2001b). *Indian planning experience: A statistical profile* (New Delhi, Government of India).

———. (2002a). "Report of the Special Group on targeting ten million employment opportunities per year over the Tenth Plan period", in *Planning Commission reports on labor and employment* (New Delhi, Academic Foundation).

———. (2002b). *National Human Development Report 2001* (New Delhi, Government of India).

———. (2006). *Towards faster and inclusive growth: Approach paper to the Eleventh Plan* (New Delhi, Government of India).

Rahman, R.I. (2003). "Pattern and sustainability of economic growth in Bangladesh", in R.I. Rahman (ed.): *Performance of the Bangladesh economy: Selected issues* (Dhaka, Bangladesh Institute of Development Studies (BIDS)), pp. 27–48.

Rakshit, M. (2001). "Contentious issues in fiscal policy: A suggested resolution", in *Money and Finance* 7: 23–60, Oct.–Dec.

Ramesh, B.P. (2004). "Cyber coolies in BPO: Insecurities and vulnerabilities of non-standard work", in *Economic and Political Weekly,* 31 Jan.–6 Feb., pp. 492–497.

Rashid, M.A. (2008). "Bangladesh", in J. Francois; P. Rana; G. Wignaraja (eds): *National perspectives on East Asia – South Asia economic relations* (Manila, Asian Development Bank (ADB)).

Ravallion, M. (2001). "Growth, inequality and poverty: Looking beyond averages", in *World Development* 29(11): 1803–1815.

Research and Information System for the Non-Aligned and Other Developing Countries (RISDC). (2003). *Indian industrial tariffs: Towards WTO Development Round negotiations* (New Delhi).

———. (2006). *Towards an employment-oriented export strategy: Some explorations* (New Delhi).

Rifkin, J. (1996). *End of work* (New York, G. P. Putnam).

Rodrigo, C. (2006). *Sri Lanka: Country profile* (Colombo, ILO), unpublished mimeograph.

Rogers, G. (2001). "Decent work as a development objective", in *The Indian Journal of Labour Economics* 44(1): 15–26.

Saloman, M.E. (2006). "The significance of the UN Task Force on the right to development", in *Development Outreach*, October (Washington DC, World Bank Institute).

Sarvananthan, M. (2004). "Labour market reforms", in M. Sarvananthan (ed.): *Economic reforms in Sri Lanka* (Colombo, International Centre for Ethnic Studies).

Scoones, I. (1998). "Sustainable rural livelihoods: A framework for analysis", Working Paper No. 72 (Brighton, Institute of Development Studies (IDS)).

Sen, A. (1996). "Employment, Institutions and Technology: Some Policy Issues", in *International Labour Review* 135(3–4): 445.

———. (2001). *Development as freedom* (Oxford, Oxford University Press).

Sen, K. (n.d.) "Globalisation and employment in Bangladesh and Kenya", Production and Poverty *Discussion Paper* No.7, prepared as part of the DFID-funded project Globalisation, Production and Poverty (University of East Anglia, UK). Available at: *www.gapresearch.org/production/Globkunalbgdken.pdf* [accessed 23 Sep. 2007].

Shah, M. *et al.* (1998). *India's drylands: Tribal societies and development through environmental regeneration* (New Delhi, Oxford University Press).

Sharma, S. and P. Bajracharya (1996). *Impact of liberalization in Nepal* (Kathmandu, Institute for Integrated Development Studies).

Shaw, E. (1973). *Financial deepening in economic development* (New York, Oxford University Press).

Sheikh, H.A. (2006). *Towards reorienting the role of government in Pakistan*, 22nd AGM, Pakistan Institute of Development Economists (PIDE), Islamabad, 19–22 Dec.

Skills Development Working Group (SDWG). (2006). *Quarterly Progress Report Q3* (Kabul) [accessed via membership in the ANDS WG].

South Asia Watch on Trade, Economics and Environment (SAWTEE). (2005). *NAMA negotiations in the WTO: Nepalese perspective*, paper presented in a workshop on NAMA negotiations in the WTO, Kathmandu.

Statistical Center of Iran (SCI). (1976). *General Population and Housing Census* (Tehran).

———. (1986). *General Population and Housing Census* (Tehran).

———. (1996). *General Population and Housing Census* (Tehran).

Sternberg, R. (1996). "Technology policies and the growth of regions", in *Small Business Economics* 8(2): 75–86.

Stiglitz, E.J. (2003). "Globalization, technology, and Asian development", in *Asian Development Review* 20(2): 1–18.

Sundaram, K. (2007). "Employment and Poverty in India: 2000-2005", *Working Paper No. 155* (Delhi, Delhi School of Economics).

Sundaram, K. and S.D. Tendulkar (2004). "Poor in the Indian labour force: Scenario in the 1990s", in *Economic and Political Weekly* 39(48): 5125–5132.

———. (2006). "Changing structure of Indian workforce, quality of employment and real earnings", in *India: Meeting the Employment Challenge* (New Delhi, Institute for Human Development), pp. 110–142.

Taee, H. (2001). *Labor demand forecasting in 2000–2009 for labor market of Iran* (Tehran, Institute for Research and Planning in Higher Education).

———. (2002). *Final report of human resources development planning and policy-making* (Tehran, Institute for Research and Planning in Higher Education).

Taneja, N. and S. Rohit (2000). "India informal trade with Bangladesh and Nepal: A qualitative assessment", *Working Paper* No. 58 (New Delhi, Indian Council for Research on International Economic Relations).

Teece, D.J. (1993). "The dynamics of industrial capitalism: Perspectives on Alfred Chandler's scale and scope", in *Journal of Economic Literature* 31: 199–225, March.

Tilakaratna, G.; P. Jayawardena and T. Kumara (2006). *Economic growth, employment and poverty reduction in Sri Lanka* (Colombo, ILO and United Nations Development Programme).

Transparency International (2006). *2006 Corruption Perception Index*, In Focus 5 Nov. Available at: *http://www.transparency.org* [accessed 01 July 2009].

Uchikawa, S. (ed.). (2002). *Economic reforms and industrial structure in India* (New Delhi, Manohar).

United Nations (2000). *Commitment 3 of the 24th Special Session of the General Assembly*, Document A/RES/S-24/2 (New York).

United Nations Development Programme (UNDP). (2002). *Nepal human development: Poverty reduction and governance* (Kathmandu).

———. (2004a). *Macro economic policy and poverty in Nepal key issues in the macro economics of poverty reduction: The case study of Nepal* (Kathmandu).

———. (2004b). *Nepal human development: Empowerment and poverty reduction* (Kathmandu).

———. 2004c. *Afghanistan National Human Development Report: Security with a human face* (Islamabad).

United Nations Office on Drugs and Crime (UNODC). (2005). *Summary findings of opium trends in Afghanistan, 2005* (Vienna).

Unni, J. (2006). "Employment trends and earnings in the informal sector", in *India: Meeting the employment challenge* (New Delhi, Institute for Human Development), pp. 215–252.

van der Hoeven, R. and M. Lübker (2006). *External openness and employment: The need for coherent international and national policies*, paper prepared for the Development Forum on Productive Employment and Decent Work, 8–9 May (New York, ECOSOC, UN). Available at: *http://www.g24.org/holu0306.pdf* [accessed 11 Dec. 2007].

Vidyaratne, D.B.P.S. and W.J. Nigamuni (2006). *Time trend of poverty indicators on population, employment and socio-economic situation: 1981–2002* (Colombo, Department of Census and Statistics).

Vijayabaskar, M. (2002). "Garment industry in India", in G. Joshi (ed.): *Garment industry in South Asia: Rags to riches – Competitiveness, productivity and job quality in post MFA environment* (New Delhi, SRO, International Labour Organisation).

Vijayashankar, P.S. (2006). "Unlocking the hidden potential of dryland agriculture", in *Seminar* 564: 15–19, Dec.

Vyas, V.S. (2002). *Our agrarian future: A medium term perspective on Asian agriculture*, paper presented at the 4th Conference of the Asian Society of Agricultural Economists (ASAE), Langkawi, Kedah, 20–22 Aug.

Winters, L.A. et al. (2002). *Trade liberalization and poverty: The empirical evidence* (Brighton, University of Sussex).

Wood, G. (2003). "Staying secure, staying poor: The 'Faustian bargain'", in *World Development* 31(3): 455–471.

———. (2004). "Informal security regimes: The strength of relationships", in I. Gough and G. Wood (eds): *Insecurity and welfare regimes in Asia, Africa and Latin America: Social policy in development contexts* (Cambridge, Cambridge University Press), pp. 49–87.

World Bank (1999). *Bangladesh trade liberalization: Its pace and impacts* (Dhaka).

———. (2000). *World Development Indicators 2000* (Washington DC).

———. (2002a). *Pakistan development policy review: A new dawn?* (Washington DC).

———. (2002b). *A Study of Financial* Sector of *Nepal* (Kathmandu).

———. (2003). *Iran: Medium term framework for transition* (Washington DC).

———. (2004a). *World development indicators* (Washington DC).

———. (2004b). *Is Sri Lanka ready for the removal of textile and clothing export quotas?*, South Asia Poverty Reduction and Economic Management Unit (Washington DC).

———. (2004c). *India: Investment climate assessment 2004 – Improving manufacturing competitiveness* (Washington DC).

———. (2004d). *Nepal development policy review: Restarting growth and poverty reduction* (Kathmandu).

———. (2004e). *Sri Lanka: Development policy review* (Colombo).

———. (2005a). *Bangladesh: Growth and export competitiveness* (Washington DC).

———. (2005b). *The investment climate in Afghanistan* (Washington DC).

———. (2005c). *Afghanistan: State building, sustaining growth, and reducing poverty* (Washington DC).

———. (2005d). *Sri Lanka Development Forum: The economy, the tsunami and poverty reduction* (Washington DC).

———. (2005e). *Nepal: Development policy review* (Washington DC).

———. (2005f). *Afghanistan: Poverty, vulnerability and social protection: An initial assessment* (Washington DC).

———. (2006a). *Pakistan: Growth and export competitiveness* (Washington DC).

———. (2006b). *India's employment challenge: Creating jobs, helping workers* (Washington DC).

———. (2006c). *Equity and development: World Development Report* (Washington DC).

———. (2006d). *Doing Business in 2006* (Washington DC).

———. (2006e). *Pakistan: Growth and export competitiveness*, Report No. 35499-PK, table 6.5, p. 111, April 25, Poverty Reduction and Economic Management Sector Unit, South Asia Region (Washington DC).

———.; Asia Development Bank (ADB). (2005). *Sri Lanka: Improving the rural and urban investment climate* (Colombo).

———.; Bangladesh Enterprise Institute (BEI). (2003). *Improving the investment climate in Bangladesh* (Washington, DC).

World Commission on the Social Dimension of Globalization (WCSDG). 2004. *A fair globalization: Creating opportunities for all* (Geneva, ILO).

World Trade Organization (WTO). (2004). *World Trade Report 2004* (Geneva).

Wu, K.B. (2005). "Increasing the employability of secondary educated workers in India", paper written for Indian Labor Conference and the Draft World Bank Report (World Bank).

Zaidi, A.S. (2005). *Issues in Pakistan's economy* (New York, Oxford University Press).

Index

B

H

I